DATE DUE

AUG 5 04			

DEMCO 38-296

Lydia Mendoza
A Family Autobiography

COMPILED AND INTRODUCED BY

Chris Strachwitz with James Nicolopulos

Arte Público Press
Houston
Texas
1993

This book is made possible through support from the National Endowment for the Arts (a federal agency), the Lila Wallace-Reader's Digest Fund and the Andrew W. Mellon Foundation.

Arte Público Press
University of Houston
Houston, Texas 77204-2090

rk Piñón

Strachwitz, Chris and James Nicolopulos.
    Lydia Mendoza : a family autobiography / Lydia Mendoza ; compiled and introduced by Chris Strachwitz and James Nicolopulos.
        p.   cm.
    Includes bibliographical references (p. 409) and discography (p. 355).
    ISBN 1-55885-065-1. — ISBN 1-55885-066-X (pbk.)
    1. Mendoza, Lydia. 2. Familia Mendoza. 3. Singers—Texas—Interviews. 4. Women singers—Texas—Interviews. 5. Mexican Americans—Texas—Music—History and criticism. I. Strachwitz, Chris. II. Nicolopulos, James. III. Title.
ML420.M3768A3 1993
782.42162'6872'0092—dc20
[B]   92-45111
                                                                          CIP
                                                                          MN

The paper used in this publication meets the requirements of the American National Standard for Permanence of Paper for Printed Library Materials Z39.48-1984. ∞

Contents

Acknowledgements

My prime thanks go to the immediate members of the Mendoza family: Lydia and her husband Fred Martínez, Lydia's sisters María and Juanita, and her brothers Andrew and Manuel. They spent many hours and days talking about their lives, remembering stories, skits, songs and anecdotes in front of my microphones. Thanks to Dan Dickey of Austin, who's fluency in Spanish greatly facilitated my recording various members of the Mendoza family individually and together. We went to Houston where Lydia talked about her life and contributed the main content of this book. On several occasions we went to San Antonio to tape María, Juanita, Beatriz, Manuel and Andrew. Andrew spent several additional days with me visiting their old homes and the neighborhoods where they used to live in San Antonio.

Thanks also to Arnaldo Ramírez ("Mr. Falcón") of Falcón Records, who personally supervised most of the recording sessions Lydia and the Mendoza sisters made for Falcón Records in McAllen, Texas. Johnny Herrera of Corpus Christi, composer, musician and one of Lydia's most ardent fans, who started his Gaviota label by producing two 78 rpm discs with Lydia. Salomé Gutiérrez of San Antonio Music Publishing Co. and DLB Records, who became an avid fan and admirer of the great Lydia Mendoza and recorded her extensively just prior to her stroke in 1989. Singer, composer, musician José Morante, owner of Sombrero/Norteño/Lira Records, almost a contemporary of Lydia's who began his own recording career as a singer and guitarist in 1937, also for Blue Bird Records.

Thanks to Philip Sonnichsen who introduced me to Ramiro Cortés (Dr. Nopal) and Frank Fouce, Jr., whose father established Spanish-language theaters in Los Angeles, both of whom had worked extensively with the Mendoza family. Philip Sonnichsen also joined me on a trip to Mexico City where he knew people both at RCA and CBS Records whose help led to my filling in important missing links in the Mendoza discography, in addition to giving me a rare insight into the inner workings of the Mexican music business. To Al Sherman of Alshire International, present owner of the Azteca masters, and his assistant Dick Ceja who supplied me with a complete catalog of the Mendoza Azteca masters. To John Philips who inherited the masters of the Ideal label in San Benito, Texas, and not only maintained the master tapes in good condition but also kept all basic catalog details. I eventually purchased the masters and tapes of this historic and important regional Tejano-owned and -operated label from John Phillips.

Thanks to James Nicolopulos who conducted further interviews with Lydia Mendoza, with Hispanic show-business veteran Rolando Morales (son of Texas-Mexican fiddler Santiago Morales) in Los Angeles, and with María

Sánchez, proprietress of the long-established Sánchez Music Co. in San Francisco. Without Professor Nicolopulos, who now teaches at the University of Texas at Austin, this book would never have become a reality. Jim's mastery of Spanish, his devotion to research and his expertise in the computer field put the content of all the tapes into a readable format. His knowledge of and familiarity with the vernacular traditions of the border country and Mexico were invaluable.

Special thanks are also due to Professor Guillermo Hernández of the Department of Spanish and Portuguese, University of California-Los Angeles, who has long taken an interest in my work of documenting Mexican-American popular culture. I also wish to thank José Martínez (husband of Lydia's half sister Mónica), Rodolfo García (of the Carpa García), Nathan Saffir (of radio station KCOR), all of San Antonio, and Joe Ramón of Houston, probably the world's number one Lydia Mendoza fan. Jim Griffith of the Southwest Folklore Center in Tucson provided constant support and sound advice. Lily Castillo-Speed of the Chicano Studies Library at the University of California-Berkeley has often gone out of her way to help with our research and graciously encouraged us to rescue the bound hardcopies of many years of *La prensa* and *La opinión* when these had been transferred to microfilm and could no longer be stored on campus. Richard K. Spottswood, world-renowned discographer, author of the definitive 7-volume discography *Ethnic Music on Records*, generously supplied us with an advance copy of the typescript of his discography of the Mendoza family's recordings up to 1939. Folklorist Archie Green has been an unfailing pillar of support and encouragement.

We also wish to thank John Minton and others at the Institute of Texan Cultures who supplied many photos, as well as Pat Jasper who worked (in 1981) for the Texas Commission on the Arts and who helped us obtain a small grant to get this project moving.

In addition, further thanks are due to, in alphabetical order: Alicia Alvárez-Villaseñor (University of California-Berkeley), Les Blank (Flower Films), Arturo Dávila Sánchez (University of California-Berkeley), Agnes Dimitriou (University of California-Berkeley), Luis García Abusaid (University of California-Berkeley), Maureen Gosling (Flower Films), Ester Jiménez, Santiago Jiménez, Jr., Professor Gwen Kirkpatrick (University of California-Berkeley), Valerio Longoria, Albert Muth (University of California-Berkeley), Héctor Ramos (University of California-Berkeley), Zack and Juanita Salem, Chris Simon (Flower Films), Juan Tejeda (Guadalupe Cultural Center), Irene Namkung Ullman (Traditional Arts Service), John Ullman (Traditional Arts Service) and many others. Above all, practically every musician and singer in San Antonio and the South Texas music scene, most of whom consider Lydia Mendoza to be a pioneer, has contributed something of importance to the making of this book.

Introduction

Every time I've mentioned the editing of a book on Lydia Mendoza and the Mendoza family to anyone from the Mexican-American community here in the West or Southwest, I've gotten a remarkably uniform response: Lydia Mendoza represents our history, she is important, she is the first star of Tejano music specifically and of Mexican-American music in general. Lydia is an institution, known far beyond the borders of her home state of Texas, a carrier and interpreter of the richest traditions from both sides of the border. The songs which Lydia Mendoza and the other members of the Mendoza family sang and recorded not only represent the singers' own personal feelings but reflect the emotions, values and literary expressions of just about everyone from just about every strata of Mexican-American society both past and present. These songs and corridos constitute the literature of the people. Some have their origins in the Spain of the Middle Ages many centuries ago, others reflect rural and urban customs and values, both past and present, from both sides of the border.

Lydia and the Mendoza family, their music, songs and life story proved to be rather special. Lydia Mendoza made her first record playing the mandolin when she was a twelve-year-old child recording with her family in a make-shift studio in a San Antonio hotel room in 1928. That first historic recording session was the result of Lydia's father carefully reading *La prensa*, San Antonio's Spanish-language newspaper, on February 28, 1928. The family, consisting of father, mother and two daughters all singing and playing in unison, was at the time traveling from town to town in the Rio Grande Valley, trying to eke out a living from their music. Here is the small ad which appeared that one time only in the classified section:

From *La prensa*—February 28, 1928.

The records, which resulted from the family somehow making their way to San Antonio for this audition at a time when the business of country music was in its infancy, were only the first opportunity, or the first little step, in a long journey which eventually made Lydia Mendoza the first star of recorded Tejano music. Six years later, after enormous hardships as migrant workers in the north during the depth of the Great Depression, the family returned to San Antonio. There, Lydia became a "star" when she recorded "Mal hombre," accompanied only by her 12-string guitar. Lydia has endured, much like the Carter Family has in American country music. She became known as "La Alondra de la Frontera" (the meadowlark of the border) and "La Cancionera de los Pobres" (the songstress of the poor), but she did not limit her repertoire to the tastes of any one social group. Lydia's songs and recordings appealed to almost every stratum of Mexican-American society. Due to her natural, clear, emotional, honest, unaffected singing style and the wide distribution of her records, Lydia's popularity spread throughout most Spanish-speaking regions of North and South America. Lydia, along with her sisters María and Juanita, recorded every type of song, from haunting tangos and romantic boleros to the rancheras and corridos which often speak of heartaches, treachery and deceit. The fact that Lydia, her sisters, brothers and parents left us a legacy of well over 1200 songs on commercial phonograph records is just one of the reasons why their songs and music will be enjoyed and studied by future generations. The songs and music are only one aspect of the heritage which the Mendoza family has handed down to future generations. An equally interesting and popular mirror of society's tastes, mores and values were the theatrical skits presented at their performances, once they had left the streets and the Plaza de Zacate and appeared in *carpas* and theaters. These skits (or comic dialogues) were not commercially recorded by the Mendoza family at that time, but several were receated for inclusion in this book.

The experiences of European immigrants have been well documented in books, films and songs, but very few who have come from south of our border have ever told their stories on paper. The saga of the Mendoza family takes us back to the era of the Mexican Revolution when many fled to escape constant turmoil, violence and uncertainty. Landless and poor, they encountered the particular prejudices expressed towards those from south of the border. Their port of entry was a bleak, barren and dry region. There was no Statue of Liberty to greet them, only the murky waters of the Rio Grande. There were no Manhattan sweat shops, but also no land grants as offered by Texas to earlier European immigrants. Even though the Mendoza family had enjoyed some social status and employment in Mexico, once on this side of the border they had to start at the bottom of the heap during times of great economic hardship. The Mendoza's story takes us from the feast days of the booming "jazz age" of the late 1920s through the famine depths of our Great Depression of the 1930s with its terrible toll on people's pride, dignity and feeling of self-worth. It goes on through the slow economic recovery and limitations of World War II, when Mexican Americans were expected to patriotically serve the U. S. (which they did with distinction), in spite of the racial and cultural prejudices they had been subjected to. This narrative carries us through the economic postwar boom era of the 1950s, when Norteño and Texas Conjunto music became enormously popular on both sides of the border and when artists like Lydia Mendoza, the Mendoza sisters, Narcisco Martínez, Valerio Longoria, Los Alegres de Terán, Tony De La Rosa, Los Donneños, Conjunto Bernal and others were selling a lot of records and were becoming popular attractions not only at cantinas, but at large dance halls, and later at auditorium and arena shows. The long tale finally brings us into the 1970s and '80s when Lydia Mendoza's remarkable contributions to the musical and cultural history of Mexican Americans were recognized not only by her own community, but finally by the surrounding world as well. In 1971, Lydia performed at the American Folklife Festival in Montreal, Canada; in 1976 she was featured in the border music film classic "Chulas Fronteras"; and in 1978 she performed for President Jimmy Carter at the John F. Kennedy Center in Washington, D.C. In 1982, Lydia Mendoza was among the very first recipients of the National Heritage Fellowship Award given by the National Endowment for the Arts to outstanding contributors to our folk heritage. Lydia was inducted into the Tejano Music Hall of Fame in 1984 and, in 1991, she was also inducted into the Conjunto Music Hall of Fame. Lydia has also performed at numerous folk festivals in the U. S. and Canada, and she toured South America on several occasions. This book also includes a catalog of the recordings, the artifacts, which the members of this family have left for future generations to enjoy.

Lydia Mendoza was the first woman performer of vernacular music to emerge as a star from the fledgling business of commercial recording of Mexican-American country music. She was the first woman from a rural background, singing in an untrained but emotional style, to gain enormous popularity via her recordings and public appearances throughout most Spanish-speaking parts of the Western Hemisphere. Most female Spanish-language recording artists who preceded Lydia Mendoza had trained voices and came to the recording studios after successes on the musical or theatrical stage. The 1920 Columbia Records Catalog for Spanish-language material lists a number of early female stars and describes their music and songs as: Populares, Cómicos, Couplets, Zarzuelas, Revistas, Operetas, etc. By the mid 1920s some of the most popular of these artists were Pilar Arcos, Amalia Molina, María Luisa Escobar, Esperanza Iris, María Conesa, Carmen García Cornejo and Margarita Cueto (who recorded for Victor). None of them were Mexican Americans and they appealed to the middle and upper classes who until the 1920s constituted the primary audience for phonograph records. Records at that time were relatively expensive: 75 cents or $1 for two songs, when you could buy a meal for 50 cents, and the machines to play them on were in the same price range as an elegant piece of furniture.

The record industry was just beginning to record and market vernacular American talent such as that of the Mendoza family when mother Leonor, father Francisco and daughters Lydia and Panchita made their first records in 1928 under the name of Cuarteto Carta Blanca. Until the mid 1920s, music patrons who owned grammophones, bought records, attended concerts and enjoyed "culture" were generally supportive of the great trained or concert voices from around the world. Francisco Mendoza himself was an avid fan of Enrico Caruso and had quite a collection of his recordings. Great male singers popular with Spanish-speaking audiences towards the end of the 1920s were the romantic voices of Juan Pulido, Guty Cardenas, José Moriche and Carlos Mejía.

The recording industry, although it had catered to immigrants' tastes since its inception, had paid little attention to the music and tastes of rural Americans until about 1918, when the first recordings were made of Texas fiddler Eck Robertson. A few years later, in 1921, the first "race" or blues record by an African-American singer was made (Mamie Smith's "Crazy Blues"). The first recordings of vernacular Mexican music were actually made by traveling American firms in Mexico City around 1908 and included selections by Cuarteto Coculense (who turned out to be the first Mariachi to record) and Rosales y Robinson, the first recorded *cancioneros*. Mexican singers began to record corridos in Mexico City about that time; the "Corrido de Macario," "Juan Soldado" and "El Huerfano" sung by the duo of Abrego and Picazo are some examples. In the United States, the first corridos were recorded in New York by Trío González in 1919, by Trío Aguirre del Pino in 1920 and in Los Angeles by Dueto Acosta in 1923. These corridos were all of Mexican origin and not from the north nor from this side of the border, and the singers had "good" voices and did not seem to be of rural background. The honor of being the first "border music" singers to perform corridos and songs for phonograph records probably goes to Luis Hernández and Leonardo Sifuentes, who recorded "El Contrabando del Paso" in El Paso, Texas on April 15, 1928. Within the next year Pedro Rocha and Lupe Martínez of San Antonio became prolific recording artists of not only corridos but other songs as well, as did the Bañuelos Brothers in Los Angeles.

The records by Mexican-American singers of rural background such as Rocha and Martínez, the Chavarría Brothers, Hernández and Sifuentes and others apparently sold well enough to begin a virtual flood of recordings of Mexican-American music during the late 1920s and '30s. The major record companies: Victor, Columbia/Okeh and Brunswick/Vocalion, after having marketed popular folk traditions from all over the globe successfully to various immigrant groups in the United States, finally realized that the rural southern Black, White and Brown public right here in the United States also wanted their own music on records and was willing but hard pressed to pay for it. The audience for rural and regional musics was not wealthy, and radio only slowly catered to their tastes and desires. This was, however, the audience which bought records of their own music with great pride and helped record companies stay in business through the depths of the Great Depression, when record sales of popular music dropped to an all-time low.

Lydia and the Mendoza family came from rural northern Mexico, where music was played and sung at home or perhaps at family gatherings, at *bailes de rancho* (ranch dances) or special occasions and festivities. The music and songs Lydia learned as a girl were passed on to her primarily by her mother. Some she learned from bubble gum wrappers where music publishers had placed them with the hope of making them popular and successful. Lydia learned her most famous song, "Mal hombre," when her father took her to see a musical show at a theater in Monterrey, N.L. (the singer was probably Elisa Berumen, who was the first to record "Mal hombre," in Los Angeles for Victor in May, 1926). Lydia already had the text of the song in her collection of bubble gum wrappers, but she had finally heard the melody to go with the lyrics! Music soon became the main tool for survival, not only for Lydia, but for the whole Mendoza family.

I see a striking parallel between the music and careers of the Mendoza Family of South Texas and the Carter Family of Virginia. Both families had a remarkably large repertoire of old and popular songs, mainly collected from their communities, which they sang in a natural, rural style, which was obviously favored by their peers, friends and neighbors. Although from very different backgrounds, both families came to commercial recording in much the same way. The Carter Family, of Anglo-American origin from the hills of Virginia, saw an advertisement in the newspaper announcing that the Victor Phonograph Co. was looking for talent for their roving recording unit, which was coming to Bristol, Tennessee. The Mendoza Family, from the plains of Northern Mexico, saw a similar ad inviting musicians and singers to audition placed by the Okeh Record Co. in a Spanish-language newspaper from San Antonio. Both families were nominally headed by a man whose singing talent was limited and both families featured women singing and playing various stringed instruments. The Carter Family experienced instant, if modest, local success and began to make public appearances which eventually brought them to the powerful Mexican border radio stations. This boosted their popularity by reaching millions of American country music fans throughout the United States heartland, making the Carter Family one of the first stars of American country music. The Mendoza family, struggling to survive and on the move, went up North following their first recording session to find work in the fields. Their first records, which included "Quatro milpas" and "Monterrey," although very popular songs at the time, gave them only slight fame, since sales apparently were not great. The Carter Family were asked back to record regularly following their first session, but the Mendozas had to wait six years before they were given another chance, and by then the recording company was primarily interested in daughter Lydia.

The story of Lydia Mendoza and the Mendoza family is the story of constant struggle by an immigrant family who fled from revolution in their homeland, economically one of the world's poorer nations, to come to the promised land of "El Norte," the world's wealthiest country. Struggling as field hands, traveling like gypsies from place to place, they finally arrived in Detroit's automobile factories just before the Depression hit. Even daughter Lydia's making of "hit" record in 1934 did not end their struggle. Unlike the Carter Family, whose copyrights, mostly of similarly traditional songs, were well represented and protected by Ralph Peer—who supervised the recordings and had the foresight to form what was to become one of the world's leading publishing companies—the Mendoza Family was not so lucky. The Mendoza family was deprived of royalties from their records by ignorant and/or deceiving middlemen, because their material was sung in a "foreign" language and because Lydia's records became popular during the Great Depression. By 1934 there was little profit to be made from the sale of records, which by then sold at retail for as little as 35 cents, and since few of the songs the family sang or composed had the potential for publication via sheet music, publishers were not particularly interested. From the start, however, records were useful promotional tools to advance personal appearances. Like the Carter Family, the Mendoza family slowly took advantage of the opportunities for personal appearances aided by growing sales of their records. For rural musicians, touring was a hard nut to crack, and they had to rely on their own wits and promotional ideas to persuade owners of church halls, restaurants and school houses of their appeal. The Carter Family eventually worked on border radio for various shady American sponsors, as did Lydia Mendoza. The Carter Family, however, was paid to travel to Del Rio and make the transcriptions to be broadcast. Lydia Mendoza was invited, but mainly to pose for photos which the management then used to promote the station while playing her records, with no financial share going to Lydia. One station even had a woman imitate Lydia's speaking voice, making the listeners believe she was in the studio. The fame achieved by daughter Lydia eventually gave the family the opportunity to develop their talents as entertainers, not only as singers and musicians, but as actors and comedians as well. Largely due to mother Leonor's strong survival instinct, these acts gave the Mendoza family the chance to share with their fellow Spanish-speaking Americans a vast body of not only Mexican but rapidly evolving Mexican-American culture and traditions.

The Mexican Revolution, although the main reason for the Mendoza family leaving their homeland, in a way contributed to the family's eventual musical success, moderate as it was. The Mexican Revolution resulted in widespread appreciation, especially among cultural and political leaders, for popular Mexican art forms, including music. Mariachi bands from the state of Jalisco were brought to Mexico City to play for the revolutionary leadership, their friends and associates. Mexico is rich in regional musical traditions and many of these began to be honored as a result of the populist direction of the Revolution. However, it must be noted that a snobbish attitude prevails even today in Mexico City circles towards the rural music of the North, *música norteña*. Mexicans, like Europeans, look down at their countrymen and women who have left for the United States as culturally deprived, even though they may envy their possibly improved economic status. Mexicans call emigrants *pochos* and accuse them of forgetting their culture and language. The same prejudices are extended to the music of the North. Many people I met in Mexico City, from scholars to recording directors to mariachi musicians, looked down on the music from the North, although they often seemed jealous of its commercial success. They seemed to wish that this "awful hillbilly music from up north" would somehow disappear! In turn, it has been difficult for most Mexican-American singers or musicians to be successful in Mexico, partially due to the fact that the audience for this music emigrates from Mexico to the United States and rarely the other way. Today it is still very difficult for Mexican-American artists to compete even in the United States with the vast number of Mexican stars who are well-publicized via films, Mexican television and records and who will play for less money and are easier to handle by promoters.

You may ask how and why did a German American get together with a Greek American and an Anglo Texan to document the struggles and culture of a musical Mexican-American family? My only explanation is that music is a universal language and that I fell in love with the regional musics of Northern Mexico and South Texas over 40 years ago. I believe the border country has given the world some of the most fascinating and haunting ballads and songs, some of the most joyful dance music and some of the most emotional, heart-felt, crying, soulful, country duet singing heard anywhere. This music may well be an ordinary daily staple for millions of Mexican Americans, especially Tejanos, but it is also very essential, nourishing, yes, even joyfully addictive, and helps to make life and work just a bit more bearable. Like blues, Cajun music or American country music, the natural beauty, direct emotional appeal, literary richness, rhythmic variety, intensity and danceability of border music is contagious and appeals to and attracts people, like myself, from outside the culture.

In the early 1970s, I decided to make a documentary film with cinematographer Les Blank. I scraped together my life's savings, and "Chulas Fronteras" was the result. I wanted to document the great names of border music who had become well-known to me via their recordings. On an initial brief trip to Texas, we filmed the two premier pioneers of recorded border music: "The Father of Conjunto Music," Narcisco Martínez, and "La Alondra de la Frontera," Lydia Mendoza. On that trip I got to know Lydia Mendoza and several members of her family, and we filmed her at various events. I wish we could have filmed this remarkable woman more extensively, but I had limited funds and I did want to document some of the other great musicians from south Texas as well as their lives and culture. A few years later, we produced a companion documentary, "Del Mero Corazón," edited by Maureen Gosling, which focused more on some of the great love songs of the border country. Ever since then I have thought about how I might facilitate Lydia Mendoza's sharing of her vast cultural treasures with a wider audience. Several friends and associates in the academic world had been tossing the idea of "oral histories" my way. Since I have long enjoyed documenting the remarkable varieties of our regional folk musics by producing recordings on Arhoolie Records, most of which I recorded in Texas and Louisiana, I decided to seriously sit down with Lydia Mendoza and other members of her family and try to collect their stories and folklore on tape.

As a fellow immigrant, having been born in Germany, in an area now part of western Poland, I had fallen in love with American music at an early age. My mother had brought back some 78s in the mid 1930s from a trip to the United States (her mother was an American) and, after World War II in 1945, I heard swing and jazz on the Armed Forces Radio until we emigrated in 1947. I attended school in California and became addicted to the radio. XERB broadcasting from Rosa Rita Beach in Baja California, opened my ears to, no, not Mexican, but what was then known as hillbilly music: T. Texas Tyler, the Maddox Brothers and Rose, the Armstrong Twins, Bob Wills, Roy Acuff, Ernest Tubb and all the rest from that era. I also listened to "Harlem Matinee" hosted by D.J. Hunter Hancock over KFVD in Los Angeles, which introduced me to the world of blues and African-American music, and on Sunday nights I would regularly listen to the gospel music of the St. Paul Church choir and services over the same station. Traditional jazz by Kid Ory, Louis Armstrong and Meade Lux Lewis, as heard in the film "New Orleans" in 1948, turned me into a total fanatic! I heard my first strains of Mexican accordion music and mariachis over a small station in Oxnard, California. I wanted to take Spanish in high school, but the principal felt that was not appropriate for someone who hoped to make it to college. The language was music to my ears from the first time I heard a ranchera on the radio. Somehow I made it through school and two years in the U. S. Army, even though I spent much of my time listening to music—especially the live variety in bars, clubs and dance halls. I was discharged from the Army at Camp Chaffee, Arkansas, and made a detour to my land of dreams, New Orleans, on my way back to California! I studied to be a teacher with the help of the G.I. Bill, and started my record company, Arhoolie, in 1960. After teaching high school in Los Gatos, California for three years, I struggled to make a go of documenting the great rural folk musics of this country.

During all those years of hearing and recording music, I also collected records with a fervor. Among those old records, which I have often purchased in large quantities from juke box operators, stores and distributors throughout the Southwest, were many by not only Lydia Mendoza but by a fierce, soulful "dueto" of two women which the label noted as Hermanas Mendoza. Once I met Lydia Mendoza, the parts of the puzzle as to who these sisters were came together. I also found out who the haunting voices were which constituted Dueto Monterrey, another one of my favorite groups, with many 78s on the Azteca label! All those great sounds recorded by various members of this Mendoza family drove me to put together this book.

As it turned out, this was easier thought than done! I contacted Dan Dickey in Austin, Texas, who had written a book about the Kennedy corridos and was obviously sympathetic to this music and who spoke Spanish. He joined me on several initial trips to Houston and San Antonio, where we collected a major part of the interviews and skits which are the heart of this book. Once I returned to California with the tapes, I had to find someone fluent in Spanish and figure out what to do with this material. At one point I thought about issuing an edited version of the tapes on cassettes, but I was not sure if I could sell these, since the only experience I had was in marketing recordings of music, and even that was very limited! I talked to a friend, Charlie Musselwhite, about my deepening involvement in Mexican-American music traditions and he suggested a friend of his, James Nicolopulos, who had lived over ten years in Mexico and was familiar with the language and the rural traditions. Jim, who was working on his Ph. D. at the University of California-Berkeley, agreed to transcribe and translate the material on the tapes, and in the process he not only became a computer expert but an avid researcher who found the little ad in *La prensa* which led to the Mendoza's first recording session. Jim also becamse an increasingly fascinated fan of the Mendoza family and their culture.

Chris Strachwitz
El Cerrito, California
March, 1993

Sources and Methods

All of the interviews with Lydia, as well as many of the others, were conducted in Spanish. I was responsible for the transcription and translation of all of the people interviewed in this project. The main structure of the Mendoza family's story slowly emerged from the interviews. Chris and I decided to follow the documentary technique that had been used in his film collaborations with Les Blank, with the protagonists telling their own story in their own words rather than having the editors rehash the material into a third person, analytical narrative. We also elected to follow a basically chronological plan, although many of the interviews ranged freely back and forth across the years. After transcribing and translating the interviews, I arranged the material chronologically, removing the interviewer's voice from the text, but always preserving the identity of the speaker.

Because it is essentially Lydia's story, and she provided the most material, she became the principal speaker. Lydia's speech also provides the overlying structure within which the other speakers' contributions are set. On two occasions, I was able to sit down with Lydia and go over what the others had said. She provided useful commentaries and transitions that helped me place the various other people's statements in context within the overall framework of her own narration.

Naturally, many of the interviewees spoke about the same subject or event a number of times in the course of the various interviews. It was, then, the editor's task to choose the "best" version for inclusion in that person's contribution on a given topic. At times I have taken the liberty of combining elements from several versions of the same event by the same speaker into one unbroken discourse in the text. Although I have attempted to avoid excessive repetition, I also felt it important that each of the central protagonists be able to offer their own perspective on important matters; thus, certain stories inevitably are retold several times. Still other material, especially some provided by persons other than Lydia, although interesting in itself, never seemed to fit anywhere in the framework of the story as it was unfolding, and was thus, lamentably, excluded.

Throughout, the speaker's own words have been left intact, although much of the inevitable hemming and hawing, false starts and repetitious "you knows," etc., particular to oral discourse, have been, of course, edited out. Nonetheless, I have made every effort to preserve the particular flavor of each speaker's utterances, even at the expense of a certain repetition or inelegant syntax. The most difficult cases were those of the speakers who were quite articulate in Spanish, but much less so in English, who nevertheless had responded in certain interviews in English. In some of these cases, I was tempted to "improve" the speaker's English grammar and syntax to better reflect their performance in their native tongue.

The most difficult challenge of all, however, has been translation. It is hard enough to accurately translate the sense of what someone has said in one language into another; communicating nuances of personal and regional style is far more problematic. Lydia Mendoza, the principal speaker throughout the text, spoke exclusively in Spanish. Lydia is not only highly articulate, she also speaks a particularly rich, rural, rooted, slightly archaic and thoroughly authentic brand of Spanish that makes a distinctive impression on the listener. One could, if sufficiently sure of the idiom, attempt to render it in a fine Appalachian, or perhaps Down East English, but no matter how well it was done, the end result would still be totally false to Lydia's reality. There is, unfortunately, no practical way to avoid reducing her superb Spanish to rather unremarkable, "standard" English.

On the other hand, Lydia is a good storyteller, and she tells a tale with originality, irony and impact. To the extent possible, even at the risk of a certain awkwardness in English syntax, I have tried to preserve the authentic character of Lydia's and the other Spanish speaker's narrative style. If any of what they say reads as ungainly or pedestrian, the fault is entirely mine.

In the course of the interviews, Lydia and her brothers and sisters occasionally sang songs and recreated comedy skits to illustrate a point in their tale. Where these have been included in the text, I have transcribed and translated them as faithfully as possible. Since many of the songs mentioned by the Mendozas have been recorded commercially by them or others, often I have been able to transcribe directly from the commercially issued recordings. In the case of the many songs reissued by Chris Strachwitz on the Arhoolie or Folklyric labels, usually I have been able to adapt the transcriptions and translations from those provided along with the liner notes of the albums.

In addition to the interviews conducted under the aegis of Chris Strachwitz, we have had recourse to other, published interviews with Lydia Mendoza (See *Bibliography* for details).

After the interviews, the next most important source of information has been the Spanish-language newspapers of the Southwest, in particular, *La opinión* of Los Angeles and *La prensa* of San Antonio. These have yielded a rich harvest of articles and advertisements that have done much to fill out many details of the Mendoza family's long career.

Lydia and the Mendoza family's story is, above all, the story of several generations of remarkable women struggling to survive in an often hostile world. Despite violent revolution, economic depression, world war, male violence and both ethnic and gender-based discrimination, the Mendoza women always seemed to find a way to preserve their family and carry on. In recent years a great deal of interest has been focused on the role and history of Mexican-American women. Although it is beyond my training and competence to comment in detail on these aspects of the Mendoza story, I highly recommend that researchers interested in these matters make full use of the treasure trove of documentary materials that we have assembled in this book.

James Nicolopulos
El Cerrito, California
January 26, 1991

Tape-Recorded Interviews

I. Mendoza, Lydia (All in Spanish.)

Tape-recorded interview by Chris Strachwitz and Guillermo Hernández. El Cerrito, California. April 17, 1978.
Tape-recorded interview by Chris Strachwitz and Dan Dickey. Houston, Texas. June 3, 1983.
Tape-recorded interview by Jim Nicolopulos. El Cerrito, California. May 4, 1985.
Tape-recorded interview by Chris Strachwitz and Jim Nicolopulos. Los Angeles, California. July 10, 1985.
Tape-recorded telephone interview by Jim Nicolopulos. Houston, Texas, and El Cerrito, California. October 3, 1987.

II. Mendoza Family (Mostly in English.)

Mendoza, Andrew and Juanita. Tape-recorded interview by Chris Strachwitz. San Antonio, Texas. May 31, 1983.
Mendoza, Andrew, Juanita, Manuel and María. Tape-recorded interview by Chris Strachwitz and Dan Dickey. San Antonio, Texas. June 1, 1983.
Mendoza, Andrew and María. Tape-recorded interview by Chris Strachwitz. San Antonio, Texas. May 18, 1984.
Mendoza, Andrew, Beatriz, Juanita, Manuel and María. Tape-recorded interview (mostly in Spanish) by Chris Strachwitz and Dan Dickey. May 19, 1984.
Mendoza, Andrew and Manuel, and José Martínez. Tape-recorded interview by Chris Strachwitz. San Antonio, Texas. May 21, 1984.

III. Others.

Acosta, Guadalupe. Tape-recorded interview in Spanish by Chris Strachwitz and Kay Scott. San Antonio, Texas. May 4, 1977.
Cortés, Ramiro [Dr. Nopal]. Tape-recorded interview in Spanish by Chris Strachwitz and Philip Sonnichsen. Hollywood, California. July 23, 1984.
Fouce, Frank, Jr. Tape-recorded interview in Spanish by Chris Strachwitz and Philip Sonnichsen. Los Angeles, California. July 24, 1984.

García, Rodolfo. Tape-recorded telephone interview in Spanish by Jim Nicolopulos. San Antonio, Texas and El Cerrito, California. October 4, 1987.

Herrera, Johnny. Tape-recorded interview in English by Chris Strachwitz. Corpus Christi, Texas. May 24, 1984.

Longoria, Valerio. Tape-recorded interview by Chris Strachwitz and Jim Nicolopulos. Oakland, California. October 7, 1990.

Martínez, José. Tape-recorded interview in English by Chris Strachwitz. San Antonio, Texas. May 21, 1984.

Morales, Rolando. Tape-recorded interview by Chris Strachwitz and Jim Nicolopulos. Los Angeles, California. July 10, 1985.

Morante, José. Tape-recorded interview in English by Chris Strachwitz. San Antonio, Texas. May 19, 1984.

Ramírez, Arnaldo. Tape-recorded interview in English by Chris Strachwitz. McAllen, Texas. May 25, 1984.

Sánchez, María M. Tape-recorded interview in Spanish by Jim Nicolopulos. San Francisco, California. June 8, 1988.

Ullman, John and Irene Namkung Ullman. Tape-recorded interview in English by Chris Strachwitz and Jim Nicolopulos. El Cerrito, California. December 3, 1988.

Lydia Mendoza:
A Family Autobiography

CHAPTER 1

"When She Announced 'Mal hombre,'
I Got Out the Gum Wrapper."

Lydia

As far as we know, the musical tradition in our family begins with our grandmother. Her maiden name was Teófila Reyna. Grandma's mother was Italian, and her father was Spanish: so we come from mixed blood.

Our grandma Teófila was raised in a little town in Mexico called Villa de Arriaga. It's in the state of San Luis Potosí about fifty kilometers southwest of the state capital on the way to Aguascalientes. During the time she was growing up, the region just to the north was still pretty wild. There were *bandidos* and occasional Indian raids, and many of the settlements were still fairly new, so there wasn't much cultural life. But the area where our grandmother lived had been part of old colonial Mexico, and the cultural *ambiente* there was very rich.

Grandmother was an educated woman—a fairly rare thing at that time. There weren't very many educated women in the Mexico of Porfirio Díaz, especially outside of the capital. She attended the *Escuela Normal*, or teacher-training school, in San Luis and eventually became a teacher there. After teaching at the *normal* in the state capital for a while, she returned to her home town of Villa de Arriaga and married our grandfather, Refugio Zamarripa. She continued teaching at what would be the equivalent of an American high school in Villa de Arriaga.

Music may have been one of the subjects she taught, but I don't know for sure. However, Grandma Teófila certainly did have some musical training, because our mother told us that grandmother was always playing music ... dances of those years, like "La negra noche," songs of that style ... very romantic songs from those years, on her guitar.

Grandma Teófila may very well have learned the guitar from her own mother, *la italiana*, since it was customary for young girls of good family to

3

learn a little music in those days. In any case, Grandma Teófila taught my mother to play the guitar, and my mother, well, she then taught me.

Our grandfather had a fairly large ranch and several houses, although it was not one of the great haciendas. He raised cattle, planted various crops and had a number of people working for him. Grandma and Grandpa would go on horseback to San Luis to take goods to market or buy things that they needed. I imagine they had to go to San Luis because Villa de Arriaga was a very small town at that time. They used to go on horseback because there was no road.

Our grandma had blue eyes, very blue eyes; her appearance was very Spanish. Grandfather was a tall man: a tall skinny man with a big nose and fair skin. He, too, looked like a real *gachupín*. They had seven children there in Villa de Arriaga: four boys and three girls. The second oldest of the girls was our mother, Leonor Zamarripa Reyna, as they would say in Mexico.[1]

Mamá was probably born sometime around 1889. She never wanted us to know how old she was. We asked her . . . we knew her saint's day was in September, but we never found out how old she was or exactly when she was born. As far as she was concerned, after she turned fifty, she never got any older; she was always fifty years old.

Mamá, like her mother, grew up in Villa de Arriaga. While she was going to school there, she met a young man named Lucio Llamas. He was a musician and older than she was. When she was about fourteen years old, her parents found out that she was seeing him—that she had a boyfriend. Our grandfather was very strict, and he ran her out of the house. She told me she hadn't intended to get married that young, and she had wanted to finish school, but Grandpa was very angry with her and refused to forgive her or let her return home. The only thing she could do was go and live with her boyfriend's parents.

When they saw that our grandfather would never change his mind, our mother married Lucio Llamas. All this probably happened around 1908–09, right before the Revolution. Mamá was still very young, and she had to marry without her father's blessing.

Lucio Llamas played the string bass, what they call the *contrabajo* or *tololoche* in Mexico, and he was also a singer. He played those old-fashioned songs, some of which are still around. The group he played with was all strings: it was just the *tololoche*, the *bajo sexto* and the violin; no other instruments were used. Mamá used to say that he had taught her how to play some of the songs she knew.

There were two children from that marriage: Mónica and Andrés. They have both died already. This boy, Andrés, is not the same person as our full-brother Andrés, or Andrew, as we sometimes call him, who lives in San Antonio and will help me tell our story in the pages ahead. My sister Mónica was seven years older than I, so I suppose she was born around 1908–09. I don't know exactly when my mother married Lucio Llamas, but she was widowed after two or three years.

Lucio Llamas used to sing in *cantinas* and at dances. He was a drinker. He stayed up all night a lot, and he didn't eat right, and then he drank, and, well, his health started to get bad. He got this disease called tuberculosis because he stayed out late, didn't sleep much and sang a lot—every night, all night long. But he didn't live long enough to die of tuberculosis. He was playing at a dance one night, there was some kind of dispute, and he was murdered.

So our mother was a widow with two small children when she was only sixteen or seventeen years old. Our grandfather died around this same time, so our mother and our grandmother were both widows. Mamá returned home to the ranch in Villa de Arriaga, but soon after my grandfather died everything began to fall apart, and they had to leave. Mamá had brothers: my uncle Juan, my uncle Baudelio, my uncle Enrique, my uncle Benjamín. But they had all married—each of them went his own way—leaving everything abandoned, and the women couldn't stay there by themselves. You have to remember that this was about the time of the beginning of the Revolution and that it could be very dangerous out in the countryside. So Grandma sold all her property—the land, the houses and the livestock: everything they had in Villa de Arriaga—and brought what was left of her family to settle in Monterrey, Nuevo León. Mamá came along with her two sisters, Concha and Jesusita, and, of course, Andrés, her son, and Mónica, our half-sister.

Mamá was a widow with two very small children, and she had to work. She found a job at the hotel that was in front of the Cervecería Carta Blanca. The hotel belonged to the brewery. It was reserved for the special guests that would come to visit the Cervecería from Germany, France, Italy and all over. Beer men, you know, they would stay in that hotel. Our mother worked as a maid there.

Our father, Francisco Mendoza Espinosa, was also working for the brewery at the time, and they used to send him over to fix the pipes in the hotel. I guess that you could call him the hotel plumber. They would call him whenever anything would break. One time when he went to the hotel to fix something, Mamá was making up the beds in the room where he was working. Papá saw her, and he fell in love with her on the spot. Well, she was young and a very good-looking woman.

Papá found out that his stepmother was acquainted with our grandmother, so he got his stepmother to speak for him. He got her to hold a fiesta at her

Francisco Mendoza with daughter Francisca (Panchita). Courtesy of the Lydia Mendoza collection.

house and to invite the Zamarripa daughters. He already knew that he wanted to meet our mother, and that was how he arranged to be introduced to her. At the fiesta he was able to speak to her and dance with her. They began seeing each other, but he didn't know that she already had two children: a girl and a boy. He thought that she wasn't married—she was still very young. This went on for a while until one day as they were talking:

"Do you love me, Francisco?" she asked him. "Well, I'm going to tell you that I was married, but I am now a widow. And I have two children, and I have my mother."

"Oh, I thought that ... ," he answered.

"Yes," she said, "if you really love me, it'll be all right, but if you don't, well ... "

So they got married there in Monterrey. The day he had first seen Mamá in the hotel, Papá had his helper with him, and this is what happened: His helper married our mother's sister. Our aunt Concha, who married the helper, is still alive. She lives in Monterrey. Her name is Concha Zamarripa de Rodríguez. She's pretty well off. She lives in the Colonia Bella Vista neighborhood where we used to live. I'm sure that she would tell you a lot of bad things about our father. She used to tell us things like, "Your father was no good! We told your mother not to marry him." Yet Concha married his helper!

After our mother and father were married, Lucio Llamas' mother wanted to take the children away from Mamá: Mónica, our half-sister, and our half-brother Andrés. Well, they were her son's children. But Mamá took her to court because neither of the children wanted to go with that woman. Mónica stayed with Mamá, and Andrés went with our grandmother Teófila.

Our daddy was dark complexioned like our brother Manuel. He was from a place called Real de Catorce, a little town way up in the mountains in the state of San Luis Potosí. It was an old mining camp way out in the mountains. They used to call it Mineral de Catorce, but later they changed the name. I don't know what it is called now.

Papá left his parents when he was seven years old. His father's name was Merced Mendoza. Grandfather Merced was a man that looked like an Anglo—he had blue eyes, and a great big moustache. His first wife, our grandmother, was Rosita Espinosa de Mendoza. They lived for a time in a place near Monterrey called Villa Aldama. They had a little ranch there, but then everything came to an end for them in Villa Aldama, and they also moved to Monterrey.

Papá didn't come back to see them until he was thirty years old. He didn't see his mother die or anything. He came to the United States for the first time on his own, before he met our mother. He was a very smart man, maybe too intelligent.

Merced Mendoza was already married to his second wife and living in Monterrey when Mamá and Papá met at the hotel. I never met Papá's mother because she had already died. Merced Mendoza's second wife's name was also Rosa, just like the first one, our real grandmother. When Papá had returned to Monterrey from his wanderings, went gone to live with his father and stepmother. He was staying with them and working at the Brewery when he met Mamá. He had returned to his family after an absence of twenty-three years.

Papá had two brothers and a sister. His sister's name was Luz, and the brothers were Jesús and Manuel. They have all died. Jesús fought in the Revolution, and Manuel died in a motorcycle accident.

Shortly after my father married my mother, they came to the United States. Their oldest child, my sister Beatriz, was born in Navasota, Texas, in 1914. I, Lydia, was born here in Houston, Texas in 1916.

The main reason they left was that at that time in Mexico one couldn't live in peace, and people were being killed. The soldiers would carry off the pretty women and all that sort of thing. When my father married Mamá it was the time of the Pancho Villa Revolution. As soon as they got married, they came to the United States. I believe they stayed here for about four years without going back to Mexico because of the Revolution. But, in those years, they didn't mention things like that around the kids. When they were talking, we wouldn't even dare ... to even stop and stand in the doorway. We'd no sooner stop, than they would send us off ... to our room. We never knew what they were talking about. But my mother would receive correspondence from her relatives, and I noticed how things were.

Many years later they did tell one story that might explain why they came to the United States at that time and didn't return to Mexico for so many years. Let my brother Andrés tell it.

Andrés

Daddy had a cousin who was a captain in the Pancho Villa Army. When Villa's troops captured Monterrey,[2] they started arresting the guys that were against Pancho Villa, and they thought Daddy was one of them. So they picked him up, and they were going to shoot him.

"You cannot shoot me," he told them.

"What do you mean we can't shoot you?" they replied.

"No, you can't," Daddy said, "because, see, I was working undercover for my cousin. His name is David Contreras Torres, Capitán David Contreras Torres. He told me to work with the enemy to get information."

"Yeah, there's a Capitán José David Contreras Torres in the Villa Army. Oh well, okay, we'll talk to the Capitán then. We'll check it out." They let him go. Mother said that his cousin came home mad! He heard about it, all right. They called him in to ask him if it was true or not that Daddy was working for him. He hadn't seen our father for a long time. That's why Mother said that Daddy had to come out of Mexico dressed like a woman. He dressed himself up in some of mother's clothes so that he could escape from Monterrey. He used to get into some real messes. My mother used to tell some hairraising stories about him. Well, they managed to get out of Monterrey, but they didn't have any money. When they reached Laredo, Texas, they found out that there was a general from the Villa Army stationed there. So Daddy went over there and told that general that he was David Contreras Torres, and that he had fought in a certain place, and in such and such a place, and that all of his men had been killed, and that he didn't have anything left. He said that he wanted to go back to Mexico to report to Villa again and keep on fighting. But he didn't have any money. So the general gave him money. So Daddy got that money, and he and Mamá came to San Antonio. From there they moved on to Navasota, where Beatriz was born, and eventually to Houston, where my sister Lydia first saw the light of day.

Daddy knew everything about his cousin. He would read the papers, and he would keep track of where he was and what he had been doing. So if he was asked any questions, he could tell them that he had fought in a certain place, that he had been victorious in such and such a place, and that he had lost in another place. Contreras Torres eventually became a colonel in the Villa Army.

Lydia

That's the way that my brother Andrés remembers that story, although I don't remember hearing it myself. I believe that Papá, even though he really loved his country and never liked to stay away too long, didn't want to return to Mexico until things had quieted down and Pancho Villa had been defeated. So the family stayed in Texas. But things weren't very easy for Mamá during this time. My younger sister María remembers a story that our mother used to tell about those days.

María

Papá had brought Mamá to the United States. He left her alone on a little ranch near Houston and went off to see what he could find. He didn't like to drag the whole family around with him at that time; he would go off by himself. He impersonated a priest, and people believed him. No one figured it out. He bought one of those priest outfits in a secondhand store. If you had seen him, you would have thought he was a priest, too. And then he went to Philadelphia on a ship, and all of the people on the ship believed that he was a priest. And as far as Mamá was concerned, well, he just forgot about her. She only had Beatriz and Lydia at that time. The rest of us weren't born yet. He just told her, "You're going to stay here." And there she stayed—she didn't move from that place. She was very young and dying of hunger, and she stayed, and she waited.

I don't know what he did there in Philadelphia, but he left Mamá there in Texas for about two months, and he didn't come for her, and he didn't leave her even a nickel or any food or anything. She didn't have any shoes, and she made herself shoes out of a canvas tarpolin. She would go out and sit herself down and watch for little birds to come down, and then she would hit them with a rock and pluck them, and they would eat them.

Finally, Papá came back, and she said, "Well, where have you been, Pancho?"

"No, now I've come back. There's nothing there—there's no work there," he replied, and that was the end of the discussion.

And what he would earn ... he would drink it all up. He did work at something up there, but he never told Mamá at what. Well, he liked to drink a lot. She used to say that she had gotten married and that her first husband passed away and that it was her cross to be like that. Mamá put up with a lot.

Lydia

My sister María spent a lot of time with Mamá in the last years of our mother's life, and she remembers a lot of stories like that. Anyway, after about three years in Texas, Mamá and Papá went back to Monterrey, Nuevo León. They must have stayed down there about two years, because my little brother Francisco was born there around 1917–18—I don't remember the date for sure. This little boy died at the age of one year and a few months. María remembers that he died of meningitis. About a year later my sister Francisca, who we called Panchita, came into the world, also in Monterrey. She was born in 1920.

Then, around this same time—around 1920—my father brought us back to the United States. It seems to me that we immigrated through Laredo. I was barely four years old. I recall that when we crossed over that time, they had a bad opinion of all Mexicans, and especially of the children. They washed my head with gasoline. They told us that we were infected with lice or some such things.

Right away they took us there in back behind the immigration station where they had a bath, one of those big ones, full of gasoline. It wasn't just me; there were several other children, all Mexicans. And they doused us with gasoline; they threw on plenty. The gasoline got in my eyes and I became very ill. I came out with red eyes. That was the last and only time they did that to me, because afterwards they stopped doing it; this was precisely in 1920.

We came to a little town in Texas called Ennis. We lived there for a while, and it was exactly there that I began to feel the impulse of the music—when I was only four years old.

We always had music in the house. My mother would take out the guitar and play whenever she got the chance. She didn't make a career of music when she was young, like I did, because her family didn't allow her to. If she were to have had the chance, she would have made a big career for herself as a great singer, because she had an exceptionally pretty voice. But her family would never have allowed her to sing in public, only at home.

But when she got married to Papá, then she began to really feel the music—it awakened within her—and my father bought her a guitar. So, after the family tasks, the dinner and all that, they would all sit down and sing. My dad also sang with her. The two of them would start to sing. And that was when I began to feel that I, too, wanted to play the guitar.

I was four years old, and I wanted to play the guitar, so much so that I tried to get hold of my mother's guitar. But she never allowed me to touch it, because she thought that I was going to pull out the strings or that I could break it. She took very good care of her guitar and was very watchful. And at my age, well, they took my interest as a childish thing, without realizing that my aspirations were real.

All right, my mother wouldn't let me get hold of the guitar. In order to prevent me from getting at it, she put a nail up real high and hung it up so that I couldn't reach it. One time when she wasn't paying attention, when she was in the kitchen, I grabbed a chair, and very carefully—just think, at four years old!—I dragged it, I pulled it to where that guitar was hanging, very carefully, in danger of falling down with the guitar and everything else—just imagine! But I climbed up on the chair; I took down the guitar very carefully, and then when I was back down on the floor, I sat myself down and started to play it with just one finger.

As soon as my mother heard the sound she burst out of the kitchen, scolded me and took it away. She told me that if I ever took the guitar down again, she was going to punish me very severely. Well, she put the fear of God into me, and I never did it again. I would just stand in front of where it was hanging and stare at that guitar. I resigned myself to just being there contemplating it.

One day when I was playing outside, there were some little girlfriends of mine—little neighbor girls—playing there with some of those little rubber bands. They would put them in their mouth and stretch them, and they would make a musical sound. So then it occurred to me, and I said to myself, "Well, I'm going to make a guitar."

I went into the patio of the house, and I found a little plank of wood. I remembered that Papá had a little can full of nails in the kitchen, and I went and got six small ones. I pounded them into the board—three on each end. And I said, "Well here is my guitar." But the strings were still lacking. So I asked my little friend if she would give me some of those rubber bands she had.

"Yes, my papá has plenty, and I brought a whole bunch," she said.

"No, I only want three," I replied.

So I hooked up the rubber bands from one end of the board to the other. And, of course, with pressure they made a sound ... which for me was the sound of a guitar. And it made me so happy to imagine—at that age—that I had a guitar. It was a guitar for me. So then my delight was to go sit down under a tree in the patio and pass the time making sounds on my improvised guitar. That was the first toy I made for myself—a guitar—when I was four years old, because my desire to have a guitar in my hands was so great, and my mother wouldn't let me touch her real guitar yet. I just imitated the way that I saw my mother play her guitar. And finally my wish was granted me, because my mother taught me how to play a real guitar when I was seven years old.

My mother didn't have a real fine guitar. It was just a regular quality one: medium, a six-string. But it sounded very pretty to me. My mother always played a six-string. The strings were always of steel.

At this time my father was working for the railroad, but not on the track, not laying track. He was a mechanic; he fixed the locomotives. Often, he was sent to different cities. I would be in Ennis, he was working there, and then, suddenly, I'd see that we were in ... San Antonio, and then, later, in Beaumont, and then here in Houston, Waco, Fort Worth ... It seems to me that he worked for the Santa Fe Railroad. The family was always on the move, sometimes on one side of the border, sometimes on the other, probably because my father worked for the railroad on both sides. I know that we returned to Monterrey again after 1921, because my sister María was born there in 1922.

As María says, it's hard to know exactly where and when any of us were born.

María

It's all mixed up, because Papá told so many different stories, it's hard to tell what's really true. He'd tell the men at the border all sorts of stories, and that's what's on our papers. The problem is that Papá didn't tell them the truth. And we had to be very tightlipped, we couldn't say anything. It was better for us not to talk.

"And you all are going to shut up, and you aren't going to speak, you're not going to say a single word," he would tell us.

And he could really get mad. So there we would be, just looking on, and he would tell *la migra* whatever he felt like.

Lydia

I remember one incident that ocurred there in Monterrey in 1922 when I was only six years old; I believe it was a miracle. I recall that on this occasion my father had told my mother that she should go pay the rent. I remember that my father had a lot of authority in those days. When he gave an order, it had to be carried out. And if it wasn't, well, God help us! So then in the morning when my father left, he told Mamá not to forget to go leave off the rent.

"All right," my mother said.

Papá went to work. My mother should have gone to drop off the rent around noon, but at that moment a visitor arrived. Mamá and her friend got to chatting, and when my mother finally looked at the clock, she saw that it was almost four o'clock. It was already very late for her to get ready or to tell the visitor. "Go away, because I'm going to go out ... on an errand."

So she told me, "Go speak to Don Remigio and ask him to come here."

Don Remigio was an old man that was always around. He was living out in back behind our house, and it was he who did many of the errands for the household or whatever came up. I went out in back and got Don Remigio, and the old gentleman came in.

"Yes Ma'am?"

"Do me the favor of going to drop off the rent for me, Don Remigio," my mother told him, "and make sure that the owner gives you a receipt."

So he went and did it and came back, and that was the end of that. Very good. The visitor left, and Papá came home in the late afternoon, and he started to read and have a few drinks and all, just as he usually did. Then he says to me, "Lydia, come here."

"Yes, Papá?"

"Did your mother go drop off the rent?"

And since I knew how he was, I said, "Yes, Papá, she did go to leave it off."

"And what dress did she wear?" he asked me.

And now I had to make it up. I don't remember which dress I said that she had worn, but he must have seen that I was very nervous—real scared. "Very well, it's all right, okay, go on and play. Go on," he told me.

I went. Later on, it was getting dark, and my father was talking to my mother, and my mother stopped in the doorway, and she said to him, "What's the matter?"

"Did you go leave off the rent, Leonor?" he said.

"Yes, I went to drop it off," she replied. And then she said, "Well, I mean that I didn't go to drop it off, I sent it, because ... "

Well, he didn't even wait for her to explain that a visitor had come over or anything. He said, "Oh! You're ... !" who knows what ... "You are deceiving me! I'm not your ... !" who knows what ...

So right then and there he was going to throw her out, to blow her away. "I'm going to kill you right now!" he shouted.

Papá always kept a carbine, behind the door, and when my mother saw that he was going to hit her with the carbine, she ran to where the baby, María, was lying. She was only a few months old—she was very, very small. And Mamá grabbed her and put her up to her breast to let her nurse. Mamá breast-fed all of her babies. At the moment that María started nursing on her breast, my father was cocking the carbine to shoot her. Mamá cried out, and María let go of her breast and turned black, all black ... as if she had died.

So then Mamá screamed at him, "Ay, wicked man, now you have killed my daughter!"

And Papá, well, as he was half drunk and not thinking very well, he imagined that he had shot her. He dropped the carbine, and he ran to where Mamá was. And Mamá was there with the baby: the "dead" baby. Mamá and Papá both grabbed little María, and they called for my grandparents and my uncles, and they all came over there. Mamá told them what had happened, and my father was very frightened. They brought the neighborhood doctor.

He came and looked at María, and he said, "This baby girl is dead. What happened?"

And they explained it to him. My father said, "My wife was nursing the baby, and one of the little girls fell down and was going to land on some scissors, and it frightened my wife, and because of that ... "

"Yes," the doctor said, "this is the result of a fright, but it must have been much greater than that ... for it to have killed this little creature."

They didn't tell him the truth. He left a certificate. In those years they didn't take the bodies to the hospital or any place like that. One would die,

Leonor Mendoza. Courtesy of the Lydia Mendoza collection.

and the doctor would just come and make a certificate, and they would leave the little dead one right there. The loved ones would take care of the body. So that was what the doctor did; he left the certificate and he went away. Well, now they picked up the little baby girl and they carried her ... they were going to lay her out on a table, when ... she started shaking and returned to life. It went on like that for about half an hour: she would have these attacks. She'd have them for about five minutes, and then she would appear to "die" again. They brought the doctor back when she had an attack and she had "died" again; he verified it.

"This baby isn't alive," he said, "she's dead."

He didn't believe that she had returned to life. So then the doctor went away again; he didn't pay any attention to what Mamá and Papá had said. And the baby was ..., well, like dead. So then I saw my mother go to another room where she had a Sacred Heart, a very large one, on an altar. She took down the Sacred Heart and brought it over to her trunk—one of those great big ones, an old-fashioned one—where she kept all of her clothes ... that she washed and ironed. Mamá raised up all of the clothes in the trunk and put the sacred heart face down at the bottom and then piled everthing back on top of it. Then she knelt down, weeping, and she said, "Sacred Heart of Jesus ... ,"—because María still hadn't been baptized—"if my daughter has to be for you ... if she's not going to be for me now, I give her to you with all my heart. And I promise you that I won't cry a tear. But I don't want to see her suffer. I give her to you. Take her. And I promise that if she isn't for me now, I won't cry a tear for her. And if she comes back to life or she dies, I'll take you out of the chest, I'll turn you right-side-up, and I'll take you to the church."

Well, the baby was "dead." We went back to the other room, and suddenly she returned to life again, and the attacks stopped. They didn't just tell me about this. I remember it very well: everything that my mother did. The little girl had "died," but she came back to life. I believe that her recovery was a miracle. That was one of the things I saw when I was a little girl, when I was about six years old in Monterrey, Nuevo León, Mexico.

Nevertheless, Papá was a very affectionate father. He cared very much for all of us, but ... I was his favorite. He was very fussy with his books, with his things, anything that he bought. Nobody could touch anything of his; he prohibited it. He would be sitting down reading—a newspaper or a book—and nobody could go in and bother him. Because he would get angry. And my mother already knew that in order for him not to get mad, nobody should bother him. But I was very daring; I *would* go where he was. But—they all understood that he cared for me very much—he would pardon me. He would allow me to be with him, even to the point of letting me look at his books, letting me turn the pages. He wouldn't allow anyone else to do that.

My mother would say, "How come you're the only one he's like that with, and not the others?"

Well, that was the way it was . . . always; that was the closeness that I had with him.

When he noticed that I enjoyed learning the guitar, he was very happy and very pleased. He helped me a lot . . . he encouraged me. He gave me support to go on with music. I felt real good because I could see that he was helping me.

José Martínez, who married our half-sister Mónica in Monterrey in 1922, remembers hearing the family play music and sing together at their wedding. It was the first time that he can recall hearing us. According to him, it was me, Lydia, and my mother and father. Mamá played the guitar, and Papá and I sang. It was a real big party; even the passers-by came in to eat and drink. Mamá used to tell us that there was a lot of beer at the party. Papá had been given several kegs by his friends at the brewery.

My brother Manuel was born in Beaumont, Texas, in 1924. So you can see that the family was moving back and forth again.

Manuel

At the time I was born, my father was working for the railroad in Texas. But shortly afterwards we immigrated back to Mexico, because my father didn't like it over here. In Monterrey, he went back to work for the Cervecería Cuauhtémoc, the Carta Blanca brewery.

My father was a . . . , what do you call it, a vagabond. He didn't like to stay in one place all the time. He just wanted to keep on going back and forth. He would get tired of being in one place, so he would want to change. He sort of commuted between Mexico and the United States. In those days, it wasn't that bad to get across. You just had to pay; it was only a dollar or two. They used to have to buy a passport to come across.[3] There were no wetbacks, nothing like that. People would just come legally to the United States, like when we immigrated through Laredo, and when we came back.

Lydia

I remember when we returned to Monterrey from Texas after Manuel was born in 1924. At that time, I could play in all the keys on the guitar and all that. When we got to Monterrey, the first thing that my father said to my grandmother Teófila was, "You have a granddaughter that can play the guitar very prettily."

It pleased him so much! After that, my mother didn't have to worry about the little that I lacked to perfect my playing, because my grandmother would work with me on it every day. My grandmother had a little guitar, and she would grab it and say, "Come on, my little girl, sit yourself down!" And she would sit with me and tune the guitar and teach me to tune and play it as she did. My grandma Teófila also sang, but only in the home—and only there. She wasn't an *artista* , an entertainment artist, or anything like that. She would only sing amongst the family. When they would have *fiestas*, she would sing at those.

For me, when I was a little girl, my only toy was the guitar, because it was what I liked the most. Musical instruments were what I most adored. That's why I learned to play the mandolin by just watching, because both music and instruments fascinated me. And then I learned the violin, also without anyone teaching me. I also learned how to play a little piano, as well. Instruments were my toys. Papá did buy, well, toys for us, but they didn't interest me. For me, when I was running around playing as a child will, I would no sooner hear the guitar than I would come running. The instruments were my toys; they were the toys that I wanted in my childhood.

When we were living in Monterrey, my father would take me to the theater. In those days it was strictly theater; there weren't any movies. Big theatrical companies would arrive from Mexico City, like the one headed by Virginia Fábregas. The one that I went to see, the one that my father wouldn't miss for anything, was María Conesa. I believe that Papá took me to see her show around 1924–25. I was very young and can barely remember. There were many artists that came from Mexico City, but the only ones that I specifically recall are Virginia Fábregas and María Conesa.

María Conesa's specialty was the *zarzuela*, and many of the *couplets* that my sister Juanita was to sing many years later in our family's stage show were first introduced into Mexico in the *zarzuelas* presented by María Conesa. The *zarzuela*, since it is mainly music, I enjoy very much. It doesn't matter what kind it might be: for me, all music is something very special. Apart from the fact that I was born with this vocation—this enthusiasm for music—I was also influenced by the fact we always had music in the family: the influence of my mother and my grandmother Teófila. Additionally, my father liked the theater and music very much, and during those times when he owned a phonograph, our home was always full of music from records as well as what we would play ourselves. For instance, when I was young I listened a lot to Caruso, Enrico Caruso. My father was a fanatical *aficionado* of his. At one time, he had the entire collection of Caruso's recordings.

One of my most important songs—"Mal hombre," which has been like a banner, for me—I learned in a very curious way. They used to print the lyrics of popular songs on gum wrappers there in Mexico. Every time you bought a piece of chewing gum, you had the chance to get a new song. I made a collection of many songs; and, of course, I didn't know the music to most of them. But I was interested in keeping them in case some day I might hear one of those songs. And I remember that I only heard the music to "Mal hombre" once. One time a variety show came from Mexico City. There was a girl, a very pretty girl, in that show, and she sang tangos and all that. And on that occasion—which was just before we came to the United States, I think it was about the end of 1926 or the beginning of 1927, there was a show at the Independencia Theater in Monterrey. My father went, and he refused to take my mother. But on that occasion—I don't know why—he took us: my sister Beatriz and me, the two oldest.

We went to the theater to see that particular *variedad*, and then, in the course of the show, that pretty girl came out and sang.[4] When they announced "Mal hombre," I became very excited. I was always very alert for the names of my songs. Wherever we went—I don't know why—I carried around that repertory just in case I heard them. She sang two tangos. One was called "Desgraciadito," which didn't stick with me, and the other one was "Mal hombre." And when she said "Mal hombre," I got out the paper, the gum wrapper. I had it with me. And I just heard the music to that song that one time, but I memorized it. As soon as I got home I began to practice it and go over it, and it stuck with me. That was how I learned "Mal hombre."[5]

Mal hombre

Era yo una chiquilla todavía
cuando tú casualmente me encontraste
y merced a tus artes de mundano
de mi honra el perfume te llevaste.

Luego hiciste conmigo lo que todos
los que son como tú con las mujeres,
por lo tanto no extrañes que yo ahora
en tu cara te diga lo que eres.

Mal hombre,
tan ruin es tu alma que no tiene nombre,
eres un canalla, eres un malvado,
eres un mal hombre.

A mi triste destino abandonada
entablé fiera lucha con la vida,
ella recia y cruel me torturaba;

yo más débil al fin caí vencida.

Tú supiste a tiempo mi derrota,
mi espantoso calvario conociste,
te dijeron algunos: "¡Ve a salvarla!"
Y probando quien eres, te reíste.

Mal hombre, etc.

Poco tiempo después, en el arroyo,
entre sombras, mi vida defendía;
y una noche con otra tú pasaste,
que al mirarme sentí que te decía:

"¿Quién es esa mujer? ¿Tú la conoces?"
"¡Ya la ves!" respondiste, "una cualquiera".
Y al oír de tus labios tal ultraje,
demostrabas también lo que tú eras.

Mal hombre, etc.

Evil Man

I was but a young girl
when, by chance, you found me
and with your worldly charm
you crushed the flower of my innocence.

Then you treated me like all men
of your kind treat women,
so don't be surprised now if I
tell you to your face what you really are.

Evil man,
your soul is so vile it has no name,
you are despicable, you are evil,
you are an evil man.

Abandoned to a sad fate,
my life became a fierce struggle
suffering the harshness and cruelty of the world;
I was weak and was defeated.

In time you learned of my downfall,
how my life had become a road to hell,
some people told you: "Go save her!"
And proving who you really are, you just laughed.

Evil man, etc.

A short time later, in the gutter,
amidst shadows, I was fighting for my life;
one night you passed by with another woman,
and upon seeing me, I heard her say:

"Who is that woman? Do you know her?"
"You can see for yourself!" you replied, "she's a nobody."
When I heard that insult fall from your lips,
you proved once again what you really are.

Evil man, etc.

Lydia

"Todo por ti" is another tango that I learned from the gum wrappers. "El tango negro," was also from the famous gum wrappers. And, then, as I have said, I came to hear them when my father took us to the theater. I was very little; but I still liked to go, anyway, because it was a chance to go hear music. So they would sing the *couplets* there; they would sing the *canciones*. And, of course, I always had my little "repertory" of gum wrapper songs with me, and I was always alert for my songs. All the *variedades* that came through Monterrey would sing "El tango negro," "La moscocita" and "Todo por ti," and that was how I learned the music to those tangos. But, of course, I adapted them to my style. Because I sing the tangos my own way. I don't sing them like they are supposed to be—I know that—but I adapt them to my style of singing.

In those years, we were living in the Bella Vista neighborhood of Monterrey. It was a very poor neighborhood back then, and it didn't have electricity on all the streets. There wasn't any musical *ambiente* at all. Every once in a while you could listen to some music when some little carnival would arrive there. They had music, but it was ... like an organ-grinder, one of those organ-grinders who had a little dancing monkey.

One time, however, something very special happened. It was very important to me, and I remember it vividly. Near where we lived in *la Colonia Bella Vista*, there was a little store on the corner that sold beer, sweets, sodas, firewood, corn—well, a little store, but they sold everything. One Saturday, my mother sent me there on an errand, and just as I was walking up, a little group arrived there that came from downtown Monterrey. They called themselves Los Aguacates (The Avocados). They were a group of about five, but they were all string instruments. It was violin, *bajo sexto, mandolón*, guitar and mandolin, I believe. They arrived there, and they found a few men hanging around the little store. Los Aguacates came inside to ask the owner for permission to sing there for whatever the people might give them. And the little old man who was the owner of the store said, "No, no, don't come around and waste my time here. I can't pay."

And Los Aguacates said, "No, we won't charge you. We just want to play for what the people will give us."

"No, no," the owner said, "there'll be some kind of disturbance and lots of drunks and fights, and the police will come and all that."

They were going on like that when I came into the store. I went up to the little old man, the owner—he knew me very well—and I said, "Don Pablito,"—because that was his name—"why don't you let them play? It will make the customers happy, and increase your business ... "

"Very well," he said—I had convinced the old fellow—"All right, it's all right. But they have to play there, out there, outside: not in here, not inside the store."

Well, my only concern now was to see what they were going to play: if they were going to play any of my songs. As soon as the owner told them that they could play, I ran and finished my errand for Mamá. Then I went and got out my little pile of songs and ran back to the store as fast as I could. I went behind the little store, and I stood back there where no one would notice me. Los Aguacates began playing, and the people started to ask them for songs of those years, like, "El adolorido," "Las cuatro milpas," "El rancho grande," "La Adelita," all those.

Since all of those songs had been printed on chewing gum wrappers, I had them. As they announced each song, I would get out the little wrapper, and there would be all of the words to the song. And that was the way that I learned the melodies to those little songs.

Because the old man had now seen that he had more business on Saturday when the group was there, Los Aguacates were able to come back and play at that little store for two or three Saturdays in a row. As you can imagine, I didn't miss a minute of it. I was there every Saturday while they were playing, and I would do the same thing: learn the melodies to my songs as they were played. I learned the words from those little improvised song books that I collected from each piece of gum I bought. The gum came wrapped up like a little finger, but there were songs printed on the wrapper.

And those were the same songs that I learned from those musicians that came every Saturday. Those songs were the beginning of my career.

* * *

My youngest sister Juanita was born there in Monterrey in 1927, and later that year, the family moved to the United States for the last time. Our grandmother Teófila and our half-brother Andrés remained in Monterrey. They both eventually died there. Grandma was coming from the market, and she wasn't paying attention. She liked to go to the market by herself, to take her basket and do her shopping. She didn't like for anyone to go with her. And Grandma was already quite old. Where she was going to cross the railroad tracks, a train was coming real fast, and it blew its whistle at her, but she didn't hear it. It hit her with the cowcatcher in the forehead and split her head apart just like that.

And it really hurt Andrés, our half-brother. Yes, he died of grief for my grandmother. It really weighed upon him. He took heavily to drink. He didn't want to live. It was because of the sadness that he felt on account of Grandma's death. He was a roofer; he repaired roofs. And one time he slipped because he was drunk. He fell off a roof and he came rolling down and fell onto a bench and opened up his skull. He was nineteen years old when he died.

José Martínez, our half-sister Mónica's husband, remembers Papá's preparations for what was to be our final trip to the U.S.

José
I don't know why Pancho, your father, decided to go to the United States that time, but he came up to me in a big hurry.

"Listen, José," he told me, "I'm going to sell you the phonograph."

"I don't have any money," I said. "How much do you want for it?"

"I'm going to give you the record player and all the records for one hundred pesos," Pancho told me. "I'm going to give it to you cheap because we're going to Texas."

In those days, the peso was worth something.

"Well, I don't have any money," I told him, "but I'll get some right away from my godfather."

I got the money from my godfather, who was the chief mechanic at the roundhouse in the railroad yards there in Monterrey. My poor godfather, I never paid him back.

Lydia

But even though Papá wanted to move badly enough to sell his precious phonograph, this time, Mamá—since just about every year we went back and forth from Mexico to the U.S. or vice versa—told Papá that she was tired of never being able to really settle down in one place or the other. She complained that we kids could never go to school and that it was too irregular a life. Mamá just got tired of living one year over here and then another year over there. We didn't really learn Spanish or English correctly; we were never in one place long enough. What could a kid learn in one year? When Mamá saw that we were starting to grow up, she said, "No! No more of this moving back and forth like gypsies!"

That's why Manuel and Juanita were able to go to school for a while in San Antonio later on. María, too, had some opportunity, but in 1927 we were growing up *burros*, donkeys. Beatriz and I, the two oldest, never went to school. Papá never sent either one of us to school. And, of course, we were constantly on the move: always going back and forth. So that last time in 1927, Mamá said it loud and clear, "If we go to the United States now, I'm not coming back here. If you want to live here in Mexico, we had better stay right here."

"No, no," Papá said, "let's go to Texas."

She told him that he had to decide where he wanted to live and that she would go along with his decision, as long as it was going to be permanent. She said she didn't care if it was one side or the other, as long as we were going to stay put.

"If we go to the United States now, I'm not going to come back here to Mexico," she told him, "I'm going to stay over there."

"Okay, all right," Papá said, "it's all right."

So we went to the United States, and we never returned to Monterrey. One of the reasons that Mamá really didn't want to live in Mexico was Papá's drinking. When we were here in the United States, the family was much happier. It was still the time of Prohibition in the United States, and Papá drank a lot less in Texas than he did in Monterrey. Drink had a very bad effect on Papá. He would get mean and beat up on Mamá—he would really hit her. He would back her into a corner, and cussing and swearing, he would tear into her—hit her real hard. She would just curl up and try to cover herself. And God help her if she ever tried to get away or run away from him while he was beating her. She would have been in danger of losing her life. He might easily have killed her.

So she suffered a lot from his drinking. When we lived in the Bella Vista neighborhood in Monterrey, Papá would get off work at four o'clock in the afternoon and come straight home. He wasn't the kind of drinker who drank in *cantinas*, no. At home, he had some of those immense *garrafones*: glass bottles like those they sell bottled water in—you know—the kind that sit on top of a dispenser and are delivered on trucks. Every week, he had delivered to the house—they used to have home deliveries—big bottles like that of *mezcal*. Every week: one immense bottle of *mezcal* and two cases of soda pop. This was every week.

Papá would get off work at four o'clock in the afternoon, and he would be fine, sane and healthy, and everything was all right. When he got home, he would sit down in the main room of the house in his big chair. He had lots of books and newspapers, and he would sit down and start reading ... and drinking and drinking. His measure—his usual ration—was a bottle that held about a liter or more that he would refill every day from the *garrafón*, the big jug. He always drank at least one like that a day: every day. He would take a swig of the *mezcal* and then take a drink of soda, and he would go on like that until the bottle was empty. When he started getting down towards the end of the liter bottle that he used as a daily measure, he would say to me, "Lydia, tell your *nana* that I want to have dinner."

Well, he was already ... well, just imagine, with that great big bottle. He would sit down to eat, and for any little thing, he would start accusing my mother of all sorts of things. It was all his imagination. And just on account of those imaginings, he would beat up Mamá.

And many times when my sainted mother had barely escaped being killed by him in his drunkenness—he would beat up on her and then he would fall down asleep—the next day in the morning he would get up and wash himself, and then, "*Ay*, please forgive me," he would say to Mamá, "don't pay any attention to me, I was just drunk. Don't answer me when I'm like that."

"But Pancho ... ," Mamá would start to say to him when he was drunk and accusing her.

"Shut up! Leonorcita!" he would yell.

"Mamá," we would whisper to her, "don't answer him, he's drunk." And if she didn't answer him?

"What am I, your fool? Your dog? What am I?" he would shout at her. "Why don't you answer me? Can't you see I'm talking to you?"

Well, what could she do? If she answered him, "Shut up!" If she didn't answer, the same. So it was an *infierno*, a living hell. There were arguments and fights every day. There was no tranquility in that place ... just because of things that he would imagine, he would want to kill her. He was very jealous, and just because he would imagine that someone had told him that she had gone out somewhere while he was at work, he would beat her up.

Because of all this, Mamá and I and all of the rest of us were scared all the time. It frightened all of us. My sister Beatriz was the most afraid. If he so much as looked at her when he was drinking, she would run and hide under the bed. And the other kids would all hide, each in their own place. I was the only one that would stay and face him. I wasn't quite as terrified of him as the others, because he cared for me so much.

"*Papacito*, please don't hit Mamá," I would beg him.

I always followed him around when he got like that, and he would reply, "No, *hijita*, you don't understand." And he would go on persecuting Mamá. And this was a *mortificación*, a living hell for all of the family.

So when we came to the United States, it was the greatest happiness we ever felt. Over here, he didn't drink, and when he was sober, he was a very nice person. But if he took a drink, God help us!

CHAPTER 2

"We're the Cuarteto Carta Blanca."

Lydia

In 1927, when I was eleven years old, my father got sick. From the age of eleven, I began to understand what it was like to struggle in life, what it was to earn each day's bread. Because when my father became ill, he couldn't work anymore. He would get these sweats, and they would make him faint. Suddenly, these fevers would enter into him, and he would sweat a lot, soaking the sheets at night, and it would take him a week or so to recover. I never found out what was wrong with him, what he had, because he never went to see a doctor. He couldn't, because we were too poor. None of us ever saw a doctor: we didn't have any money. We just lived from day to day.

So Papá couldn't do anything, he couldn't work, and that's when I saw the tightness and poverty of everything. While he was working, we were poor, but we never lacked for the essentials; we didn't suffer calamities. But when he could no longer work, we really began to notice the things we no longer had. And, well, we were without education, without a way to go to work someplace to earn money. We didn't know anything but music.

At that time, I only played the mandolin in the group. My mother played the guitar, and my little sister Panchita, a little triangle. Papá, Mamá and I all sang, but Panchita just played her little triangle; she was very shy. Papá also helped us by playing the tambourine. Papá wasn't much of a musician or dancer, but he played the *pandero*, the tambourine. He used to do sort of a march while he played it. It's not really dancing, it's more like walking. He played the tambourine very well, and he could also play the triangle. That one march was the only dance that he knew how to do. That was the Cuarteto Mendoza of the very first years.

I, too, tried to help out by teaching María. She was the first one that I taught to play the mandolin. María eventually learned to play it very prettily.

27

When she could play the mandolin, then I started playing the violin. I learned to play by just watching, but that was a couple of years later on. In 1927, María and Manuel were still too young to perform with the group, and Juanita, of course, had just been born. I was always trying to build up the group in order to earn more money for the family. I was never a rebel like my sister Beatriz.

The first time that I remember going to play music with the family in public was in 1927 when we left Monterrey and immigrated to the United States. We started singing in restaurants, barbershops, on street corners and in little places like that. We would arrive at a place and ask permission to sing, and, sometimes, they wouldn't give it to us, and we would have to move on and find another spot. If we were given permission, however, and if it was a store or a barbershop, we would set up and play outside. They would put out some chairs for us, and we would play and sing out in front of the place for whatever the people cared to give us. Sometimes, too, we would play for family get-togethers, private parties, and then we would go inside and play for the people in their homes. We sang songs like "Rancho grande," "Las cuatro milpas" and "La Cucaracha."

When we left Monterrey, we first went on up to the border, and we ran through all the little border towns on the Mexican side—Reynosa, Río Bravo, Matamoros, places like that—singing and trying to get up enough money to come across. On the Mexican side, of course, there was no Prohibition, so there were *cantinas*, and we could play out on the sidewalk in front of them. And we sang in front of bakeries—all sorts of places, anywhere there were people who would listen—and even, at times, just on a street corner. We would just sing for whatever the people felt like giving us. When Papá thought we had gotten together enough money, we crossed over through Reynosa to McAllen, Texas. And then, we roamed like that all over the Valley of Texas for all of 1927.

At that time, it still wasn't as difficult for Mexicans to cross the border as it is now. Papá paid the passport for Panchita, María and Juanita, because they were born in Monterrey. We crossed over all together, but he didn't have to pay for Beatriz, Manuel and me, because we had been born in Texas.

María

It wasn't until 1950, when you had to have a green card, that Mamá took me down to the Immigration Office. All the *rinches* were there, and they started to question Mamá.

"Where was your daughter born?" they asked her.

"Well, María was born in Monterrey."

"How come our records don't say she was born over there?" one of them said, because they were investigating the births. Then he just said, "Come!" He wanted us to come back in two weeks because they were going to investigate me because we had crossed through Reynosa, not through Nuevo Laredo. They searched their records, and they found over there, among all the people who had crossed in 1927, there we were: Francisco Mendoza and his three daughters: Panchita, Juanita and me. And it said in those records that Juanita had been born in Cuba, and that I had been born in Argentina, and only Panchita had been born in Monterrey.

So those *rinches* didn't believe us. But I sure don't look like I came from Argentina, and Juanita, from Cuba? Who knows? Maybe if you were to color her hair lighter, clearer, right, maybe ... No, of course not.

"Don't you go and pay any attention to that old stuff that my husband had to say," Mamá told them, "because I'm the one that gave birth to them; I know where they were born."

Papá was smart. As long as we could pass, he just paid. At that time you just paid about five dollars, and that's all. He would pay for the ones born in Mexico. It's all on the immigration records.

Juanita

I just got my baptismal certificate, and it says I was born in 1926, and my name is Margarita, not Juanita. It says: Margarita Díaz Mendoza—and my name is Juanita Mendoza! On my I.D. and immigration papers I have Juanita Zamarripa Mendoza, that's what I use.

Andrew

Because of what my birth certificate says, I can't use my real middle initial, which is Z, from Zamarripa. I cannot use it because Daddy put Andrew Díez Mendoza on my birth certificate. Then my mother changed it to Díaz. Papá used Díaz because that was his grandfather's name. He did lots of crazy stuff like that. He put it down that Beatriz was born in Cuba, although she was really born here in the United States. But he said that she was born in Cuba. And he said that María and Panchita were born in Minnesota. He would take us across to Mexico with letters—no passports, nothing like that, just letters. They used to believe him and let us come and go. It was the same thing in the United States, he would start showing those letters; I don't know what he had in those letters.

If he said something, they used to believe him. Papá used to really tell some stories. He was talking to this couple one day, a man and his wife, and he told them, "Well, you know, I had a good trip. Oh yes, we did. We were coming from Cuba, and the only one that got sick was my wife. She couldn't stand the boat, and she got seasick."

"Oh well," they replied, "we understand that, she's not accustomed to riding on a boat."

And the lady of the house asked our mother, "You got sick on the boat, eh?"

"What boat?" Momma replied. "I have never been on a boat in my life."

Lydia

When we first arrived in Texas, we resided in McAllen, because my mother had some cousins there, some relatives of hers: the Zamarripas. We stayed there for a while—probably about two months. Then, we went to live in Weslaco and, after another little while, we moved on to Harlingen.

We barely made enough to eat. We were a large family. It was Beatriz, me, Francisca, María, Manuel and Juanita—there were eight of us in the family, including Mamá and Papá. When we arrived in McAllen, we didn't have to pay rent because we were with relatives. Then we went on to some other relatives of my mother's in Weslaco. We stayed there for a while, and then from there we moved on to Harlingen. We didn't have any relatives in Harlingen, so we had to pay rent there. We had two little rooms for the whole family. But, in any case, we were always traveling from one place to another in order to make a living. We'd grab the instruments and just go on the bus. We paid to ride on the bus from, for example, McAllen to Brownsville. We would go on the local buses: not the Greyhound or anything like that.

On this side of the border, people would give us American money: pennies, nickels, dimes. At the most, we'd put together about five dollars in one day in 1927.

María

We went to Weslaco, Texas, over there in the Valley. We lived there with our godmother, Jesusita. We stayed with her when we passed over here to the Valley. I remember during the daytime, I would go over there to help my godmother to get some water from the *noria*, you know. We didn't have water in pipes, it all came from the well. I would help my mother and my godmother during the day, and at night the group would go to some town to sing, but I wouldn't go along. Manuel, Janie and I were still too little, so we stayed home with our godmother. She would take care of us while Mamá and Lydia and the rest went out to sing and try to make a little money.

Lydia

We stayed in the Valley for a year, singing and playing with our instruments. When I saw that my father could no longer work, and that we were lacking for essentials, I tried to help Mamá build up the music so we could live from that. We were roving all over the Valley. María was still very small, and I hadn't yet taught her to play the mandolin; I would still play the mandolin in the group.

After a while, we moved to Kingsville. We were there for New Year's in 1928, *allá vimos nacer el* 28. We were living there in Kingsville. One day Papá was reading *La prensa*, the Spanish-language newspaper from San Antonio, and when he turned to the page that had the *aviso clasificado*, the classified ads, he exclaimed, "We're going to San Antonio!"

"What, Pancho?" Mamá asked him. "What are you talking about?"

"We have to go to San Antonio right away, as soon as possible, that's what I mean," Papá replied.

It was then that he read us the advertisement. The OKeh Record Company announced that it was going to be recording Spanish-language musicians in San Antonio for two weeks. They wanted anybody that knew how to sing and play instruments. As soon as Papá saw that ad, he was convinced that we had to go straight to San Antonio.

Papá asked this man he knew in Kingsville if he could take us to San Antonio. You see, we didn't have any way to get there: no transportation or anything. This man had an old Dodge. It was an old car and didn't have any windows: it was open. It looked like a Model T, but it wasn't a Ford, it was a Dodge. We didn't pay him a single cent up front, because we didn't have any money. Papá told him that we were going to record, and that we could give him something when we got to San Antonio.

The man thought very highly of us: "Don Francisco, I'll be very happy to take you to San Antonio, if you'll just buy the gas," he told Papá, "but I don't have very good tires."

"Well if you don't have good tires," Papá replied, "we'll just buy some tire patches."

"All right, we'll get there on patches, but it will be all right," the man said, "because the motor is very good. The tires are the only problem, they're very old."

So that's how we got there. I think that we bought about fifteen cans of patches. We started out, and you know how many flats the poor guy had on the way? He had about twenty flat tires on the way, believe it or not. Every time one went he would tell Papá, "Flat, *compa'*." Bump, bump, bump, bump, bump . . .

They were those skinny little tires like they used to have, and he had about twenty flats on that trip: just to get us to San Antonio. We would go for a few miles, and then we'd get another flat. We'd have to stop, and they would get out and raise up the car with a jack, and Papá would take off the tire, and they would put another patch on it. It took us two days to get to San

Antonio, and it's only about one-hundred-and-fifty miles from Kingsville. When it started to get dark, we didn't want to take the risk of having more flats without the light, so we stopped for the night. The next day we started off again as soon as the sun started to come up. We finally arrived in San Antonio in the afternoon.

We were lucky that the OKeh people gave us a chance to record. After we had auditioned, and they had decided that they liked the way we sang, we were told through their interpreter that they were going to give us $140 for twenty songs—that is, for ten records—and that they would pay for our trip to San Antonio. The ad in *La Prensa* had just said that the OKeh label was looking to record *artistas*, singers, who knew how to play instruments and how to play Mexican music. But it didn't say exactly how much they would be paid or that they would be given transportation: nothing like that. However, when Papá had a chance to speak to the company representative, he explained how we had gotten to San Antonio from Kingsville. The Mexican who was acting as interpreter for the OKeh company told them to give us so much money. He also told us that they would provide lodging for us, and that we should immediately find a hotel, and that they would also pay for our food. So Papá told them to give the man who brought us from Kingsville fifty dollars. The record company bought the man four tires and gave him fifty dollars for having brought us and to cover the cost of our return. All this, of course, was after they had listened to us and accepted us, and the contract had been signed.

The truth is that they paid us very little, but what did we know about these things? To us, $140 dollars was a fortune. But the big thing, what we were really happy about, was that we got the chance to record, that they accepted us. The amount they paid us wasn't really that important, what we were after was ... a beginning, a start.

The OKeh record company was recording lots of people in San Antonio at that time, and we thought we were very fortunate that right away they let us make some records. Unfortunately, we never heard any of those records after we made them. I didn't get to hear any of them at all until Chris Strachwitz played a couple for me when he was getting ready to put them out on an album. In all, we recorded eleven sides for OKeh back then. It seems to me that we did "Monterrey" and "Las cuatro milpas."

When we went to record, the OKeh people asked Papá, "What's the name of your group? You have to have a name or we can't record you."

Papá thought for a minute—because the group had never had a special name before—and then he said gruffly, "We're the Cuarteto Carta Blanca. Carta Blanca, just like the beer."

Before we came to record, when we were just roaming around singing

Cuarteto Carta Blanca: Leonor Mendoza, Lydia, Francisco and Panchita. Courtesy of the Lydia Mendoza collection.

in the streets, we didn't have a name or anything. We were just the family: *la familia Mendoza*. Papá must have thought of the name "Carta Blanca" because he had worked at their brewery in Monterrey.

On those OKeh records, I played the harmony part on the mandolin, my mother played lead on the guitar, my sister Francisca kept time with a triangle, and Papá banged away on a tambourine. That was the Cuarteto Carta Blanca. María still wasn't playing yet; she was very little, only about five years old. The lead voices were Mamá and Papá, as you can hear on the recordings. You can barely hear me on those at all, because I just sang the harmony and didn't really sing very much. The *dueto* was Mamá and Papá. You can actually hear all of our instruments on the records, you can even hear the little triangle.

Naturally, we were feeling pretty good then, because we had recorded and everything. And, of course, word got around that we had made some records, and we started to get more little jobs. We were beginning to get a little better known.

But then, a month or so after we made those records, someone, I don't know who, gave Papá the idea that up North they were making real good money with music, that a lot of people were going up there to work in the fields and that there wasn't much of anything up there in the way of music. And that was the way it actually was, too. There were lots of people going up there to work the sugar beets at that time, and I guess someone talked it up so much to my father that he got all excited and couldn't think about anything else. So, well, Papá got the idea of going up North. And one morning he came and said to Mamá, "We're going to go up North, to Michigan."

"Listen you, are you crazy?" she replied. "How are we going to go so far away? With what?"

And it was true: we didn't have anything. We didn't have any money; we lived from day to day. So my mother told him, "Ah, what's the matter with you, Pancho? You're dreaming."

"You'll see," he said, "we're going to go." Well, *dicho y hecho*, said and done. He left for the street. Three days later he came back with some papers, and he said, "Here it is."

"And this ... what's this? Some music contract?" my mother asked him.

"No," he said, "it's a labor contract, an *enganche*. We're going to work the beet fields."

He had gone and signed us up. The same thing happened when I came in and saw all the papers, the contract, and I asked him, "Where are we going to work, Papá?"

"We're going up North," he said.

"Where to? Which theater?" like a *loca*, I asked him.

"No theater," he replied, "we're going to the beet fields."

"Well, I don't know what we're going to do up there," Mamá told him. "What do we know about field work, about beets?"

"Oh, I know what I'm doing," he replied.

My father had signed up, I think, for four workers: my sister Beatriz, me, and himself and Mamá. But my mother, she said no, and my other sisters and Manuel were still too young.

"I'll cook your food," Mamá told him, "but I'm not going to go work in the fields. I don't know anything about all that."

But it didn't matter what any of us said, he had signed us up for an *enganche*, a contract to go work the beets.

Manuel

They had a railroad station on Flores Street in San Antonio, and we were going to leave from there. While we were waiting, I was running around the train yards, playing, and I saw this coach, so I got on it. Then it started moving, and Mamá started hollering: "Get out of there!"

I had gotten on the wrong train all by myself. When I heard Mamá hollering, I just closed my eyes and jumped. That's all I remember until we got to Michigan.

María

I remember that we were just waiting over here to go to Michigan, just waiting for the train to leave. And then, my little brother Manuel and my little sister Janie got down from the train to play on the ground—they were just little kids. And then, the train was going to start to go, and my father was scared.

"Where is Manuel? Where is Janie?" he started hollering.

I ran into the coach and my father was real mad, he really came down on me.

"Hey! Don't you have any sense?" he yelled at me. "Do you see your brother and your sister? See them over there, why don't you tell them to get on the train? It's going to leave without them."

Manuel jumped right up, but Janie hurt herself on the door, she was bleeding all over the place. She still has the scar.

Papá said that the trains were old, the engines and coaches were old, even for that time. He knew all about trains because he had worked for the railroad. At least, there were chairs in the cars for us to sit on.

They had food for us there on the train. They gave us "lunches" of bologna sandwiches and sodas. They gave food to all of the people who were going on the contract. Everyone on the train was going for the *enganche*; the train was special for the labor contract. The contractor sent along his representative, a guy who was in charge of the whole group.

Lydia

The trip up there wasn't too bad, but when we arrived in Michigan, they sent us out to a little ranch near Pontiac. Well, there we were. My mother was the *comisaria*, she brought food to us, and she put some pants on us, and: off to work!

And, well, what did we know about any of this? Those little plants—we had never seen anything like that before. The little beet plants were real small, but they were starting to put out leaves. We were told that each plant should only have two leaves. No foreman went with us that day, they just told us that we had to work down the rows, taking off all the leaves except for two, that had to be just so. Well, we'd tug on the leaves ... , and we'd yank out the whole plant. Who knows how many plants we murdered that day? It was hard work, and we weren't very good at it.

They had these old railroad cars set up as houses for the workers to live in. Our family was put in one. Everybody used to sleep in the same place: it was the whole blessed family in one room. We only had two beds for the eight of us. Manuel recalls that he had to sleep on the floor. At least they had a stove. Except for the two beds and the stove, there was no other furniture; it was just like the inside of a boxcar.

A week or so went by like this. In the afternoons we didn't have to work. Papá would sit outside with Mamá and her guitar and me with the mandolin. We would join together there to sing—it was our only real happiness in that place.

At the end of the week, they would have sort of a little fiesta out there, and all of the people that were working on the farms around there would come. One Saturday, some Mexicans who were working on another ranch passed by, and they stopped to hear the family sing. After listening to us for a little while, they told Papá, "Listen, what are you doing here? You can make more money with this music than by being stuck way out here. Wouldn't you like to go to town with this music? You'll make good money."

"Well, yes, we'd go, but we don't have any way of going—we don't have any transportation," Papá replied.

"Would you like to go next Saturday?" one of the men said to my father.

"Well, yes, we'd like to ... "

"Good, the boss where we are has a little old car," the man said. "He's a very nice *americano*, he'll take us."

Said and done. Yes, Saturday those Mexicans came, and they took us into town in the morning—their boss, and all of them, too. It was Mamá, Papá, Panchita and me. María, Manuel and Juanita stayed out on the ranch with Beatriz to look after them. Those men and their boss took us into Pontiac. We got there, and we caused a sensation, *un furor*. People came and stacked up piles of silver money for us—like so, so high—one silver piece after another: one silver dollar and then another and then still another—because there was a lot of silver money around. We didn't even have to pass the *pandereta* around like we usually did: they just piled up the money for us after each song. One man would say, "Sing *El rancho grande* for me ... ," and another would call out, "Sing *Cuatro milpas* for me. ... "

As soon as we finished a song, all of them, each person, would add another *peso*—one of those big silver dollars they had in those days—to the pile. You see, they used to pay off the workers with silver dollars in those days. This was right before the Crash of '29—the beginning of the Depression. In 1928, even the field workers were paid with real money: silver dollars. They didn't know anything about checks or paper money, and everyone still felt very prosperous.

We were singing in a little restaurant there in Pontiac—the only Mexican restaurant in town. The lady that owned it was delighted because her place filled up with people, and they bought lots of food and everything. We were there all afternoon playing, and we made, I don't know, I think, about two hundred dollars. We made a lot of money. We'd no sooner finish one song, and in a moment, there they were again: piles of coins. Well, the afternoon went on. The owner of the restaurant said, "You all aren't going back to the ranch, are you?"

"Well," Papá told her, "we have a contract."

"Well, don't ... ," she said, "don't worry about it, because a lot of people come up here on *enganches* like you did, and they leave the camps, and nobody goes out looking for them."

She didn't have to tell Papá twice. That same day or the next day, Sunday, they brought a truck and moved us into town from the ranch, because we didn't have anything, just our clothes. They brought us to town, set us up and gave us a place to stay.

Manuel

The owner of the ranch gave us some time to make the move. He let Papá out of the contract that he had signed. He told him, "You know what? You people ain't worth a damn to work in the fields. You should go soon and do some singing someplace. Go earn your living singing someplace, because I don't think you'll make it, you won't make a living at this work. It'd be better for you to go and sing, you're a lot better at singing than you are at this."

So Mamá, Papá, Lydia and Panchita went to Pontiac, and the rest of us—María, Juanita and I—stayed behind with Beatriz. She was the one that took care of us. She was only about fourteen or fifteen years old. We stayed out on that farm in the little shack. We used to have a dog there, we called it Fifi. At night, Beatriz would bring Fifi inside to sleep with us in bed; she was afraid. And you know what we used to eat? Those cans of pumpkin, you know, canned pumpkin, that's what they used to feed us: great big cans of pumpkin. That's all we used to eat. We survived, though.

We stayed there like that for—it seemed to me like it was weeks, but I think it was probably only two or three days—while they were gone to Pontiac. They went there to sing and make some money and find a place to stay. They found us a place, and then they came back and picked us up. I remember, they brought a little truck, a little Model T, and picked up all our belongings, and we went to Pontiac. We were driving by one of the big Michigan lakes, because I could—I thought we were near the sea someplace—because I could smell the water, you know. You know how it smells, like fish? And I wanted to look out—we had a canvas over the top of the truck—but my mother wouldn't let me look out. I wanted to see where in the hell we were, because there was this smell of water: water with fish. When we got to Pontiac, we went to this house—there were these people that let us stay in their house. And then, Mamá and Papá started making plans for renting a house of our own so we could take in boarders.

Lydia

We really created a sensation up there in Michigan, because there were no other groups playing Mexican music, and there were a lot of Mexicans working up there at that time. In those years, a lot of Mexican people were going—many workers—to the jobs up there, especially in the beet fields.

In the little towns like Pontiac, where there was a little Mexican restaurant, even though it was a very small one, all the people would get together on Saturday. Everybody from the fields would come to town. It was the same way in Detroit. When we got there, there weren't any other Mexican singing groups around. I don't remember running into any others up there; we were the only ones. We stayed in Pontiac for a while after that, and there we saw the birth of 1929. But we didn't stay there too long.

Papá started to feel a little better, and he wanted to go see if he could work some, and he wanted for us to go to Detroit. So we went to Detroit, and he got a job there. He worked at the Ford factory in Dearborn, Michigan. If my father was working, like when he was working at the car factory there, then things weren't so bad. When he had a job, everything was all right:

we didn't need to sing in order to stay alive. But we would still play music; there wasn't a *fiesta* that we wouldn't be asked to play at. But there weren't any bars—because of Prohibition—and I don't even think that there were any Mexican restaurants in Detroit. But people noticed that there was a family from Texas that played music, and well ... we didn't lack for work: in people's homes, at family get-togethers, in private houses. For instance, the very first day we arrived in Detroit, we stopped on a street corner and sang there for what the people would give us. That's how we started out up there.

When Papá got that job at the Ford plant, Mamá found a house to rent. It was a big, two-story house on Michigan Street, right in downtown Detroit. Since it was the custom in those days to rent out rooms—to take in boarders— we took in a few boarders and served meals. Mamá would prepare lunch and dinner for our boarders, and my sisters and I had to clean the rooms and help Mamá prepare the food. It seems like there were always about three or four of those boarders; they were all men.

Manuel

There were a lot of *polacos*, Polish people, around there. It was Prohibition time, and now when I see Elliot Ness, you know, *The Untouchables*, when they are breaking bottles and all that, it brings back the memories from when I used to be a kid. I used to watch the Federal men smashing beer bottles on a big tree trunk and all of those Polish women cussing like nobody's business. Those women would even beat up those Federal men sometimes.

Papá stayed with us the whole time we were up in Michigan; he didn't run off anywhere. We lived in a two-story house on Michigan Street. It was right on the corner; there used to be a drugstore kitty-corner to the house where we used to go and buy ice cream cones with a little cherry on top. The house had a big basement, and Papá had to stoke the furnace. Well, all the houses in Michigan, in Detroit, they all had furnaces in the basement. That's how they heat the places up.

I'll tell you one thing, Mamá, she had me very sissy-like. She used to hate for me to play with anybody; she thought that they were going to hurt me or something. I used to hang around with a kid by the name of Elmo. I was about five or six, and he must have been about eight or nine years old. One day, we were playing out there on the porch of the house on Michigan Street, and Mamá was going to take a bath, so she told me, "You stay right there! Don't move from that porch until I get out of the bathroom. I'm going to take a bath."

So she went inside, and then this kid, Elmo, tells me, "Hey, Manuel, let's go. Let's go see the toy store."

"No, no, my mother ... she'll get mad."

"Aw, come on, we'll be back by the time that she gets out of the bath."

"Okay, let's go," I said.

So we went over to see the toy store. It was about five or six blocks away, right on Michigan Street—right where Michigan Street is one of the main streets of downtown Detroit. When we got over there, I kept on looking at all of those toys: they were sure something. I was really amazed to see all those beautiful toys in there, and before I knew it, that kid Elmo was nowhere around. When I ran outside, I saw that he was running like mad, going towards the house. He left me at that toy store; he did it on purpose.

And there I was. Well, I started running after him. I wasn't crying; I wasn't panicking, either. I was just running, following Elmo. I wanted to see where he was going, so I could find the way back to my house. When we were getting closer to my house, I could see Mamá standing on the porch. I remember it as if it were yesterday.

She had her hands on her hips, and she said, "¡*Oiga*! Listen you!" she yelled at me. "Didn't I tell you not to go anywhere?"

"Listen, Mamá," I said to her, "Elmo said we were just going to see the toys and come right back, but he ... "

"Watch what you say, *cabrón* !" She got so mad. "Come here!"

When she got me inside the house, she got out a big belt, and she whammed the heck out of me. Man, she beat the hell out of me. It was so bad, I felt sore where she had whipped me for days. And you know, that did me some good, because whenever I used to leave the house I would wait for Mamá to say, "*Anda con Dios*," "Go with God," or "*Dios te bendiga, mi hijo*," "God bless you, son."

I wouldn't leave the house until she would say that.

Lydia

Manuel remembers those things, of course, because he was still a young child. My sisters and I had to work, helping our mother. Sometimes in the evening, though, we would get together and sing. Lots of people would come by to listen, even some of the *americanos*.

Up in Michigan we didn't play much with the other children, except with the Mexicans. If there were Mexican children around, we could play with them, but if they were children of other races, we couldn't. One thing I remember very well was that when we were living in Detroit, someone, I don't remember who, invited us to see the first talking movie. It was playing there in Detroit. My mother and I went, and one of my sisters, the oldest: Beatriz. The film was called the *Jazz Singer*, and it starred Al Jolson. We just went for the curiosity of seeing a talking picture. I didn't understand it very well—in those years, I didn't understand any English at all—but we had a good time.

My older sister Beatriz was growing more and more rebellious all the time. Beatriz never sang with us. She has a cleft palate; she sort of speaks through her nose. Beatriz swallowed a marble when she was real little, and when Mamá stuck her finger down her throat and pulled it out, she split her uvula. You can hardly understand anything she says, so she could never go out singing with the rest of us. Beatriz was a little older than I, and she lived in rebellion. She said that she was going to get married to the first man she ran into, because she wasn't going to go on with the kind of life that we had been leading. She didn't want to help us struggle.

One of our boarders was a young man from Chihuahua named Ignacio Montoya. He was about twenty-two years old, and he had gone to work up there in Detroit at the Ford factory. Papá met him at work, and Ignacio became one of our boarders. When Ignacio and Beatriz told Papá that they wanted to get married, he got mad. Oh man! He got real mad. Papá said that he had taken Ignacio in first as a boarder, and that now he was taking advantage of the family. I'm telling you, Papá used to blow his top. He told them he didn't want Beatriz to get married. But she said that if they didn't let her, she was going to run away. Then my father, cursing and grumbling, said, "If you run away, I'll have you put in reform school."

Then Mamá grabbed my dad and told him, "Look, it's impossible ... she wants to get married ... let her. We're going to let her get married. Why should we want to keep her by force? Let her go however she likes. Put her in jail? What for?"

Mamá finally convinced him. And so Beatriz got married at the age of ... she was barely fifteen—she was very young.

Beatriz

I liked the music that Mamá and my sisters played, but I couldn't sing with them. Mamá wanted to teach me how to play the violin, but I never learned it. So even though I was the oldest, I was always left behind to take care of the little children when the family would go out to sing.

I didn't get married in church, we just got married. At first Ignacio, my husband, and I stayed on at the boarding house my parents had. But when I got pregnant, Ignacio took me to an apartment, and I took my sister Francisca, Pancha, along to help me. My mother sent her to help me because I was very young at that time. And then my husband used to lock me up, and he would go away. If I said anything to my father, Ignacio would beat the hell out of me, you know, beat me up. I was so afraid, I wouldn't tell my father anything. I got married too young.

And then, when I was expecting my first child any day, Ignacio took me to my mother and left me with her, and he didn't even pay for the child's birth. It was the beginning of the Depression, all the men got laid off at the Ford factory and Ignacio couldn't find a job.

Lydia

That's how my sister Beatriz remembers 1929 in Detroit, although my own recollections are a little different. As I recall, Ignacio was laid off from his job at the Ford plant, but he was always on the look-out for any little job that he could find, and he did what he could. He always brought home whatever he earned and shared it with the whole family as long as he and Beatriz were living in our house. But one time when their newborn baby was still very small, Ignacio couldn't find any work, and Papá ran him and Beatriz out of the house. That's why they had to go out and find another place to live. And to be honest, I never saw him mistreat her while they were living with us. But it's Beatriz's own life, and I'll let her tell her own story in her own way. My brother-in-law Ignacio wasn't all bad by any means, though.

Manuel

Ignacio was a hustler; he used to work. I mean he used to drive a dump truck, and deliver bread, and do all sorts of little jobs after he got laid off at Ford. Ignacio used to be a hard-working man; he changed after he went back to Mexico. But you know, he used to be a pretty good man.

That was the beginning of the Depression. Everybody got laid off from the Ford plant. We used to get some help from the Welfare up there—the Relief, whatever you call it. They used to give us some coal and some money to buy food with, but eventually the family had to start singing for a living again.

Lydia

In 1929 when the Depression came, when a lot of people began to lose their jobs, my dad also lost his job. Finally, Papá said, "No, we're not staying here." The winter was very hard, very cold. "We're going back to Texas!"

We left right away. It must have been around 1930, because my youngest brother, Andrés, was born there in Detroit just before we left. Both he and our half-brother who died in Monterrey that same year had the same name: Andrés.

Mamá kept on writing to our half-sister Mónica over there in Sugarland, Texas. Mónica had stayed behind in Mexico when Mamá and Papá came to the United States the first time. But after she got married, she and her husband, José Martínez, came here to the U.S. By 1930, they were living over there in Sugarland, not far from Houston. She kept on writing back to Mamá, asking us to come and stay with her. So we decided to go down there.

Mamá sent a letter to Mónica in Sugarland, letting her know we were going to come. Then Mónica and José sent us some money so that we could buy them a car up there in Detroit—they were very cheap up there—and bring it down to them. They wanted a closed car, so we bought them a Chevrolet sedan. That was the car that Mamá and the youngest children rode in. Ignacio bought a great big old Dodge—a convertible, an old used one, that was also very cheap. And finally, we sold everything we had up there, and Papá bought us a little square Model T truck which he was to drive all the way down to Houston. So we loaded everything up, and we started the journey back to Texas in a little caravan of three vehicles: the little truck and the two cars.

We left Detroit in October, and we arrived in Houston in December. We spent almost three months on the road, traveling. Because we left with so little money, we'd have to stop in the towns along the way, play some music to get some money, and then buy food and fill up the cars. We'd arrive at a town, and we would be running low on gas, so right there we would look for a place to sing. That was the way that we came, and that was how we made our trip until we arrived here in Houston.

On the road from Detroit to Houston we camped out most of the time. When we did arrive in a city—we looked for cities where we thought there might be some Mexicans—we would go and ask them for help. When they saw how we were traveling, what kind of shape we were in, that we needed help, well, they would organize *reuniones*, get-togethers, or little parties in some family's house. We would sing for them, and they would ... help us. That's how we would get money together for traveling. We'd fill up all the cars with gasoline, and we'd hit the road, *y caminábamos*.

But since the towns were often distant from one another and sometimes pretty far from the highway as well, we would buy bread, cold meats, and we'd eat what we could on the road. At times we would have the desire for something cooked, so, well, we'd improvise a fire in the woods or fields by the side of the road, and there we would cook our little dinner, and we would eat, and then get back on the road. We didn't go to restaurants. We didn't give ourselves any luxuries. We usually contented ourselves with having a slice of bread and a piece of bologna or something—whatever we could afford. Occasionally, however, we would treat ourselves to something special. One time, for instance, Ignacio told Mamá, "I feel like eating flour tortillas."

"Well, I'm not going to mix the dough and all that," Mamá said. "It's too much work out here on the road."

"I'll mix it, I'll make them, Mamá," Ignacio told her—he always called her "Mamá."

So he went to the store and bought flour and brought it back to where we were camped. Somehow he rigged up an old piece of sheet metal over the fire, and he made tortillas right there. That was a real treat for us.

Most of the time we slept in the cars out near the road. We almost never went into a town to spend the night. We did stay in St. Louis, though. We had to stay there because the little truck got lost just as we were arriving. Papá took the wrong way; he took another road. The rest of us in the two cars arrived in town together, but the little truck never caught up with us—we never saw it. My dad and my brother Manuel were riding in that truck. Manuel was still pretty small, and Mamá was worried about him. So we couldn't go on. We had to wait for them and see what had happened, but we didn't know where to go or what to do.

So then, we went to a firehouse where all the *lumbreros*, the firemen, were. They were all *gringos* there at the firehouse, but we asked them where the Mexican neighborhood was, and they told us where to go. There was a man with us who had agreed to drive the other little car, the Chevy, if we would take him back to Texas. He spoke pretty good English, and he did all the talking for us. He was the one who asked the firemen where the Mexican *barrio* was. We went over where the firemen told us to go, and at the first house we stopped at, we met *una santa familia*, a blessed family, that gave us some help. They saw what kind of shape we were in, and they told us to come in and stay there. They put the whole bunch of us up in their house and gave us food to eat. We were hungry and didn't have any money, we were all lost and frightened, and that sainted family helped us out a lot then. They also helped us find la *"dichosa" troca*, the confounded little truck.

This is how my brother Manuel remembers that trip and getting separated from the rest of the family:

Manuel

I rode with Papá. We would spend the night by the side of the road in the truck, or we would camp outside: just lay on the ground. It was really cold, but we covered ourselves as well as we could. I remember sleeping in the back of the truck. I always wanted to stop. I was small; I was a little, bitty guy. At night Papá would take some of the luggage out of the back of the truck—we were carrying everyone's luggage in the truck, so there would be more room in the car—and we would sleep up there. Then in the morning, he would have to put everything back. So everyday Papá would have to load and unload that little truck a couple of times. And sometimes he would get it all loaded up, and then when he started to drive off, one of those big old-fashioned trunks we had would fall off the back of the truck, and he would have to stop and load it up all over again. Papá would really start cussing when that happened. Ignacio tried to help him a few times, but finally he gave up because Papá would get so mad and get to swearing so much.

We bought stuff to cook along the way—we cooked on the road. Our brother-in-law, Ignacio, was a good cook. One time, before we got to Sugarland, Papá and I got behind, and when we finally caught up with the rest of them, we saw Ignacio's Dodge parked by the side of the road, and there they were, making tortillas right by the side of the road. I don't know how he made the dough, but he was making flour tortillas. They sure tasted good to me. Another time Ignacio killed a rabbit, and he cleaned it and cooked it like barbecue over a fire by the side of the road. He was a cook, he was a jack-of-all-trades, that guy. You know, he went bad when he got back to Mexico.

And Mamá used to cook beans and rice for us; that's why it was so nice to have those tortillas to eat them with. We also ate crackers and canned sardines—stuff like that. And one time we passed a farm where the lady was milking a cow. It was very cold, and there were a lot of children there. When the lady saw all of us children, she gave Mamá a big jug of milk for us.

Just before we got to St. Louis—I was riding with Papá—he took the wrong damn road. My father was stubborn, he was stubborn as hell. He thought he knew everything, but he wasn't as smart as he thought he was. So we were going towards Minnesota while the rest of the family was heading for Texas. I just kept on saying to myself, "Oh hell, I'll never see my mother again."

I was just a little kid, and I used to be too close to my mother. So I started crying and saying, "Where is Mamá?"

"*Oh, ¡no estés chingando!*" ("Oh, quit your griping!") Papá would yell, and he kept hitting himself on the head. He was cussing like mad. And then, every once in a while, he would shout, "Where in the hell is Ignacio? He must have taken the wrong road!"

But it was Papá who had taken the wrong road. So, finally our brother-in-law, Ignacio, just turned back and came back the other way to see if he could find us. We had all of the luggage—everybody's—with us in the back of that truck. We were driving up towards Minnesota when Ignacio finally caught up with us. It was cold, colder than hell! And, you know, that truck didn't have any windows or anything; it just had those little canvas panels that you could cover up the openings with. Man, was it cold! It was the winter of 1930—probably November of 1930.

María

When we had almost got to Sugarland, Papá got in a wreck; he crashed the little truck. And we didn't have any way of carrying all the luggage. After we got to our half-sister Mónica's house, she went with Papá in another little truck to get it, but some black man had already come and picked it all up and was bringing it to us.

We stayed there in Sugarland with Mónica for a while and passed Christmas and the New Year at her house. The whole family stayed there for about a month or two. My mother wanted to stay there because it had been a long time since she had seen my sister Mónica, and my sister, Mónica, was so happy to see Mamá again. But my father and my brother-in-law José didn't get along very well. Papá, he was a mean one.

Lydia

As María says, it wasn't possible for us to stay there too long. While we were living out there in Sugarland, we still had to go into Houston and sing in barbershops and restaurants. Mamá could leave little Andrés with either Mónica or Beatriz, because they were both nursing small babies then. We were able to get a little money together, but transportation was really a problem. We had no sooner arrived in Sugarland than all of our cars broke down. Ignacio's, also. So it was a big hassle for Mónica and José to bring us into town every day and then come and get us when we were finished singing. For that reason, if for no other, we couldn't really stay in that little town of Sugarland.

José and Mónica had one of those houses that the Imperial Sugar Company used to give to the workers a long time ago over there in Sugarland. It was a company town, and they lived in a company house. They had about five rooms, that's all. We were too big a family for that house. Mónica and José had six children, and you have to remember that we had Ignacio and Beatriz and their little Charlie with us, as well as our whole family, including another very small baby: our youngest brother, Andrés.

Manuel

Our cousins, Mónica's kids, they were mean to us. They didn't like us being there; so we had to leave. They used to fight with us a lot. Those kids used to be very selfish, and very jealous of what they had. They had a house, and we didn't. They didn't want us to touch anything: none of their toys, or anything. We were just kids. A kid doesn't care whether it's somebody else's toy; he's going to try and play with it. They didn't like for us to handle their things.

All of José and Mónica's kids used to go to school right there. They had a beautiful school; I used to really like that school. And those kids used to look at us with ... like with resentment or something like that. Our own cousins! They're here in San Antonio now; they're all grown up and married.

Mónica's husband, our brother-in-law José, used to work with Imperial Sugar. He used to pack figs there at Imperial, and he loaned money. He did that in Monterrey before coming to the United States, and he did it up here too. José and Mónica had another business on the side, too: they made beer. Mónica knew how to make beer. You see, it was during Prohibition, and they used to allow her to make beer—3.2 beer, I guess it was called—but just to sell to people whenever they ate. They wouldn't sell it to people to get drunk.

There used to be some Federal men who would come to drink beer and eat at her house. I was just a kid, and guns used to scare me. I used to see the guns, you know, right there on the guy. Maybe, for all I know, it might have been some gangsters. But they said that they were Federal men. They would come in and drink the beer Mónica made. José and Mónica didn't miss out on any way to make an extra buck. All along, José's been sort of a businessman. Years later he had a bakery here in San Antonio.

José Martínez

When Mónica and I came here to San Antonio from Monterrey, we went looking for Pancho and Leonora. I knocked on the door where I had heard they were staying. I had to pick up a rock to knock louder, to see if someone would come out. Finally, a lady came out and said, "Who are you looking for?"

"Pancho Mendoza," I said.

"Ay, Mister, they just left. They left this morning for Michigan."

So we went on over towards Houston to see if we could find work. We were in Houston when a man came to look for pickers, for cotton pickers to pick the cotton harvest. So I signed up—without taking Mónica into account. And I told her, "Listen, Mónica we're going to *las pizcas.* ... "

"We're going to go where, you say?" she said.

"Well, *a las pizcas de algodón*, we're going to go pick cotton."

"Where are we going to go pick? But we don't know anything about picking cotton, man! What do you mean we're going to the cotton harvest?"

"Well, they'll teach us how when we get there."

"All right, whatever you like," she finally told me.

And we picked up our spirits, and we went off to pick cotton. When we got there, I didn't like that ranch. So, I finally went to work sharecropping for a man from Sugarland. He had a lot of land planted in cotton. There were a lot of pickers there, and I was also there with Mónica. I made pretty good money during the harvest, *en las pizcas*. That's how we got established in Sugarland. It was purely business, really. I never worked in the fields. I didn't pick the cotton myself; I had other people do that. I was the boss. I did that for three years before going back to Monterrey.

Lydia

Well, our brother-in-law José, he was really a businessman; he was always a businessman; it was business all the time. At that time, most of the population over there in Sugarland was Black. One house after another, they were Blacks, and they were all working for Imperial Sugar. José, our brother-in-law, used to lend them money. He was like a *prestamista*, a moneylender or loan shark. He and Mónica also made beer and sold it to those sugar workers. I guess that, in a small way, you could have called him a bootlegger. He and his family were doing pretty well, and we didn't have anything. So we decided to go back to Houston.

Mónica and José helped us to move and install ourselves here in Houston in Magnolia. It seems to me that it was in Magnolia near Avenue B— that was where we lived, not right here in town. Most of the Mexicans in Houston lived in Magnolia in those days. It was the *barrio*, the Mexican neighborhood, although it no longer is today. At that time there were no Mexicans living in the central part of the city, like where I live now. The neighborhoods were separated in those days, because Mexicans couldn't live where there were Americans. We lived here in Houston during 1931 and part of 1932, almost two years.

I never thought about making a solo career for myself in those days because what I wanted was ... for the group, to build up the group real strong, *formar aquel grupo bien formado*. At that time I was singing *la segunda* to Mamá: the harmony part. I was the second part, *yo era la segundera*, the accompanist. Of course, when we started to record later on, they dragged me up to the microphone so that she became my *segundera*. But my mother was still the lead singer in those days in Houston. I never had the ambition to want to be a solo singer. No, I just wanted the group to be strong.

The group was now starting to shape up pretty well. I had been teaching María to play the mandolin since 1928. When she had mastered the mandolin sufficiently well, I took up the violin on a full-time basis. That was when

María became a regular member of the group. This happened around 1931. So the group was really taking shape, because María played the mandolin, I played the violin, we had the guitar, the triangle and the tambourine; now there were five of us. The mandolin would play the lead melody, I played the *melodía segunda*, the harmony part, on the violin and Mamá played the bass part on the guitar. When we were singing, I would do the harmony, and my mother would sing the lead.

It was here in Houston that I taught myself to play the violin. One Cinco de Mayo we went to a *fiesta*, and I saw some musicians playing there, and one of them was playing a violin. I really liked it a lot. So, just from watching him, I saw how it was played. Somehow I got a hold of a violin, and I taught myself to play by remembering what I had seen at that *fiesta*.

Well, then I also started learning to play more on the guitar. I didn't know if I had a voice, if I could really sing. But then, right here in Houston, in 1931, while we were living in Magnolia, I started picking up the guitar whenever I got a chance. I liked to study and learn more about the guitar, and one day as I was practicing, I started to sing one or two little verses of a song that my mother sang. And as I began to sing, I noticed that I could sing solo. But I didn't give it any importance. That was the first time that I sang one or two verses, for myself, while playing the guitar. But that was all.

During this time, I also helped Mamá teach my sister Panchita the guitar so that Mamá could rest sometimes. We were a group mostly of little girls—I was only fourteen or fifteen, and Panchita and María were even younger—but I think that helped. People were more likely to help us because we were children.

We sang songs like "Trigueña hermosa" ("Beautiful Brown-Skinned Girl" and "El ingrato" ("Ungrateful Man").[1] Many of the songs that we sang were written by my mother. Mamá composed them. "El ingrato" and "Pero paloma" were both her songs. There was another one they go around singing nowadays that was Mamá's, "Yo fui el primero" ("I Was the First").[2]

Yo fui el primero

Yo fui el primero que besé tus labios, y la primera sonrisa enamorada, y de sus ojos la primera mirada, y de sus pechos un suspiro virginal, y de sus pechos un suspiro virginal.

Me duele el corazón de tanto amarte, y de adorarte, mi bien, con tanto amor. Vengo a pedirte que por compasión derrames una lágrima que calme mi dolor, una lágrima que deje engañado el sol.

Porque a otro hombre tu corazón le has dado y que le amas con delirio a ese hombre, ¡guárdale pues, tu dignidad y tu nombre! ya que nada existe entre los dos, ya que nada existe entre tú y yo.

Aquí te envío estas marchitas flores y los rizos de tu frente que me diste y las cartas que en un tiempo me escribiste, ya que nada existe entre los dos.

I Was the First

I was the first to kiss your lips, and the first to receive your first enraptured smile, and from your eyes the first glance, and from your breast a virginal sigh, and from your breast a virginal sigh.

My heart aches from loving you so much, and from adoring you, my love, with so much passion. I come to beseech you to be compassionate and let fall a tear that might assuage my pain, a tear that will deceive the light of day.

Because you have given your heart to another man and you love him deliriously, entrust to him, then, your dignity and reputation! now that nothing more exists between the two of us, now that nothing more exists between you and me.

Here I'm sending you these wilted flowers and the lock of your hair that you once gave me and the letters that you once wrote me, now that nothing more exists between the two of us.

"Yo fui el primero" was originally a *danza*, but now they've made it into a *corrido*. You see it all over. "Pero ay qué triste" ("But Oh How Sad") was also by my mother, but people have stolen many of her songs from her. Those are both songs I recorded.[3] She had *danzas*, and she had *rédovas*; she had a bunch of different kinds of songs. We sang all of them.

The people would all gather around to hear the music when we would play out in front of those little stores. And then we would pass around the tambourine that Papá played, and they would throw us the money. It was a very pretty sight, and very special because we were women and very young.

It attracted a lot of attention, because we were a family and most of us were very young girls.

In Houston we continued going around singing—all of us. We would play in the little restaurants and stores, just like before. Sometimes we would also go out and sing in some of the other little towns around there, like, Richmond, Rosenburg, New Gulf. We would also go to Baytown, Texas City and, very often, down to Galveston. Especially during *las pizcas*, the harvests, when there would be a lot of Mexican workers out in the fields, we would go out and travel around to try and make a little extra money. At first, we had to go on the bus or the streetcars, because we no longer had a car of our own. Manuel was a little older now—he was now an *hombrecito*—so we gave him the triangle, and he would go along and help, too. It was still the Quinteto Carta Blanca.

Manuel

When we moved to Houston, that was rough. We had a hard time. There was no work—nobody was working—and it was still winter time. We used to live in a house, and I remember that Ignacio, my brother-in-law, and I used to go out at night in his little Model T Ford and steal railroad ties to build the fire to heat the house and cook. It was very cold in those days, and we didn't have any coal or wood, so we used to go steal those ties. And you know, the guard that used to be there, he wouldn't bother us when we were picking up the ties and putting them in the truck. I guess he realized that times were pretty hard. We got those ties over by the railroad station. We would load them into the back of the little truck and take them home and then cut them into pieces and put them in the fire. That's how we kept warm. You have to make it somehow.

Lydia

But we also used to go out and cut firewood in the countryside. Mamá and I went along with Ignacio many times. I don't remember them ever stealing railroad ties. We used to go out to the bayous to cut firewood for the house.

Manuel

We lived in Magnolia. That's sort of a suburb of Houston. But we were still living like Gypsies. Except for that really brief time in Detroit, none of us went to school yet, we didn't go to school at all. Mamá wanted to send us to school, but Papá said, "What the hell do they want to go to school for? I didn't go to school and I can take care of myself, why should they go to school?"

But Mamá wanted to send us to school, so there was a controversy there. She tried to teach us, but she hadn't had the chance to get too much schooling herself, and so we mostly had to learn by ourselves.

I was about seven years old. At first, I didn't even play the triangle yet, I was just taken along when the family went around singing. We used to go out and sing in places like this little hamburger place right there at an underpass in Houston. We used to get up there and sit there and sing while all of the people would be coming in and buying hamburgers. Oh, those hamburgers smelled good! But we couldn't afford to buy any, we were just playing music and singing there to try and get a little money. And, oh man, it would take us a long time. You know, not too many people could afford to hand out money in those days. There used to be a lot of colored guys hanging around there buying hamburgers at that place where we used to sing. I don't know what they thought of our music, they would just stand right there looking at us. I don't know whether they enjoyed it or not, but there they were. I guess it kind of struck them as funny.

While we were living there in Magnolia, Papá finally bought another little old car, and we started traveling to places like New Gulf and Old Gulf, little places not too far south of Houston, down right close to Matagorda. They make sulfur there in New Gulf.

We'd do all right. We'd stay there a week at a time. My mother had a friend that had gone to school with her in Mexico who was living in New Gulf, and the family would stay with her while we were there. We used to make good money, because the people would pay to hear us sing. The people that worked for the sulfur company were mostly Mexicans, so we used to make what was a lot of money for us at that time in New Gulf. They used to treat us real nice; they were real good people. Everybody lived in company houses. There's nothing much else around that place; they have to pay people to live there. It stinks like hell around New Gulf because of the sulfur plant, but we used to sing there. We would go in places like barbershops or in some restaurant, outside the restaurant or just outside. ...
But we made good money. We would go down there and work for about five or six days, and then we would be able to come back to Magnolia and relax for about a month. We would make enough money to pay the rent and buy food.

Mamá was a good bookkeeper. She used to buy a lot of food all at once and store it away to save money. She was a good planner. I don't know how she used to make enough money to take care of everything.

We would never eat in restaurants ourselves if we had to pay, or spend any money unnecessarily. I'll give you an example of how we used to travel. One time during this period, we were out working on the road, singing, and we had been traveling all over South Texas, around Corpus, and we were coming back. We stopped at this little ranch because we were hungrier than hell; we hadn't eaten in a long time.

My father asked the lady at that ranch if she would like us to sing a few songs so that maybe they could give us something to eat. I guess they felt sorry for us, and they told us to come on in. So we went in, and this man liked the way we sang, and he served us some real fresh milk. It was still warm. I even went with him while he milked the cow outside. That's the best milk that I ever drank. I've never again drunk milk like that. And they gave us fresh baked, sweet bread to eat, too.

Once in a while we even used to enjoy ourselves, like when we used to go to the movies. Lydia, Mamá and I would go, but they would make Panchita and María stay in the house to take care of Janie and Andrew. The little girls liked to draw to pass the time, and we would call them *"Las '¿qué hago?'"* the " 'what is there for me to do?' girls."

But on the whole, it was real hard there in Houston; we had a rough life over there. And then we had some bad luck. My father had bought that little car, and we had a covered box on the running board where we used to put the instruments. One time we were going somewhere to sing, and this guy came and hit us broadside: bang! It tore up all the instruments. That really put a hardship on us, to get some more instruments. So when we finally got some more instruments, we started thinking about moving on again.

Lydia

I don't think Manuel is exaggerating. When we were living in Houston, times were really hard and there was very little work. Several times we couldn't pay the rent, and the landlord kicked us out. We'd try to rent a single room somewhere for the whole family until we got up enough money to rent another house. Papá didn't even go looking for a job, because he had already said that if we didn't go back to Mexico, he wouldn't work. But Ignacio would get up every morning at 4 o'clock and walk about five miles down to where the produce market used to be in those days. He would get there when the trucks arrived at 5:00 AM, and he would help unload the trucks and then do odd jobs around the market. Then in the evening he would come trudging home with his dollar that he had earned and a big sack full of potatoes, onions, chiles, tomatoes, lettuce—all kinds of produce that they would give him where he worked. Sometimes he would get mad when he got home: "Look! Look at what I've brought," he would tell Papá. "Why didn't you get up and come with me?"

"Ay, cabrón," Papá would say, "you go ahead, but not me. I'm not working for these damn *gringos* anymore."

But Ignacio would always go and bring back whatever he could. Both up in Michigan and back in Texas, Ignacio really helped us a lot. There in Houston, when things were really bad, it was what Ignacio brought home that kept the whole family alive. But he finally got tired of fighting it. There still weren't any jobs, so he and Beatriz and their little family went back to his *tierra*: Chihuahua.

At this same time—1932—our brother-in-law José, Mónica's husband, decided to leave Sugarland and go back to Mexico. His parents were in Monterrey, and he said that he wanted to see them again while they were still alive. José went into Houston and bought a brand-new little truck—a bright red one that he still remembers with pride—for seven hundred dollars cash, and started preparing for the journey.

When Mamá found out that Mónica and her husband and family were returning to Monterrey, she asked them, "Well, how about taking us along and leaving us off in San Antonio? We want to move over there."

Mamá had been talking about moving to San Antonio, because she thought that it might be a little easier for us to make a living there. San Antonio had more *ambiente*, because there were a lot more Mexicans living there than in Houston. For that reason, Mamá figured there might be more interest in our music—more possibilities—in San Antonio. The one thing that was certain was that we had to do something—make some kind of change—because we couldn't go on the way we had been any longer.

But Papá had his own ideas. In fact, ever since we had decided to leave Detroit, Papá had been trying to talk the family into returning to Monterrey. After he had worked for the railroad, he had gone back to work for the brewery in Monterrey. There he wasn't just an employee, he was a contractor. He contracted to do repair and maintenance jobs on the pipes, tanks and machinery. He had a lot of independence, and it was very good work. He had his own crew; he was the boss. On pay days he used to sit behind a big table loaded with stacks of coins—real money—and pay off his men one by one as they came up to him. Everyone had treated him with respect. Back in Monterrey, he gave the orders; he didn't have to be ordered around. So by this time—1932—he was sick and tired of being treated like a second-class person in the United States. Ever since he had been laid off at the Ford Plant in Dearborn, he just said, "Here in this country, I'm not going to work." And every so often he would start to say, "Well, I think I'm going to go to Monterrey."

In the past, he had always gone on ahead of the family to make sure that he had a job and a place for us to live before we all arrived. "I'm going to go to Monterrey and get a job and set up a house for the family to live in," he would say.

"Remember what I told you," Mamá would tell him, "I'm not moving back to Mexico anymore."

Mamá had told him when he wanted to leave Monterrey in 1927 that it was going to be the last move, and that we were going to have to live permanently on one side of the border or the other. And for reasons that I have already explained, Mamá and all of us children much preferred living in the United States, and Prohibition was still on here in the U.S.

"You're not coming back to Mexico with me?" he asked.

"No, no, I'm not moving from here, not anymore," she answered. "Remember what I told you!"

"Well, then, I'm not going to work!" he replied. "I'm not going to work for these damn *gringos* anymore. I'm going to Monterrey, that's where my job is. I have work over there."

"Well, go ahead and go," Mamá told him, "but you're going to have to go by yourself, because I'm not leaving this country."

Then he would ask us children, "Do you want to come with me to Monterrey?"

"No, Papá, we want to stay here," we would tell him.

"Well, I'm going," Papá said, "and if you don't want to come with me, well, you can all just stay here."

Well, I guess he wasn't really ready to leave without the family yet, because he stayed with us—cussing and complaining—but he never did work at a regular job again. He said that he was through with having *gringos* order and push him around. He kept on saying that he had his own job back in Monterrey, where he wouldn't have to put up with any guff or discrimination.

So when Mamá told him that José and Mónica were going to Monterrey, and that they were going to drop us off in San Antonio on their way, naturally Papá said, "No, we're going to Monterrey, too!"

Well, it was the same argument all over again, only worse: "No, we're not going to Monterrey," Mamá insisted, "we're going to San Antonio, and that's that!"

Well, Papá wasn't very happy about it, but for the time being he had to go along with the rest of us. Papá was very patriotic, and for that reason he really missed Mexico. It hurt him a lot not to be able to go back there to live. And sure enough, soon as we got to San Antonio, Papá said, "Bah, it's rotten here, it'd be better for us to go back to Mexico. At least I'd have a good job there."

"No," Mamá and the rest of us kids said, "we don't want to go back there."

"Well, you can stay here, then," he said, "but I'm going."

And he went. But two weeks later, he was back. He didn't even last two weeks down there by himself. But Beatriz and Ignacio and José and Mónica all did go back to Mexico at this time. When the Depression got real bad up here—there wasn't any work and the discrimination got a lot worse—I guess many Mexicans headed back for the other side.

CHAPTER 3

La Plaza del Zacate

Lydia

When we got back to San Antonio in 1932, the first thing we did was take part in some *concursos*, singing contests, that were going on at the Teatro Nacional. They were sort of like amateur music contests: mostly for children. The man who was in charge was a very good friend of Papá's, who he had got to know many years before. So Papá went over there when we got to town, and he told his friend, "Look, I've got this little group here, they're my children, could they possibly enter the contest?" "Sure, of course, lots of people are taking part in these contests," Papá's friend told him.

There really were quite a few people singing in those contests, and they were mostly boys: young boys who played or sang. There was one girl, however, I remember, because she played a twelve-string guitar.

We entered the contest, and I wanted to do some of my songs by myself, to sing them alone, without the rest of the group. The guitar that we had was a six-string, and it sounded real bad—it was a very old one. So, Papá asked that girl if she would lend me her twelve-string so I could sing a song. However, that girl didn't want to loan it to me, because she thought that she was going to win the contest.

All of the groups came out singing in turn, and then I went out with my violin, and my sister María with the mandolin and my other sister, Panchita, with our old six-string guitar. Manuel and Juanita even helped out on that occasion. Manuel played the triangle and Juanita danced; she was only five years old. We won the first prize, which was a five dollar gold piece. It was a five-dollar coin, but of gold! That was the money we used to settle ourselves in San Antonio.

The first thing we did was rent a little house, and then we bought some chairs, some old chairs, (this was when Papá ran off to Mexico) and we went down to the Market Plaza—where the Mercado is now. It was called the

Plaza del Zacate. It used to be open air, and there used to be some chili queens down there. They used to call them chili queens—they sold menudo and chili and all that sort of thing. And at night, there used to be a whole bunch—I mean a lot—of people singing down there: singers with guitars and everything. So we set up our chairs, and we sat right there and started singing, too. Then we used to pass the *pandereta* around. Really, just our same old routine, but now we were singing in the famous Plaza del Zacate. And, you know, believe it or not, we used to make enough money there to pay the rent and buy clothing and food and everything.

There were a lot of groups in the Plaza, but they were all men. We were women; we were the only women singers: my mother, my sisters and I. We were also the only group that was a family. The rest were strictly male trios or duets ... with their guitars ... singing ... making their living like us. Only a lot of those groups didn't get too much business. There were ... more than ten groups there all spread out through the open area of the Plaza. And they'd just be hanging around there playing dice at the tables; waiting for someone to turn up. There was an entrance through the middle of the Plaza where cars could come inside and stop at the edge of the tables where the hot food was sold. The people could get out of their cars there and eat if they wanted to, so they would drive in there and eat enchiladas and all that sort of thing at the little tables that were set up along the side of the little street that ran through the Plaza. As soon as a car would enter, everybody, all the musicians, would run and crowd around to see.

"Can I sing for you? Me? Can I sing for you? Do you want to hear "La Adelita"? Can I sing "Rancho grande" for you?"

Well, times were hard, and those musicians all made their living the same way we did: just from what people would give them. Everybody was chasing after the *centavos* in those days.

Americans and Mexicans—everybody—would come down there to eat and listen to music. As for us, well, we couldn't run after the cars like the other singers. We would just be sitting in our little corner, waiting for the people to come to us. A man who had a corner spot, a place where he put up his table and sold his food, gave us permission to sit at the edge of his stand. We had our little chairs; unlike the other groups, we played sitting down. Anyone that wanted to listen to us had to come on over to our little corner; we didn't go chasing after them like the others. The cars would arrive, and the people would get out to hear us. They would form a little knot around us and listen to us sing, while the other groups would run around as best as they could.

My sister María would stand there with her little plate that we took along, and she would take it around, and she would call out: "Échale, échale."

Some of the people would throw in pennies, two pennies, a nickel. ... We would put together fifteen, twenty, twenty-five cents a day. We played every night; that was our daily income. We would start to play as soon as it began to get dark. Summer and winter, *la familia Mendoza* sang in the Plaza every night.

The only reason we would ever miss a night was if it was raining very hard. That was just about the only reason we wouldn't go there. We would go even if it was very cold; and in the wintertime, it was very cold. But since the people would form a circle around us, we didn't feel the cold as much. Anyway, Mamá had this little can, and she would buy a nickel's worth of charcoal, and before we left the house, she would light it and get the coals burning nicely. Then when we went down to the Plaza, she would carry along the coals in the little can, and we would put it next to us on the ground. We would finish singing and playing a song or two, and of course our hands would start to get numb while we were waiting for our next customers. Then we would warm our fingers over the coals, so we didn't get too numb to play our instruments.

The whole night would pass like that until twelve o'clock. We had to get out of there a little before midnight. The Plaza had to be cleaned out by twelve because the trucks would start arriving then from the Valley with the fruit and vegetables. After the trucks came in, the people that had produce stands or grocery stores would begin to arrive, and they would buy their boxes of tomatoes and other produce and their crates of fruit there in the Plaza. That would go on all day. But by around six o'clock in the evening, this place—*La Plaza*—had to be empty again. Then the people who sold cooked food there would start coming in with their carts, their little tables, their chairs and their braziers, and they would start setting up for the night. Shortly after the food vendors set up, the singers and musicians would start to drift into the Plaza, too.

The groups that played in the Plaza made the people happy. Nobody had to ask permission from the authorities to sing. It wasn't necessary for the musicians, just for those who sold food. Never, that I can recall, was there a fight or a loud argument or anything like that in the Plaza. Everything was very peaceful ... very nice. There were never any difficulties of that kind.

In those days there were just local groups playing there in the Plaza. There weren't any musical shows, revues or anything like that. No groups from Mexico came to play in the Plaza, either; it was just the trios from around San Antonio and South Texas: strictly local groups. Of women, nobody! Just us, we were the only family and the only women there.

Groups and artists like Los Trovadores Tamaulipecos and Las Hermanas Águila passed through San Antonio and gave performances there in those

La Plaza de Zacate (Haymarket Plaza), San Antonio, Texas, 1920s. Courtesy of *The San Antonio Light* collection at the Institute of Texan Cultures.

days, but we didn't have any money to go to theaters. And besides, we had to sing ourselves in order to earn a living, so we didn't get to see them. As I have said, we sang in the Plaza almost every night.

Some of the other people who were singing in the Plaza at that time were Pedro Rocha and Lupe Martínez, Los Hermanos Chavarría, Gaytán and Cantú, Manuel Valdez, El Ciego Melquiades and Santiago Jiménez. All of them have recorded, and some of them became quite well known. They all started in the Plaza.

Actually, most of the groups in those days were trios, or, at least, they started out as trios. Sometimes, though, one of those trios would lose one member and become a duet. That, for instance, was how Pedro Rocha and Lupe Martínez became a duet. The Hermanos Chavarría were also originally a trio that lost one member to make a duet.

José Morante, musician, composer and, for the last twenty years, owner and impresario of the Sombrero, Norteño, Lira, Tesoro record labels, used to play in the Plaza himself on occasion.

José Morante
The first time I saw Lydia Mendoza was down in the Market Square in San Antonio where they used to sell *menudo* and *chili con carne*. It was all open air in those days; there was no building, no roof, no nothing: it was just the people there.

I used to hang around with some other people about a block away from where the Mendoza family would set up their chairs and sing. One night I walked up one block from where I was, and I just went up there to see the Mendozas play. Lydia was real young, real young.

Those Mendoza girls didn't follow people around like the other musicians did, they just sat with their mother. And the people would go over to them, come up and drop a dime, a nickel, pennies, you know, into their little plate. That's the way they were doing it. They didn't make too much, but it was enough; in that time, a nickel was enough.

The Mendozas weren't the only group working the Plaza, there was a bunch of musicians and singers down there every night. At that time, there was no work for people; it was the Depression. And those guys in the Plaza . . . some of them just had their guitars just to look like they were going to play, but they didn't really know how to play the guitar, they just sang. But they would carry guitars to identify that they were singers.

Before the Mendozas showed up down there, the people used to congregate where those other groups were singing. But when the whole tribe of the Mendozas—and there were a lot of them—started singing in the Plaza, everybody would go over where the Mendoza family sat. Those Mendoza kids would really get the money. And it was very curious, because as soon as they appeared, people started taking to them. They really brought in the audience.

I remember the Mendozas very well, although I wasn't playing yet myself. I was still pretty young—I'm a couple of years younger than Lydia. Most of the other singers in the Plaza were young people, very young. Not all of the people there, but the people that I got to know were young—although there were also a few old-timers. I remember one group in particular: the Model T Band. They were three old men, and they called themselves the Model T Band. Their only instrument was the guitar. Sometimes it would be three guys and only one guitar, because there were also some people who couldn't get an instrument, even if they knew how to play it.

But the Mendozas really stood out; there just wasn't anyone else like them around at that time, not a whole family that played music and sang together. I remember that Lydia's mother used to sing most of the lead parts, and it's funny, but what really intrigued me at the time was that triangle.

After that first time, I didn't see them again for a while. We were like everybody; comes the cutting time—you know, the cotton is ready to go—everybody starts going to the fields. We would go to, say, Austin and Lubbock; it would depend on the transportation that we could get. And the Mendozas were the same way; they would go to different places: down to the Valley, and I don't know where else they went to. But they disappeared for a while, and then they'd come back again.

Lydia

Many years later, my sisters and I recorded some of José Morante's songs, and we even made some records for his recording company. But I don't remember him from those days back in the Plaza. As he said, he wasn't playing yet, and I was concentrating on the music.

When it was cold, Mamá would make a fire in a little grate, and everyone would gather around to stay warm. Mamá also bought big leather jackets with fur-lined collars for both Manuel and me. I would wear mine with the collar turned up, and Manuel would wear his the same way, too. Manuel's jacket was so big, and he was so small, that the fur collar would completely cover his head when it was turned up like that. Consequently, Mamá couldn't tell if he had fallen asleep or not, and, quite often, he would slip off to sleep in his chair as the night went on. Then when Mamá realized that he had nodded off, Pow! She would whack him on the head to wake him up. He was real young—he wasn't even ten years old yet—and he really felt the cold. Our hands used to get real cold while we were playing. It seems like it was colder in those days. They used to have what they called *hielo prieto*, black ice, and you would see everybody falling down as they tried to walk along. It was slick, really slick.

Manuel

Mary and I, we were crooks. She might not admit it, but I will admit it now. When we used to pass the plate around, and people would put their little dimes or quarters in, we would slip a few into our pockets—we were just kids. Then we would go to the movies the next morning. Heck, I used to go to the movie show, and all the kids would see me giving away cookies and candy, and that was real unusual in those days. We were so poor, everybody was so poor, and they would see me going to the movies and eating candies and crackers and cookies ... it was really something. María and I used to fight to see who was going to pass the hat around, to collect the money!

María

I would take the dimes and the quarters and put them in my shoes. Mamá couldn't see what I was doing because of all the people that would crowd around to hear us sing. Mamá and the others would be sitting in the middle while I went out to collect the money. When I got way in the back of the crowd where she couldn't see me, I'd stick a few of the coins in my shoes. I'd take all of the dimes.

Manuel

It's a good thing that Mamá never caught us. Ohhh man! It would have been hell. We didn't realize that it was wrong, but Mamá was the head of the family then, and she needed that money to buy us stuff to eat, to pay the rent and to get us clothing. We were just irresponsible—we were only children.

The people used to ask to hear certain songs more than others. They would ask for "El rancho grande" a lot, and a song that Manuel Valdez wrote, "Los tres aventureros," and "María, María," "El capiro," and "El buque de más potencia." They were old songs, real old songs. They wrote pretty songs in those days. Nowadays, people don't like them like that anymore. They were songs that were popular in those days, that everybody knew.

María was already playing the mandolin, and I played the little triangle. They forced me to do it, I didn't want to. "You're going to play this!" Papá told me.

Panchita had played the triangle before I took it up, but she played it so much that she got a boil on her elbow, and she couldn't do it anymore. So they made me do it. Panchita played the guitar better, anyway. She used to play good guitar. She would go: boom, boom, boom, boom, boom. ... She used to really hit it. She played it real hard. Everybody used to tell her that she was going to bust out those strings the way that she was hitting it. But she used to play good, man. But Panchita was very bashful, she didn't like all the people looking at her. She used to wear a little cap to try and hide herself. When she saw the people coming, she wanted to run away. Mamá had to force her to come with us; sometimes she had to whip her. That's why Panchita finally stopped appearing with the group: Mamá didn't want to have to keep on forcing her to perform.

María

I remember those times very well. It was fun for me. I was the one that wasn't embarrassed in public. I wasn't shy, I was little and I would stand up to play the mandolin and sing, and the people would be curious about me. As I played I would begin to tap my feet, to do a little dance to the rhythm of the song. Those were old-time songs, but you could play along with them any old way on the little triangle, and Papá also played rhythm on the tambourine. We never used the *claves* in our *conjunto*, but Papá did play *los güiros* a few times. He got a *güiro* someplace, who knows where, and he would play it sometimes along with the tambourine. Mamá certainly didn't like the *güiros*. "Don't you go playing that thing," Mamá would tell him.

But no, he would play it to the rhythm of what we were singing.

When I first learned how to play the mandolin, I would join with Mamá and my sisters on some of the songs. We would play waltzes, lots of waltzes, like "El Salón París" and "San Pedro vacilando."

Lydia and I played the melodies, she on the violin, and I with the mandolin, and Mamá and Panchita accompanied us on their guitars. We all played in harmony, all together. And all the people were laughing about me, because I wasn't bashful, *no me dio vergüenza*, it didn't embarrass me. And then, when I finished, I passed the tambourine around to the people, and they put in some money.

Manuel

When Mary and I were singing in the Plaza, we used to compete with each other to see who could sing the loudest. You could hear us all the way down to the Tower, I bet you.

Juanita

I was about five or six years old when I started singing. The first time that I sang was in the National Theater. They took Manuel and me there to sing and dance. The people threw some money to us while we sang.

I remember that my mother always played the guitar. And I especially remember that my daddy didn't work—he never worked. I'm going to tell you the truth: he used to drink. It was a tough life. Everybody used to say that he was an alcoholic, and that he was our stepfather. They thought he was our stepfather because of the way he treated us. But he wasn't our stepfather, he was our real father. But the way he treated us … well, he didn't really care—maybe because he drank too much. When we were little, we started to see things, to notice the way he treated our mother, and the way she tried to keep on going. And Papá didn't seem to care.

The family didn't just play in the Plaza. They also played in a place here by the name of La Villa del Carmen. It was a little grocery store. They used to play there for a few dollars. They didn't take me most of the time, just once in a while, because I was still too small—I was only about five years old. But I remember that I liked to go along. The Villa del Carmen was just a little grocery store, but a lot of people would go there, because my sisters and my mother were singing. My mother was the head of the group.

The owner would set them up in a little corner of his store. It was Lydia, María, Francisca, my mother and Manuel. My mother played the guitar. Lydia played the violin. María played the mandolin, and Francisca also played the guitar. Manuel played the triangle. The owner set them up some chairs to one side of the door, where you would enter the store. But I usually had to stay home with my little brother, Andrew. When I did get to go along, they gave me cookies or some little candies. I was very little, but I liked to sing.

María

That's right, we used to go and sing in the Plaza at night, but sometimes during the day we would go and play at little neighborhood stores and restaurants. After 1933, some of those little places that sold beer became sort of like *cantinas*. On the weekends, especially, a lot of men would go into those places and drink beer. One place, La Villa del Carmen, was owned by a man we called Don Domingo. We used to play there while we were still working in the Plaza at night. Another place, it was almost like a *cantina*, they mostly sold beer, was called the Monterrey Cafe, it was run by Tito Garza. I can remember playing there the same year that Lydia got married, 1935. We also played at the Liverpool on Dolorosa Street.

Juanita

We managed because they started going to La Villa del Carmen to sing for a little extra money. They went every Sunday, sometimes on Saturday.

And then they would play in the Plaza at night. So it got a little better. It was not too good, but it was better. We were happy because when Mamá came home, she would give us two or three pennies ... so we could buy little treats.

But they had to stop singing at La Villa del Carmen, because my daddy went over there and told the owner that his family didn't have to sing there because he worked, he had a job. But it was a lie. He didn't have a job: my daddy didn't like to work.

He didn't sing with them there at the Villa del Carmen, either. When my father would go along with the family to the little places like that little grocery store, he just went along to fight with my mother. She would tell him not to go. He liked to sing with them, but he would make them mad. He couldn't control himself.

We never hated our father. My mother just used to say, "Well, he's your father until God ... " My mother had a rough time.

One day when I was little I asked him, "Why don't you work, Daddy? Help Momma?"

And he hit me. He got mad. "What's it to you?" he said.

Andrew

We have to understand my father. It was the Depression that sent him to drinking so much. It was a hard time to make a living. You know, during the Depression a lot of men died inside because they couldn't get a job.

It happened to me, too. I know how it feels to not be able to have a job. I'm going to tell you the truth. If you don't have a job, you can go and stand in any beer joint, and there'll be somebody that's going to buy you a beer. But they won't give you a dollar to take home. And that's the truth.

"You want a beer?" anybody will ask you. They'll buy you a beer. But they won't say, "You don't have a job? Here's fifty cents ... a dollar."

They won't say that.

And that's what probably happened to him. Anybody could offer him something to drink, but they wouldn't give him anything to bring home. He didn't have an easy life. You have to understand that.

One time, the group was singing at this beer joint, right after Prohibition had been repealed, and one of the men who was drinking there tried to get fresh with Panchita. "Don't do that! She's my daughter," he told the man.

The man turned to my father and knocked him flat.

When Juanita and I had to stay home while they were out singing, we would eat peanut butter, because we were so afraid of being alone. We thought that by eating peanut butter with our fingers ... we wouldn't be so afraid. It was a big house. My mother used to say that she used to pay five dollars a month rent for that house. When they would take Juanita along, they left me with my father.

I was left alone so many times. It's impossible to erase from my memory. You don't remember something when you had a good time, but you do remember something you went through . . . bad times, you know.

I played by myself a lot. I had imaginary friends that I talked to. There was really nobody there, but to me they were friends. When I started growing up, I used to play with clothespins. I made people out of them, and soldiers; I would make like they were fighting.

You can imagine in a two-story house. There were about six, seven, eight . . . about ten rooms, and a big porch outside the house. And lock up a little boy, about four years old, and leave him alone . . . all night. You can imagine how that kid felt.

Juanita

I stayed with you, Andrew!

Andrew

Not all the time. Afterwards, they left you with me, but at first they didn't. You all used to leave me with Daddy. When you used to go out on the *giras*, the tours, that's when you left me with Daddy. When you used to go out and leave town to play around here: San Marcos, New Braunfels, little towns around here. I understood. It hurt my mother more than it did me. She knew that I was a little boy, a little kid, and she knew I needed her. And she knew that she couldn't stay with me because she had to support the family.

Juanita

And things could get pretty tough. I remember one time when it was real cold, and we didn't have anything to eat. Momma walked with us all the way across town to the Relief. We didn't have any coats or anything, and we were very cold. We stood on the steps and rang the bell. It was freezing. A man finally came to the door and let us inside, and the people there gave us food and some little coats for us children.

Sometimes, we didn't have money to pay the rent. We had to use kerosene, and sometimes, candles. . . . It was a very tough time. We moved around a lot. We didn't have much furniture, so it was easy. Especially, I believe, for the grown-ups, it was really rough.

Andrew

This house where we all lived in San Antonio at that time was close to the Washington Plaza over on Monterrey Street. It was a big house. And not too far away, over in front of Washington Plaza where the truck drivers would park and leave their trucks, were the nightclubs.

It was a big house for five dollars a month. Five dollars a month! You can imagine the way the Depression was at the time. The whole family was living in that house. At one time we even had an uncle staying with us: my father's brother, Jesús. He had been a lieutenant in the Pancho Villa army back in Mexico. Jesús only stayed there with us for a little while, though.

At the time, they used to have prostitutes in that neighborhood. But it was the only place we could afford to live. Juanita and I used to go visit the prostitutes, and they would give us good food: hot cakes. It was a luxury for us.

Juanita

They'd give us a nickel.

Andrew

They were very nice. They would treat us very nice. They liked us. We were kids.

María

That's true. When we were little girls growing up in San Antonio, we used to live in a neighborhood that was full of streetwalkers, prostitutes— around Matamoros Street. They would be up walking around all night. It was where the *clandestinas* were, the places that sold bootleg beer and liquor. It was pretty loose in those days, and it was all mixed up, spread out; there weren't special places for that sort of thing.

Sometimes the prostitutes used to give us and our little brother, Andrés, things to eat, to feed us. I used to do errands for some of them, and they would give me a dime. Me, what I wanted, was the dime. I would go over there to Garcita's Drugstore on the corner of Matamoros and Pecos to run an errand for one of those girls, and from there I would go home and tell Mamá, and she would say, "All right." And I would be off again. Those women used to tell me: "Te doy una peseta" ("I'll give you a quarter").

Oh, I really liked that *peseta*. They used to send me down to Garcita's to buy them perfume, and I would bring it right back for them. They were all right.

Juanita

We used to see men in there, but we didn't really know what was going on. Once we went over to see one of those women, and there was a man there, so my brother and I left. We went around back to see what we could find, and that woman threw some water at us. And then they gave us a nickel and told us, "Whatever else you do, don't tell your momma. Here's a nickel for you, and don't tell her anything."

They always used to give us something. They felt sorry for us. It's not the same nowadays, but at that time everyone was poor, everyone was the same.

I had one good friend, she was a prostitute, and she was real nice with us. La Chiquita—they used to call her La Chiquita. She was really strong; she was the head of us, of the girls in the neighborhood. She had a lot of money, and she used to help Mamá. She gave our mother some money to buy ... some things, because we didn't have anything to eat. But she was murdered, they killed her. Those people used to fight a lot, but we didn't.

María

Mamá used to invite all of those girls to the house. They all liked Mamá, and sometimes she would do ironing for them. They used to say to her, "Mrs. Mendoza, please iron for us, and we'll pay you."

And Mamá would invite them up. They really liked Mamá, and they knew that Papá didn't work, and that he drank too much. That was eventually the death of him.

Manuel

When we lived down there on Matamoros Street where all the prostitutes were, I used to be an errand boy for them. They used to give me nickels and dimes. They used to send me to get cigarettes or matches or salt or sugar— things like that. They used to cook right there. Most of the prostitutes were Mexican girls. There were one or two Anglos, but most of them were Mexican girls.

They were real quiet; they didn't have music in their houses or anything like that. They were legalized, though, because the cops even used to go in there—the detectives that I used to know. They were pretty quiet, and they didn't have any fights. Sometimes these old men, real old men, used to go over there to see those girls.

There were some of them, though, that would cause trouble. There was this bunch of taxi drivers that got killed over something like that back in the 1930s. They wrote a *corrido* about that, "Los chóferes." It happened on Texas Street. We used to live about a block away from where it all happened. We could hear all the shooting. These taxi drivers were fighting over some women, some prostitutes. I don't remember how many of them got killed. I went to see them when they were having them in the coffins, right over there on San Saba Street. It was a sad thing.

There was a bunch of *cantinas* over there on Conchos Street. And across the street from the Market Square, *La Plaza*, there were several *cantinas*; there was Sapos and the Cinco de Mayo. And right next door to the Cinco de Mayo there was a great big house, a two-story house, and they used to have cockfights in the backyard. I used to go and watch them. It was illegal, but they used to have them, anyway.

And there were a lot of bootleggers, too. You could hear the noise when the Federals would come and break all the bottles. It was right before Prohibition ended.

There was a boy, his name was Johnny, and his mother was a prostitute. He and I used to play cowboys around the neighborhood together. He was the number-one cowboy because he had the boots, the chaps and the spurs, and he had extra guns and those wooden horses. He used to lend them out to the other guys. He got to be number one, though, because otherwise he would take the guns away from us, and he wouldn't let us play with them. The rest of us kids used to run around barefoot most of the time. Until Lydia was discovered, I went barefoot just about every day.

Another thing I remember from those days was Andrew's baptismal party. He was still just a little kid, and they baptized him. You know, in those times it was hard to make any parties of any kind, so my mother went and bought fifteen cents worth of cheese, the yellow cheese, to make some enchiladas. We used to have some friends, some other little kids, and there was this one little guy who was about my age. And while everyone was out in the front room talking, this little friend of mine went into the kitchen and ate all the cheese. He ate all the damn cheese, man, and just left the tortillas. Oh, my mother got so mad! Poor guy. That was the ironic part of it. He had gone and eaten all the cheese, and then my mother came up to me and gave me a good whipping, because she thought I had done it.

Andrew

That reminds me of another thing that happened back then. There was this man, Lydia didn't like him, but this man was in love with her. He was a young man who was called El Capino. He used to work in a restaurant. The guy wanted to make an impression with the family, so he would tell Daddy, "Mr. Mendoza, if you have a chance, go in back of the restaurant, and I'm going to give you a few things there ... in the trash can." "Okay," Daddy would say.

Daddy would go out there, and El Capino would give him oranges, eggs, you know, something to eat. And Daddy would bring it over to the house, and say, "I bought this food for the family."

So finally one day, the young man must have said to himself, "Well, I guess I've proven myself to Señor Mendoza by now." So he came to the house, and he told Daddy, "Mr. Mendoza, you know me now, you know what kind of man I am, and I would like to ask your permission to ask Lydia to be my steady girl friend."

"What!" yelled Daddy. He really blew his top.

El Capino ran from our house like he was shot from a gun. Our old man was really something.

Juanita

We couldn't have a girl friend, nobody. Lydia didn't have a friend; Panchita didn't have a friend. ... Because if they tried to have a friend, Daddy would say, "She's a bad girl. I don't want you associating with her."

And Momma would get so mad, because he would always say, "She's no good, I saw her ... " this and that.

Momma had a friend, an old lady, that she always passed the time with. Her name was Amalita, and she was about eighty years old. She was real nice. She loved my mother. She would always bring her little things, little presents. Then one day Daddy was drunk, and Amalita came to visit Mother, and he started yelling. "You get out of here! Get out of here, you're a bad woman! I saw you dancing in the *cantina* one night."

Mother got real mad. That poor woman was eighty years old! Then Amalita got mad, and she started yelling back at him. "¡*Eres un mojado*! You're just a wetback!" "*No estoy enojado*, I'm not mad," Daddy replied.

She had called him a "*mojado*," which means "wet," and is short for "wetback," but he thought that she had said "*enojado*," which means "mad" or "angry." "No, I'm not *enojado*," he said, "I'm just telling you the truth. I don't want you with my family."

He didn't want anybody to have any friends, not even Momma and not even Lydia. She couldn't invite anybody over to the house because he would run them off. For him, everybody was bad. He would cuss a lot, he was cussing most of the time. He was mean, my father. ... He always treated us like that, strictly swear words, all the time, and he used them with my sister María and me, too.

Lydia

Papá didn't even want us to be baptized. I don't know what his religion would have been called. But this I do know, he just believed in Christ. Every day, before going to bed, he would have us older children kneel down. We couldn't go to bed if we didn't kneel down with him, sing praises and say our prayers.

My mother wouldn't kneel down with us like that. My mother and my grandmother, all of the family on that side, were very Catholic. My father never opposed my mother's religion, although he didn't agree with it. We were baptized to please Mamá, but for his part, he said that since they hadn't baptized Christ until he was thirty years old, how come we should be baptized when we were small? Those were his beliefs. But what stuck with us the most, with all of us, was the religion from my mother's side. She never missed a Sunday at church. That was the way she taught us, impressed on us, her religion, her ideas. My dad made us kneel, and we sang and all. . . . But he didn't believe in saints nor candles nor in the Church nor the priests nor any of those things.

Never, never, did my father send us to a school. But my mother taught us to read at home. When she saw that my father didn't want to send us to school, she bought some blackboards. And there she began to teach us the . . . ABC's . . . the alphabet, and we came to know the letters and all. Everything she knew, she taught to us. Every day she would schedule a time for us to study. And we learned . . . , all of us, to read. Naturally, we lack spelling; we lack a lot of things. She taught us everything, but it didn't stick with us.

Then, later, I wasn't satisfied because I didn't know which were the capital letters, what was . . . the way to begin a letter, how to pronounce. . . . So I became interested in buying books to improve a little on what my mother had taught me. I sent to a bookstore in San Antonio called Lozano, and bought books on spelling, letter writting, arithmetic, accounting. . . . Wherever we were, I always went and bought my books or sent for them. When I put myself to study, or when I'd just be reading a newspaper, and I'd see that some word or letter that I had written wasn't correct, I'd copy it. And that's how I taught myself. Somewhat, I improved a little. My brothers and sisters didn't, they didn't worry about it. It's too bad, because my mother was fairly well-educated. All of her brothers and sisters had been to school, because my grandmother was a teacher. My uncle Enrique, my uncle Benjamín, my uncle Juan, my uncle Baudelio and the three sisters, they all studied.

María

Papá was raised in Mexico, and he never went to school, but he could speak English. He could really tell some lies. Papá didn't believe in school. Mamá was the one that made an effort, and that only for Juanita and Manuel. Mamá sent them to a Catholic school here in San Antonio for a while.

Juanita

Papá believed that when you grow up, you have to work. Mamá used to tell him, "Pancho, why don't you work?" "I already gave them their lives," he would answer, "now it's time for them to work."

You see? So . . . we had to work. I only went to the third grade. Actually, one of the first things I remember is when I was about six years old and my mother put me in school. It was a Catholic school, and since I liked to sing and dance, Mamá didn't have to pay. The school was here in San Antonio.

The sisters at the school loved me. They didn't care if Mamá paid for me or not. It didn't matter to the sisters that we didn't have anything and couldn't pay. They paid my way for me because I taught the other little girls to dance and to sing. And Mamá used to ask the sisters, "How is Juanita doing?" "She is doing pretty well," they would reply.

And the sisters would make my report card good, when it was really bad. I taught them how to dance, so they let me pass everything. I would dance the "Jota aragonesa," a Spanish dance. I used to dance a lot of Spanish dances.

I didn't learn very much. I learned how to read by myself. I read a lot of books. I learned with the books *Junglemen* and *Love Story*—books like that. I don't know how to write English; I wish I could now. I can read and write in Spanish, and I can read English very well.

Manuel

My mother wanted for us to get an education. She didn't want to put us in a public school, though, so she sent us to this Catholic school, parochial school. I really loved going to school; it made me very happy, but Papá used to complain about it. He always used to say that we didn't need any schooling. He didn't have any schooling himself, and he had made it by himself, he would say, so he didn't care about us going to school. My mother was the one that was always trying to get us educated, and she finally enrolled us here in San Antonio, right here at Immaculate Heart of Mary. I think she only used to pay a dollar a month, or two dollars a month, I don't remember how much it was. But she didn't have to pay for Janie, because she was pretty talented. They used to use her in plays, singing and dancing. She was real cute and kind of chubby. She used to be very talented, she used to sing a lot, so they didn't charge her for her tuition, just mine. She was in the first grade, and I was in the second grade.

All of the classes were taught in English, although there were only one or two Anglos in the school. Almost all of the kids were Mexican, and most of them didn't speak much English. For instance, my teacher was Sister Mildred, and she didn't speak a word of Spanish. The only one that could speak Spanish was Sister Mónica, a Mexican nun. Sister Mónica was Janie's teacher, she was the one that had her start appearing in some plays.

As far as learning how to read, we did it by ourselves, you know, by reading the newspaper. Papá used to buy *La prensa* and different Mexican papers, and we all learned. I don't know how in the hell we did it, but we did learn. I learned to read Spanish by myself. I can read in Spanish and in English, both. The only education that I have now is that I went to either the second or the third grade at Corazón de María.

We didn't stay in school too long because we started going out singing. My mother started making us some costumes so that we could appear in shows. There used to be a theater called Randolph's, down at Zarzamora and Guadalupe. Soto's Café is there now. The building is still there; it's been turned into a restaurant. But the theater form is still there. We put on some stage shows there. It was before Lydia got pretty well-known; it must have been right around 1932, or 1933. Then there was another theater, across the street from where the Guadalupe Theater is now, the Progreso. It used to have a great big stage, but there wasn't any place to dress or any backstage area; they just used to have a great big stage, a big platform. And we used to put on some shows there. And in 1932 we sang at yet another place called the Venus Theater with a variety show.

I was the comedian along with Janie; we used to do a comedy duet. We used to sing comedy songs, funny songs, like "Las cuarenta cartas." We also played some tent shows like the *Carpa García*, the García Tent Show. There were two big tent shows in town: there was a Cuban, and there was the García's. They used to put them in different places in town. We used to go to both the Cuban, *La Carpa Cubana*, and the García. Papá didn't go with us to those theaters or the *carpas* because he was always taking off and heading for Mexico.

Juanita

Papá would take some things from my mother . . . and take them to Mexico, and sell them over there—little things of my mother's. He'd take towels, he'd take sheets, he'd take everything and he'd go. He took everything he could. Mamá was in the Plaza playing, and he took everything—bedspreads and everything. And he left . . . for a month. And then when he finished, he came back. "I'm sorry, I'm sorry. Let me see my kids, I miss my kids."

He'd cry and cry and ask my mother for forgiveness. Mamá took him back. He just spent it all. And then he'd just do it again. And Mamá always let him come back.

Andrew

One time we were living beside the railroad tracks, and our father had gone off and left us. I don't know where he went that particular time, but he had left our mother to take care of us on her own. We didn't have any food to eat. But Mamá knew that the train would pass by at a certain time each day. There were a lot of pigeons around there, and when the train went by it would strike and kill some of the pigeons. She would go out, pick them up, and bring them over to the house. She would have boiling water ready, she would clean the birds and make something for us to eat. She fed us with the pigeons that got killed by the train.

Juanita

Every time Daddy got drunk and started to raise a fuss, Mamá would call the police. But he was pretty sharp, because when he saw the police car coming, he would run out the back and go hide out. The police would come in and say, "Well, where is he? Why isn't he here?"

"Well, he was here. ... "

And the police would go back outside. They usually didn't find him. After they had gone, he would come in again by the back way.

Lydia

In those years of the Depression, there wasn't any work, and we felt the effects in every way. People didn't have money to enjoy themselves with. We were in debt. Sometimes we had to go to the Welfare where they would help you out, give you something to eat. We would go there and sing so that they would give us something to eat, and they gave us food to take home. In those days, times were very hard. There wasn't any money; there wasn't anything. All the people were suffering. Times started to get better when President Roosevelt came in and the businesses opened back up and all that.

Also, after Repeal, when they started selling alcohol legally again, there was more work for musicians. There would be dances and *cantinas* and more places to go sing.

Although things were pretty rough for us, we sometimes had our little pleasures, too. It may seem strange, but one of the things that I most enjoyed, besides playing music, was washing dishes. Sometimes we would be invited to some meal, a dinner, with some families that were acquaintances of my parents. We would arrive, and we would dine, and then the men and the ladies would all go out into the living room to chat and all. And we girls would all go to the kitchen and wash the dishes. I couldn't wait to do that, and I would put myself to washing them right away because I like doing that. That was when I was young, just a little kid. I like to soap them up and wash them like that and rinse them. I don't remember much of anything else that I took pleasure in from those days because my mind was completely given over to the music. I wasn't interested in playing children's games—none of that attracted me. Mostly I just wanted to learn, and what fascinated me the most was the music.

I believe that if I celebrated my birthday once during my childhood, it would have been a lot. We didn't have the money. Christmas would come, holidays, whatever; for us they didn't exist. It was all we could do just to get enough to eat. Festivals like the Sixteenth of September, Mexican Independence Day, or Cinco de Mayo, and also the New Year and Christmas were the days that we made a little more money. We did especially well when the Fiesta de las Flores, the flower festival in San Antonio, would come around in April. It's a very big festival that lasts for a week. They have lotteries and all that. We would be playing there in the lotteries or in some tent where they put on variety shows.

We also sometimes got work in the year-round tent shows. Some of the tent shows that existed at that time, like *la carpa* of the García brothers and La Carpa Cubana looked for sites outside of the city or empty lots to set up their tent theaters. But they were different from the tent shows they would have during the Flower Festival. This was the city's carnival. Different acts would come, some of them would put on variety shows, stage acts, and sometimes they would hire Mexican acts. So we also came, in time, to work there. And those were the times of the year when we made a little money.

We worked in the *carpas* around or after 1932, about the same time that we got to San Antonio. In the Mexican *carpas* they had a trapeze, and they had clowns and tightropes. They had pantomimes, chorus dancers, two or three girls that danced—a variety of everything. They had comedy skits, all of that kind of thing. Also, in 1933-34 when my name started to get better known, the group and I returned to sing in those *carpas*.

I was now playing the guitar. Just to learn for myself. I didn't let anyone know, and no one noticed, that I wanted to sing by myself. I wanted to accompany myself as well. *Chueco o derecho*, crooked or straight, whether I did it well or not, I wanted to accompany myself on the guitar.[1]

So when we arrived in San Antonio in 1932, we went directly to the Plaza, the famous Plaza del Zacate, with the group—mandolin, guitar, tambourine and triangle, all just as I've described it to you—and we started singing there almost every night.

Then, since I had already tried out singing solo by myself, when I was alone, I learned some songs that I could perform solo. So after the whole group had sung one or two or three songs—since nobody knew us there, we were just like anybody else there—I took the guitar from Mamá and I started to sing some of the songs I had learned. We still didn't have a twelve string guitar yet; I just played that same old six string that we used to have. I did this for several nights. I did this _sin darme cuenta de nada_, without noticing anything special about it. I would sing a few songs like that, just by myself, and then the group would start back up again.

And then something happened. I think that someone had heard me sing by myself once before, and then he came down to the Plaza with some of his friends one night and told us, "Well, we want the _señorita_ to sing us this song."

Of course! I grabbed the guitar and sang the song he had requested, and he gave me twenty-five cents. In those days twenty-five cents was a lot of money. And the nights passed by like this. And since I saw that they were asking me for songs, and that they were paying a quarter, well then, I started to learn more songs: _tangos, boleros, rancheras_, all kinds of songs.

I learned those songs in order to at least be able to earn more money. But not thinking—God knows—not thinking that I might want to stand out, or be a . . . star. I looked at it from the point of view that they were paying more. The night finally came that the group didn't play at all. I sang by myself the whole night, because everybody paid me a quarter for each song that I sang solo. That's how I started out there, and that's how the gentleman from the radio station discovered me.

His name was Manuel J. Cortez. He was the father of the man who used to own KCOR, the big Spanish-language radio station that we have now in San Antonio.[2] Mr. Manuel J. Cortez was the gentleman who had the Voz latina, a half-hour radio program that was on the air in San Antonio back in those days. The show was broadcast from above the Texas Theater. The rest of the day the station had American programs. The "Voz Latina" came on at seven o'clock at night: it was on from seven to seven thirty every evening.[3]

So Mr. Manuel J. Cortez came down to the Plaza with his wife to eat dinner one night and heard me sing. That was when he told my mother that I had a very pretty voice and that I would be a big star if I went over to the radio station so they could hear me.

"Well, how much will they pay if she goes there?" Mamá asked him.

"No, no, they don't pay anything," he replied.

And Mamá told him that I couldn't go, because that was our livelihood there in the Plaza. "Well, in that case, if we were to go to the radio station, we would lose out," Mamá answered. "If we were to do that, what would we eat? This is our living here, and we live from one day to the next."

Of course, they weren't going to pay me anything for going to the radio station, and what Mamá said was true. Every day we would make our twenty-five, thirty cents there in the Plaza, and that was what bought our food for the day. On Saturday and Sunday we made the dollar and twenty-five cents we needed for the rent.

Then Mr. Manuel J. Cortez said, "Look, Señora Mendoza, it will be good for you to let Señorita Mendoza go to the radio station. She will gain more popularity. Moreover, for you all that sing here, well, it will be good for you, too. And I promise that it won't take very long. I'll take her over there and bring her right back. It won't take more than ten or fifteen minutes, you won't lose that much time."

And it was true, the station wasn't that far away, it was just nearby. And I said to my mom, "I want to go, *Mamacita*, why don't you let me? Let's go … what'll we lose?"

What I wanted was to go and sing on the radio. Well, in the end my mother told him: "Well, it's all right, we'll go."

The next day Señor Cortez came very early, picked us up, and took me over to the radio station. He took Mamá and me over to KABC where I sang, and then I went back to the Plaza just as if nothing had happened. That first night I went, I only sang two songs—that was all—but I felt very happy when I finally got to the station and was able to sing on the radio. Two or three days later the gentleman came back.

"Mrs. Mendoza, I've had so many telephone calls! With just that one day on the radio "—because all of San Antonio listened to that program—"I'm getting tired of answering the phone. They're wearing me out. People are calling and saying that they want to listen to Miss Mendoza again. They want to hear that voice."

"I'm very sorry, but the day we went to the station we lost out on earning some money, and this is our living," Mamá told him.

"Well, what if I can get her an advertising sponsor that will pay her to go and sing?" he replied. "A business that will pay her for the time?"

"Well," she said, "if it's like that, yes, she can go, but no other way."

Well, he got it. He went and got me an advertisment for a tonic that was very popular in those years: Tónico Ferro-Vitamina. He got it from a Mr. García, who said that he liked my voice. Mr. García said, "I'll pay, I'll sponsor her program."

Mr. García gave me three dollars and fifty cents a week. Well, with that three-fifty, we felt like millionaires. Now at least we could be sure of paying the rent. Because to get the rent together, which was one dollar and twenty five cents a week, we had to play … two days. We had to play Saturday and Sunday to put together the rent. And sometimes we didn't even get it together. Now with three-fifty, we had the rent for sure.

When Mr. García started paying me that three-fifty a week, I had to sing on the "Voz latina" for Ferro-Vitamina every night. I would only sing about two or three songs a night, though. The show was only half an hour long, and there were a lot of advertisements and announcements that took up a lot of the time, but I sang every night. And then Mr. Cortez got to thinking, and he said, "It shames me that Lydia Mendoza should be singing in the Plaza del Zacate. I'm going to take her out of there."

"Well, that's impossible. This is our living," Mamá told him.

"Well," he said, "I'm going to look for jobs for you ... just as long as they're not here in the Plaza. I'm going to make Lydia Mendoza into a big star, and it's not right that she should be singing there in the Plaza del Zacate."

And he got us Friday, Saturday and Sunday in the restaurants ... one hour in one, another hour in another ... and like that until he got us out of the Plaza completely. The jobs he got were for the whole group, for all of the family. I couldn't go to the Plaza anymore because he was resolutely against my continuing there. And my fame began from there. That was in 1932.

One of the places we worked after my name began to get known from singing on the radio was the Carpa García, one of the semi-permanent tent shows in town that I've already spoken of. Mr. García, the owner of the Carpa García, was a very curious person. He had lots of acts working for him, but he didn't pay them a fixed wage. He calculated each act or artists's pay according to how many people had paid to enter, and according to the type or class of the act. He paid me more than the rest. Often he would give me twenty-five cents, which was a luxury wage. To the others, he would give a nickel or a dime, depending on the person and the circumstances. Sometimes, for instance, the whole group of us would perform, and if the attendance was very good, Mr. García would pay me a dollar, Mamá fifty cents, Juanita, María and Manuel each a nickel. But most of the time, my pay was a quarter, which was considered very high.

Every night, at the end of the show, Mr. García would walk around with the money in his hand, and to each person he would personally hand their pay: to this one, a quarter, to that one, a dime, the other, a nickel.

Almost all of the performers in the Carpa García were related to the García family: brothers, sisters, cousins, etc. They were *vedettes*, chorus girl style dancers, and they put on pantomimes and all that kind of thing. The whole family were artists, even Mr. García himself. They were all *artistas*. Every once in a while, he would hire someone who wasn't part of the family, like us, but on the whole, his tent show was a family affair. Mr. García hired us because of the exposure I got on the radio.

Rodolfo García grew up in that *carpa* and can tell us a little more about it:

Rodolfo García

I was born just upstairs from the Teatro Morelos in San Antonio in 1917, so you could say I was born into the theater. The Teatro Morelos was on the ground floor, above it was a hotel, and above that, they had a gambling parlor.

My father had a circus, in a *carpa*, a tent, that traveled all over the state of Texas: La Carpa de los Hermanos García. We would go to Corpus, Houston, Laredo—many places around here. We were always going from one town to the next. Sometimes our family would appear in theaters, and sometimes in the tent. Our show included *variedades* (variety acts), comedians, comic actors and actresses, and circus acts—highwire, trapeze, many things. Ours was a one ring circus, a small circus.

My father, Manuel Valero García, was originally from Saltillo, Coahuila, and came to the United States around 1910 when the revolution broke out in Mexico. He had been orphaned when he was about twelve years old and began working in a circus there in Mexico when he was very young— that's where he learned the arts of the circus. He married my mother, Teresa González García, in Monterrey; she, too, was a circus performer. They had two children while still living there before coming to the United States when the revolution broke out down there. Here in Texas, they continued in the same line of work: the circus. We were all one big family working together in the circus, the *carpa*: brothers, sisters, cousins, in-laws, etc. We were, of course, the *artistas*. The *mozos*, the roustabouts, who would put up and take down the tent, that kind of thing, were another group altogether.

In the circus, my father had monkeys, other animals; he even had an elephant. My dad rented it from an American animal trainer, mostly so he could use it to advertise our *carpa*. Of course, Dad had to feed it. My father would have the *americano*, who was the elephant's "driver," parade it through the streets when we did our *convite*, announcing our show through the streets of the town or neighborhood where we were going to play. Lots of people would come just to see the elephant. But finally, my father and the elephant trainer got into difficulties, and the result was that my dad ended up owning the elephant, but he couldn't keep it anymore. You see, when we shut down the circus for the winter, it was too expensive to keep on feeding the elephant. That darn elephant ate three bales of hay a day! So they had to give the elephant to a zoo or take it out to some ranch; I don't really remember exactly what they did with that elephant.

During the winter, when the really cold weather would set in, our family troupe would return home to San Antonio, because it would be too cold to keep on touring around and performing in the tent. My family would take advantage of those times to send me to school. All the other kids at school knew very well that I was working in a circus. They would call me *"maromero,"* and it would make me very mad. *Maromero* means "acrobat," and when I was a little boy, I really didn't like it when the kids at school used to call me a *maromero.*

Back then in the '30s, we would move our *carpa* from one neighborhood to another. We would set up in one *barrio* for a week, in another for a month, and so on, but we would always move on to somewhere else.

The Mendoza family came to work for us in the *carpa* here in San Antonio. After Lydia became known around San Antonio, she would sometimes do the Saturday and Sunday shows in the *carpa*, and lots of people would come to see her. In those days they didn't charge very much for admission into the tent. The best seats were about fifteen cents and the general admission was only a dime, or even a nickel for standing room. But our tent could hold a lot of people, maybe even a thousand in the course of a day and night. My dad would collect the ticket money and then give each of the artists their share. He also had to pay the other workers—the roustabouts who didn't perform. Even during the worst years of the Depression, our tent would always be full of people. The admission was pretty cheap, and back in those days there wasn't any television or anything like that for people to do.

The Mendoza family started out singing in the Plaza del Zacate, which a lot of people used to call "La Plaza del Menudo," because there were a bunch of tables there where they would sell *menudo* and *chicharrones* and every kind of Mexican food. There must have been eighty or ninety of those tables. From there Lydia and her sisters went on to sing in a theater down on Guadalupe that's since been torn down—the Teatro Venus. My sisters Consuelo, Aída and Gilberta also worked there. They were in charge of the *variedades* that used to be presented there. They had started working there sometime between 1925–1930. My sisters brought Lydia Mendoza down there to perform in the early '30s. This was during the winter when our family would return to San Antonio, *cuando invernábamos.* We would take our circus on the road during the hot weather, and, when it started to get cold, all the circuses would close down. So during the winter we would work in theaters, wherever we could. The owner of the Venus Theater knew us very well and understood our situation, so he would give us as much opportunity to work as possible. At this time, of course, I was still too young to be working in the family show; it was my sisters who would work at that theater.

In my father's *carpa*, even though it was mainly a circus, he would also put on *variedades*. He even had a little stage, a place with a curtain where my sisters and others would come out to dance and sing. There was also *la pista*, what you call the "ringside." The seats were arranged around the ringside.

My sisters sang and danced in the family *carpa*, and, whenever they got a chance, in the little theaters as well. They would do a *pasacalle*, what was called a "potpourri"—a medley of different songs and dances. For instance, they would dance "La Diana," and then a *jarabe tapatío*, "Las espuelas," "Las chiapanecas" and so on. My mother taught my sisters all those songs and dances. They would dance *jotas aragonesas* and another dance you almost never hear about around here anymore: "El garrotín." It's a Spanish dance where the dancers tap out the rhythm with castanets on their fingers and with their shoes on the dance floor.

We learned many of our comic skits from our older relatives who had been doing the same kind of thing, first in Mexico and then in the U. S., for years. For instance, my uncle Miguel, who was also an *artista*, used to work with the Trío Hermanos González back in the 'teens and 'twenties when they came here to San Antonio. It was the Hermanos González who brought all those dances here from Mexico. My uncle Miguel and my aunts Micaela and Carmen were *artistas* who used to perform all kinds of dances, all sorts of *jotas aragonesas* and *pasodobles*—Spanish dances—and sang *couplets*. Carmen, for instance, would do those songs where she would pick out people in the audience and sing to them, talk to them each in turn, just like Juanita Mendoza was to do later on with the Variedad Mendoza. My aunt Carmen taught my sisters how to do those *couplets*, and Juanita Mendoza learned them from my sisters when her family was singing in our *carpa* back in the early '30s.

Another of my brothers was also in comedy, not as an *actor cómico*, comedian, but as a clown. He would work *la pista*, what you call the "ringside" in English, in my father's circus. There's a big difference between a comic and a clown. A clown works the "ringside" and a comic appears on a stage. I was never any good as a clown, for instance, but I did make a career as a stage comic, "Don Fito, El Vato Suave."

Another comic team working around San Antonio back in the '30s was Netty and her brother Jesús Rodríguez. They worked as "Don Suave y la Netty" in the Teatro Nacional, the Teatro Zaragoza, many theaters around town. My sister Consuelo used to work in the circus and the *carpa* with Jesús Rodríguez, also.

Netty and Jesús even made trips to work in theaters as far away as California. They loved to do parodies as well as comic skits, parodies of popular songs.

My older brother and sister were sort of the directors of our show, but we didn't really do a lot of rehearsing like some artists do. We were always ready to improvise. For instance, my sister Consuelo would tell my other sisters and the sisters-in-law and the cousin, "Let's do the 'Pasacalle de las colombinas,' " or "Let's do the 'Pasacalle del jaripeo,' " which was a song and dance routine where they would all come out dressed up as *charros*, cowboys, and *charras*, cowgirls, and they would all start jumping around. And then the comics would come out. And then my sister would tell my brother, "Then we're going to do a *dueto*," such and such a song, etc. Since we already knew all the material, why should we rehearse? We would do brother/sister duets exactly like those Manuel and Juanita Mendoza used to do in the Variedad Mendoza.

Lydia

The Carpa Cubana was a higher-class operation. We sort of "graduated" to working at La Cubana after we had been with the García's for a while. La Cubana paid me five dollars a night, and the others were also paid well compared with the Carpa García. Juanita and María didn't do duets yet when we were singing in the *carpas*. I did my solo numbers, and the family appeared as a quartet. My sister Juanita also remembers working in those *carpas* in San Antonio:

Juanita

Where we really started out as a stage act was in the *carpas*, the tent shows. The Carpa García was the first one that took us on. We went and auditioned, and Mr. García decided that he wanted us to sing there, so he took us on. He didn't pay us very much. They used to give me a nickel. Mamá would get fifty cents and Lydia, a dollar. Well, at that time everything was very cheap. It was at the time when Mr. Cortez from the radio station didn't want us to play in the Plaza. At that time, if you were to give Mamá a dollar, oooh! It was a big thing. And to me, a nickel! I would have walked the tightrope for a nickel. Because I did whatever I was told, see. Pantomimes? They would paint me up—it didn't matter to me. And Manuel, they had him lifting weights or whatever it might have been, for a penny. That was the first time we really got our act together—in La Carpa García.

There were other artists too, and all kinds of acts. Mr. García's daughters were all *artistas*; his whole family, in fact, were performers. We used to do some of the acts with them. They would tell you, "You have to go out when Señor García whistles," and they would tell my brother and one of the García boys, "You have to act like the boyfriend, and you have to be the husband."

"Yes, yes," we would say.

"Do it, and we'll give you something."

"What are you going to pay?" we would say all together.

Señor García would have a little table by the door to the tent, and he would get everybody together, and he would say, "A nickel for you, a dime for you," and so on. And he would give Mamá fifty cents or a dollar.

I wasn't at all bashful like my sisters; I really loved performing in front of an audience. From there we went on to the Carpa Cubana. It was a little higher class operation. And there they paid us three dollars. Just like in the Carpa García they had all kinds of acts in La Cubana: tightropes, trapeze, all sorts of things.

Lydia

Those *carpas* declined during the late '30s and finally disappeared completely. The Carpa Cubana was a fine theater, but it eventually fell apart and passed off the scene.

Then after we had been out of the Plaza for a little while, working *las carpas* and the restaurants, Manuel J. Cortez, the same man who had the "Voz Latina" radio program, organized some singing contests for me to take part in. There were two contests: the first one was sponsored by the Ferro-Vitamina Tonic, and the second was for Pearl Beer. This was in 1933.

The first contest was actually put together by Mr. García (my radio sponsor, not the tent show impresario) for the Tónico Ferro-Vitamina with the help of Mr. Cortez and was held at the Teatro Nacional. Mr. Cortez advertised for contestants over the radio. The people who wanted to sing had to come and try out, and if they were good enough, they got a chance to take part in the contest.

I didn't win the first prize in that contest. Another group called the Hermanitos Cárdenas won first prize. They were some young boys who sang very well and played their guitars. All kinds of people entered the contest, but it got down to only three at the end. I don't remember who the other finalist was. I won the second prize; I believe I won a watch, but I was very happy. Well, it was the public's choice, they made the decision, and I was happy to abide by it. And well, winning that contest, even if it wasn't first prize, was another step up for me. But Mr. Cortez wasn't satisfied and said that he was going to organize an even bigger and better contest so I could win first prize. And that was the one sponsored by Pearl Beer. It was a lot bigger than the Ferro-Vitamina contest, and the prizes were worth a lot more. The contest ran for three months.

There were a few men singers in the contest at the beginning, but most of the contestants were women. The men didn't last. The finalists were all girls. The first presentation was at the State Theater. All of the contestants were presented. There were twelve of us singers in the show, all girls, and according to the number of votes each singer received, they were progressively eliminated until only three remained. When there were only three of us left, it kept on going for two months to see which of us would come out in first place.

Every so often—every week or two weeks or month—they organized a show to present the front-runners to the public, to announce who had the most votes and all that. The shows were presented at midnight, but they would fill up with people. The public was accustomed to those hours.

All of the major clothing stores of San Antonio—La Feria, Joskes, Franklins, etc.—loaned a dress to be exhibited by a contestant. The dresses were to be worn with a big sash or ribbon across them bearing the name of the store. It was like an advertisement. Each store would give five dollars—a fortune at that time—to the singer who wore its dress. So in that way they dressed all of us up in different dresses from the various stores.

Amongst the group of us contestants, the others were very jealous of me. It wasn't my fault that everyone voted for me, or that the public preferred me. At that time, my hair was very long, and I wore it very high in braids. But the other girls in the contest used to make fun of me because of the way I looked and dressed. I only owned two dresses. And those other girls? No, every day they went out all dolled-up, showing off jewelry and all that. And I didn't have anything like that, but they were still very jealous of me.

On this occasion when all the stores provided the dresses, they brought some very pretty outfits. So then I arrived, and the woman who was in charge there in the theater asked me, "Haven't you put on your dress yet?"

"What dress?" I replied.

"Well, the one you're going to wear for the show," she told me.

"Oh, I didn't know. ... "

Well, all of the other girls were already walking around with some extremely beautiful dresses, and they gave me a really ugly white one. It was very plain, there wasn't anything fancy about it. They had left the ugliest dress for me. They not only gave me the ugliest dress, they didn't even give me the five dollars. Well, that didn't bother me.

"Here's your dress," the wardrobe girl said, "but are you sure that you've taken a bath?"

"Well, I might be poor," I told her, "but yes, I did take a bath."

"Well, if you get it dirty, you're going to have to pay for it," she said.

So the other girls went out on stage showing off their fancy dresses, but the audience just gave them a little light applause, just a little polite clapping. And when I came out in that shabby dress, whooo! the roof almost flew off the theater. The public didn't care how I looked, they just wanted to hear me sing.

My brother Andrés has even suggested that it helped me not to look as fancy as the other girls. Times were still very hard then, and perhaps the audience loved me even more because I represented the poor people.

You see, the *directora*, the woman in charge of the show, didn't like me either. All of the other girls sang with the piano. *La directora*, she would accompany them on the piano. And I, of course, accompanied myself on the guitar. So that woman would try, on purpose, to arrange the show so as not to leave me time to do my songs. But the audience began to protest, "We came to hear Lydia, we want to hear Lydia for more time!"

And even on the radio, since there was only half an hour for twelve singers to sing, well that was no time at all. In half an hour's time, twelve of us contestants would all congregate there in the studio. Each one would only get to sing a little piece of a song. The *directora de música* was a woman named Estela González. She would have it arranged so that when I arrived, there wouldn't be enough time for me to even sing a little scrap of my number. She practiced with the other contestants, and she had it figured out so that they would take up all the time. That *directora* who played the piano, that Estela González, would make her numbers very cute and very long on purpose, to the extent that sometimes I wouldn't be able to sing more than the first verse of my first song before the time was up. They always put me on last. The audience began to complain that they wanted to hear more of my songs. Of course, that just made the others that much more jealous.

Finally, the public, who really wanted to hear me, protested, and Mr. Cortez reprehended her. "Señorita González," he told her, "you have to be more careful in the rehearsals to measure the time so that there will be enough time for all of the contestants—principally for Lydia Mendoza—because the public is demanding to hear her."

Well, I guess that Miss González got angry, because after Mr. Cortez spoke to her, she disliked me even more. It was also she who gave me the ugly dress at the presentation.

The way the votes were cast was *muy curioso*, very curious. This was at the time when President Roosevelt came in. Prohibition had just been repealed, and the breweries were back in business. They started selling beer legally again, and the bars opened back up. Each contestant would sing on the radio, and the people would listen to us. In all the bars, lounges, they would have a box, and the customers would put the votes there. All of the *cantinas* would have a great big book, I mean a really big one, full of these coupons. Each coupon was printed with the name of one of the contestants. Every time you bought a beer the bartender would ask you, "Who are you going to vote for?"

Everybody already knew what was going on, about the contest, and the customer would say, "Well, I vote for Miss ... so and so. ... "

Just that, and that was all there was to it. And almost all the votes were for Lydia Mendoza—everybody voted for me. As I recall, I had something like thirty-five thousand more votes than the runner-up.

The first prize was a very pretty bedroom set, complete with everything: with mattresses and blankets and everything. Second prize was a radio. And I believe that the third prize was a watch. I won the bedroom set. And actually, we didn't have one, and, well, I felt really good about it. I still wasn't married at that time. I was living at home with my parents and the family.

Mr. Manuel J. Cortez was my first promoter, and he really helped me out a lot. He was the first one to take charge of building up my career. Of course, he also made some good money for himself by helping me, because I didn't make anything from all this at the time. It didn't bother me that after that contest he bought himself a brand-new car or that he made a lot of money off me.

But all of the people used to say "There goes Cortez with Lydia Mendoza's money." That's what they used to yell out as he drove by.

For sure, when I did that second contest for Pearl Beer, I told him that I would only appear on the programs as long as I was paid. If I wasn't paid, I wouldn't continue. And of course, all of the rest of the contestants were against me, because I was the only one being paid.

Because of those contests, my name became very well known, but just in San Antonio and the immediately surrounding area. And eventually wealthier people even started to hire me to play at their parties. For instance, there was a dairy, La Escovedo, that was owned by the Flores family. I got to play at their festivities. The Flores brothers had a lot of businesses. As you can see, my first success and my first hits were in San Antonio. But they were nothing compared to what was to follow just a little later during the next year, 1934, also right there in San Antonio.

CHAPTER 4

"Mal hombre"

Lydia

In 1934 Blue Bird Records was making an experiment to see if it could produce a star from its first recording sessions. And since they knew that there were a lot of groups in San Antonio, well, they gave an opportunity to everyone there as long as they could play an instrument or sing. They gave everybody a chance, but the Blue Bird people didn't advertise in the newspaper for artists like the OKeh did in 1928. Mr. Eli Oberstein was the first one who came to San Antonio for Blue Bird Records, and he relied on his music business contacts in the area to bring him artists.

There was a woman who worked at San Antonio Music ... I think her name was Beatriz Morín, although I'm not real sure about her last name. She was a salesgirl there at the music store. She became the interpreter for the Blue Bird recording company when Mr. Oberstein came to San Antonio. From that time on, whenever the Blue Bird recording team would come to San Antonio from New York—it was an American outfit, of course—they would employ this woman Beatriz as their interpreter to deal with all of the Spanish-speaking *artistas* who were going to record.

At this time, my name was becoming well-known around South Texas due to my appearances on the radio and the contests. So this woman, Beatriz Morín, came to our house to see me and talk to my father. "Mr. Oberstein wants to give all the best singers a chance to make a record. I can't promise you anything except that he'll pay you fifteen dollars a song for anything you record," Beatriz told us. "After that, it all depends on how your records turn out."

"Well," Papá told her, "if he'll pay us, we'll go and talk to this Mr. Oberstein."

Then she took us to see Mr. Oberstein. That led to my going to record. They arranged the day and the time, and then on March 27, 1934, we went on down to the Texas Hotel for the first session. The Texas Hotel was just a house—it was a hotel, but it was just a house with a sign that said: Hotel. It was a very large house, but it wasn't a big building of many floors nor was it right downtown. The Blue Bird people rented two rooms there and improvised their studio. That was where all of the groups recorded.

That first day only three of us went down to the "studio." Just Mamá and Papá came with me to look after the business—so it wasn't really the group, but just me as a solo act. They only let me record four sides the first day.[1] Two of the songs were "Mal hombre" and "Al pie de tu reja."

"Al pie de tu reja"[2]

Al pie de tu reja,
allá en la noche oscura,
estoy, bella Carmen,
pulsando el laúd.

Como trovador
vengo a tu ventana,
del sueño a robarte
la dulce quietud.

Y entreabre tu reja,
abriga el encanto,
verás mi instrumento
en sus vibraciones.

Levántate, ¡oh Carmen!,
y anima mi llanto,
porque eres el ángel
de mi salvación.

In the Dark Night

In the dark night,
at the foot of your window,
here I am, lovely Carmen,
playing the lute.

Like a troubador
I come to your window,
disrupting the quiet
of your gentle sleep.

Open your window
and listen to the sound,
hear the resonances
of my instrument.

Wake up, oh Carmen!
bring cheer to my lament,
because you are the angel
of my salvation.

They only let me do two records. That's what they were doing with everybody. Two records, and get out of here: go home and let someone else record.

Oberstein was recording everybody that showed up, whether they sang well or not, it was sort of like a recorded audition. It was, "Oh, you play the guitar? Into the studio!"

They made *una infinidad*, a whole bunch, of records—some good, others bad, but they recorded them all. When I got there, I was just like everyone else. They treated me exactly like they were treating all the others. "You sing?" they asked me. "Okay."

And I made my recordings, and they paid me, and then, "*Vámonos*, let's go. Next please!"

Just as Beatriz Morín said they would, they gave me fifteen dollars a side. The records came out about two months later. As soon as "Mal hombre" was issued, it made a big impact. Lots of people began to hear it and buy it; it was an instant hit. So then, after the record had been out for about a month, and they had seen the success that it was having, that woman, Beatriz from San Antonio Music, came back to the house with Eli Oberstein, the agent for Blue Bird, and they spoke with Papá. They told him that they were going to give me royalties for that record they had paid me fifteen dollars for. They were going to pay me royalties for "Mal hombre" and "Al pie de tu reja." And they also said that they wanted me to sign a contract with them so that I wouldn't record for anyone else. Because after "Mal hombre" first hit it big, other companies began to ask me to record for them, too. But Mr. Oberstein of Blue Bird Records didn't want to record the family group. He said the company only wanted to record my singing. When I saw that they didn't want to record the whole group, the rest of my family, then I told Mr. Oberstein that if he didn't give one or two opportunities to the group, that I would no longer record for him. Around this time Decca[3] was there ... and other companies ... that wanted me to record for them. There were other companies that were interested in me and the group, as

Lydia Mendoza. Courtesy of the Lydia Mendoza collection.

well. I didn't have to tell Oberstein twice, and right away the whole family was included in the deal.

So anyway, Papá signed a contract for me with Blue Bird. The deal was that they weren't going to pay me by the record, but they were going to give me royalties: two cents for each record sold. Well, I continued to record for them, and time passed, and they never made an accounting to us of the royalties. When they came back to San Antonio two months later to record again, Papá told them that he didn't want royalties. He didn't want me to continue to record on a royalty basis. Well, we didn't really know anything about all this sort of thing. We didn't really understand about royalties or managing money or anything like that. Papá just told them, "It'll be better if you just pay me."

"Fine," Oberstein answered, "if you want, we'll make another contract on the basis just how you say. If you want a contract, well, we'll pay you forty dollars for each record: for two songs—forty dollars."

And they made a new contract like that. And I continued to record for them on that basis: forty dollars per record. And as for those first records—the ones that they were going to pay me royalties for—well they just paid us off at forty dollars each, and that was the end of that. This was in 1934.

But at the end of the year, the government tried to charge me about thirty thousand dollars in taxes because of the enormous quantity of records that had been sold.

I got married on March 3, 1935. After I had been married for one or two months, the Blue Bird was going to return to San Antonio to record again. Before the company got to town, this woman Beatriz came over to let me know they were coming. She found out where I was living with my husband, and when she arrived at our house, she was accompanied by an *americano* who I hadn't met before. At this time, Mr. Oberstein no longer came for Blue Bird, but this man Medaris was coming in his place. It was Medaris who came to our house with Beatriz, the woman from San Antonio Music. They came in the evening when my husband was home, and they said, "We brought over these papers," they told us, "since Lydia Mendoza has now married, you have to re-sign the contract. The old contract was signed by Señor Mendoza, her father, but now we need your signature."

There were two copies of the contract. They gave one to my husband Juan to sign and the other to me. "You sign this copy, Señor Alvarado (my husband), and Lydia, you sign this other one," she told me, "and then everything will be all fixed up."

Well, my husband was pretty ignorant, and I wasn't so sharp either: we signed. After we had finished signing, "Well, here's ten dollars for your signature," they told us.

They gave us ten dollars. Well, to be sure, we didn't even have electricity in the house, and so I went and got us hooked up with the ten dollars. That ten dollars paid for our electricity, and that's how it ended up: well, nothing.

That contract that they had brought over was where it said that I ceded all the royalties that were due to me—I didn't even notice, because it was all in English—to Mr. Medaris. Of course, I believe that Medaris gave something to that woman Beatriz, because she was the one that interpreted everything. And shortly afterwards, she took off for Mexico, and nobody ever heard from her again. We never found out exactly where she went. Although we searched for her later on, we never found her. That paper they had us sign said that the royalties that were due to me from the first recordings, the ones I did before Papá renegotiated the contract with Oberstein (including "Mal hombre," etc.–the biggest selling hits), were ceded by my husband and me to Mr. Medaris. If they would have had to deal with Papá, Papá—he spoke English—he would have known what was going on, and we never would have signed. But Juan and I were ignorant, and that's what happened. So at the end of the year—1935—the government came looking for the taxes I supposedly owed on those royalties. That's when I figured out what they had done to us.

The next time the Blue Bird came to record, well, Medaris didn't come with them, some other man came in his place. So then I told them about what had happened and I protested what their agent had done to us. "Oh, Medaris," they said, "oh, Mr. Medaris, he went off to Germany or someplace. He's not with us anymore. We don't know exactly where he is. But leave this tax bill with us, we'll take care of it for you, we'll fix things up."

And that was the last I heard about it. The government never bothered me about it again. I don't really know what the Blue Bird people did about it, how they arranged things with the government. They did just about whatever they felt like with me, because I didn't know how to deal with things like that in those days.

If we had been a little bit more on the ball, if we had gone to see a lawyer or something before we signed, we could have saved ourselves. If we even could have read it ourselves ... , but, of course, we couldn't even speak English, much less read it.

When we got that tremendous tax bill, both my husband and I were very frightened. "They're going to grind us up," we thought to ourselves, "we're finished."

"No, no," other people told us, "you didn't receive any money. You can't be liable."

I think that Medaris and that woman probably forged my signature on the tax forms and on the checks. Those two ended up with all the money.

*   *   *

The first impression that I felt when my first recording came out was that I had made a mistake. "Now they won't come to listen to me in person," I said to myself, and that there, it died, I was dead now. "Who is going to come to hear me if they already have the record?"

And of course it was completely to the contrary because it helped me out. Well, I didn't know ... making a record gave me a lot of pleasure. I felt happy. But when the record came out, I was a little disappointed. "Who's going to hire me now?" I said to myself.

We had a little wind-up Victrola. As soon as the first record came out, my father became my first booster, and he advertised my record. There wasn't a house that he didn't stop at, "My daughter recorded, Lydia Mendoza recorded! Do you want to hear her?"

He would put the record on right then and there. And as soon as the people heard it, they would buy it. The first thing that Papá would do was grab that Victrola and walk from house to house all around there where we lived, nearby, and play everyone the record. We were living on Monterrey Street in San Antonio. It was a two-story house, and we lived upstairs. That was where I got married in 1935.

I met Juan Alvarado in the Plaza del Zacate when we first started to play there in 1932. He was one of the people that came to listen to us there. Papá was *muy delicado*, very touchy, about me. He didn't let me go out anywhere by myself. I was never alone, and certainly not outside of the house. So Juan made use of my little brother Manuel. Juan sent me letters. He sent me three letters. He would pay Manuel a nickel to pass me a letter in secret. "Look, kid," Juan would say, "I'll give you a nickel if you'll slip this letter to your sister."

I never really had noticed him in particular before. I just noticed that there would always be some men standing there near us, listening to us sing. But I never raised my eyes to look at anyone. I never noticed any of them individually. But then, one time when no one could overhear him, Manuel told me, "Listen, the guy from the gas station," Manuel always called Juan "*el de la gasolinera*," because Juan worked as a shoemaker and he wore a dark colored shirt with the initials of the shoeshop on it, and Manuel thought that it was some gas station shirt. "Listen, haven't you noticed the guy from the gas station?"

"No, which one is he?" I replied. After all, there were so many young men around there.

"Well, he says that he likes you," Manuel told me.

"*No, estás tú loco*, no, you're crazy," I said, "get out of here."

So then one night when we got home from the Plaza, Manuel told me, "Take this."

"What is it?" I asked.

"The young man from the gas station sent you this letter," Manuel replied.

Well, in that letter, Juan told me that he liked me and that he wanted to meet me. He said that he had been in love with me since the first time that he saw me and that he really liked the way I looked and carried myself and that I was the woman that he had always been looking for—things like that. He wrote the letter in Spanish, and I was able to read it, although I had never been to school. All right, when I saw what it was about, I tore it up and threw it away. "Oh, the guy's nuts, *está loco*," I told my brother as I ripped up the letter.

Juan wasn't the only boy who was interested in me during those days in the Plaza. Of course, there were many boys who tried to make time with me. They all made use of my brother Manuel—they entrusted him with letters for me. Manuel was a little go-between, that was how he earned his nickels.

"This boy sends you this letter," he would say.

I didn't pay any attention to any of them. Except, of course, eventually, to Juan—he must have been my destiny. Although many of the young men who came to the Plaza and saw me singing there used to send me letters, nobody sent Panchita any letters, because by this time Manuel had replaced her in the group, and she didn't come very often to the Plaza. She was a girl who didn't really like music very much; she only played because she had to. Of course, after I got married, she was obliged to rejoin the group for a while, but she never did like music. She was very odd. She was very timid, very shy. If people came over to the house—like when they would come with singing contracts for me—she would be sitting there, and as soon as she saw that someone was coming, she would run and hide behind the stove or in the closet so that no one would see her. She was a very strange girl. But lots of boys would send me letters through Manuel.

Neither Mamá nor Papá knew what was going on—they hadn't noticed anything. A few days after Juan had sent me that first letter, "Listen," Manuel whispered to me on the sly—because he knew that Papá was very touchy— "that guy from the gas station is asking me: 'What happened about the answer to my letter?'" "Tell him that he's crazy!" I said. "What answer?"

Well, Juan sent me another letter telling me the same things. Then he sent me another one after that. "See him? See him over there?" Manuel would always tell me as he pointed Juan out on the corner. "That's the guy from the gas station—he's always standing over there listening to you sing."

So I began to look at him. And, I guess, I liked him, because after he had sent me three letters, I finally answered him. And I told him, "Yes."

For a while after that, he would just look at me there in the Plaza, and I would just look back at him. We never spoke to each other face to face. We became boyfriend and girlfriend strictly by letters. We only spoke to each other by letters. Juan would write everything he wanted to tell me in a letter, and I would answer him and tell him what I wanted to tell him in the same way, and then he would write back to me, and so on. That was the only way we communicated—that was how we decided to go steady. This happened in 1932. Our courtship lasted for three years—he was my steady boyfriend for three years before we got married.

After I had answered his letter, and we had decided to go steady, I spoke to my mother about him, and so did my brothers and sisters. Finally Mamá told Papá that I had a boyfriend.

"Well, she's not going out to see him," Papá said, "but if he wants to come over here and talk to me about it, maybe he can come over and visit her here at the house, but only here at the house with all of us."

And that's how it happened, that's how it was for three years. Juan came and told Papá that we liked each other and that he had honorable intentions, and he asked Papá for permission to come over and visit with me at the house. So Papá granted him permission to come to the house, and Juan began coming over to visit with me. But I never went out with him anywhere. Finally, after Juan and I had been going together for two years, one day Juan told Mamá, "Well, I would like for Lydia to come with me to the movies."

"Yes, of course," Papá interjected, "but her mother has to go with her."

"Well, that's no problem," Juan replied, "it's all right if Señora Mendoza comes with her. What I want is to take Lydia to the movies."

So that was how it was. We got to the theater—the three of us—and Mamá got one up on me. She sat in the middle, and Juan and I had to sit on either side of her. So there we were. Every once and a while I would look over at him, and he would look over at me, but, well, there was Mamá in the middle. Well, finally there was a little slip-up, because Juan was able to slip his arm around behind the seats, but he had just barely touched my shoulder when Mamá suddenly turned toward him and gave him a real dirty look. Immediately, he took his hand off of my shoulder, and he never tried to touch me again for the rest of the show. And that was the only time we ever went out together.

That was how Mamá was, that's how she and Papá were, and that's how my courtship was with Juan. Three years of going steady, and up until the day I married him, I was never alone with him for a second. The day we got married was the day I went with him.

When Juan and I decided that we should get married—that it was the right time—then I went to Mamá and told her the date that we were thinking about for the wedding. It was sometime in the month of November, 1934, when I first mentioned it to Mamá. "They are going to come and ask for my hand, Mamá," I told her, "so that we can get married early next year."

"Well, that's all right," she said, "let them come."

So my mother already knew that they were coming to ask for me. But my father didn't know. My mother had already agreed, but my *papá* didn't know anything about it. So when the gentlemen came to get their petition, Papá had gone to take a bath. He was in the bathtub when they knocked on the door. It was Juan's father, Mr. Alvarado, and Mr. Acuña, the owner of the furniture store, and another man who worked for Mr. Acuña. There were three of them. Papá always made the contracts and took care of all the business that people came to see about, so he stuck his head out of the bathroom and called out to my mother: "Who is it?"

"Oh no, it's just . . . some gentlemen . . . " my mother said. Mamá already knew who it was and what they had come for, but she didn't want to tell him. "What do they want?" he said. "Well," she said, "I don't know . . . what they've come about. Take your bath!"

And he went back in the bathroom again. And the gentlemen came on into the house. Then I guess that he must have heard something of what they were talking about. I don't know for sure, but he just had to see what was going on. He just wrapped a towel around himself, and he came out like that. When he saw who they were, at first he was very pleased. Papá thought that they had come about some contract, because people were coming over all the time with singing contracts for me, and Mr. Acuña was a big man in San Antonio in those days.

But when they announced what they had come about, Papá stopped short and really threw a fit. "My daughter, Lydia Mendoza," he growled, "is going to marry this *tomatero*?!"

He called Juan a "*tomatero*" because his father sold tomatoes. They were poor folks. Juan, too, was a poor boy, *un muchacho humilde, un piscador*. He had been a field worker, a migrant picker or harvester himself at times. It was just that finally Juan was able to get into the shoe shop and he learned to be a shoe and boot maker, and he was able to work at his trade.

So Papá refused. He said that he wasn't going to give me up for anything in the world, that I was a great artist and too good for someone like my fiancé. He opposed it categorically. "No, Señor Mendoza, you should be honored that your daughter wants to get married here in our town," the gentlemen told Papá, "and that we have come to ask for her hand in the correct way."

But no, Papá said, "Well, no . . . "

"But we want to know," they replied.

"I don't know," Papá finally said, "come back in December. Come back in December, and I'll tell you one way or the other."

Well, as soon as those men had left, Papá grabbed me, "Oh, so you want to get married? Well, I'm going to send you to reform school! You'll see!"

Ah, he told me all kinds of things, he told me so many things like that. Well, I was eighteen years old, but he still said that he wasn't going to allow me to marry Juan. But Mamá began to slowly try to convince him.

And Papá lasted to the end of the year like that ... before he decided to give me up. And so then, at this point, when it was going back and forth between ... he wanted to give me ... he didn't want to give me ... As I was considering all the difficulties, I wanted to poison myself. Believe me, I'm telling you straight from the heart, if I was going to poison myself, it wasn't because I was so in love, or because I was afraid of losing Juan. Something just came over me—to see my father so reluctant, and everything so upset. So it just came to me: well, so there won't be any more problem, I'll just poison myself.

I was by myself in the kitchen, thinking those thoughts, and my little sister Panchita was sitting there staring at me. God alone knows how I must have looked, because Panchita wouldn't take her eyes off me. I was talking to myself: what I have just said about poisoning myself. I was standing there, saying to myself that I should take poison and put an end to all of the discord in our family. Well, God in Heaven knows that I was going to do it because I was desperate. I didn't know what to do. I wanted agreement. I wanted Papá to approve of my getting married. I didn't want all of those arguments and disagreements and bad feelings. It wasn't because of some great love or in order to get married for love, no, the reason that I wanted to go, to leave this world, was because I couldn't stand all that disagreement and disapproval ... mainly from my father.

So, then I left the kitchen and walked to the bathroom. There was a bathroom in that house, and in the bathroom there was a bottle that contained a white liquid of some kind ... but it had a skull and crossbones on the label. Who knows what it might have been? But the bottle had a skull and crossbones, which means that it contained poison, right? Well, I looked around to see what I could find, and I saw that bottle.

"Well, for sure, I'll swallow that stuff," I told myself, and I snatched up the bottle.

As soon as I had left the kitchen for the bathroom, Panchita had run as fast as she could to find Mamá and tell her about my intentions—about what I had been saying to myself.

So I left the bathroom and walked back into the kitchen. The moment that I raised that bottle to my mouth to swallow it down, Mamá came rushing into the kitchen and slapped it away from my lips, knocking it to the floor. If Mamá hadn't arrived in time—as they told me afterwards—I wouldn't have died, I would have just burnt my throat. That stuff wasn't sufficiently poisonous.

"*¿Estás loca*? Are you crazy?!" she yelled at me, and she slapped me again, "What's the matter with you?"

And I started to cry and scream at her: "Mamá, you must think that you have another daughter who's gone bad on you," I told her, "but don't you go thinking that I was going to do this on account of Juan or anything like that! It's the situation that I find myself in: my father, you, everybody quarreling and fighting so much because I'm going to get married. That's why I was going to do it. Look, *Madrecita*, I could just put an end to the whole mess, let me put an end to it!"

Well, that shook her up; it really frightened her. Papá had also come into the room by this time, and he, too, was very alarmed. "Look! All on account of you!" Mamá yelled at Papá. "It's all your fault, you're the cause of all this!"

And well, she finally made him understand. So when the gentlemen came back in December, Papá reluctantly gave his permission for Juan and me to marry.

The day set for the wedding finally arrived. Papá dressed himself up very nicely, very correctly, and when it was time to go to the church—well, he had to deliver me and hand me over to the groom—he just took me there in the car, brought me into the church, left me at the altar and went on out by the back door. He just went in one door and went out by another. He returned immediately to our house and shut himself up in a room, and we didn't see him again. I was married, and they took our picture, and we went back to the house.

My husband's whole family was there waiting. It was just a few close relatives who had come for the wedding meal that they had prepared for us. It was just going to be a dinner. Papá wouldn't permit any formal reception or celebration. When we got there, Papá had already shut himself up in a room, and nobody could get him out of there. He didn't come out to greet anyone or see anyone or anything, not even to give me his blessing, nothing, nothing at all. He didn't want for me to get married.

And so it was a very sad wedding for me. There was no dance, there was no party, there was no big reception—nothing but a dinner. A dinner was prepared, and then the judge came and married us, and around six o'clock in the afternoon, Papá—who had remained shut up by himself in that room all day—came out and said, "All right, now! Now we have done our part, now please do me the favor of leaving. Everyone! Everybody out!"

Even me. He ran everybody out. That was my wedding. He threw us all out: the guests, the godparents, Juan and me, everybody. He didn't want anybody there in the house. And everybody was crying. Instead of beginning with joy, my marriage began with tears. That was my wedding.

We had gotten together a little two-room house over on Frío Street, and so I already had my house. I had everything prepared. But it was ... a very hard thing for me. That whole experience seemed more like a funeral than a wedding. It was all tears, all laments. It pained me to leave in that way, to leave my home like that. It hurt me so much that I was almost sorry for having gotten married. My wedding was very sad.

Juan Alvarado was my first husband's name. He worked for a man who had a shoe shop there in San Antonio and who had taught him his trade. Juan worked for that man for a whole year without receiving a cent in wages just so he could learn the trade. Juan, my husband, had been a harvester, a field worker. He used to be very good at it. He would go pick the crops with his whole family. They worked in the area around San Antonio, and all over. But when he got to be about fifteen years old, he decided that he didn't want to stay in that line of work. Juan decided that he wanted to learn a trade. He didn't even go to school, his family didn't even send him to school. Because in those days people used to take their kids out of school and take them off to work in the fields all the time. It's not done nowadays, but in those years, it was very common. That was the way it was for Juan and his brothers. If his family was leaving to go pick the harvest or do some other field work somewhere, they would just pull the kids out of school, and off they would go. Finally, the last time, Juan just said that he wasn't going to go. "Okay," his father told him, "stay here if you want to."

And they went off to work without leaving him a cent or food or anything. He was only fifteen years old. So Juan made friends with this man who had the shoe shop and he would go down there and try to help out around the place.

Finally: "Why don't you teach me the trade?" Juan told the man. "I would really like to learn it."

"Okay, I'll teach you," the shoemaker told him. "You seem to have some aptitude for the work, but I'm not going to pay you. You can help me out here and learn the trade, and I'll give you fifty cents a week or something, but I can't pay you wages."

"Don't worry about it," Juan told him.

And Juan worked like that for one year while he was learning to be a shoemaker. After he had learned, then he received a salary. When we got married, he was earning seven dollars a week.

The first year after I got married, there were two reasons why I left the group. Upon marrying, my husband's family were opposed to my continuing my career, and they really worked on my husband about it. They told him that I had now married and that I ought to stay at home with my husband. They put a lot of ideas into Juan's head, to the point that he wouldn't let me work anymore. Contracts, opportunities to work would come up, and Papá would come over and tell Juan about them. There were lots of contracts to go and sing in all the towns around San Antonio and South Texas in theaters and at dances—that kind of thing. The people would come to see Papá about them, but the condition was always that I had to appear. But Juan didn't allow me to go and take advantage of those jobs. He had got the idea that I was going to cut off my career.

And then, of course, I got with family right away. I got pregnant soon after we were married, and so, for the moment, the idea of not working didn't bother me too much. Then when God gave me health, and I had my little girl safe and sound, I wanted to continue to follow my career with my family, like always. Then Juan did oppose my career some, but not on his own account—he was a good man—but because of his family, his parents. They kept on telling him that I was married now, and that I had to dedicate myself to him and to my home, to my little girl. They told him that all of my going around singing wasn't the proper life for a respectable married woman ... who knows what all. They put it into his head like that, that he shouldn't permit contracts and that he shouldn't allow me to perform in public.

It was in 1936 that my records started achieving really big sales, and it was raining contracts from all over, but at my parent's house. But the people and the promoters wanted me as well, not just the group. When they saw that I couldn't go, then the family was left without work and had to go back to singing for tips in the Plaza.

Things were pretty rough for Juan and me, too. He was a shoemaker, but he earned very little; he still only made seven dollars a week. We could barely get by, and then not too well, on seven dollars a week, and we now had my little girl to think about, too. "What necessity is there," I asked him, "for us to be struggling and suffering like this, when the offers and music contracts are piling up over at Papá's? Lots of people are still trying to get me to sing, and here we are, barely scraping by. Why shouldn't we take advantage of the opportunity?"

But he was reluctant. He didn't want me to do it because his family had been after him so much and put all these ideas into his head. "Look, don't pay any attention to them," I started to tell him ... "We're going back to singing. Look, right now we can make very good money."

Finally, Juan started paying attention to me and he got the point. He decided to ignore his family's opinion, and we started to really work all out at singing. We joined up again with the whole family, and we started to work together. We all worked together for about the next seven years. We would no sooner get back to town from one tour, than we would take off on another. It was raining contracts, and we didn't spend much time in San Antonio.

I also continued to record for Blue Bird, and just about every song of mine that they released became a hit. I recorded with them for six years, year after year without a break. They would come to San Antonio every three or four months to record. One time it even happened that I was in Monterrey, Nuevo León, México, and they came and recorded me there. That was in 1940.

When I used to go into the studio for them at the Texas Hotel, and later at the Blue Bonnet Hotel, it didn't take me very long to record. It took some of the other groups a lot longer. The most difficult thing about recording in those days was that the people making the recording would be behind a little window there, and we would be over here on the other side. And we would have to begin our number just as soon as this light bulb lit up ... and we would have to finish ... when it went off. Some people made a lot of faulty recordings because they would still be in the middle of their number when the light went off, and they would have to do it over again—they wouldn't be on time. I didn't have this problem because as soon as they told me how many minutes they wanted the song to be, I would take the time, and we would put ourselves to practice my numbers ... with Papá with a watch in his hand. We would measure the songs—approximately—so that they didn't go a full three minutes. We had to be alert to the turning on and off of the light bulb. Many of the other groups, well, they didn't practice or they didn't know; for whatever reason, they would make a lot of faulty recordings. At that time you recorded in wax. They were round disks of wax about sixteen inches wide. That was the master. It was recorded there crooked or straight, *chueco o derecho*, good or bad: there it went. And unlike nowadays, you couldn't do anything about it. It was much more difficult to record in those days. One mistake during the recording would ruin the whole thing.

María

Papá had a very strong voice, just like my brother Manuel, exactly the same, and they had to put him all the way in the back of the room when we recorded, because otherwise it would come out all his voice. And Mamá had a very thin voice. My brother Manuel and I had just about the same voice at that time, and Lydia also had a voice like Mamá. Well, they put those two—Lydia and Mamá—together, and my brother Manuel and I were put together because we were about the same. I always used to sing the second part, *la segunda voz*. I can sing first now, but I always used to sing second with the family, and later with Juanita and with Lydia on Azteca, when we were the Dueto Monterrey.

Lydia

When I went to record, they never told me, "Record this, record that." I recorded the songs that I brought with me, many of which were the songs that my mother sang. When I came to record, I recorded a lot of her repertory, like "Pero ay qué triste," "Al pie de tu reja"; those songs didn't come on gum wrappers.

Pero ay qué triste[4]

Pero ay ¡qué triste! Y es amor sin esperanza; en mi pecho, mi corazón latiendo.

De mis ojos una lágrima virtiendo, Y desde entonces no hay consuelo ni esperanza para mí.

Pero ay ¡qué triste! (etc.) De mis ojos una lágrima virtiendo, (etc.)

Pues, si no me quieres, pues ¿para qué me miras? ¡O, qué misterio encierra tu mirada!

But Oh, How Sad

But oh, how sad! And it's a love without hope; in my breast, my heart is throbbing.

From my eyes a tear is falling. And ever since then there is neither hope nor consolation for me.

But oh, how sad! (etc.) From my eyes a tear is falling. (etc.)

Well, if you don't love me, well, why do you stare at me? Oh, what mystery your gaze contains!

And "Los besos de mi negra," "Deliciosa," "No puedo dejar de quererte"—all those were my mother's songs. She would sing them when I was a small child and later with the group when we were traveling around singing in the streets. I believe that most of those songs would be from the time when my grandmother was also singing them.

"Los besos de mi negra"[5]

Los besos de mi negra son amargos, y más amargos que la ley de la traición. Me jurastes que me amabas, y sin embargo, ya no tienes en tu pecho el corazón. (Se repite la estrofa.)

Y, ay, quién pudiera generarte un beso y arrancarle a tu espíritu las alas. Tan fácil es amar como se olvida; ya no tienes corazón, y lo regalas, ya no tienes corazón, y lo regalas.

Todo se acaba, mujer, en esta vida: la riqueza, el amor y la hermosura. Tan fácil es amar como se olvida; el reposo sólo está en la sepultura, el reposo sólo está en la sepultura.

"My Dark-Skinned Woman's Kisses"

My dark-skinned woman's kisses are bitter, even more bitter than the law of treachery. You swore that you loved me, but nevertheless, you no longer have a heart in your breast. (The stanza is repeated.)

Oh, if only I could really kiss you and clip the wings of your spirit. It is just as easy to love as to forget; you no longer have a heart, but you still give it away, you no longer have a heart, but you still give it away.

Woman, everything in this life comes to an end: wealth, love and beauty. It is just as easy to love as to forget; the only place there is peace is in the grave, the only place there is peace is in the grave.

In any case, my mother already knew that whole repertory, so when I went to record, I did all of those songs.

But my biggest song, my signature, was always "Mal hombre." Although some people have said that I must have sung "Mal hombre" because of some personal disappointment in love, how was I to have been in love? When I learned that song I wasn't even ... nine ... or ten years old. I was just a little girl then, and my biggest ambition was to learn songs. But that I had suffered an amorous disappointment and then sang about that—of course not.

During that first year of my marriage—1935—things had been pretty tough for my family. Not only did they have to go back to singing for handouts in the Plaza, but there was a fire that burned my parent's house down. I got married in March, and their house burned down in August.

Juan and I were living over on Matamoros Street. Right after we got married we lived for a while in a little house on Frío Street, but we soon moved to Matamoros Street, and that was where my first daughter was born. But since I was pregnant I used to go over and visit with Mamá and my sisters pretty often. The family was living on Pecos Street at that time. Well, this one day I was over at the house with my parents, and the fire occurred that afternoon. Their part of the house was upstairs, and there was only one exit. There was a big balcony, and there was a room there where I was lying down because it was a very hot day. The house caught fire and started to burn by the stairs—the only exit. Everyone figured out what was happening, and they all managed to get down, but I was asleep—I was still upstairs. When Mamá remembered about me, that I was in the last room up in front, she came running back into the building: "Lydia! Lydia! We're burning up! Let's get out of here!" she was yelling.

But when we got to the stairway, we could no longer get down, because the flames were too intense. So we ran out onto the balcony, and finally someone—probably the firemen—got us down with a ladder. If Mamá hadn't remembered that I was up there, I probably would have died in the fire—I would have burned to death up there. I hadn't even noticed that the house was burning. I was sound asleep.

So, things were real tough for the family. They lost everything in that fire, and they had to start over again from scratch. What made it worse was that I still hadn't rejoined the family act, and pickings were pretty slim for them down in the Plaza.

Manuel

After Lydia got married, we had to start going to the Plaza again because she wasn't with us anymore: because she was married. It was just Mamá, Panchita, María and I; Juanita was still too young, and Papá was already in pretty bad shape. We just kept on going the best we could, and slowly we started to make a living for ourselves again, but it was real rough going, and we'd already had a taste of better things before Lydia got married. So Mamá decided that it was much too hard work singing in the Plaza, and that we could do better than that, that maybe we could put on a stage show. I guess we first got the idea for that when we were working in those *carpas* right before Lydia got married. When Lydia talked her husband into going back into show business, well, that really helped get us going, too. And you know, because Lydia had gotten a name for herself by the records, people started knowing about her all over the United States and in Mexico. So we started to form a stage show.

Lydia

What Manuel says is true, I first recorded in 1934, and by 1936 my name was very well-known by the public which listened to the radio. My records were very widely played on the radio, so we were able to get lots of little jobs around San Antonio, but that was all there was because we were very ignorant of ... of how business could be done, how to work in theaters or wherever it might be. We didn't know anything about all that, but everywhere Mexican music was heard, people were beginning to be aware of my name and of the group that I had. The opportunity was there, but we didn't know how to take advantage of it by ourselves.

This was when Mr. Antonio Montes joined up with us. Antonio Montes was a person that took an interest in helping us. He became our master of ceremonies and our teacher. He taught us all about the theater and presenting variety shows, what they call in Spanish *variedades*—sort of like vaudeville shows—because what did we know about all that? We knew about music but not about comedy routines or anything like that. So between Mamá and Mr. Montes, we were able to organize a little group that could put on real stage shows from among the family. And that was how we began to work out on the road, eventually touring all over the United States.

Antonio Montes is dead now, but he was the one that started us out as a touring *variedad*. He was singing *tangos* there in San Antonio when we met him. He had traveled for a number of years with some big-name variety shows—the biggest and most popular Mexican acts of that time— but he eventually came to sing with the strolling groups there in the Plaza del Zacate. Mamá and Papá met him by hearing him sing one night when Antonio Montes came down to try and make a little money in the Plaza del Zacate, like so many other *artistas* in those days when times were really hard. He sang down there for a while, mostly *tangos* and *boleros*, sometimes by himself and sometimes accompanied by some of his friends from among the singers there. I didn't really know him very well at that time, and I don't know exactly why he became aware of us, but he went and spoke with Mamá down there in the Plaza.

Later, when he became aware of my fame, and that of the group, he came and presented himself to us. He said that he could help us find jobs because he knew a lot of halls and theaters. He said that he could join up with us as a representative, as an artist, as a driver ... as ... in any capacity, helping us out in every way.

Well, Antonio Montes did join up with us, and afterwards we came to see him, not as an agent, but as a ... member of our family, as a friend, a brother.

We became very fond of him because, only a couple of years later, my father died. Antonio Montes joined up with us in 1936 when my father was very sick, and he helped us to take care of Papá a lot and all of the problems of working on the road. When my father finally died in 1938, Montes stayed on with us. Shortly before my father died he instructed Antonio Montes not to abandon us. Papá entrusted us to Señor Montes so that his children would not be abandoned, so that they would have someone to care for them, and Mr. Montes never forgot it.

We all traveled and toured together like that with Mr. Montes for the next five or six years. Montes was the one that opened up the field for us to work outside of San Antonio ... for El Paso ... all that stretch of territory. He was the one that took us to the state of Colorado, to the state of New Mexico and to many other places that he had worked before. It was Montes that taught us the ropes of professional show business, because we didn't know anything about any of that. My brothers were still very small and Papá could no longer really help us. My mother had her little car when we went out on the *giras*, the road tours, and Montes was her driver. It was Montes that took charge of the advertising, of the announcements and of putting us up, finding us a place to stay. He even helped us to present comedy skits in our stage show. We went around like a family. Of all of the people who helped us during our career, Antonio Montes was the principal one.

Juanita, María and Manuel were starting to grow up, and they had a lot of talent and enthusiasm for comedy, so Mamá started to put them into *esqueches cómicos*, comedy skits or sketches. They had first started to do that kind of thing back when we were with the Carpa García, but only in a very rudimentary way. We all still had a lot to learn about professional, stage-quality show business. So Mr. Montes really helped out with the comedy skits. He was really a teacher to them, a *maestro*. The youngsters were trained by Montes and Mamá.

Mr. Montes had toured as a singer, and he had a lot of experience in that field. He had toured with Elisa García—a very big star in Mexico at that time. Leonardo García was the director of the company, and Montes learned a lot from him. Leonardo García was one of the very best *apuntadores*, theatrical prompters, in Mexico in those days. Leonardo García's family had one of the biggest theatrical companies in Mexico. Antonio Montes had first come to the United States on a tour with the company of Elisa and Leonardo García. So Montes had seen lots of skits and routines and he remembered many of them, although he hadn't performed in them himself.

When Montes joined up with us, we didn't really know what to do. How were we going to make money? My name was well-known, but we had to fill out an entire show with something. It was Mr. Montes who saw the

La Familia Mendoza: Lydia, Juanita, Leonor, Manuel and María. Courtesy of the Lydia Mendoza collection.

way to put together a complete *variedad*. Montes had noted that Manuel had the makings of a comic, and he thought that there was a way that we could come up with a complete show. Juanita, also, had shown early signs of comedic ability. Ever since she was five years old, she had sung, "*Adiós, mi chaparrita.*" She had a really winning way, and a lot of talent for comedy.

In the beginning, even Mamá would go out on stage to do the skits with Montes and Manuel—it was a three-person skit. But Montes kept on training Juanita and Manuel, and eventually they took over almost all of the skits. As Andrés got a little older, he too began to do some comedy. Andrés actually began with parodies, singing parodies of popular songs, before he got into the skits. María would occasionally get into the act, too, but I myself never did any comedy—I was strictly a singer and musician.

Montes would teach Manuel and Juanita the skit, and then Mamá would say, "Practice it, study it well!"

"Oh, Mamá," Manuel—who was always very lazy—would say, "we know it already."

"Study it well!" Mama would say, again.

"We've got it now, Mamá," Manuel would say a little later.

"You better have, because if you go out on stage tonight and you haven't learned it and you make a mistake, you'll see what'll happen to you. ... "

"No, Mamá," Manuel would answer, "I know it real well now."

And he would run out to play. When the time came to put on the skit, I remember that Mamá used to stand just behind the curtain on one side of the stage ... with a razor strap in her hand. Well, Manuel, the poor kid, just seeing Mamá there with the strap made him start to get nervous, and of course, he would make a mistake in the skit. The minute the skit was over and Manuel walked off stage, Mamá would grab him and start really laying that strap on him. "Mamacita! Mamacita!" he would cry, but he didn't rebel, he didn't fight back. "*Mamacita*, what can I do?"

And he would have to go back out and do another number. So he would try to get his costume straight and stop crying and regain his composure while Mamá stood there with the strap in her hand, and he would go back out on stage. That's how Mamá taught them to be good comics. It was the same with Juanita. She would be on stage and she would do something, and then she would turn around, and there she could see Mamá waiting in the wings with that strap in her hand, the poor kid. I'm going to let Manuel and my sister Juanita themselves tell you a little about those first stage shows we started putting on in 1936.

Manuel

We presented our very first stage show at the Venus Theater at the corner of Zarzamora and Guadalupe right here in San Antonio. It was right on the corner where the Soto Café is now. Mamá taught Juanita and me how to do a little skit with a little song in it. Everything was set—the stage was all set—so Juanita and I came out. She went out first, and I came out behind her. We stood there looking at each other for a moment, and then we burst out laughing. We just stood there laughing our heads off. "Ha, ha, ha, ha. ... " Nothing came out—none of the lines of the skit we were supposed to be doing, just, "Ha, ha, ha. ... "

Well, then Mamá said from backstage, "Come here. ... " Pow! She started hitting us on the head. She conked the hell out of me, I even got some bumps on my head, she got so mad. I'm telling you. That was the first time that I was ever out on stage.

Juanita

Mamá always stayed just behind the curtain waiting for us while we were out on stage. Manuel and I would get real scared if we ever did anything wrong, because she would be waiting for us right there. She would punish us like that right away, and that was what happened the day we started doing the comedy skits together.

Manuel

Well, I don't think that I did the skit that day, because I couldn't do anything that day: I was too embarrassed. But then we played at the Progreso. That was another theater, right there at Brazos and Guadalupe. We went to play there, and that's where Juanita and I sang "Las cuarenta cartas."

Las cuarenta cartas[6]

LUPE: Oiga, amigo, si le choco, bien se puede largar. Que al cabo el dicho lo dices, pero menos engorda más.

REGIM: No es tanto como Ud. dice, porque yo siempre he pensado que más vale estar solo que mal acompañado.

LUPE: Pos yo, como dijo Chencha, que hombres hay en dondequiera, y no como Ud., correlón.

REGIM: A una mujer como Ud. las enaguas le vienen flojas. El que nació pa' tamal, del cielo le caen las hojas.

LUPE: Y a Ud. tan enamorado. Pero eso sí, cuatezones, ni a mí me compra zapatos, pero ni él carga calzones.

REGIM: No jale que descobija. Ni me canten la de molde, si no quiere que le saque sus trapitos al sol.

LUPE: Pues si es tan pantera, jugaremos un conquián, y así pierda quién perdiera, la suerte decidirá.

REGIM: Y el perico ha de ser verde aunque levante la pata. Y ¡Ay, cilantro, no te seques! ¡Porque se te va el jedor! (De aquí en adelante se canta, con música.)
AMBOS: Ay, no te revientes, reata, antes de llegar a tu edad, jugaremos un conquián con una baraja nueva.
REGIM: Adiós mis cuarenta cartas, también contaré los ases. Si tienes algo, amigo, por eso ni caso me haces.
LUPE: Adiós mis cuarenta cartas también contaré los doses a la hora de dar el "gano" es cuando me desconoces.
REGIM: Adiós mis cuarenta cartas, también contaré los treses, cuando más te necesito es cuando desapareces.
AMBOS: Ay no te revientes, reata, antes de llegar a tu edad, jugaremos un conquián con una baraja nueva.
LUPE: Adiós mis cuarenta cartas, también contaré los cuatros, ya estoy cansada de ti, que no me compras zapatos.
REGIM: Adiós mis cuarenta cartas, también contaré los cincos, estando el suelo parejo, ¿para qué son tantos brincos?
LUPE: Adiós mis cuarenta cartas, también contaré los seises, cuando te pido dinero, es cuando desapareces.
REGIM: Adiós mis cuarenta cartas, también contaré malilla, donde andan los gavilanes no rifan las aguilillas.
LUPE: Adiós mis cuarenta cartas, también contaré la sota no te lo digo de veras que tú solito te alborotas.
REGIM: Adiós mis cuarenta cartas, también contaré el caballo, con mujeres como tú, dondequiera me las hallo.
LUPE: Adiós mis cuarenta cartas, también contaré los reyes, porque nos dan las medidas, por eso los hacen güeyes.
AMBOS: El conquián ya terminó, ya vimos los dos la prueba, ya te canté tus versitos con una baraja nueva.

"The Forty Cards"

LUPE: Listen, friend, if I offend you, you can just leave. In the end, you just say what's said, but less fattens more.
REGIM: It's not really so much like you say, because I've always thought that it's better to be alone than in bad company.
LUPE: Well, I agree with what Chencha said, that there's men everywhere, and not like you, coward.
REGIM: On a woman like you, your petticoats fit real loose. He who was born to be a tamale, the corn husks fall on him from heaven.

LUPE: And on you, loverboy. But one thing is true, buddies, he doesn't buy me shoes, but he doesn't wear the pants either.

REGIM: Don't tug the blanket because you're uncovering too much. Don't go singing your usual song, either, if you don't want me to hang your own laundry out to dry.

LUPE: Well, if you're such a panther, we'll play a game of bluff, and whoever loses, luck will decide.

REGIM: And the parakeet has to be green even if it lifts up its leg. And, ay, *cilantro*, don't dry out! Because you're losing your stench!

(From here on, it is sung, with music.)

BOTH: Ay, don't drop dead, buddy, before your time, we'll play a round of bluff with a brand new deck of cards.

REGIM: Farewell, my forty cards, I'll count the aces, too. If you've got something, friend, don't pay any attention to me.

LUPE: Farewell, my forty cards, I'll count the twos, too; when it's time to say "I win," that's when you'll disown me.

REGIM: Farewell, my forty cards, I'll count the threes, too; when I most need you, that's when you disappear.

BOTH: Ay, don't drop dead, buddy, before your time, we'll play a hand of bluff with a brand new deck of cards.

LUPE: Farewell, my forty cards, I'll count the fours, too; I'm already tired of you, who doesn't even buy me shoes.

REGIM: Farewell, my forty cards, I'll count the fives, too; the floor being flat, why are there so many bumps?

LUPE: Farewell, my forty cards, I'll count the sixes, too; when I ask you for money, that's when you disappear.

REGIM: Farewell, my forty cards, I'll count on the seven, too; where the hawks fly, the baby eagles don't fight.

LUPE: Farewell, my forty cards, I'll count the Jack, too; I'm not really telling you that, you get riled up by yourself.

REGIM: Farewell, my forty cards, I'll count the Queen, too; women like you, I can find them anywhere.

LUPE: Farewell, my forty cards, I'll count the Kings, too; because they give us the measures, that's why they make them cuckolds.

BOTH: The game of bluff has now ended, now we've both seen the test, now I've just sung you verses with a brand new deck of cards.

"Las cuarenta cartas" is an old song that Mamá taught us, and that we used to sing in the Carpa García.

In those little theaters they used to show a movie first; then after the movie came the stage show. First María would play the piano, and then the announcer would come out and welcome the people and tell them about the show, that it was headed by whoever it was, the main star, like Lydia.

Then Janie and I would come out and do our comedy skit. After the skit, María played something again on the piano, then Juanita would come out and sing the mirror song. She had a little mirror, and she would dance around shining the mirror at some of the men in the audience, one after another, and sing that song to them.

Show business veteran Rolando Morales remarks:

Rolando Morales

The "Mirror Song" is a Spanish *couplet*. When María Conesa came to Mexico, she brought all of these *couplets* with her.[7] Antonio Montes toured quite a bit with Selma Villagrán. Selma Villagrán used to do all of those *couplets* that María Conesa brought over from Spain. All the Garcías also used to do all of those *couplets*. Everything that La Conesa did, the Garcías used to do in the Carpa García. They did "Mírame, mírame" ("The Mirror Song"), they did all of the material that was known as *la zarzuela chica*, sort of light musical comedy stuff.

I used to see Juanita Mendoza when she was justing starting out—when she was just starting to perform—sitting in the front row at the Zaragoza Theater in San Antonio with her attention riveted on the stage. She really liked show business, she was really attracted to it. This was in about 1937. But where she probably learned all of those *couplets* was with the Garcías at the Carpa García, because the Garcías sang all of those *couplets*. There was also a *salón* at the corner of Matamoros Street and Pecos Street in San Antonio where they used to show movies and put on variety shows, where all of those *couplets* would be sung.

Mírame, mírame[8]

Como el cielo de mi patria
que está cubierto de azul.
Por eso las mexicanas
tienen la gracia de Jesús.

Una mirada que mata,
un corazón que ama mucho,
unos ojos que enamoran
y unos labios que enamoran.

Mírame, mírame, mírame, mírame,
mírame con tus ojitos.
Porque si tú no me miras,
Amor, me voy de fijo.

Me canso de estar soltera,
y he decidido casarme.
Pero tengo mucho miedo,
pues, pudiera equivocarme.

Joven, me gusta Ud. mucho.
¿Me quisiera hacer feliz?
No se ponga colorado,
que lo quiero hacer reír.

Mírame, mírame, mírame, mírame,
mírame con tus ojitos.
Porque si tú no me miras,
Amor, irme voy de fijo.

Me gustan mucho los viejos,
de veritas se lo digo,
porque son muy consecuentes
y muy blandos para el castigo.

Aquí estoy yo viendo a uno,
tiene cara de bendito.
Y si no se me enojara,
le diría más bajito:

Mírame, mírame, mírame, mírame,
mírame con tus ojitos.
Porque si tú no me miras,
Amor, irme voy de fijo.

Look at Me, Look at Me

Like the sky of my homeland
which is all covered with blue.
That's why the Mexican girls
have the grace of Jesus.

A glance that kills,

a heart that loves a lot,
some eyes that fall in love
and lips that fall in love.

Look at me, look at me, look at me, look at me,
look at me with your little eyes.
Because if you don't look at me,
Love, I'm leaving for sure.

I'm tired of being single,
and I have decided to get married.
But I'm real scared,
well, I could make a mistake.

Young man, I like you a lot.
Do you want to make me happy?
Don't you blush,
because I just want to make you laugh.

Look at me, look at me, look at me, look at me,
look at me with your little eyes.
Because if you don't look at me,
Love, I'm going to leave for sure.

I like old men a lot,
truly, I tell you,
because they always spoil me
and don't get too rough with me.

I'm looking at one here,
he looks like a sweet man.
If he weren't getting mad at me,
I would tell him more softly:

Look at me, look at me, look at me, look at me,
look at me with your little eyes.
Because if you don't look at me,
I'm going to leave for sure.

Juanita

When I would say that I liked the old men, or the young men, I would shine the light from the mirror on different men in the audience, and all the people in the audience would start laughing.

Manuel

Then María would play something again while Juanita changed her clothes, and then Juanita and I would come out dancing together. We had to change real quick! We would dance "¡Viva Jalisco!" We used to sing it, too. And we used to sing "Yo tengo la casita," "La guía"[9] and "El queretano," a song that went: "I'm a Queretaran gentleman. ... " And we used to sing "Atotonilco," and we would dance "Las jícaras de Michoacán."

Las jícaras de Michoacán[10]

Ay, qué lindas florecitas
traigo en mi jicarita
de Tepic, Michoacán.
Da da da dan, da da da dan.

Un amor tengo en el alma
que me ha robado la calma.
Pues mi vida es un volcán,
da da da dan, da da da dan.

Por eso le quiero,
por eso le adoro,
porque es mi ranchero,
sin duda un charro mejor.

El es el primero que ha
ido en mi corazón.
Porque siempre vivo
pensando en su amor.

Bamp ba bampa, bamp, bamp, bamp.

The Gourds of Michoacán

Ay, what pretty little flowers
I bring in my little gourd
from Tepic, Michoacán.
Da da da dan, da da da dan.

I have a a love in my soul

that has robbed me of my peace
So my life is a volcano,
da da da dan, da da da dan.

That's why I love him,
that's why I adore him,
because he is my *ranchero*,
without doubt the best cowboy.

He is the first one that has
gone into my heart.
Because I live always
thinking about his love.

Bamp ba bampa, bamp, bamp, bamp.

Manuel
    We used to have to practice all of those routines a lot. We worked real hard on them. Then at the end the whole family would go out together, and we would all sing "¡Qué malas son!" or, sometimes, "Mariquita," which goes like this:

Mariquita[11]

Vámonos Mariquita,
a bailar esta polquita.
Acuérdese de sus tiempos
aunque sea Ud. la abuelita.

El corazón no envejece,
está alegre y ya palpita,
nomás que se acuerda
de una música bonita.

Viejos y muchachos,
todos a bailar
esta linda polka
que se va a tocar.

Doña Mariquita
ya se está animando,
y una cana al aire

quiere soltar.

Yo tuve mis veinte abriles,
me complazco en recordarlos.
¿Para qué les digo nada
de esos tiempos juveniles?

Se bailaba la cuadrilla,
la mazurka y los espejos.
Acerca de esos bailes viejos,
casi no se ha quedado nada.

Viejos y muchachos,
todos a bailar
esta linda polka
que se va a tocar.

Doña Mariquita
ya se está animando,
y una cana al aire
quiere soltar.

Mariquita

Let's go Mariquita,
and dance this little polka.
Remember how it goes even
if you're a grandma.

The heart doesn't get old,
it'll be happy and start beating,
just as soon as it remembers
a pretty song.

Old men and boys,
everybody dance
this pretty polka
that's going to be played.

Doña Mariquita
is getting wound up,
and now she wants to cut
loose a gray hair into the air.

I have seen my twenty Aprils,
it makes me glad to remember them.
Why shouldn't I talk about
those youthful times?

They used to dance the quadrille,
the mazurka and the "mirrors."
About those old-time dances,
almost nothing has remained.

Old men and boys,
everybody dance
this pretty polka
that is going to be played.

Doña Mariquita
is getting wound up,
and now she wants to cut loose
a gray hair into the air.

Juanita

The people really loved the way that Manuel danced. He did some really funny things. He did the footwork in a real funny way, but they gave him a lot of applause because he did it very well. And Mamá brought him a beautiful *chinaco*[12] suit from Mexico, and when he would come out, all the girls would whistle.

Manuel

I was a skinny guy. I used to weigh a hundred and forty pounds, and now I weigh two hundred and twenty. I'm twice as big as I used to be.

Lydia

We had never worn costumes when we were singing down there in the Plaza del Zacate. We would just be there singing in whatever clothes we had. But when we started to put on a real show, to do salons, halls and theaters and all that, we realized that we needed costumes. We didn't have any way of going to Mexico and buying costumes, so my mother got the idea of making them herself because she was a very good seamstress. She sewed very prettily.

Mamá would make the costumes for my brother Manuel, so that he could go out to sing his numbers with my sister or put on his dances. She bought him some black pants, and she altered them so that they would be like a *charro* outfit. For adornment she bought buttons, those silvery ones, to simulate those silver fasteners, *conchos*, that they use on *charro* suits. She adorned all of his clothes; she made his jackets. The only thing that she bought ready-made was a hat: an ordinary cheap one. Mamá made everything else. The same for my sisters. For Juanita, she bought a *rebozo*, one of those Mexican shawls, and made it into a Mexican outfit.

I also began to make my own costumes, or Mamá would buy a little dress somewhere cheap, and then she would fix it up for me to wear on stage. That was how we began. Afterwards, we had the opportunity to go to Monterrey and to Nuevo Laredo. We had money. So then we would buy costumes there on the other side of the border like the other big Mexican acts.

But in the beginning, we had to make everything for ourselves. Mamá would make blouses out of shawls. She wove with a hook, she knew how to do that needle work, and she also did embroidery. Mamá arranged the wardrobe the best that she could when we didn't have the money to buy it ready-made. That was how we began. Then slowly we started to buy clothes. ... When we went to New York in 1941, she bought a brown *charro* suit from some singer here in San Antonio, and fixed it up for Manuel.

Manuel

When Mamá decided to try to put on a stage show, she made us some costumes. I'm telling you, they were real ugly. You should have seen the *china poblana* outfit she made. She pictured herself as wearing a typical Mexican costume, one of those fancy ones like the famous Mexican *ranchera* singers wear. It had a skirt with sequins. Antonio Montes, who used to be our manager, he used to laugh, and he'd say it looked like a "tubercular eagle ... ," a little skinny eagle. He used to make fun of those costumes. But Mamá, you know, she did the best she could. She made all of our costumes, every costume, at that time. Then later on she started hiring a lady that used to make costumes; her name was María. She was an Indian, and she used to make some real good *chinas poblanas*.

CHAPTER 5

La Alondra de la Frontera

Lydia

In 1936 when Mr. Montes joined up with us, my name was starting to get big, and people wanted us to go play in different places. Antonio Montes would go and book places for us like church halls or society and association halls to put on an hour or an hour and a half of variety show.

Mamá managed all of the money on the tours. Mr. Antonio Montes got 35% for his work. He was the master of ceremonies, he got us the jobs, he was the driver of my mother's car and he helped us in the family out a lot—so we gave him 35% of the gate. Of what was left, I gave half to Mamá, and I kept half. We worked on that basis.

That same year—1936—before we went out on our first big tour to Colorado, Montes took us around South Texas on sort of a little tour—a warm-up for what was ahead. One day Montes just said, "We're going out on a tour."

"All right," Mamá said, "but we don't have any money."

"That's all right," replied Montes, "let's just see what we can do."

We went down to Mr. Acuña's furniture store, and they helped us make up some programs, some printed flyers. We had about 2000 programs printed. They were just a regular sized piece of paper with a list of the artists and acts in their order of appearance in the show and the name "Lydia Mendoza." And for the date, they just said: "Tonight." But we didn't print the actual date. When we arrived in a town, the afternoon before the show, we would all get together and write in the name of the town and the *salón* (the hall) and the date, and then Montes would hire a couple of kids to hand out the programs. We had two cars: mine and Mamá's. My husband Juan drove my car, and Montes drove the other.

"There's a little town down near Laredo, Texas," Montes told Mamá, "and it's a very good little town; there are a lot of Mexicans there. There's not much work, it's true, but many of the people who live there have money, they're pretty well off, and it's a real nice town. I worked there a few years ago when I used to be with the *variedad* of Elisa García, and we did real well there."

"Okay," Mamá said.

So we went on down there, and when we arrived, the place looked very bare, very empty, but there was a great big hall, and Montes said, "That's the *salón* where we played here before. It's a great hall, but I don't know if it still belongs to the same owner."

So Montes went around asking, and somebody told him where to find the owner. We went to the address and found a very fat man sitting in a swing, swinging himself back and forth and fanning himself because of the heat.

"What can I do for you?" the fat man asked us.

"Are you the owner of the *salón*?" Montes asked.

"Yes, of course," the fat man said, "it's mine."

"Well, you know," Montes told him, "I've got this *variedad* here with me ... "

"Yes, yes," the fat man broke in, "but, well, it's been a long time since we've had anything like that around here."

"I've brought Lydia Mendoza," Montes said.

"Lydia Mendoza! The one who sings? The one we've heard on the radio?" the fat man asked.

"Yes, her, the same."

"Really?"

"Yes, really, I've got her here, in person, right here. And I've got a whole variety show that goes with her."

And so Montes started telling him all about the show.

"Oh, that's real good, that'd be great," the fat man said, "but I just remembered. The hall, because it's been years since it's been used, doesn't have any electricity and there aren't any chairs."

"Well, how can we work there?" Montes asked him.

"Well, not too long ago," the fat man replied, "some acrobats, some *maromeros*—in those days the *maromeros* still toured around the country-side; they were the wandering artists who roamed from place to place or circus to circus—came through here, and they worked in that hall, and lots of people came to see them. I don't think there'll be any problem, the people around here are accustomed now. When a show comes along, they are all very eager to see it. They'll even bring their own chairs and their own lamps. If they don't have chairs, they'll bring benches or crates or something to sit on, but don't worry, they'll manage somehow. Of course, the *salón* is yours. You can put on your show for sure, just give me five or ten percent, it's not that important how much, the thing is that we all want to see Lydia Mendoza."

Then the fat man gave us some brooms so that we could clean the hall up a little bit. When we got there, the place was empty, and there weren't any chairs or anything—it was just a great big, empty room. There was no stage, no backstage area: nothing. Well, we always brought some tarps along with us, so Mr. Montes was able to improvise a dressing room for us. He drove in some nails in the wall in the back corner and ran some rope between them so that he could hang up the canvas to make a little room for us to change in. And Mamá got my sisters all dressed in their costumes, and the owner went out and made the rounds of the town, announcing the show and distributing the programs.

So there we were at about four o'clock in the afternoon, sitting there waiting to see what would happen. And listen to me, at about six o'clock that afternoon, when it was just starting to get dark, we saw what looked like a religious procession coming toward us through the streets of the town. It was really something, and it was very beautiful. Each person or little group was carrying their own lantern—those gasoline lamps they used to use in those days, like a Coleman lantern—and they lit the place up like it was daytime. And they were all carrying something to sit on. If one person didn't have a chair, they'd have a bench or even a wooden crate. Every person was loaded down, and they all brought something to sit on.

So they arrived in the hall and arranged their chairs and set up their lamps—what a light!—which really lit that place up. And that's where we played that night. We really packed them in, and we had a very good gate. That was how we worked. We didn't have any promotion by radio or in the newspapers. We'd just arrive in a town and work there that same night.

Papá no longer appeared with us very often at this time, but once in a while when he was feeling well enough, he would still come along. I especially remember one incident that occurred during that same first time we went out on a little tour around South Texas with Antonio Montes. I think the town was Beeville, Texas. This is when we were just starting out with the variety show, and we still hadn't appeared in any theaters. We got to Beeville.

"I know the priest here very well," Antonio Montes said, "and I'm sure he'll let us use the church auditorium to put on the show tonight."

Montes went to see the priest. "Oh, of course," the priest said. "Lydia Mendoza? Of course, that'll be no problem. But you'll have to come and clean up the hall, because last night we had a function in there, and it's still a real mess. Yes, you can use the *salón*, you can even have it for free. As long as you clean it out when you're finished, you don't have to pay me anything. Just go ahead and use it."

The priest had a lot of pictures in the hall. He had pictures of Lincoln, Washington, Hidalgo, Juárez, etc. —patriotic pictures, both Mexican and American—hanging all around the inside walls of the *salón.*

"One thing I want to tell you," the priest told Mr. Montes, "I don't want any of those pictures removed. Leave them just as they are. I don't want them touched."

"No," our manager, Montes, said, "we're not going to touch anything. We're just going to use the *salón* to play music and put on our show."

"Okay, that'll be fine," said the priest.

So everything was arranged. We were going to first clean up the hall and then put on the show that night.

"Señor Mendoza," Antonio Montes said to Papá—Papá was traveling with us this time—"can you stay here and clean up and arrange the chairs while we go and do the *convite*, drum up some business?"

"Oh, yes," Papá said, "I'll fix everything up, don't worry. You all go take care of everything else. I'll stay here."

So the rest of us all went off and took care of the *convite*, the flyers and their distribution, all of the advertisement for that night's show. When we got back to the hall—it was still early, it was still light outside—Papá was sitting in a chair out in front.

"There's not going to be any show tonight," Papá said as we came up, "because I just told the *padre* to go to hell."

What had happened was that when Papá went in there and saw all those pictures hanging on the walls of the *salón*, he decided that he wanted to use some of them for the patriotic monologue that he was going to present as part of our show. So he went and borrowed a ladder and put it up there, and he started taking down those pictures. He had already taken down two of them, and he was bringing down another one when the priest walked in.

"What! Don't! I don't want you to take those pictures down! I told that man I didn't want those pictures down!"

Papá just turned around and said, "You go to hell!"

And then when he saw that it was the priest, he went out in front and waited for the rest of us to arrive. When we drove up, Papá told Antonio Montes, "Montes! We're not going to be able to play here tonight."

"Why, Pancho?" Montes replied.

"Well," Papá said, "I already told the *padre* to go to hell."

Well, after that, we were always afraid to take Papá along with us on the tours. "No, Señor Mendoza," Antonio Montes told Papá, "I'm sorry, but it would be better if you stayed at home."

And from that time on, Papá would stay in San Antonio while we went out on the tours. Papá didn't put up too much fuss about it. They told him that it would be better for him to stay so that he could watch out for the house, that somebody might try to break in, and finally, they convinced him to stay behind.

He wanted to come with us because he also presented his numbers. He did monologues. He had a wig with gray hair, and he would sort of get made-up, put on stage make-up, and he would sit down in a chair on stage and start talking about Mexican history and all sorts of things. He used to speak with so much real feeling! Well, the people used to listen to him with attention and pleasure. He would talk about Cura Hidalgo and Benito Juárez—things like that from the history of Mexico. When he was talking like that, you could even hear the noise of a fly, the people were so attentive and absorbed in what he was saying.

In San Antonio, on the sixteenth of September and on the fifth of May, Papá never was missing from the *tribuna libre*. He would go and present monologues and stories from Mexican history. He wasn't a very educated man, because he ran away from home when he was thirteen years old for some reason or other, and so he grew up on his own, but he really liked to read—he was a self-educated man—and he was very knowledgeable. He knew a lot of things from what he had read in books and novels and all those kinds of things. If you were to have talked with him, you would have said, "Oh, this is a very well-educated man—¡*qué barbaridad*!—he expresses himself so well and so courteously."

So although he had no formal education, he knew lots of stories and monologues about Mexican history from his reading. On the sixteenth of September, he would stand up and declaim salutes to *la bandera,* the Mexican flag—he was very patriotic—and other things of that type. As far back as I can remember, he was like that. Even back in Monterrey when I was just a little girl, or wherever we might have been, when the patriotic festivals came around, like Cinco de Mayo, Francisco Mendoza would be up on the platform to speak in the *tribuna libre*.

I remember that they really used to organize the celebrations of the patriotic festivals in a nice way. Nowadays it's strictly commercial—it's all business. Back in the old days when the sixteenth of September came around, they would put up a platform in the park, and anybody who wanted to express their thoughts or memories or affection for the *patria* or make a *saludo* could get up and say their say. That was called the *tribuna libre*. Well, Papá was one of the best. He was so good that people used to seek him out to make patriotic speeches and presentations like that. Papá was very patriotic, and for that reason he really missed Mexico.

Andrew

When we returned to San Antonio after that first little tour through South Texas, Daddy was very proud, and he would go on by the Plaza, where we started, and he would stop there and holler to the guys who were singing, "After three weeks of going on the road, we're back. After three weeks!"

He was proud. We were rich, you know, and they weren't. We had gotten out of there, now we were bigger.

Lydia

But Papá was starting to get sicker and sicker every day, and even back in the days before Blue Bird and "Mal hombre," he would just come with us to the Plaza part of the time. And later on, especially after I started recording, he would mostly just stay at home. Back when we used to go play in the Plaza, he would come along and play his tambourine sometimes, but he used to give Manuel and María a hard time. He was always shouting at them "¡*Tóquenles bien*! Play it right!" he would yell, and he would always cuss at them—he would use a lot of bad words.

"But Pancho!" Mamá would try to whisper to him, "can't you see that we're out here in public? Everyone can hear how you're talking to the kids."

"What's it matter to me?" he would reply in a loud, gruff voice. "It's nobody's business how I talk."

Well, people lost respect for him, and finally Mamá just didn't want him to come along with us anymore. All it took was one little drink, and he would start to talk bad, to cuss and swear up a storm.

We would send him money for the expenses of the house and to spend on himself when we were on the road, so he didn't really have anything to complain about. We didn't want him coming with us on the tours, because he would start arguments—like with that priest in Beeville—and get into disputes with the management where we would be working. We couldn't really work if he was with us.

"It'll be better for you to stay at home," we told him, "and we'll send you the money you need."

Antonio Montes really helped us a lot. And a little later on, after we returned to San Antonio from that first little tour around South Texas, he really opened up some new opportunities for us. He had traveled with touring theatrical companies out West before, and he already knew all the little towns out in West Texas and New Mexico—places we had never been before: Marfa, Pecos ... towns like that. We had polished up our act during the tour of South Texas to the point that Mamá and Montes decided that we were ready to take it out on the road in the West.

Before we left San Antonio to go on the western tour in 1936, we would go to merchants, like Tomás Acuña or Señor Acosta, and ask them if they would help us to prepare the printed programs. They used to prepare their own advertisments and so they would help us lay out and print up 1000 or 1500 or 2000 flyers. They would just print "TODAY" and "SALON" with blank spaces after the words—that was all. We would fill in the date and the name of the hall later on as we got to each little town.

So we got ourselves together—with the same two cars, just like before—and we headed west out of San Antonio. We would arrive at a town, a little town, Marfa, for example, that is on the way to El Paso, and Montes would go directly to the church to speak with the priest, "Do you have a hall, ¿*un salón*?" Montes would ask the *padre*.

"Well yes, yes, we have one," the father would reply.

"Well, listen, I've got Lydia Mendoza here," Montes would tell him. My name was already well known to most everbody in the Spanish-speaking community by that time. "Lydia Mendoza and a variety show group. We put on an hour and a half of variety show. It's a family group."

"Of course," the priest would say.

And right away he would give us the hall. We would usually have to agree to give the priest ten or twenty percent of the *entrada*, the gate, for the use of the hall. That priest in Marfa, for example, wanted ten percent. Then the *convites*, the invitations, would be put out. First, we would all, all of us, sit down and write in the date and the name of the town or the church on some of the printed flyers that we brought from San Antonio. Then Mamá would dress Manuel up in a little *charro* outfit and Juanita in a "typical" Mexican dress, and Montes would drape a couple of colorful *sarapes* over the front fenders of one of the cars. When everything was ready, Mamá would seat Manuel up on one fender and Juanita on the other, and Antonio Montes would then drive slowly through the town announcing the show through a big cardboard megaphone. He would hire the little boys of the town. "You want to go see the show tonight, *muchachos*," he would ask them. "You'll get to see all kinds of stunts."

"Yes, yes," the little boys would tell him.

"All right," Montes would tell them, "you can get a free pass if you walk along beside the car and leave a flyer off at the door of each house as we go along."

"Yes, of course."

So the car would go slowly down the street with Juanita and Manuel on the fenders while Montes called out through the megaphone: "Tonight! Lydia Mendoza! Comedy! Big variety show! Don't miss it!"

All of the people would come out to see what was going on, and the little boys would hand them a flyer as Montes drove past with Manuel and

Juanita. And that night, the hall would be full of people, and we would get together ... well, fifty or sixty dollars—it was a lot of money at that time. And for us, who were just starting out and didn't know anything, it was good money. When we got to the next town, we'd do the same thing. We used to always work the night of the same day that we arrived in town. The priests would almost always allow us to sleep in the hall after our show—we always carried lots of bedding and pots and pans—and then early in the morning Mamá would prepare breakfast, and we would hit the road again for the next town.

We left San Antonio without any money, just enough to get to the first little town where we could play. Montes would get the hall for us, and right away we would have money. Then we could buy gas and go to another town, and we would go along doing the same thing. We went around like that, I believe, all of the year of 1936.

So the family road show went on like that—working the *salones* of the little churches—until we got to El Paso, Texas. When we got to El Paso in 1936, we also played in the church hall there. That's where some people from Colorado noticed us. Some people from Trinidad were around, some *aliancistas* and they saw the variety show. They told us that I had a big audience up in Trinidad, Colorado, and they invited us to go up there. They told us that we could put on our show in the Alianza Hispano-Americana halls over there in New Mexico and Colorado. So Montes arranged a contract with them, and off we went. We put on our show as we usually did—in the church *salón*—in Las Cruces, and then the Alliance presented us in Santa Fe, Ratón and, finally, in Trinidad.

After we played in Trinidad, we returned to San Antonio. That was as far as we got on that first tour out West. We worked our way back the same way we had come out, stopping here and there to put on our show and make a little money, and then pushing on to the next town. It was all churches— church halls. Since they were Mexicans, all Montes had to do was say, "It's Lydia Mendoza." And the priests would give us permission to use the hall. We would work that same night, then put gas in the cars and push on early the next morning.

We couldn't get in the theaters yet because the theater owners and managers—almost all *americanos*—wouldn't give us a chance. Although I had a big name with the Spanish-speaking people, the Americans, they, well, they didn't know who Lydia Mendoza was. They would say, "Well, she is probably a great artist, but ... " They wanted more proof of my box-office potential; they weren't willing to take any chances with something they didn't really understand. So if the theater wouldn't let us play, Montes went to the church hall or to *la sociedad*, the Mexican cultural society or wherever, but somehow he would get work for the group. After we returned to Texas from our trip to Colorado, we roamed all over the Rio Grande Valley and South Texas. Montes really helped us a lot.

In 1936, just after we returned from Colorado, my second little girl still hadn't been born yet; I was just expecting her. I went to sing in Houston one night. Francisca, my little sister, always came along because she took care of my baby girl, who is now Lydia, who was only two years old at the time. I sang at a church hall here in Houston, and after the function, some of the organizers invited us to a dinner in my honor. We came out of the church of Guadalupe here, and in front there was a restaurant, and they gave us the dinner there. When we left the restaurant it was almost two o'clock in the morning. We shouldn't have even left that night, but my husband was very stubborn, and he said, "No, we're going back to San Antonio tonight."

It was sprinkling a lot and it was foggy. The highway that existed at that time had just been recently paved: it was new. You know this fence that they have at the edge? Well, it was still not very well finished. Well, we set out for San Antonio, and my husband liked to drive like crazy, real fast. We were going very fast, and in Luling, not too far from San Antonio, the car went off the road because of how fast he was going. And when he tried to get it back on the road, since it was raining, the car skidded and flipped over. It threw us all around, and Francisca hit herself. She was the most battered one in that accident. Nothing happened to the rest of us, just to her. I was yelling at her as the car was rolling over, "My daughter! My daughter!" "Don't worry, sister," Panchita was saying, "here. ... " She grabbed the little girl, and Panchita received all of the blows so that nothing would happen to my little daughter. Panchita covered little Lydia with her body, and so she was the one that eventually was taken away.

After the wreck, we went on to San Antonio. Panchita started feeling ill, and, since we were unable to care for her properly because we were always on the road, Mamá and I took her to my sister Mónica, who was living in Monterrey. But Panchita just got worse down there, and that's where she finally died of tuberculosis in 1938. Francisca was only eighteen years old when she died.

*   *   *

When my Blue Bird recordings started coming out, they very rapidly became available in all of the border towns. I don't know why, but Blue Bird didn't pass over to Mexico—they were just sold here in the United States. However, the broadcasters from the other side of the border would come over to this side, and they would buy the records and take them back across. In Piedras Negras, Villa Acuña, Reynosa, out there by El Paso in Cuidad Juárez, all along the border, the radio stations had my recordings, and they would play my records constantly on the radio. For instance, there was a program that came on at three o'clock in the morning that was broadcast from Piedras Negras and also from Reynosa and Villa Acuña. They would put this program on at that hour of the morning on those really powerful stations—XER in Villa Acuña was licensed for 500,000 watts!—that carried Dr. Brinkley's shows during the daytime. They used to say that I was there in person in the studio during the broadcast, that I was singing live. And they would ask "Lydia Mendoza, which song are you going to sing?" and things like that.

And I was never there. They had a person, a woman, there who played the role. That program was so popular that someone took on the rôle of being me, so that they could pretend that I was actually there.

But when I started to make tours in the *salones*, and a little later in the theaters around the Valley, for example, and all that, people started to say, "But how is it going to be possible for her to appear here in person if she is over there, if we hear her every morning live from Villa Acuña?"

So we had to put a stop to that—not to the programs, just to their announcing that I was there in person. We hired a lawyer in order to prevent them from pretending that I was there in person, and they stopped doing that. They continued to play my records, but they no longer announced that I was there at the studio, and they no longer asked questions, nor had anyone pretending to be me.

Fred Martínez (Lydia's present, second husband)

I heard Lydia sing for the first time in 1937. That was after I had married my first wife. Lydia used to come on the radio from Piedras Negras at about three o'clock in the morning. My father-in-law used to like to listen to her, so he used to get up about three o'clock in the morning and make some coffee, smoke cigarettes and listen to Lydia Mendoza on the radio. That's when I first heard her. But I didn't know her. I had never met her personally. I didn't even have any of her records. When I was a young man, I didn't care much for music.

Ramiro Cortés

In Del Rio there was a big, strong, very strong radio station; they tell me that you could hear this radio station all over the world. A Dr. Brinkley was the owner of that station. He used to advertise the glands, he was transplanting glands, a lot of bull, you know. There was a program there, every day, that played Lydia's records. And then this fella, somebody, not

Brinkley, but another guy who rented some time from this radio station, he was advertising, he was selling Lydia Mendoza's photos for one dollar. "Mail me one dollar, and I'll mail you an autographed picture of Lydia Mendoza." He made, like, a million dollars. He made it rich, because the dollars would come in the mail by the thousands every day, by the thousands. But, still, Lydia didn't get nothing from that.

Lydia

My voice and my songs on those Blue Bird records were heard all along the border, and I believe that the idea of calling me "La Alondra de la Frontera," the Lark of the Border, was born from that. Because they only listened to me along the border; they didn't know of me in Mexico. They only got to know of me through those recordings with that beautiful blue bird design on the labels that all of the broadcasters from the border towns brought across and played on the radio. From Matamoros, Reynosa and Villa Acuña all the way out to California, all along the border, my recordings were there. I believe the name they gave me was born from that. Who exactly started it? I have never known.[1] Many people still call me "La Alondra de la Frontera" to this day.[2]

We did two series of recording sessions for Blue Bird in San Antonio during 1937, one in February at the Texas Hotel—our last there—and then another at the Blue Bonnet Hotel in September. Shortly after those September sessions, towards the end of 1937, we heard that they wanted us to go to California. We got back to town from one of our little road trips around Texas and found out that we had received a phone call from Los Angeles about going out to be presented—in a theater!—out there. The date they gave us was December 3, 1937, at the Mason Theater in Los Angeles. So a month or so ahead of time, we left San Antonio and headed back out west. The family road show began by following the same route out to El Paso that we had taken the year before. We stopped and worked in all of the places we had been on the first tour, all the little *salones* and society halls.

In those days our cars would often break down on the road. They weren't new cars; they were second hand, the best that we could get. We always had problems, mostly with the tires. Sometimes the tires would be very defective, and we would go along strictly on patches. In those days it wasn't like it is now: you always carried a jack, an air pump and your can of patches. If a tire went flat, the men and boys would get out, they would take it off, they would patch it and put it back on. We traveled like that.

Now, when we went to California, it was a little different. We bought a brand new car. It cost us seven hundred dollars, and it was a new car! Of course, it didn't have air conditioning, because in those years they didn't even install air conditioning in cars. And, well, it didn't have any luxuries, or extras; it was just a little car ... very simple. But it was new, and we were really happy. We bought a new Chevrolet to go to California, so at least one of our two cars was pretty reliable. As before, Montes would drive Mamá's car, and my husband would drive my new car.

We used to take advantage of the time while we were driving from one town to the next to practice and improve our material. For instance, if we had some new skits, my mother would coach the kids: Manuel, María and Juanita. Everyone would ride along studying their parts, memorizing them, so that when we would arrive at the place where we were going to work, they would already know them. In the same way, like at midday, after the meal, Mamá would have them try out the routines that they were going to present. I, also, would learn and practice new songs on the road. We all took advantage of the time that was spent driving on the road.

Just like on our previous trips, we would either sleep in the church halls or camp out by the side of the road. Mamá, María and I used to do all of our cooking. Mamá always liked to steer clear of hotels and restaurants—partly to save money—partly to avoid discrimination. There was a lot of discrimination in those days.

When we got to El Paso, we found out that Mr. Calderón, the owner of the Colón Theater, had noticed how well we had drawn at the local church hall on our first tour.[3] Antonio Montes, our master of ceremonies, knew Mr. Calderón slightly from his days with the *variedad* of Elisa García.

So Montes went to see him. "You know what? We're running into lots of difficulties," Montes told Mr. Calderón. "We have to work in *puros salones*, just strictly in church halls, because they don't want to give us a chance in the theaters out here. It's those *americanos*, they still haven't heard about Lydia Mendoza."

"Don't you worry," Mr. Calderón replied, and right then and there he told Montes that he would give us a chance to appear at the Cine Colón. We presented our *variedad* there for two or three days and really pulled in the crowds. After the last show, when we went to collect our pay, Montes and Mamá were talking with Mr. Calderón—I was there, too—and Calderón was saying, "Oh, ¡qué barbaridad! What a show! What a success!"

"Well, it's too bad, Señor Calderón," Antonio Montes told him. "Now you've seen the *variedad* that we put on, and seen how successful it is, but the bad thing is that we still can't get into the theaters in the other towns. Because the owners and managers—all those *gringos*—don't know about Lydia Mendoza and her variety show, they won't give us a chance."

"What? How could that be possible?" said Mr. Calderón, who was hooked up with a chain of theaters; they had them in Las Cruces—in all, about four or five towns. "Just you wait and see!"

And Calderón picked up the telephone and put through a call to Las Cruces. Montes had tried to get our show into the theater there in Las Cruces several times, but—just like in all the other towns—we couldn't get in.

But when Mr. Calderón made that call and spoke with the owner of the theater over there in Las Cruces, we were able to appear in that theater where we had been denied a chance before. And it was a tremendous success. The man in Las Cruces phoned the man in the next town, and so on, and we went along like that, opening up a whole chain of theaters where we were welcome to appear. Now this *americano* theater company realized they had good admissions, that they made good money with us, and so then they recommended us to the theaters in Phoenix and in Tucson.

In this way, from El Paso all the way out west to California, we now started to work for all of the theaters. When we went to a new theater, the management would ask us where we had played before, and we could say: this theater, that theater, etc. Upon seeing the other places we had worked, they would give us a chance. That's how we broke into show business and the theater circuit. That was how Antonio Montes and Señor Calderón opened up the way for us in the movie theaters.

On our trip out to California, I met Tin Tan, who later became, along with Cantinflas, one of the most famous Mexican film comedians. I met him in Ciudad Juárez. He was the announcer on a radio station there. I happened to go to that program, and I met him there. He came to see our show on the other side of the border, but we didn't work together at that time. Many years later, in Los Angeles, I did appear with Tin Tan and Marcelo one time when I was out there at the Million Dollar Theater.

In those days, the luxury price of admission at most of those theaters was twenty-five cents. But at the Mason Theater in Los Angeles, which was a real fancy place, the price that they would charge was forty cents for general admission, thirty cents for the two balconies and ten cents for children. In the little towns and at the church halls, it was more like a dime, fifteen cents or even just a nickel, (laughs) and those *salones* didn't usually have nearly as much room for people as a big movie theater. So breaking into the theaters was a tremendous step up for us.

Eventually, the theaters took charge of advertising and promoting our shows in the different towns. They would contract with us in advance for specific dates, so they could advertise ahead of time for a certain movie and the *variedad* on a specific date. The Mason Theater in Los Angeles was the first one to advertise for us in advance like that; when we arrived there in December of 1937, they had already been running ads in *La Opinión*, the

Spanish newspaper out there, for several days.

We opened there at the Mason Theater on a Friday [December 3, 1937], with two shows: one at 7:00 pm and another at 9:30 pm. We alternated on stage with a live theater group made up of local actors which presented some comedy or other.[4] The grand master of ceremonies was the well-known screen actor, Carlos "Dracula" Villarias. Mr. Frank Fouce, Sr., the owner of the theater, had been running large ads on the entertainment page of *La Opinión* for days before we arrived, as well as advertising extensively on the radio.[5] Señor Fouce even arranged for me to drop by the offices of *La Opinión* the day before we opened to give an interview that was published the morning of our opening night.

La Opinión, December 3, 1937:

Lydia Mendoza entrevistada en 'La Opinión'
Es una mujer modesta, que tiene un gran cariño por los niños

Sencilla y modesta como cumple a una artista identificada plenamente con el alma popular mexicana, Lydia Mendoza estuvo departiendo con este cronista ayer, al hacer una visita a las oficinas de LA OPINION, desde las cuales envió un saludo cariñoso a la colonia en general, por conducto de sus columnas.

La mujer que ha electrizado a las clases populares del "México de Afuera" con sus canciones, no parece haber sido afectada por su inmensa popularidad. Viste y habla con sencillez, rehuye comentar sobre su propia personalidad, y manifiesta sólo un inmenso cariño hacia la niñez mexicana. En muchas ocasiones, ha actuado y cantado gratuitamente, a beneficio de los pequeños, en diversas poblaciones de los Estados Unidos. Su mayor afán es el de ser algún día madre de muchos de ellos, **"para inculcarles**—dice—**el más grande amor por México y por la raza en general"**. Otra de sus grandes aspiraciones es la de visitar México en el futuro. Hasta hoy, su actuación solamente se ha extendido por los estados fronterizos—Texas, Arizona y hoy California—y solamente ha cantado ante los micrófonos de una estación de Radio, contra todo lo que pudiera esperarse. Esa estación es la de San Antonio, Texas.

Nativa de San Antonio, Texas

Porque Lydia es nativa de la pintoresca ciudad del Alamo, en cuyas escuelas se educó elementalmente. Miembro de una

familia de artistas por abolengo, desde muy joven sintió una
grande afición a la canción popular, y hace apenas tres años
inició su carrera, grabando para la casa Víctor la canción "Mal
hombre" que desde luego conquistó para ella una arrolladora
popularidad. De ahí en adelante, los discos se han ido multipli-
cando y ella misma no tiene idea, en la actualidad, de cuántos
habrá impresionado. Lo cierto es—y eso no lo dice ella—que
en todos los hogares del "México de Afuera", su nombre es
querido, y sus canciones son conocidas por toda la familia.

Cuando le preguntamos cuál era su canción favorita, vaciló
un poco antes de contestar. Le parecía que "posaba" si lo hacía
inmediatamente. Al fin nos manifestó que era cierto huapango
que para ella fue escrito por un compositor de Texas, y cuya
primera copla dice:

"Cancionera de los pobres
cancionera y nada más:
Mi guitarra es compañera
de mis cantos de arrabal ... "

Y es verdad. Lydia Mendoza es esencialmente la cancionera
del pueblo, en una época en que el movimiento social va en-
caminando a la dignificación de ese mismo pueblo. De ahí su
fama. De ahí que sea el ídolo de los trajabadores. Conociéndola
personalmente, se da uno cuenta de su plena identificación con
ellos. Nada hay en ella que revele la consciencia de su nom-
bradía. Nada que indique que el prestigio de que goza se le haya
"subido a la cabeza".

Y esa es, a grandes rasgos, la "Alondra de la Frontera", cuya
primera presentación en California, Estado al que ama por lo
que de él ha oído, se efectuará esta noche en el teatro "Mason"
de la Broadmay [sic], entre la calles Primera y Segunda.

El público que asista podrá mejor que ningún crítico, aqui-
latar el verdadero valor de su arte.

Lydia Mendoza interviewed by *La Opinión*
She is a modest woman who has great affection for children

Simple and modest as befits an artist completely identified
with the soul of the Mexican common people, Lydia Mendoza
was chatting with this writer yesterday. She was visiting the
offices of *La Opinión*, from which she sent out an affectionate

greeting to the entire Mexican colony by way of the columns of this paper.

The woman who has electrified the common people of "Mexico Abroad" with her songs doesn't appear to have been affected by her immense popularity. She dresses and speaks with simplicity, she shies away from talking about herself, and she is outgoing only with her tremendous affection for Mexican youngsters. On many occasions she has performed and sung without remuneration in many parts of the United States to benefit children. She is very eager to be someday the mother of many children herself, " ... in order to inculcate in them the greatest possible love for Mexico and *la raza* in general." Another of her greatest aspirations is that of visiting Mexico in the future. Up until now, she has only performed in the Border States—Texas, Arizona and, now, California—and, contrary to what one would expect, she has only sung before the microphones of a single radio station, one in San Antonio, Texas.

Native of San Antonio, Texas

Lydia is a native of the picturesque city of the Alamo, where she received an elementary education. As a member of a hereditary family of performers, from a very early age she felt a great attraction to the songs of the common people. And just three years ago she began her career, recording for the Victor company the song "Mal hombre," which immediately earned her overwhelming popularity. From then on, the records have multiplied, and she herself has no idea how many she might have recorded by now. What is certain—although it is not she who says so—is that her name is revered in all the households of "Mexico Abroad," and her songs are known by the whole family.

When we asked her what was her favorite song, she hesitated a little before answering. It seemed to her that she would be striking a false pose if she did it right away. Finally, she told us that it was a certain *huapango* that was written for her by a composer from Texas, the first stanza of which goes:

"Songstress of the poor,
a songstress, nothing more,
My guitar, companion of my songs
from the poor outskirts of town."

And this is, broadly drawn, the "Lark of the Border," whose first performance in California, a state which she loves for what she has heard about it, will be tonight at the Mason Theater on Broadmay [sic], between First and Second Streets. The public which attends, better than any critic, will be able to judge the true value of her art.

Editor

Señor Fouce had just acquired the Mason Theater, formerly an opera house, which when added to the three movie theaters he already owned, really put the icing on the cake. Unlike the other three theaters, the Mason had been designed from the beginning for the presentation of live performances and really added an element of class to his operation. Señor Fouce, whose family was from Galicia, Spain, was sincerely committed to furthering Hispanic culture in Los Angeles, and had already taken the unprecedented step of devoting all three of his big, downtown theaters to exhibiting Spanish language films on a full-time basis. The appearance of the Mendozas at the Mason, a "live" *variedad* in a first class theater, was a really important event for the Hispanic community in Los Angeles. Something of this can be seen from an article that appeared a few days following the Mendoza's opening at the Mason Theater.

La Opinión, Monday, December 6, 1937:

LYDIA MENDOZA HA TRIUNFADO: Millares de personas han ido a oírla cantar en el teatro "Mason": Un triunfo en toda línea. Un par de llenos como nunca se habían visto en el teatro "Mason" en funciones de carácter mexicano, fue lo que saludó a Lydia Mendoza, la prestigiada cancionera de San Antonio, Texas, al presentarse en Los Angeles por primera vez. El éxito fue rotundo. En las funciones del sábado, tuvo que devolverse mucha gente, por falta de localidades.

La lealtad del elemento trabajador mexicano hacia esta su artista favorita, ha sido notable. De los poblados vecinos, de los campos, de los barrios más apartados, ha estado afluyendo la gente en grandes cantidades. El tópico de sus conversaciones es ella: Lydia Mendoza y nada más. El resto del espectáculo parece importarles poco, a pesar de su excelencia. Todo se concentra en ella, en la favorita, en la cancionera que tiene ese "no sé qué" que arrastra a las multitudes.

LYDIA MENDOZA HAS TRIUMPHED: Thousands of

people have gone to hear her sing at the Mason Theater: A tri-
umph in every sense of the word. Lydia Mendoza, the famous
singer from San Antonio, Texas, appearing in Los Angeles for
the first time, was greeted by a succesion of two full houses
such as had never been seen before at the Mason Theater in
Mexican-oriented shows. The success was overwhelming. For
Saturday's shows, many people were turned away at the door
due to a lack of seats.

The loyalty of working class Mexicans to Lydia Mendoza,
their favorite artist, has been especially notable. From nearby
towns, from the fields, from the most out-of-the-way neighborhoods, great numbers of people have been pouring in to see
her. Their only topic of conversation is Lydia Mendoza: her
and nothing else. The other parts of the show, despite their ex-
cellence, seem to matter little to them. Everything is focused
on her, on the favorite star, on this singer who has an indefin-
able 'something' which exerts an irresistible attraction on the
multitudes.

Lydia

We played the Mason Theater for ten days straight: two shows a day on
week nights, three on Saturdays and four on Sundays. The comedy presented
by the troup of local actors changed several times, but our show remained
essentially the same, although of course, Mamá and Montes did their best to
vary our material. Naturally, my public wanted to hear the songs they had
heard on the Blue Bird records, so I had to repeat certain songs fairly often.
Señor Fouce continued to run large ads in *La Opinión* every day of our stay
there, and every day there was also some sort of article about our show,
usually on the same page.[6] Finally we gave a special farewell performance
and brought our first Los Angeles engagement to a close.[7]

After our success at the Mason Theater, we got a lot of jobs from other
theaters all over California. We even went up as far as San Francisco, San
Jose and all over the place.

We worked in Fresno and all the other Valley towns in California—
anywhere there was a Mexican theater. We were in California for three
months, working all over the state. December, January and February, we
spent in California. We returned to San Antonio at the end of February or
the beginning of March, and I recorded again for Blue Bird back at the Blue
Bonnet Hotel.[8]

When we got back to San Antonio, well, I guess that my name had spread from my recordings, the family show and, especially, from our highly publicized tour to California, so then the local press began to come to my house. I was even interviewed by the *San Antonio Light* and, unlike the paper in Los Angeles, I didn't have to go to them, they came to my house. One time, they even took a picture of me and my two little girls. It was probably around 1938. It was a photograph of me seated with my two little girls at my side.

San Antonio Light:[9]

> The class will now come to order: and who knows the feminine singing star who really goes to town when it comes to doing business for the Victor Recording company?
>
> Connie Boswell? Frances Langford? Maxine Sullivan?
>
> Nope, your musical I.Q. is next to nil. The gal who sells more records than any other solo artist is none other than Lidya Mendoza, Latin American citizen of San Antonio.
>
> For four years she has been strumming her guitar and singing her Spanish songs in front of Victor's recording machines and the results are heard around the world.
>
> Her records are sold all over South America, in Spain and other parts of the Spanish-speaking world. She is called "the poor people's song bird."
>
> Miss Mendoza, who lives at 306 North Leona street, doesn't know how many thousands of records have been sold since she does not receive a commission but she has put some 400 songs on the black disks.
>
> Surprisingly, she can not read a line of music. She is self-taught, never had a music lesson, and plays and sings entirely by ear. She works out her own arrangements.
>
> Besides the guitar, she plays several string instruments, including the violin. She has appeared on radio programs here.
>
> Her most popular song?—"Bad Man."

Lydia

It came out in the *San Antonio Light*, the most important Anglo paper in the city, and probably in all of South Texas.

We kept on touring as much as we could, always returning to San Antonio for the Blue Bird sessions, of course, but working the road for all it was worth. For instance, the first time we went out to California, we were on the road for four or five months. As soon as we got back to San Antonio, we rested for about two weeks, and then we got another contract to go to Colorado.

It was still the same show we had taken to California: basically just Montes and the family. I already had my two girls: Lydia and Yolanda. They were still very small at this time. I took them with me when we went on the road—I never left them. We would travel just as we had before: I brought my own car and my mother took her car. Mamá traveled with my sisters, and I traveled in my own car with my husband and my little girls. And I also took along a person that cared for them now that Panchita was no longer with us. My husband always went along with me and drove our car, although he wasn't an artist.

It was around this time that they started to call us "Gypsies." It was when we started to go out on the road and work in theaters that we started to stay occasionally in hotels, but some of them wouldn't give us rooms because they said we were "Gypsies."

My mother sort of looked like a Gypsy: she had Italian blood, a long nose, and she was very tall. She always wore mascara and her hair was done up in a very unique way. And she always wore big gold earrings and a gold medallion. So I guess she looked like a Gypsy. When we would arrive someplace, they would see us as "Gypsies" and they would say: 'Oh no, no Gypsies here!"

Manuel

We used to meet up with some discrimination on those trips: like when we used to go rent the tourist court. They must have thought we were Gypsies, so they wouldn't rent us a place. We had a hard time trying to find a place to stay. Man, we had a hard time! I used to dread going into the office of the tourist court. I was the one who was told to go in to rent the damn place, and half the time they wouldn't give us any rooms. I remember once when they wouldn't rent to us. They had a vacancy, but they told me in the office they didn't have any vacancy, and the sign right outside said "Vacancy" plain as daylight. When some Anglos drove up, well, they got a room right away.

Another thing that made me uncomfortable about renting those tourist courts was that we would hide Andrew. Yeah, so they wouldn't count him. He was little, he was a young kid, but they would count him as another person.

Lydia

Despite a few ugly things like that—the discrimination that all Mexican Americans encountered at that time—we had a happy life: quiet; very contented. Because we had lived many years with constant calamities, when we lacked for everything, including, at times, even food and all, now when we started to work in real theaters and all that—when my name started to get big—well, now we felt we had what seemed to us like the life of millionaires ... because nothing was lacking for us compared to what we had lived through before. So then, whether we were earning a little or a lot, we felt that it was all right. At least we had the wherewithal to keep on living the basic necessities of life. We at least had the means of clothing ourselves and food to eat, the ability to have a tranquil life. It was like that. We lived happily, and I was very content because I was with my mother, my brothers and sisters and all of my family: my husband and my little girls. We were going around ... enchanted with life. Traveling like that was a very beautiful thing for us; we weren't suffering like we had been before.

Still, traveling all the time had its rough side, too. In addition to the discrimination—which we pretty much avoided by cooking our own food, staying out of restaurants which often would refuse to serve us, anyway, and wherever possible, staying in people's homes or in tourist courts where we could cook for ourselves—there were the hardships and dangers of being on the road in those days. For instance, later on in that same year of 1938, we went up as far as Nebraska, playing in movie houses for the Mexicans who spread all over the Midwest for the summer's field work. We had an engagement to appear in a theater in Lyman, Nebraska, one evening, but we had spent the previous night in Scottsbluff—about forty miles of dirt road away. Well, Mamá and Montes left first with their car as usual, since they had to put on the first part of the show. As was our custom, Manuel, Juanita and María all rode with them. Juan, my little girls, the baby sitter, Montes' cousin Henry (who lived there in Nebraska, and with whom we had stayed) and I all were to follow a little later on in my car.

Well, Mamá and the rest got to the theater, and by show time we still hadn't arrived, so they went ahead and started without us. After all, my part in the show was always the last, just before the grand finale with the whole family. But as the show went on, they really started to get worried because we still hadn't arrived, and my part in the show was coming right up.

Well, we finally made it, and just in time to finish the show, but only after having been in the hospital, the Emergency Room, and all that. We had left Scottsbluff a little late, and Juan as always liked to drive real fast, anyway. Those back country Nebraska dirt roads weren't very well-made or very safe, and when Juan took a corner a little too fast, the car flipped over and slammed into some kind of pole—like a telephone pole—and even busted it in half. Everyone said that Lady Luck must really have been on my side that day, because I got out of it with only a cut on the head, and no one else was seriously injured. When I finally got to the theater, they were really going crazy: the audience, because I hadn't performed yet; my family because they didn't know what had happened to me and because they were frantically trying to find ways to keep the show going without me. Well, I rushed straight on stage, with the bandages fresh on my head, and I wrapped up the show.

The family received still another blow that year, as well. As I have already mentioned, Papá had been staying in San Antonio while we were on the road for the last couple of years. We were now able to rent a large house for the family there that we kept year round—whether we were in town or not—and that's where Papá stayed. We would always send him money for the rent and whatever else he needed. But he was very sick, and things weren't very good for him.

Andrés

We had a big house there in San Antonio, and my father was receiving money from the family out on the road every month. And then on Christmas, my mother bought him a suit; Lydia bought him a suit. They sent him the suits, they sent him the money, and then when we got back to San Antonio and we went to the house, he wasn't there! He had moved into the garage so that he could spend the money. Yeah, he was spending the money. My mother was sending him rent, but he didn't pay the rent, he was spending the money. But at least he got all the furniture and put it in the garage. That's where he was living. Boy, he was really something. He sold the suits that they sent him. He was just getting the letters at the house. He would come and pick them up so he could get the money, and that was it. He spent it all on drink, all of it. He was something, my *papá*. That was mainly what destroyed him. The Depression came in, and he didn't have a job, he couldn't support the family, and the only thing that he would find was somebody to give him something to drink. I think that that destroys a man when you cannot support your family. I think that destroys you from the inside.

Juanita

"You know I suffer a lot," Mamá used to say, "but someday God is going to give me the peace I need. Someday, I don't know when."

Mamá was still young when Papá died, but she never got married again.

Lydia

Well, I don't really remember that part, but it was certainly true that he was getting worse all the time. Nevertheless, it was still a shock to return home from a tour in 1938 and find him gone for good. The poor man had finally passed away while we were out on the road. We buried him in the

San Fernando Cemetery, in the same plot where both he and our mother are today. That was a sad time for us, but we had to keep on going, in spite of everything.

We were touring constantly, and I recorded for Blue Bird again there at the Blue Bonnet Hotel in San Antonio several times in 1938, the last time in October. The next year, 1939, we went back out to California, following the route we had taken in 1937; only this time we were able to appear in movie theaters all the way. We arrived in Los Angeles at the end of July, and I made my first appearance of that summer at the California Theater—also owned by Señor Frank Fouce.[10] He was showing a very popular Mexican film, and another, English-language movie. We would present our *variedad* between the showings of the movies. My fame and popularity had increased even more since our previous visit in 1937, due to my recordings and radio broadcasts. So, our opening was eagerly awaited by the public, and the response was tremendous. Also, unlike the first time, Señor Fouce's ads in *La Opinión* for our appearance were combined with ads for my Blue Bird recordings. There was only one price of admission—thirty cents—and we did three shows a night, alternating with the movies. The first film was shown at noon, and we did our first stage show at two o'clock, then again at six-thirty and once more at nine-thirty.[11] We only stayed at the California for a week, giving our "farewell" show on Sunday,[12] and then we returned to the road, playing all up through the Central Valley and as far north as San Francisco before returning to Los Angeles at the end of the month.[13]

We stayed out there in California for a few months, and then we returned to San Antonio. The last year we all worked together was 1941. From then on we could no longer make tours because there wasn't any gasoline. And then they called my husband and my brother Manuel to the Army. During the time of the War, we all retired, including my family as well, but in 1941 we went to the Hispano Theater in New York. Mr. Montes went on that tour, and it was the last one.

Manuel

We were working in Walsenburg, Colorado. I remember it as if it were yesterday. We were staying in this tourist court, and Montes, he was really up on the war in Europe and Asia, and all that. And he came out saying, "You know what happened? They attacked Pearl Harbor!"

Well, nobody knew where Pearl Harbor was. I, just like a lot of other people, didn't even know where Pearl Harbor was. But I was listening on the car radio to the news they'd attacked Pearl Harbor. I used to enjoy listening to our car radio. We'd come in from giving a show, and everyone would pile out of the car to go to bed as fast as they could, but I used to enjoy staying

Quarter page ad in Los Angeles' *La opinión*, August 2, 1939, for a Mexican film and a performance by Lydia Mendoza, billed as "the champion Mexican recording artist."

in the car and listening to the radio, listening to music. I used to catch that WOAI from San Antonio all the time, right there in Colorado; they played Anglo music, popular music.

From Walsenburg we went on to Denver, and we had a little time off—I don't remember why, but we had a little time off. I used to like to dance a lot, I always have liked to dance. I'm considered a pretty good dancer, you know, I mean ballroom dancing. So I went into this place they called the Eldridge Gardens, right there in Denver. And you know who was playing there? Glenn Miller. Of course, at that time, I didn't realize who Glenn Miller was, until later during the war when he got famous. I went to dance, yeah, with this Anglo lady. The young lady, she told me what a good dancer I was. She wanted to go out with me again the next day. I was really looking forward to that, but then my mother said she had to go someplace. I had to take Mamá instead. I had to go back to the tourist court without seeing that pretty young Anglo lady again because of Mamá. I lost out on that occasion. I had a lot of fun that night I went dancing with that young lady. Sometimes I used to enjoy myself.

We played in Denver, and then we went to Chicago and Detroit. In Detroit we got a contract to go work in New York at this Hispano Theater. I was doing the comedy act then. This was in 1941, just as the war was starting. We went all the way to New York from Detroit.

We had an incident while going over there. When we left Detroit to go to New York, we drove a long time. I thought we'd never get there. On the way, we stopped in some place—maybe it was Pennsylvania—but it was in a little town that had some tourist courts. There was a gas leak during the night, and if we hadn't been lucky, we'd have all died.

When we got to New York, that's when my brother-in-law (Lydia's husband Juan) and I went to see this fight between Joe Louis and Lou Nova. We only played at the Hispano Theater one week. But, you know, in that place there weren't too many Mexican people; there's only Spanish, Puerto Ricans and Cubans. So we played one week at the theater. It came out all right, there were a lot of people there. And our numbers went over, everybody seemed to enjoy themselves. That's all we did at the Hispano Theater, one week, and then we had to rent a hall by the Alianza Hispano-Americana on Twenty-First Street, where we put on another show. That's where most of the Mexican people lived in New York; there were not too many of them. So we played there, and then we came back. Man, we had some hard times after we finished from that week at the Hispano Theater.

Lydia

Antonio Montes had to retire from the group about 1941 because he began to suffer from high blood pressure and heart trouble. He went to Mexico with his family. We were then left on our own. Before the war put a stop to our touring, we all had worked together for about seven years; after those seven years I retired a little bit. My girls were of school age by then, so it was actually good for them. In any case, soon after the war started, you couldn't get gasoline or tires anymore, and we had to stop touring, whether we wanted to or not. My husband Juan went back to making shoes, and the family stayed in San Antonio.

CHAPTER 6

Juanita y María, Las Hermanas Mendoza

Lydia

When the War began, my husband had to sign up for the Draft, and he could have been called away at any time. We couldn't leave the city. There wasn't any gasoline or automobile tires; we could no longer travel. So that's when I retired ... for about, I believe, six years. From 1941 when the War began, I spent about six years without doing anything, dedicated to my daughters. I did sing occasionally around San Antonio at *fiestas*, things that would come up. For instance, every year, the thirteenth of February was the anniversary of the newspaper, *La Prensa*. During the '40s, just about every anniversary Señor Lozano, the owner, would hire my sister María and me to go and sing at the *fiesta*. María would go along so that it would be two guitars. We played at family affairs, political events or in family homes, but just in San Antonio; we didn't make any recordings, and we didn't do anything out of town.

At least my husband Juan had a job, making shoes, so he and I were able to survive during the War, but at first it was pretty rough for Mamá and my brothers and sisters. My brother Manuel had gone into the Army, and the little that he earned and what Juanita and María made, that was it for six years. Juanita and María will tell you their own story.

María

When Manuel went into the Army, Mamá was left with a problem. There was nothing for us to do. Lydia's husband, Juan, went to work with Lucchese, at the Lucchese Boot Shop; Lydia was raising her children and working for Mamá. She cleaned house and did the cooking and all that for Mamá, but she had to stop singing. I couldn't work at most jobs because I didn't speak English. Juanita spoke a little more than I could, but she couldn't find work either, and Andrés was still too young.

147

We were really up against it, and somebody had to do something, so I went and tried to work at the Sunshine Laundry, but I couldn't do it. I couldn't speak English; the work was too hard and I wasn't used to it. I tried packing pecans: the same thing. Then I went to the cigar factory, and I came out of there with a headache because I had to peel the tobacco. It was real hot and stuffy in that place. When I got home, I didn't even eat, I just went straight to bed—the smell of the cigars made me sick. They only paid me thirteen dollars a week; it was nothing. So I told Mamá I couldn't take it anymore. "Listen, my daughters," Mamá said, "we've got to do something. We've got to go looking and find something where we'll make better money."

So one day she went downtown with Juanita and me, and we passed by the Club El Bohemio on Dolorosa Street. Arturo Vásquez, the owner, already knew of us—he had heard us sing—but he didn't know us personally. On this particular day he was sitting out in front of the club talking to some people as we came walking past. Arturo knew a lot of people that worked at the courthouse, and he knew most of the constables, a lot of people like that. So he was talking to some men there, and we were conversing with each other as we walked past, and all of a sudden he called out, "Listen! Mrs. Mendoza, come over here." And then Arturo Vásquez said, "Are these your daughters?"

"Yes."

"The ones that I've heard singing?"

"Yes, yes, they are."

"Well, let's hear them in here," Arturo said.

So we went in. I didn't have my guitar with me, but Arturo Vásquez had one there. I was very shy and embarrassed, and Juanita was also very nervous, because it was the first time that we had ever gone into a place like that to sing. We were scared. We used to sing, but never in a night club. It was not exactly a club, it was a *cantina*. There were a lot of people in there, and we were afraid, but Mamá was with us.

"Let's see!" Arturo Vásquez said. "Sit down right here! Who plays the guitar?"

"My mamá and I," I answered.

Arturo sat down next to us, and he said, "Sing me a song! Let's see, sing me ... 'Petrita.' "

So we sang that for him; it was a song that we later recorded for Imperial. And we also sang another song for him, one that goes, "De fecha de mañana te doy mi despedida ... " ("As of tomorrow I take my leave of you ... ") It's called "Paloma consentida."

After we finished the songs, all the people in the club applauded. They really liked the songs, and they gave us a lot of applause.

"You know what ... ?" Arturo said to Mamá, "What are the girls doing these days?"

"Nothing," Mamá replied.

"Bring them over here! They can sing here. I'll give them ten dollars a night."

"Well, look, I don't know," Mamá said, "where are you going to put them in here?"

"*Mire Ud., Señora* Mendoza, just so that you won't have to worry, we're going to put up a little fence here, so that the people will have to pass by on the other side, and we'll put up a little stage behind it. Who plays the piano?"

"She does, María does," Mamá said, pointing at me.

"Well I'm going to put the piano up above, and the guitar will be a little bit below it, just like this. ... " And Arturo promised Mamá that he wouldn't let anybody bother us. He used to come and pick us up and then bring us home in his car, just so there wouldn't be any problems.

Arturo was a musician, he played the piano himself—he's made lots of records and everything—and when we did *boleros*, he would accompany us with the *maracas* or sometimes on the *congas*, and after we finished our set, he would play the piano.

Arturo Vásquez was very popular himself, but the War was going on at that time, and there were so many soldiers around. The soldiers were the ones who would go and hang out in the beer joints, drink beer, and Juanita and I were girls. They would go into the club on account of us.

Arturo Vásquez and his wife Josie owned El Bohemio Club. Well, they didn't own the building, they had a lease, but everything inside was theirs. They made good money with us. They sold a lot of beer when we were singing. Sometimes Josie sold so much beer that she would run out of beer to sell. After they saw how popular we were, they started to pay Mamá fifteen dollars a night. But we didn't care about the fifteen dollars; what we liked were the tips. Mamá made a lot of money there, and sometimes we, the two of us, would take a few of the *pesos*, you know, one for you María, one for you Juanita, and then one for Mamá, because Mamá didn't give us anything. She would grab the kitty, the box they put the tips in, as soon as we stopped singing and started to get off stage.

"Give me the box! I'll take it. I'll take care of it."

So when we could, each of us would take a little bit for ourselves. When the soldiers would give me a quarter or fifty cents or a dollar, Mamá would say, "*¿Qué te dio?* What did he give you? Let me see your hand!"

And oooh, so much money, so many soldiers! There was a lot of money. ... So of course, the other musicians all got jealous.

Juanita

A lot of soldiers used to come into the Club Bohemio. After we started singing, there were even more. So then a lot of musicians started going to Arturo and telling him that they would work for nothing, just for the tips. They saw that there were a lot of people coming in because we were singing there.

So then Arturo Vásquez told us, "Let's forget it for a little while. I'm going to put in this combo, and you're not going to work for a while. I'll call you back."

But Johnny García was just around the corner at the Pullman Bar. It was just a couple of blocks away. The Pullman Bar was a *cantina*, a lot like the Club Bohemio. Johnny García heard that we weren't working with Arturo, so he came to talk to us at our house. He said that if we wanted to work for him we could start right away. So we worked with Johnny García for a long time. The soldiers really loved us at the Pullman Bar. It was during the War, remember, and on Friday night you would see all those boys lined up out in the street to come in and hear us sing.

Andrew

Johnny García would charge fifty cents at the door. He would charge you fifty cents just to go in there and drink beer. He would have a couple of guys at the door, and sometimes they wouldn't let you go in. Because even though he was charging fifty cents, the place would still be full. There would be so many people trying to get in, there wouldn't be any more room inside. People would have to wait their turn outside.

The show was just the two girls singing. Johnny put a little fence around the stage so that nobody could come close to them or bother them. Then he put a piano up on that little stage for María.

Juanita

María would play the piano, and when I sang *boleros*, I would play the *maracas*. Momma played the guitar. All the soldiers started coming over there to see us at Johnny García's; they forgot all about Arturo Vásquez. Then Arturo came back, he wanted us back, but it was too late.

We left Arturo Vásquez's club because the combos came over and told him that they would play for nothing. Arturo had to pay María and me, and those combos would play for free, just for the tips. Arturo thought he already had all the customers, but he made a mistake, because when they

Las Hermanas Mendoza: Juanita and María. Courtesy of Arhoolie/Ideal Records.

all heard we were at the Pullman ... Arturo was left alone, all by himself. All the soldiers came over to the Pullman to see us. So Arturo would come over and try to talk us into going back to his place, but we didn't go back, we stayed with Johnny.

Since we weren't married, all of the soldiers would ask us for a date. Of course we never went anywhere. We couldn't go out with anyone because Johnny brought us to work and took us home. I was young— about eighteen years old—and not married, and all of the boys ... they were crazy. María and I still have some of the letters they used to send us.

Once there was a troop, you know, a bunch of soldiers, and they had to go overseas. They came up and told Momma, "We love you like our own mother, please give us your blessing." And then they said, "Put out your kitty"—the little kitty we had for the tips—"because the whole troop wants to give you their money."

And they put in all the money they had on them, because they were leaving to go overseas the next day. We bought a house with the money we collected in the kitty, which was a little cigar box with an opening in the top where the people could put in a nickel or a quarter or whatever when they wanted us to play a particular song.

María

That's right, Mamá bought us a house. Mamá would always put that tip money away in jars. Even though she didn't let us have much of the money we were earning day-to-day, she did buy us a little house. My brother has a friend they used to call El Chiflán, and he was going to be transfered someplace, so we bought it from him. It was a three-room house, a real old one, right there on Hess Street; it's still there. That was the first house that we owned, and we were happy. It was a tiny, little bitty one, but we were very happy to have it. El Chiflán gave it to Mamá for two thousand dollars. Later on, when she had finished paying for it, we told Mamá, "Mamá, we have a lot of money, and we're getting real famous. Mamá, we need a bigger house."

So then we bought a beautiful house on Lubbock Street. It was a two-story house, beautiful. And we bought some furnishings, nice furniture, not brand new, old, you know, second hand, because Mamá never liked to spend too much. She was the manager, she knew what she was doing.

Juanita

Having our own house really made a big difference. The problems we used to have before we finally got our house! For instance, back when we were still working for Arturo Vásquez, we were living in a place that was upstairs from a *cantina*, a bar, on Arbor Place. They used to call this *cantina* downstairs the Río Grande Bar. It was owned by this certain lady. Mamá had a little icebox, the kind you have to put ice inside and a little bucket under for the water to drip into as the ice melts. One day we went to town, and Mamá forgot to empty the bucket before we left. When we got back from town, we had to pass by the door of the *cantina* to get to the stairs that went up to our place. The door of the bar was open, and that lady came over when she saw us. She was a little bit drunk, and she was real mad because the water from our icebox had been dripping down into her *cantina*. That woman said some bad things to Mamá; she really insulted our mother. "You shouldn't say things like that," Mamá told her.

"You should do honest work," that woman replied. "You shouldn't sell your daughters to the men at El Bohemio!"

Mamá went to Arturo Vásquez: 'You know, Arturo," she told him, "I don't believe we're going to stay. I don't think we can keep on singing here because this so and so … "

"What's happening here?" Arturo asked.

"Well they're telling me I sell my daughters here!"

Our brother, Manuel, wasn't there with us; he was away in the Army, so we didn't have anyone else to look out for us. "You know what?" Arturo said, "we're going to have to go to court. We're going to go to a doctor and get him to prove it's not true. We're going to take that lady to court."

It was really tough, because we took her to court, and she lost. They found out it wasn't true. My sister and I were young, and we weren't married, but they found out it wasn't true. That woman tried to defend herself, but she didn't have a case. The judge fined her. I think she had to pay five hundred dollars, but we didn't get anything—the lawyers got it all. Her lawyer was Jimmy Tafoya, and Arturo had Albert Peña. If anyone besides the lawyers got any money, it was probably Arturo. But the court told that lady not to say anything to us or talk about us anymore.

It was tough for us, because all the people thought bad about my sister María and me. They used to call Mamá those names they call people that sell girls and all that. They used to say she was making business with her daughters. But my mother wasn't like that!

María

People used to say a lot of ugly things. They used to say we were just whores, *puras putas*, and that Mamá would charge money for us—things like that.

Juanita

It's pretty hard because everybody talks about you. If you're a woman alone, they talk about you.

María and I must have worked for Arturo Vásquez for about two years, and we were with Johnny García even longer. But it all came to an end because of Johnny's wife. Johnny García, the owner of the Pullman Bar, fell in love with me. He was older than I was. I didn't know anything about it, but he told my sister. Then Johnny started giving me presents, and he would tell my sister, "This is from a soldier," this and that ... , but it was really from him. And he cried and everything, but I didn't know about it. Johnny García was in love with me, and then his wife found out. They let us go; it was just because of jealousy.

Later on, Johnny straightened it all out, and he brought his wife over to apologize because there was really nothing ... nothing wrong going on. But she divorced him, anyway. I would never have married him. Maybe I should have married him—he liked me the way I am—but he was much older than me. He was about thirty-six or thirty-seven, and I was just about eighteen.

*   *   *

Manuel

About six or seven months, maybe a year, after the War started, they began rationing gas, and you couldn't buy tires anymore. That was when we said we weren't going to travel anymore, so I decided to go out and look for a job by myself. I started working at a place that was called Dairyland at the time; it's Foremost Dairies now. I went over there with a friend of mine, a guy named Joe Panelli who was already working there. We were loading those great big fifty-gallon cans of milk onto trucks. I started out pretty strong because I thought I could take it. I thought I was real strong; I must have loaded about a hundred of those cans. I worked all day. The next day, I didn't go to work because I couldn't even get out of bed. Oh, my arms, my back, my legs—everything! I wasn't used to hard labor. I didn't even go collect what I had coming for the one day's work. "Aren't you going to work?" Mamá asked me.

"Hell no, I'm not going to work that damn job."

I didn't go to work that day, but as soon as I could move again, I decided to go look for another job. So then, I went to work for the Iron Works, right here on Colorado Street, hitting rivets. Man, that was hard work! It was those hot rivets; it was hitting rivets and then throwing them to another guy so he could rivet them into something that they were building. That's what a guy with no education, no profession, has to do; that's the kind of jobs he can get.

I was working there at the Iron Works when they drafted me. When I found out I had been drafted, I went and told my mother, and we had a party before I left. I was gone for thirty-six, thirty-seven months, and I spent twenty-four of those months overseas.

When I went into the Army, I had never been out of my house. I mean, I had never been away from my family at all before I went in the Service. I felt lost the first time I had to sleep here at Fort Sam [Houston].

The Army was segregated at the time; there were no Negroes, just Whites—just *gringos* and Mexicans. I was very embarrassed a lot of times in the Army by Anglos. Like when I was in Basic Training, me and this other guy—he was from Arizona, and his name was Munguía—we had gotten a haircut here at Fort Sam, but when we got over there to Alabama, this sergeant says, "Look, if you guys don't get a hair cut, I'm not going to give you a pass to go into Anniston, Alabama."

He wasn't going to let us go out on a pass from Basic Training. So me and this guy Munguía got so mad, we went and took all of the hair off of our heads: bald-headed. We came to the sergeant, and we said, "How do you like it?"

Oh, that son of a gun started laughing at us, "You know what? You guys think you're smart? Well, you're not going anywhere until you grow some damn hair."

And I'm telling you, he didn't let us out of that damn camp because we didn't have any hair. Well, our hair started growing up a little bit every day. We were supposed to stay in Basic at least thirteen weeks, but we only stayed ten weeks. So by the fifth week, our hair grows up a little, so we finally went on a pass.

When I was in Basic Training, we used to get into a lot of fights with some of the *gringos*, especially those guys from Texas. One time, some of those Texas *anglos* even beat up my friend Munguía over there in a beer garden. A lot of the soldiers used to get drunk at the beer garden and get into fights.

I remember one guy especially, his name was Nunn. I remember him completely. He was mean as hell to us. He used to call us, "Mexicans! Hey, Mexican!" It used to make me feel inferior, you know. He was from College Station, where Texas A&M is. He was an ex-ROTC man; he knew a lot about the Army. I think he had been going to college when he was drafted. He was drafted just the same as I was, and we were in Basic Training together, but he used to look at us with contempt, you know, like we were the lowest thing there is to walk around. He used to enjoy calling us "Mexicans, Mexicans!" Well, what the hell, we were soldiers. We didn't have to be called "Mexicans."

But I got over that feeling, though, because there were some nice *anglos*, too. My sergeant right there at Fort McClellan, Alabama, where I did my training, liked music. He used to have me and another guy from San Antonio sing in his quarters. The other guy's name was Henry Rodríguez; he used to play the guitar. We would get together right there in the barracks and sing. When this sergeant, our platoon sergeant, heard us, he started inviting us over to his barracks so we could sing there. He used to get a bunch of girls and lots of other guys and make us sing there for him until all hours of the night after we had finished the day's training.

And then we went to town, they had a USO over in Anniston, and we sang there, too—Hank Rodríguez and I. I don't know what happened to him, because after we finished Basic Training, we were sent to Pennsylvania.

When we got there, Hank told me, "Hey, you know what? Let's get out of the Service."

"What do you mean, get out?"

"Go to town with me, and I'll tell you what to do. Then, when they start shipping the rest of the guys out, we won't be with them!"

I didn't want to go with him, I wanted to stay with the guys, the rest of the guys that had taken training with me. So Hank went to town, and the next morning, I'll be damned if they didn't take him out of sight and discharge him. I don't know what he did, but he just got out. I stayed with my unit—might as well go wherever they send me.

From Pennsylvania we went all the way across to Seattle, Washington. That was the POE, the Port of Embarcation. From there they sent us to the Aleutian Islands to take an island that was supposed to have Japanese on it, but when we landed, there were no Japanese there. That's Kiska Island—I don't know whether you heard about it, they even bombarded it. But the Japs had left overnight. They left a whole bunch of us guys there to mop the place up, to look for Japs, but we couldn't find any. So a bunch of us, a whole platoon of us stayed there. All we could find were some Japanese dogs. After a while, they sent some more troops in there and they moved us to another island: Adak Island.

On the way to Kiska Island I had a little guitar, and I was playing it on the ship. These Navy officers were with a bunch of nurses in one of the compartments, so they asked me to come over and play for them. They were dancing while I was playing "La Cucaracha," songs like that. One of those officers I met that day got killed over there in the Aleutian Islands. He used to fly a PBY.

Once when I came home on furlough, my sisters were singing at Arturo's El Bohemio. My mother was there with Juanita and María; they were singing there. I was in uniform, I went over to the club, and these guys started ... you know, they were giving Janie some drinks, so I got into an argument with them. And I saw one of them pull a damn razor blade, one of those barber's razors. He got it out of his pocket, and I said: "Uh oh." So I got out of that damn place right quick. There were about five or six guys there, and I was by myself, so what chance did I have? I just told my mother,"I'd rather get out of here. I don't want to mess around with these damn guys and their razors."

It was hard for women to be singers in there. All these guys would come and flirt with them. That was it. And there were some real fresh guys that would come into that club.

We were finally discharged from Seattle. But the company commander made a mistake. Instead of sending me to Fort Sam Houston in San Antonio, where I was supposed to go, they sent me to Fort Bliss in El Paso. I had some money saved, I had it in money orders, but I exchanged everything to cash. I put it in my wallet, and I went to bars. Well, it only lasted me about an hour. Somebody put a mickey on me, and they took the damn money. I didn't have that much—about four hundred and fifty dollars. But you know, in those times, that was money. It's a good thing that I had my ticket for the train to come home, right here in my jacket. So I traveled all the way from El Paso to San Antonio without even a thin dime. When I got home, the girls were already singing at the Pullman Bar.

My mother was very religious; she used to believe in this Señora de los Milagros. I used to go with Mamá to pray to her, and when I came back from the Service, we went to San Juan de los Lagos, a big shrine over in Mexico. Mamá had promised the Virgin to take me there if I came back alive from the Army. I came out of the Service in 1945.

Lydia

In 1947, after the war had been over for a while, Mamá and I went downtown one day, and we ran into an impresario from California, Ramiro Cortés, who would take on artists. In those years, they used to call him *Doctor Nopal*, "Dr. Prickly Pear." He would get people, *artistas*, from Mexico and all over together and take them on really big, enormous tours. He knew me from before the war, but I had never worked for him. When he saw us, it made him very happy, and no sooner did he run into me than he said, "Hi, Lydia! It's been years since I've seen you, where have you been hiding? What are you doing these days, Lydia?"

"Well, nothing, hanging around here," I replied. "Circumstances have just obliged me to stay here; I haven't been able to leave town."

"¡*Ay, qué barbaridad*! ¡Lydia Mendoza!" Doctor Nopal replied. "Wouldn't you like to make a little tour out to California?"

"Oh forget it," I said to him. "It's been six years now since I've done anything, and the people probably don't even remember me anymore."

By this time I had forgotten all about the theater and all that.

"I'll revive you Lydia. They'll go for it!" he told Mamá and me with enthusiasm. And he looked at Mamá as if to ask for her response.

"Well, I don't know. Let's see what Lydia says," Mamá replied.

"Look," Ramiro told me, "if you feel like going, I'll take you out to California right now."

Well, I had been out in California in 1937, which was the first time that I came out to the West Coast, and again in 1939, which had been a great success. But it was now in 1947 that Dr. Nopal was asking me if I wanted to go back out there.

"*Pues, vamos a ver* ... let's wait and see ... ," I told him. "Well, I'm going to California real soon," Ramiro Cortés told me, "and I'm going to see what I can do."

"Well, all right," Mamá told him, "let us know if you can come up with something."

"All right," he said, "I'll let you know."

About four days later, Dr. Nopal came over to the house. "Well, everything's ready," he said, "do you feel like going?"

"It's all right," I told him.

"You're going to start in El Paso, and then you're going to appear in Las Cruces and all of those other places."

Well, he was as good as his word. He got me a contract to begin with at the Colón Theater in El Paso. And then Las Cruces, another one in Phoenix and from there to California. He set us up a very nice tour that eventually brought us all the way out to California. He booked us into the Mason Theater in Los Angeles where we opened on August 4, 1947. And we worked out there real hard for about three months.

"Doctor Nopal"—that's what we called him. He is a *compadre* of mine. My husband and I baptized one of his little girls. He lives in Hollywood nowadays.

When Dr. Nopal told us about this tour, we started to get our costumes and clothing together—after all, we had forgotten about all that. So we went out to Los Angeles and we worked the Teatro Mason—the whole group, the whole family, just like before the War.

Ramiro Cortés

I first heard Lydia and the Mendoza family group back in about 1933 or '34 when they were singing in the Plaza del Zacate in San Antonio. She was playing the violin back then—very sweet music, very beautiful music—all types of waltzes, you know, fox trots. ... And then, Lydia would sing solo, that's when the people got around her. When she started singing, why, everybody would quit all the tables and come over to where Lydia was, because she sang so beautifully. That's where she was picked up by this Blue Bird Company to make records and by this Cortez boy, who worked with the radio station. At that time, I just followed her, but I didn't do any business with her, I didn't talk to her, or nothing. I just admired her.

But years later, it was a little after the War, I ran into her in San Antonio and invited her to go out on one of the big tours I was arranging in those days. I told her that I was going to do my best for her, because, about that time, everybody had almost forgotten about her. Because, you see, the public thought that Lydia was the one that got killed in the car wreck that caused the death of her sister Panchita. Everybody thought that Lydia was the one who died. They didn't think that it was the sister, Panchita, because Lydia had disappeared and hadn't been heard from for so many years. Lydia disappeared from the stages, from the public, so everybody thought that Lydia was the one who died in this accident. So when I started to try to book her in theaters, nobody wanted to believe me. They'd say, "Oh, no, what's the matter with you, you're trying to fool everybody now, you're getting out the sister," thinking that Lydia is the one that had the name, "so we don't want you."

One time we were playing—this is funny, this is real funny—in a little town called Sonora in Arizona, where the copper mines are; there are a lot of people there. While Lydia was singing on the stage, I was out in the lobby getting ready to count the money and check up, because we had to leave for another town the next day. I was talking to the manager there, waiting for the show to be over, when here comes an old woman and hit me with an umbrella on my head. And it broke my head; blood came out and everything. I was taken to the hospital, and there were three stitches in there, because she really hit me with this umbrella, with the handle of the umbrella. "What the hell's the matter with you?" I asked her.

"You should be ashamed!" she says—she was cursing me. She says, "bringing this woman to sing here ... using the name of people who are already dead! Lydia Mendoza is in Heaven now! And you bring somebody else here, thinking you could get away with it ... telling us that it was her. You should be ashamed!"

And she kept on hitting me with this umbrella. She was still thinking it was not Lydia, see. I couldn't convince her; they took me away in an ambulance. I was all bloody, here, all over my suit and everything.

"You should be ashamed!" that old woman kept on yelling, "Bringing somebody else here. That's her sister."

And that's on account of those five years she hid from people. Things like that happened many times. I had big trouble, lots of effort, to put her in theaters again. But, still, I got her in the theaters, and the people responded and they saw it was really her when they heard her sing. She has such a beautiful voice.

Anyway, on that first tour in 1947, we played El Paso, Texas, at the Colón Theater, one whole week, and then, we came over to the Mason Theater in Los Angeles. At that time, we weren't playing the Million Dollar yet, which was still an American theater for American shows. The Mason Theater belonged to Mr. Frank Fouce, who also owned the California and several other theaters. The Mason had two thousand five hundred seats. That's where she played the first time. I'm telling you, that was a historic night, the night she opened there. There were so many people in the streets that the firemen had to come over, and the police, and they had to send some soldiers, because there were so many people and they all wanted to get in to see Lydia. They couldn't open the theater because they were afraid that the people would burn the place down, throw down the doors and everything. Even Frank Fouce, the owner of the theater, didn't think that she would be so incredibly popular, that she would bring so many people. Even from Tijuana, they came over to see her, from San Diego, from San Francisco and everywhere, and they all tried to get in at the same time. It was bad. The firemen with the big trucks were there. I mean to tell you, it was something big, and nobody, nobody ever had, not even the big stars from Mexico ever had attracted such a crowd; not even Cantinflas or ... nobody. She was really something; that show was really something.

Lydia

So that's how we went back on the road: the whole family, all of the group. Manuel went with us. He was back from the Army, and he hadn't gotten married yet. And my children also went. I never left them; I would take them along. So it was my mother, María, Juanita, Manuel, Andrés and me. Andrés was the one who sang parodies. My mother and I were in charge of everything, and we tried to get each of them into doing something in the show. Of course, the show started with the whole *variedad* together, with everyone. The master of ceremonies would tell a few jokes and introduce the first act. Then Manuel and Juanita would do comic sketches (skits) and put on Mexican dances. They would dance and sing. And María was the pianist, she accompanied the *couplets*, the songs that Juanita sang solo. Then the *dueto* would come on—Las Hermanas Mendoza—Juanita and María. Then my number would come up, and I would sing. Then another number would go out, and then we would go on with the *dueto*. I would accompany Juanita and María, but I wouldn't sing, just the two of them. And then at the end when we finished, all of us would go on at once together. We would put on a number with a quartet. We had it arranged so that it was all variety. Our show lasted for two hours.

We played strictly in theaters; theaters and movie houses, just us by ourselves. The variety show would come on after the movie. In some of the theaters we played, we would be scheduled to put on a variety show at two o'clock in the afternoon ... mainly on Saturdays and Sundays. There in Phoenix, for instance, we would put on three variety shows at the old Aztec Theater, which I believe is no longer there. We began the first show there at two o'clock in the afternoon. Then we would do another one around six o'clock, and the last one around nine. The number of performances depended on the place. It would be the Colón Theater in El Paso, and then the Azteca in Phoenix, and then the California Theater in Los Angeles. We worked for seven years—from 1947 to 1954—seven years.

I never took part in the comedy routines; my part was to sing and to accompany the group. I helped Juanita and María out on the guitar. María was also an accompanist; she didn't take part in the skits either. But Juanita, Manuel, Andrés, my mother—the four of them took charge of doing the comedy.

For example, sometimes they would do a skit where there was a couple who owned a little store, and the wife had a little brother. Manuel would be the husband, and Juanita was the wife, and Andrés was the wife's little brother who came to stay with them and didn't want to work.

Juanita

We used to call that sketch "La tienda," "The Store." It was a real good one. Andrew would play my brother, and I was married. I was running this little store, and my brother had come to visit and never left. My husband and my mother-in-law were tired of him hanging around; they wanted to send him away. They said they couldn't stand him anymore. So I tried to get him to help with the store, so they wouldn't mind him staying. This is how the part Andrew and I did used to go:

La tienda[1]

JUANITA: Tú sabes muy bien que mi esposo y mi suegra

ya no quieren que estés aquí. Ya no lo quieren. ¿Qué quieres que haga yo?

ANDREW: Que se vayan ellos.

JUANITA: ¿Cómo que se vayan? No, es ... es que tú no eres pa' trabajar.

ANDREW: Ahora, ahora, yo no vine porque yo quise. Yo vine porque Uds. me invitaron a pasar unas vacaciones.

JUANITA: Sí, sí, unas vacaciones.

ANDREW: Pues sí.

JUANITA: ¡Y tienes dos años!

ANDREW: Sí, hermanita ...

JUANITA: Esas no son vacaciones. Ya tienes dos años. ¿Y te vas a buscar trabajo?

ANDREW: No hay, hombre.

JUANITA: No hay trabajo ... bueno, mira, ¿por qué no hacemos una cosa?

ANDREW: ¿Qué?

JUANITA: Mira. Tú sabes bien, tú sabes muy bien, Chapulín, que yo te quiero mucho. Te quiero mucho porque eres el más chico de la familia.

ANDREW: Pues soy el bebito de la familia, el coyotito.

JUANITA: Tú eras el bebito, sí, pero ya no eres bebito.

ANDREW: Soy el más chiquitito, el coyotito.

JUANITA: El coyotote, porque ya estás muy grande.

ANDREW: Bueno, pues, estoy de cuerpo, nomás, pero yo siempre soy ...

JUANITA: No, no, ya estás grande. Bueno, mira ...

ANDREW: Mi mente todavía está igual.

JUANITA: Mira, mira, te voy a decir una cosa. Para que mi suegra, y mi marido ...

ANDREW: ¿Tú sabes? ¿Sabes qué, hija? ¿Sabes que tu suegra es una metiche, que es más metiche que la fregada, que yo ... ?

JUANITA: ¡Pero es mi suegra!

ANDREW: Todo, todo le cae mal. Si como, ¿por qué como? "¡No! ¡Viejo! ¡Que come! ¡Hombre! ¡Que traga mucho!" ¿Quién sabe qué ... ? ¿Y si no como? No, pues: "No le gusta la comida. Pues siquiera ha comido en un restaurante ... " No, esa vieja, no entiendes, hombre, es muy ...

JUANITA: Ahora ¡ahora voy a hablar yo! O te vas, obra, te voy a decir una cosa. Tú sabes bien que tenemos una tienda, ¿verdad?

ANDREW: ¿Hmmm?

JUANITA: Sabes que tenemos una tienda, ¿verdad?

ANDREW: Oh, sí, yo sé que tenemos una tienda.

JUANITA: No, no, no, no, no. Tenemos una tienda.

ANDREW: Pues sí, tenemos una tienda.

JUANITA: No, tú no tienes nada.

ANDREW: ¿Cómo, no tengo nada?

JUANITA: No. Yo y mi esposo ...

ANDREW: ¿Entonces, entonces, dónde quedó lo que dijimos cuando estábamos chiquillos?

JUANITA: ¿Cuándo ... ? ¿Cuál? ¿Qué?

ANDREW: Cuando estábamos chiquillos yo y tú.

JUANITA: ¿Qué dijimos?

ANDREW: Que prometimos ... , dijimos: ... , "Mira, hermano", tú me dijiste, "mira, manito, cuando yo crezca, todo lo que ... , todo lo mío es tuyo". ¡Acuérdate! Tú dijiste ...

JUANITA: ¿Sí ... ?

ANDREW: Yo te dije, "Hermana, si todo el tuyo va a ser mío, todo el mío va a ser mío".

JUANITA: Bueno, ya no sabes nada. Yo digo que te voy a decir una cosa ...

ANDREW: Tenemos la tienda.

JUANITA: Bueno, está bueno ¡pero tenemos la tienda! Oye, para que ya mi suegra no diga nada, y no te corra ... , porque yo no quiero que te vayas, no quiero que te vayas ... Pero vas a tener que ir ... Pero, mira, ¿por qué no hacemos una cosa? ¿Por qué no trabajas tú en la tienda?

ANDREW: ¿Por qué?

JUANITA: ¿Trabajar?

ANDREW: ¿Que yo trabaje en la tienda ... ?

JUANITA: Sí, trabajar ...

ANDREW: ¿Y este dependiente que tienen allí?

JUANITA: Se fue.

ANDREW: También no le pagan, hombre ...

JUANITA: ¡No te importa! A ti no te importa si le pagamos ...

ANDREW: Quiere que la gente trabaje sin pagar ...

JUANITA: Oye, Chapulín, oye Chapulín, a ti no te importa si le pagan, o no le pagan. Yo te estoy hablando de esto, ahora te estoy hablando yo. Tú podrías trabajar. ¿Quieres? Tienes que trabajar en la tienda.

ANDREW: Pues, yo nunca he trabajado en una tienda, hermana.

JUANITA: Pues, tienes que agarrar a una cosa u otra. O te trabajas o te vas.

ANDREW: Yo trabajo si me enseñas.

JUANITA: O trabajas o te vas.

ANDREW: Pues, si me enseñas ...

JUANITA: Yo te enseño, es muy fácil.

ANDREW: Oh, bueno, pues, tú me enseñas, yo aprendo ...

JUANITA: Bueno, mira. No hay problema, es muy fácil, y yo te enseño.

ANDREW: *Okay*, ¿a ver qué vamos a hacer?

JUANITA: Vamos a suponer ...

ANDREW: ¿Qué vamos a poner?

JUANITA: ¡No vamos a poner nada! ¡Suponer!

ANDREW: Suponer, ah, suponer.

JUANITA: Vamos a creer como éste es la tienda.

ANDREW: (Childish voice.) Vamos a jugar a la tiendita.

JUANITA: (Speaking with clenched jaw.) No vamos a ... ¡Ay! ¡No, hombre! Vamos a estar en la tienda. Éste es la tienda.

ANDREW: Ya estamos en la tienda.

JUANITA: Ya estamos en la tienda. Y esto que ves aquí tú es el mostrador. Y ésta es la puerta. Por acá se abre la puerta, por acá se abre, y se levanta así. Te vas pa' allá, vienes pa' acá, el mostrador está aquí ... ¿Qué miras?

ANDREW: Te estás volviendo loca.

JUANITA: No estoy ... no estoy loca. Te estoy explicando para que batalles ...

ANDREW: Pues aquí no hay nada. Mejor ponga mostrador. Mira, hay nada. No hay nada aquí, hombre.

JUANITA: De imaginario. Imaginación, no más de mentiritas.

ANDREW: Oh, de mentiritas, para que yo aprenda, en una palabra, ah ...

JUANITA: ¡Ándale! Chavo, eres buen chico.

ANDREW: Ah, bueno, explícate. No, porque ... aquí hay mostrador, y que aquí la puerta, y aquí está quién sabe qué ...

JUANITA: Pues ... pero es no más de mentiritas. Así es que, bueno, así es que yo voy a ser la dependienta, y tú vas a venir a comprarme ...

ANDREW: Tú eres la dependienta, y yo ...?

JUANITA: Y tú vienes a comprarme ...

ANDREW: ¿Voy a comprarte?

JUANITA: Andale, sí.

ANDREW: Bien. Muy bien. (Pausa.) Ya vine.

JUANITA: Buenas tardes.

ANDREW: Buenas tardes.

JUANITA: ¿En qué puedo servirle?

ANDREW: Pues oiga, hombre, en verdad, Ud. no me sirve a mí pa' nada.

JUANITA: Oye. Oye, espérate tantito. Oye, ¿pues qué modo es ése de tratar a la gente? ¿Dónde has visto que vas a una tiendita, y le dices que, "Para mí no me sirve para nada"?

ANDREW: ¿Pues qué pregunta me estás diciendo? Pues: "¿Pa' qué le puedo servir?" Pues, pa' nada.

JUANITA: Pero tienes que ... que tratar a la gente con cortesía, con una sonrisa, y bien, ¡hombre! ¿Cómo que vienes a comprar algo, y "A mí no me sirves para nada"?

ANDREW: Pero yo no vengo a comprar, yo no vengo a comprarte nada.

JUANITA: No le hace, ¡porque tienes que tratarlos bien! ¡*Geez*!

ANDREW: Bueno, déjame hacer el dependiente, y tú vienes a comprarme algo.

JUANITA: No sabes comprar ¿y vas a saber vender?

ANDREW: Bueno, vamos a ver si ... si tú compras mejor, y yo soy el dependiente ...

JUANITA: Ora, otra cosa.

ANDREW: ¿Ehhh?

JUANITA: Cuando llegue alguien a comprar algo ...

ANDREW: Ummmm hmmmm ...

JUANITA: ... Si no lo tenemos, lo que ... siempre lo hacen en todas las tiendas, lo que quiera la gente, véndeles algo parecido para que no se vayan. ¿Ves? Para que no se vayan sin comprar nada.

ANDREW: No, si ellos llegan aquí, yo los amarro hasta que compren algo ...

JUANITA: Tú no vas a amarrar a nadie, tú vas a venderles bien. Así es que, ahorita, entonces, ahorita vengo, ya me voy.

ANDREW: Bueno. Cierra la puerta.

JUANITA: ¡Pues! ¿qué es eso?

ANDREW: Pues, cierra la puerta.

JUANITA: ¿Cuál puerta? (Molesta.)

ANDREW: Pues la que pusiste ahí.

JUANITA: (Angry sigh. Clears throat, loud.) ¡Ay! ¡Chi ... ! ¡Ay!

ANDREW: ¿Qué quiere? (Pausa.) Hábleme pronto porque yo estoy ocupado.

JUANITA: Oye. ¿Qué es eso?

ANDREW: Yo tengo cosas que hacer.

JUANITA: ¡Oye! ¡Ay! ¿Así vas a correr a la gente? ¡Ríete! Una sonrisita muy ... tú sabes, alegre. Así. ¡Ríete! Con esa cara, ¿me entiendes?

ANDREW: Pues yo te boto ...

JUANITA: Pues, ¡ríete! Ya me voy. Voy a venir otra vez, hombre. ¡Ah Hmmm!, ¡Ah Hhhggmmmm! ¡HHHHGGGGM-MMMM!

ANDREW: Hhgmmm, hump, hhggmmm.

JUANITA: Ya estoy aquí, ¡hombre!

ANDREW: ¿Ya llegó?

JUANITA: Dime que "¿Qué quiere?"

ANDREW: ¿Qué quiero?

JUANITA: (Angry voice.) ¡Cómo que "¿Qué quiero?"!

ANDREW: Pues sí, pues ¿qué quiere?

JUANITA: Oh. Pues ... ¿tendría Ud ... ? ¿tendría Ud ... ? Favor de darme ... ¿tiene ... eh ... clavos para comer?

ANDREW: ¿Clavos ... pa' comer?

JUANITA: Clavos para comer. Sí. Clavos para comer.

ANDREW: Un momentito, voy a ver. (Pausa.) ¿Sabes qué? Me vas a dispensar ...

JUANITA: No tiene, bueno.

ANDREW: ... Pero se nos acabaron.

JUANITA: Se acabaron ...

ANDREW: Se los acaban de vender. ¿No quieres algo parecido?

JUANITA: Ándale, ándale, ya estás aprendiendo. ¡Qué bueno!

ANDREW: (Bright, happy voice.) Ya, sí tenemos clavos pa' clavar.

JUANITA: ¿Para clavar?

ANDREW: Sí.

JUANITA: Mira, mira, te voy a decir una cosa. Mira, Chapulín, ¡voy a venir otra vez! ¿Cómo vas a venderme clavos de clavar si te pido clavos de comer?

ANDREW: Pues los clavos pa' clavar, pues clavos pa' comer ... pues si puedes comerte un clavo, te puedes comer el otro. Todo es una cosa. Hmmm. ¿Qué diferencia de clavo a clavo? Si te puedes comer uno, clavo, puedes comer el otro.

JUANITA: Mira, voy a venir otra vez. Vale más que aprendas, porque, mira, te vas a ir de patas para la calle.

ANDREW: ¿A volar?

JUANITA: ¡A volar!

ANDREW: ¿A volar sin alas?

JUANITA: O con alas o sin alas, pero te me largas.

ANDREW: No, ya aprendí, hermana.

JUANITA: ¿Ya aprendiste? ¿Estás seguro?

ANDREW: Ya, ya te juro, ya seguro que sí.

JUANITA: A ver.

ANDREW: Vas a ver cómo ya te aprendí.

JUANITA: Ah, bueno ... ¿Qué estás haciendo?

ANDREW: Estoy limpiando el mostrador.

JUANITA: Oh, ándale ... Ah, sí. Oh, ándale. Ya sí. Sí, ya estás aprendiendo. (Ambos riéndose.) Buenas tardes.

ANDREW: Buenas tardes.

JUANITA: ¡Ándale! Anda, así. ¿Cómo le va? ¿Cómo está su familia?

ANDREW: Buenos días. ¿Cómo le va? ¿Cómo está su mamá? ¿Está bien?

JUANITA: Está bien, gracias.

ANDREW: Qué bueno.

JUANITA: ¿Y la suya?

ANDREW: Pues, ¿qué le importa, verdad? Está bien. ¿Qué se le ofrece?

JUANITA: Pues, ah, ¿no tiene Ud. suelas para zapatos? ¿Zapatos? Tú sabes, ¿suelas? ¿Suelas?

ANDREW: ¿Suelas pa' zapatos?

JUANITA: Zapatos ...

ANDREW: Suelas pa' zapatos ... Vamos a ver ahorita, un momentito.

JUANITA: Ándale.

ANDREW: Pues, mire, me vaya a dispensar, pero no tenemos suelas para zapatos ...

JUANITA: Oh, no ...

ANDREW: ... Ves, porque, como no es zapatería aquí, ves, se acaban muy pronto.

JUANITA: Pues, muchas veces las venden en estas tienditas ...

ANDREW: (Cheerful, upbeat voice.) Pues sí, tenemos un par de llantas, ¿siquiera lo sirve? Así los puede hacer, y saca más.

JUANITA: Mira, Chapulín, te voy a decir una cosa. Ésta va a ser la última vez. ¡Eres un burro de primera!

ANDREW: Pues ...

JUANITA: (Angry voice, increasing volume.) Ora sí te digo que es la última vez que voy a venir. Y si esta vez no aprendes, te vas a tener que ir para afuera. Ora sí, ya me dio coraje. Ya ... ya me enojo, Chapulín.

ANDREW: ¿Voy a tener que ir a California?

JUANITA: (Almost yelling with anger.) Pa' ... pa' ... California, para donde te ocurra, pero ya no te soporto. No sirves para nada. ¡Ahí voy ya!

ANDREW: Está bueno ... A ver, ¿dígame ... ?

JUANITA: Buenas tardes.

ANDREW: Buenas tardes. A ver, ¿dígame Ud., en que le puedo servir?

JUANITA: Hágame el favor de darme un rollo de papel del ... del ... del ... de *toilet paper*. Quiero un rollo de *toilet paper*.

ANDREW: ¿Un rollo de *toilet paper*?

JUANITA: Ah huh, *toilet paper*.

ANDREW: ¿Un rollo de *toilet paper*?

JUANITA: (Raising her voice.) ¡Sí, señor! ¡De *toilet paper*!

ANDREW: ¡*Toilet paper*! ¿*Toilet paper*? Oye, ¿dijo Ud. "*toilet paper*"?

JUANITA: Sí, señor, le dije *toilet paper*".

ANDREW: ¿"*Toilet paper*"? ¿Para qué ... para qué se usa eso?

JUANITA: ¿Eh?

ANDREW: ¿Para qué ... para qué es? (Pausa. Chapulín comienza a reírse.) Ha, ha, ha, ha, hee, hee, hee, oh, oh, oh, ahorita vengo, ahorita vengo ... Ahorita voy a ver. (Pausa.) Óigame, me vaya a dispensar, pero se acaba de acabar el "*toilet paper*".

JUANITA: ¿No tiene ... ?

ANDREW: No. Pero tenemos algo parecido.

JUANITA: ¿Qué tiene?

ANDREW: Tenemos un papel de lija número ocho.

JUANITA: Ya no más, maldito ... !

The Shop

JUANITA: You know very well that my husband and my mother-in-law don't want you to stay here any longer. They don't want you around anymore. What do you want me to do?

ANDREW: Let them leave.

JUANITA: What do you mean, let them leave? It's not ... it's that you just don't want to work.

ANDREW: Now, now, I didn't come here because I wanted to. I came because you all invited me here for a vacation.

JUANITA: Yes, yes, a vacation.

ANDREW: That's right.

JUANITA: And now you've been here for two years!

ANDREW: Yes, little sister ...

JUANITA: That's no vacation. You've been here for two years already. Are you going to go out and look for a job?

ANDREW: There aren't any, man.

JUANITA: There's no work ... all right, look, why don't we do this?

ANDREW: What?

JUANITA: Look. You know, you know very well, Chapulín, that I love you very much. I love you very much because you're the youngest in the family.

ANDREW: Well I'm the little baby of the family, the little coyote.

JUANITA: You used to be the little baby, yes, but you're not a little baby anymore.

ANDREW: I'm the very littlest, the little coyote.

JUANITA: The great big coyote, because now you're very large.

ANDREW: Well, just my body is, but I'm still . . .

JUANITA: No, no, you're grown up now. All right, look . . .

ANDREW: My mind is still the same.

JUANITA: Look, look, I'm going to tell you something. So that my mother-in-law and my husband . . .

ANDREW: You know what? You know what, babe? You know your mother-in-law is a busybody, a nosy, meddling old bag, and that I . . . ?

JUANITA: But she's my mother-in-law!

ANDREW: Nothing pleases her. If I eat, why am I eating? "No! Old man! How he eats! Oh man! He drinks too much!" Who knows what all . . . ? And if I don't eat? Well, no: "He doesn't like the food. Well, he's never even eaten in a restaurant . . . " No, that old broad, you don't understand, man, she's very . . .

JUANITA: Now, now I'm going to talk! Either you go, or, now, I'm going to tell you something. You know very well that we have a store, right?

ANDREW: Hmmm?

JUANITA: You know that we have a store, right?

ANDREW: Oh, yes, I know that we have a store.

JUANITA: No, no, no, no, no. We have a store.

ANDREW: Well yes, we have a store.

JUANITA: No, you don't have anything.

ANDREW: What do you mean, I don't have anything?

JUANITA: No. My husband and I . . .

ANDREW: So then, so then, what happened to what we said when we were little kids?

JUANITA: When . . . ? Which? What?

ANDREW: When you and I were little kids.

JUANITA: What did we say?

ANDREW: We promised each other we said: "Look, brother," you told me, "look, little brother, when I grow up, everything that I . . . , everything of mine is yours." Remember! You said . . .

JUANITA: Yes . . . ?

ANDREW: I told you: "Sister, if everything of yours is going to be mine, everything of mine is going to be mine."

JUANITA: All right, you don't know anything anymore. I'm saying that I'm going to tell you something . . .

ANDREW: We have the store.

JUANITA: All right, it's all right, but we do have the store! Listen, so that my mother-in-law won't say anything, and run you off ... , because I don't want you to have to go, I don't want you to go ... But you're going to have to go ... But look, why don't we do something? Why don't you go to work in the store?

ANDREW: Why?

JUANITA: To work?

ANDREW: Me, work in the store ... ?

JUANITA: Yes, work ...

ANDREW: And that clerk that you have there?

JUANITA: He left.

ANDREW: You don't pay him, either, ...

JUANITA: That's none of your business! It's none of your business if we pay him ...

ANDREW: She wants people to work for nothing ...

JUANITA: Listen, Chapulín, listen, Chapulín, it's none of your business if he get's paid or not. I'm talking to you about this, right now I'm talking to you. You could work. Do you want to? You have to work in the store.

ANDREW: Well, I've never worked in a store, sister.

JUANITA: Well, you've got to choose one thing or the other. Either you work, or you leave.

ANDREW: I'll work if you show me how.

JUANITA: You either go to work, or you leave.

ANDREW: Well, if you show me how ...

JUANITA: I'll teach you, it's very easy.

ANDREW: Oh, all right, well, you show me, I'll learn ...

JUANITA: All right, look. There's no problem, it's very easy, and I'll show you how.

ANDREW: Okay, let's see what we're going to do.

JUANITA: We are going to suppose ...

ANDREW: What are we going to put down?

JUANITA: We're not going to put down anything! Suppose!

ANDREW: Suppose, ah, suppose.

JUANITA: We're going to pretend like this is the store.

ANDREW: (Childish voice.) We're going to play store.

JUANITA: (Speaking with clenched jaw.) We're not going to ... Ay! No, man! We're going to be in the store. This is the store.

ANDREW: Now we're in the store.

JUANITA: Now we're in the store. And this that you see here is the counter. And this is the door. Here's where you open the door, it opens here, and it raises up like this. You go out through there, you come in through here, the counter is here . . . What are you looking at?

ANDREW: You're going crazy.

JUANITA: I'm not . . . I'm not crazy. I'm explaining it to you so that you won't have to struggle . . .

ANDREW: But there's nothing here. It'd be better to put up a counter. Look, there's nothing. There's nothing here.

JUANITA: It's imaginary. Imaginary, just pretend.

ANDREW: Oh, make-believe, so that, in a word, I'll learn, ah . . .

JUANITA: There you go! Kiddo, you're a good kid.

ANDREW: Ah, all right, explain yourself. No, because . . . here's the counter, and this here's the door, and here's who-knows-what . . .

JUANITA: Well . . . but it's just make-believe. So, all right, so I'm going to be the clerk, and you are going to come in to buy something from me.

ANDREW: You're the clerk, and I . . . ?

JUANITA: And you come in to buy something from me . . .

ANDREW: I'm going to buy something from you?

JUANITA: That's right, yes.

ANDREW: Good. Very well. (Long pause.) I already came in.

JUANITA: Good afternoon.

ANDREW: Good afternoon.

JUANITA: Can I help you?

ANDREW: Well, listen, man, the truth is that you're no help to me at all.

JUANITA: Listen. Listen, wait a minute. Listen, well what kind of way is that to treat people? Where have you ever seen that, you go into a little store, and say, "You're of no help to me at all?"

ANDREW: Well, what question are you asking me? Well: "How can I help you?" Well, you can't.

JUANITA: But you have to . . . to treat people with courtesy, with a smile, and good, man! What do you mean, you come in to buy something, and "You're no help to me?"

ANDREW: But I'm not coming to buy, I'm not coming to buy anything from you.

JUANITA: It doesn't matter, because you have to treat them right! Geez!

ANDREW: All right, let me be the clerk, and you're coming in to buy something from me.

JUANITA: You don't even know how to buy, and you're going to know how to sell?

ANDREW: All right, let's see if . . . if you're better at buying, and I'm the clerk . . .

JUANITA: Now, another thing.

ANDREW: Ehhh?

JUANITA: When someone comes in to buy something . . .

ANDREW: Ummmm hmmmm . . .

JUANITA: . . . If we don't have it, what . . . they always do in all the stores, is sell the people something similar to what they want, so they won't go away. See? So they won't go away without buying anything.

ANDREW: No, if they come here, I'll tie them up until they buy something . . .

JUANITA: You're not going to tie anybody up, you're going to wait on them right. So now then, I come in right now, here I go.

ANDREW: All right. Close the door.

JUANITA: Hey, what's that you say?

ANDREW: Hey, close the door.

JUANITA: Which door? (Angry.)

ANDREW: The one that you put there.

JUANITA: (Angry sigh. Clears throat, Loud.) Ay! Chi . . . ! Ay!

ANDREW: What do you want? (Pause.) Speak up quick because I'm busy.

JUANITA: Listen. What's all this?

ANDREW: I have things to do.

JUANITA: Listen! Ay! Hey, you're going to run people off like that? Smile! A little smile . . . very . . . you know, happy, like that. Smile! Put a smile on your face, understand?

ANDREW: Well, I swear . . .

JUANITA: Well, smile! I'm going now. I'm going to come in again, man. Ah Hmmm! Ah Hhhggmmmm! HH-HHGGGGMMMMM!

ANDREW: Hhgmmm, hump, hhggmmm.

JUANITA: I'm here, already, man!

ANDREW: You already came in?

JUANITA: Say to me, "What do you want?"

ANDREW: What do I want?

JUANITA: (Angry voice.) What do you mean, "What do I want?!"

ANDREW: Okay, what do you want?

JUANITA: Oh. Well ... would you happen to have ... would you have ... please give me ... do you have ... eh ... some cloves?

ANDREW: Cloves ... for cooking?[2]

JUANITA: Cloves for eating. Yes. Cloves for cooking.

ANDREW: Just a moment, I'll look. (Pause.) You know what? You have to excuse me ...

JUANITA: You don't have any, all right.

ANDREW: ... But we just ran out.

JUANITA: You ran out ...

ANDREW: They were just sold. Wouldn't you like something similar?

JUANITA: There you go, that's the way, now you're catching on. How nice!

ANDREW: (Bright, happy voice.) We do have nails.

JUANITA: Nails?

ANDREW: Yes.

JUANITA: Look, look, I'm going to tell you something. Look, Chapulín, how are you going to sell me nails if I ask you for cloves?

ANDREW: Well *clavos* for nailing, *clavos* for eating ... well if you can eat one *clavo*, you can eat the other. It's all the same. Hmmm. What's the diference between *clavo* and *clavo*? If you can eat one, you can eat the other.

JUANITA: Look, I'm going to come in again. You'd better learn, because, look, you're going to go feet first out into the street.

ANDREW: To fly?

JUANITA: To fly!

ANDREW: To fly without wings?

JUANITA: With wings, or without wings, but you'll be amazed.

ANDREW: No, now I've learned, sister.

JUANITA: You've learned now? Are you sure?

ANDREW: Yes, yes, for sure. I swear it.

JUANITA: We'll see.

ANDREW: You'll see how I've learned now.

JUANITA: Ah, all right ... What are you doing?

ANDREW: I'm cleaning the counter.

JUANITA: Oh, there you go ... Ah, yes. Oh, that's the way. Now you've got it. Yes, now you're learning. (Both laughing.) Good afternoon.

ANDREW: Good afternoon.

JUANITA: There you go! That's how it's done. How's it going? How's your family?

ANDREW: Good day. How's it going? How's your mother? Is she well?

JUANITA: She's fine, thanks.

ANDREW: How nice.

JUANITA: And yours?

ANDREW: Well, what's it to you? She's fine. What would you like?

JUANITA: Well, ah, do you have soles for shoes? Shoes? You know, soles? Soles?

ANDREW: Soles for shoes?

JUANITA: Shoes ...

ANDREW: Soles for shoes ... We'll see right away, one moment.

JUANITA: There you go.

ANDREW: Well, look, you're going to have to excuse me, but we don't have soles for shoes ...

JUANITA: Oh, no ...

ANDREW: ... You see, because, since this isn't a shoe store here, see, we run out of them very fast.

JUANITA: Well, lots of times they sell them in these little stores ...

ANDREW: (Cheerful, upbeat voice.) Well, yes, we do have a set of tires, perhaps they'll do? You could make them out of those, and get more for your money.

JUANITA: Look, Chapulín, I'm going to tell you something. This is going to be the last time. You're a first class donkey!

ANDREW: Well ...

JUANITA: (Angry voice, increasing volume.) I'm telling you, this is the last time that I'm going to come in. And if you don't learn this time, you're going to have to get out. Now you've got me mad. Now ... now I'm getting angry, Chapulín.

ANDREW: I'm going to have to go to California?

JUANITA: (Almost yelling with anger.) To ... to ... California, wherever you like, but I can't put up with you anymore. You're a good-for-nothing. I'm going now!

ANDREW: It's all right ... Let's see, can I help you ... ?

JUANITA: Good afternoon.

ANDREW: Good afternoon. Tell me, what can I do for you?

JUANITA: Please give me a roll of paper for the ... the ... the ... of *toilet paper.* I want a roll of *toilet paper.*

ANDREW: A roll of "*toilet paper?*"

JUANITA: Ah huh, *toilet paper.*

ANDREW: A roll of "*toilet paper?*"

JUANITA: (Raising her voice.) Yes, mister! Of *toilet paper!*

ANDREW: "*Toilet paper!*" "*Toilet paper?*" Listen, you said, "*toilet paper?*"

JUANITA: Yes, mister, I told you, "*toilet paper.*"

ANDREW: "*Toilet paper?*" What ... what do you use that for?

JUANITA: Eh?

ANDREW: What ... what's it for? (Pause. Chapulín begins laughing.) Ha, ha ha, ha, hee, hee, hee, oh, oh, oh, I'll be right back, I'll be right back ... I'm going to look right away. (Pause.) Listen, you're going to have to excuse me, but we just ran out of "*toilet paper.*"

JUANITA: You don't have any ... ?

ANDREW: No. But we have something similar.

JUANITA: What do you have?

ANDREW: We have some number eight sandpaper.

JUANITA: That's enough, you damn ... !

Andrew

I don't know where my mother got all those, but she got the ideas somewhere. Mamá taught us all of those skits. She must have seen them at other shows, or she picked them up someplace.

Lydia

Mamá also sang at times, or between the five of them they would do something. Señor Montes had originally taught them some of those skits. Montes knew them because he had traveled with some variety shows that had comedies, and all that. He had learned quite a few of them. Montes would say, "Look, I know this skit. Just that it has to be so many people. Good, there are three of us."

And Montes chose the performers for each part. The majority were skits that he knew. My mother would take part in the skits sometimes when they needed five people in the comedy. For example, when the '*compadre*' would die, and Mamá was the wife, and the other '*compadre*' would then arrive. Mamá would also give ideas.

"We're going to do it like this. . . . " or, "I don't like it that way, it would be better if we do it like this. . . . "

The skit would be rehearsed and discussed. If Mamá didn't like something about it, she would say, "No, better yet, let's do it like this."

In the same way, she baptized Manuel with the stage name of Manolo. And Andrés, she baptized him with the name of Chapulín, which means "grasshopper." Mamá would also help out a lot in choosing the numbers that they were going to put on. And she was the one that would say, "All right, you go first, this number goes on first, and then the other one goes on."

She would arrange the program. She arranged the whole show. The thing is that everything varied, and Mamá was the one who coordinated it all.

We tried to vary our presentations every day. For example, when we would play in Phoenix, they would give us three days. The program would be varied each day for those three days. It wasn't put on the same way two days in a row. So if the same people were to come twice, they wouldn't see exactly the same show. My mother tried to arrange it so one skit would be presented on the first day, another on the second day, and the program would be varied in such a way that it wouldn't be the same. I would change my songs around, and the Dueto would do the same. Mamá put a lot of thought into everything.

My mother had the whole schedule of everything that we would put on, and she knew it very well. We rehearsed everything the day before it was to be presented. Mamá would put those of us who were going to be doing a particular act as if they were on stage. The dances were the same way. Everything was rehearsed the day before. In that way, I was always ready when we got to the theater, and everything would go in the order that it was supposed to.

*   *   *

When we first returned to Los Angeles in 1947, Señor Peláez, the owner of Azteca Records, came with his wife to the Mason Theater to see the show. Afterwards they came backstage to my dressing room to talk with me.

"You still sing very well," Mr. Peláez told me, "what have you been up to all these years?"

I told him what had happened, how we had stopped touring because of the war.

"Well," Peláez said, "why don't you come over to our studios? I'd like to listen to you and see if perhaps we could make a few recordings."

"Yes, of course," I replied.

"Very good. You don't have a contract with anyone, do you?" Peláez asked me.

"No, I don't have a contract," I told him. "Okay, that's very good," he said.

So later on, we went over to the Azteca studio, and I sang a song for him, and he liked it very much. Right away, he started recording me. I recorded with him for quite a long time—a lot of records. And then, after I had started recording with him, I mentioned Juanita and María to him: "My sisters, Juanita and María, sing very well, why don't you give them a chance to record, too?"

"No, no," Mr. Peláez replied, "I'm not interested in them, I'm only interested in you."

Well, I didn't insist the first time, but not long afterwards I asked him again. "Go ahead," I told him, "give them a chance. After all, what can you lose?"

"Well, all right," Mr. Peláez finally told me, "I'll give them a recording session."

Well, after just one record, he gave them a contract, and they continued to record for him for a long time.

María

We heard the Padilla Sisters on records, and Carmen y Laura, and then we came in: Juanita y María. The Padilla's were still real popular when we started. We worked from Texas, you see, and we hit Texas like a bomb. All the companies wanted to get us right away.

Mamá and Lydia had sung together for years, but that's not a *dueto*, you see, because they sing in the same voice. A *dueto* is where you have a first and a second voice—different. If two girls or two men sing the same, with no second vocal part, just the first, that's not a *dueto*. Juanita and I didn't make any records as a *dueto* until after the war. We made some *dueto* recordings for Azteca, and I also made some with Lydia as the Dueto Monterrey for the same company.

Mamá wanted to raise us up, to build us a career that would be as big as, or even bigger than, Lydia's. But it wasn't easy. For instance, when we went to this big theater, the California, a beautiful theater with all of the stars, we didn't have any clothes. Our costumes weren't fit for that theater. They weren't rich like the costumes the others had who had all come from Mexico.

Juanita

I heard some people laugh. I heard some people say, "¿No te gusta esta volada?" ("Don't you like this goofy gal?") When we came with those costumes we were nothing, but we sang. And Mamá told Lydia to ask Peláez to give us a chance. And that's when Mamá told him to give us something for the record.

"I'm going to give you fifty dollars," he said.

"Okay," said Mamá.

When Peláez heard that record, "Morena morenita" and "Corrido de Laredo," he loved it. "It's good," Peláez told Mamá, "and the voices are pretty. I like it, and I'm going to send it to San Antonio. And you know what, I'm going to give you seventy-five dollars, not fifty, seventy-five for each record. I'm going to send this record out right away."

Those were the first songs that we recorded as a dueto. Santiago Jiménez wrote "Morena morenita," it's a *canción ranchera*. Santiago really got mad at us for recording it, but they gave him the royalties for the song.

After we finished at the Mason Theater, we went on to Santa Ana and then to Fresno, California. After the record had been out for a few weeks, Peláez called Mamá in Fresno, and he told her, "Mrs. Mendoza, I want you to bring Juanita and María back to Los Angeles because I want to record them some more."

And then Mamá made a contract for us with him. We had recorded for a label called Globe before, but the records didn't come out very good. The man from Globe heard us singing at the Bohemia Club, and the recording was done here in downtown San Antonio at a music store called San Antonio Music; it's still here.

María

Then later on we made some recordings with Sam Murray for Discos Álamo. We sang with the *conjunto* of Leandro Guerrero. We made a song with him, it was a real good song for the war: "Una carta para Corea." I think it was written by a policeman. Leandro Guerrero played the accordion, Juan Viesca was on *contrabajo*, string bass, and I played the guitar.

Una carta para Corea[3]

Esta carta yo la mando
a los frentes de Corea,
ojalá ahí que la recibas
para que pronto la leas.

Se llevaron a mi amor,
y quebraron mi corazón.
Te daré mi bendición
para que regreses pronto.

Pero amor, amor, amor,
a mi Dio' le pido por ti
que te traiga buena suerte
y que pronto estés aquí.

Se fue a peliar por la paz,
lo llamó el Tío Samuel,
pero a mí no se me olvida
el querer rezar por él.

Desde que él me dijo adiós
yo relloro mi pasión,
porque el día que se marchó,
se quebró mi corazón.

Pero amor, amor, amor,
rezaré mucho por ti,
que la Virgen te acompañe,
es el deseo de mí.

A Letter to Korea

I'm sending this letter
to the front in Korea;
I hope you will receive it there
so you can read it right away.

They took my love away

and broke my heart.
I will give you my blessing
so you will return soon.

But my love, my love, my love,
I plead to God on your behalf,
that He bring you good luck
and that you'll be back here soon.

He went away to fight for peace,
Uncle Sam called him away,
but I don't ever forget
to pray for him.

Ever since he told me goodbye
I have been crying over my love,
because the day he went away
my heart was broken.

But my love, my love, my love,
I will pray so much for you;
that the Virgin always be with you,
that is my desire.

We also recorded "Qué suerte la mía," which is by José Alfredo Jiménez. We really liked that song, it's a good song. We also did "La prisión del colorado." Another *corrido* that we recorded with them was "El Güero Polvos."[4]

El güero Polvos

Año de mil novecientos,
cuarenta y ocho al contado,
mataron en San Antonio
al güero "Polvos" mentado.

Por la calle Guadalupe,
en cantina de Simón,
lo sacaron ya sin vida
para llevarlo al panteón.

El güero dijo a Simón,
antes de hacerse la bola,

—Te juro que sólo muerto
me quitarán mi pistola.

Llegaron dos condestables,
llegaron por mala suerte;
para poder desarmarlo
tuvieron que darle muerte.

Simón le dijo a Rodolfo:
—Rodolfo, no seas así,
entrégales la pistola
y yo voy a hablar por ti.

Pero el güero contestaba,
sin dejar de forcejar:
—Los que quieran desarmarme,
pos me tendrán que matar.

Nada más con un disparo
el güero quedó tirado.
Así acabó con su vida
el güero "Polvos" mentado.

El güero dijo a Simón:
—Este anillo es para ti,
quítamelo de la mano
pa' que te acuerdes de mí.

Rodolfo era su nombre,
González su apelativo;
decidido y muy valiente,
de San Antonio nacido.

Dusty the Blond

In the year of nineteen hundred,
forty-eight to be exact,
they killed the notorious *güero*
known as "Dusty" in San Antonio.

Down on Guadalupe Street,
in Simón's *cantina*,
they brought him out already lifeless

to take him to the cemetery.

El Güero told Simón,
just before it all went down,
"I swear they won't take my pistol
as long as I'm alive."

Two constables showed up,
unluckily they arrived just then;
in order to disarm him
they had to kill him.

Simón told Rodolfo:
"Rodolfo, don't be like that,
hand over your pistol,
and I'll go downtown to vouch for you."

But *El Güero* answered back,
without ceasing to struggle:
"Anyone who wants to disarm me,
they'll just have to kill me."

With just one shot *El Güero*
fell stretched out on the floor.
That's how the notorious *güero*
called "Dusty" ended his life.

El Güero told Simón:
"This ring is for you,
take it off my hand
so that you'll remember me."

Rodolfo was his (*El Güero*'s) first name,
González was his family name;
determined and very courageous,
he was born in San Antonio.

We also recorded for Manuel Conde during this period, for either Columbia or OKeh.[5]

I think we started with Azteca about 1947. When we were recording for Azteca, Mr. Peláez just sent us the songs he wanted us to record. He chose most of the songs we did. Sometimes when we recorded for Discos

Falcón, they also would choose the songs for us. They were popular songs. Mr. Oberstein of Blue Bird Records was different. He never told us what to sing. Whatever Lydia and Mamá wanted to record was all right with him.

Lydia

Mr. Peláez was a very good person. He both treated and paid us well. He gave us royalties, and we always received what we were owed without difficulty. Mr. Peláez didn't tell us how many records we had sold, but we noticed because of the royalties that we received. They were good; we made good money. Azteca would pay us in advance: fifty dollars for each record. Peláez was a very good *empresario* and he always behaved very correctly with us.

Sometimes Señor Peláez would send us records with songs he wanted us to record so we could practice before we got out to Los Angeles, but when I first started recording for him, he was primarily interested in having me do all of the material I had recorded for Blue Bird. So this was the second time I recorded all of my songs—the songs from my personal repertory from the Blue Bird days: "Pajarito herido," "Mal hombre," "Mundo engañoso." Just about everything I had done for Blue Bird, I recorded again for Mr. Peláez.

But after we had done all of that repertory, Peláez started sending us new songs to record. I also came up with new songs to do. And we continued to record like that. It was the same way with my sisters: Peláez gave them some of the songs, and we in the group came up with others.

Since we recorded with Peláez for such a long time, we developed a real friendship. When we came out to make the records, it wasn't just business. We would always visit with his family, his wife, and we would always go out to have dinner, and we would go and visit them at their house and like that. We were a lot closer with the Peláez family than with any of the other recording companies that we worked for during the long years of our career.

CHAPTER 7

The Variedad Mendoza

Andrew

There had been a lot of trips at different times when I was a little boy, and I enjoyed them all, because I didn't have to do anything—I didn't have to work—but eventually the time came when I had to help out, too. When I started to grow up, Mamá asked me, "What about you? You don't sing, you don't do anything. You're going to have to do something in this house, you know."

"Well, what do you want me to do?" I replied. "You need to teach me something."

Mamá taught everybody something except me, because I was the youngest. So she said, "Well, you're going to learn how to announce the stage show."

So I really started paying attention to how they would announce the *variedad* and to how my brother Manuel and the others would tell jokes and do comedy routines. But I didn't get my first chance to actually work on stage until one time when we were staying in Ratón, New Mexico. We would play in Ratón, and then we would play in Trinidad, a town which is only across the mountains in Colorado and close to the highway.

So, one night we were in Trinidad. We were playing in a movie theater like we generally did at that time—alternating with the film. When our show ended, Manuel went out somewhere with some friends. I don't know where he went, but he went out and didn't come back in time when our next show was going to start. The movie was almost over, and he still wasn't back. My mother didn't know what to do, and they were going to have to start the show any minute. They were the first number, see: Manuel and Juanita. But I knew all the material, so Mamá told me, "Well, you had better go ahead and do it. Do you know how to do it?"

Juanita, Manuel and María Mendoza. Courtesy of the Andrew Mendoza collection.

"Well, okay," I said, "if you let me drink one beer, I'll do it. I'm pretty sure I know how to do it."

I'd seen it done a lot of times, and I knew everything. So I went out there, announced the show and played Manuel's part in the skit. Instead of saying "Manolo," they called me, by mistake, "Chapulín." I kept that name, *Chapulín*, "grasshopper."

In show business, when you go out there on stage, you have to control the people. The people can't control you. You better not let them control you, because if you do, you're going to get nervous, and you're not going to say anything, and you aren't going to be able to do anything. So you have to control the people. You have to tell the people what to do. If they start hollering at you and all that—because they will start hollering, a lot of guys whistling at you and telling you jokes and all that—you have to wait until they finish talking. Suddenly, well, they realize that they have to shut up. And they do. When they do, you say, *"Buenas noches*, good evening, ladies and gentlemen . . . " and then you wait for just a minute, and then you say, "I said: 'Good evening!' " so that the people answer you back: "Good evening!" "All right. Now we're all here. Now we're going to start the show," I would tell them. "We hope that you're going to have a good time and a good pleasure."

It sounds different in Spanish, but I'm telling you in English. In Spanish it goes something like this:

> Muy buenas noches, respetado público. Vamos a tener el gusto de presentar nuestros humildes trabajos, esperando que sean al agrado de cada uno de Uds. Primeramente vamos a tener un *estage*-cómico por Juanita y Manolo. Vamos a recibirlos con un fuerte aplauso para que agarren ánimo. ¿Eh? ¡Vámonos!

> Good evening, respected public. We are going to have the pleasure of presenting our humble works, hoping that they will be pleasing to each and every one of you. First we are going to have a stage comedy by Juanita and Manolo. Let's receive them with a hearty applause so that they get inspired. Okay? Let's go!

And everybody would clap, the people would start applauding. And then Manuel and Janie would usually come out and start doing their stage show. You're only nervous before you go out. Once you're out there on stage, you forget about it. I mean you're not nervous anymore, you're at ease.

So anyhow, I went out in Manuel's place, and everything went fine. Then Manuel showed up—he came late—and took over. There was that number, and then another number, and then Manuel and Juanita were supposed to go out again. When the time came, Manuel was ready to go out, and he went out, but then he realized that I was a better comedian than he was. After the show, Manuel told my mother, "I think Andrés is a better comedian than I am, and I think we should let him get in the act now."

So that's when I started acting as a comedian. At first Manuel and I would work together, but soon Janie and I were completely on our own with the comedy routines.

We were in Fierro, Colorado—it's a mining town. We were playing there, and Manuel received a telegram from his wife—he was already married by that time—telling him that she was having a baby, she was having a little girl. So he had to return to San Antonio right away; he had to leave us out there.

Manuel

Mamá wanted to get us tangled up with somebody with the same kind of profession. I guess that's the reason she didn't like my wife, because my wife wasn't in show business. I met her at a dance. I love to dance; it's one of my weaknesses. I love to ballroom dance.

María

He used to dance like a feather.

Manuel

I met my wife at a dance. It must have been about 1946 or '47, right after I came back from the Service. I had met another girl I would've married, but she went and got married to someone else. When she got married to somebody, I sent some flowers. My wife didn't like that.

Anyway, when my first child was about to be born, I had to leave the show and go back to San Antonio, and Andrew had to take over as the main comedian.

Andrew

We worked together for a while, though, and we used to do some of the stuff that Manuel had originally done with Antonio Montes before the war. One of our favorites was the skit we called *The Lover*. This is how it used to go:

El Amante[1]

Muy buenas tardes, señoras y señores. Vamos a tener el

gusto de presentarles un bonito programa que esperamos que sea al agrado de todos y cada uno de Uds.

Vamos a presentar primeramente, antes de seguir el programa, un bonito *"esquit"* entre yo, su servidor, Manuel Mendoza, y aquí, el Chapulín. Esperamos que sea del agrado de Uds., y si acaso cometemos algún error, queremos que nos perdonen. Y que sea ... , ojalá que les guste. Con permiso, eh, ahí vamos.

ANDREW: ¡Eh Manolo! Manolo ¡te ando buscando, hombre!

MANUEL: ¿Cómo que me andas buscando?

ANDREW: ¿Cuándo me vas a ... me vas a vender eso que cargas tú?

MANUEL: ¿Cómo que vender qué? ¿Que ya te dijeron que ya me andaba robando yo?

ANDREW: No, no, no, no, pero, pero tú tienes algo. Yo quiero aprender ... a ver cómo tratar a las muchachas.

MANUEL: ¡Ohhhh! ¡Vaya!

ANDREW: Ay, tú todo el tiempo ... las muchachas, todo el tiempo luego luego caen contigo, y conmigo no quieren caer.

MANUEL: No pues, hermano, pues fíjate, mano, mira, la persona tuya, y la mía, la persona yo. ¿Cómo quieres que se fijen mejor en ti que en mí? ¿No soy más simpático yo que tú?

ANDREW: ¿Por qué? ¿Qué tienes tú que no tenga yo? (Riéndose.)

MANUEL: Ah bueno, bueno. ¡Bueno! Pues soy más bien parecido yo. ¿No es cierto?

ANDREW: Cuando estaba chiquito, ¿todo el tiempo no me decían que era muy bonito ... ?

MANUEL: ¿Ya me dijiste otro día que te usaban para Niño Dios? ¿No?

ANDREW: Pues sí, también ...

MANUEL: ¿Y ahora?

ANDREW: Pues ahora, no sé por qué no ... , es algo que tú cargas. ¿Tú cargas algo?

MANUEL: No hombre, no es nada, no es nada ...

ANDREW: Tú cargas alguna cosa, porque ...

MANUEL: No, mira, déjame decirte, hermano, mira, todo lo que tienes que saber es ... cómo tratar a las mujeres. A las mujeres les gusta que tengas que maderearlas. Tienes que ...

tratarlas ... con mucho ... , ¿cómo te diré? Bueno, decirles palabras bonitas, palabras dulces. ¿Sabes palabras dulces?

ANDREW: Seguro que sí ... , ¿cómo no ... ?

MANUEL: A ver, échame unas cuantas palabras dulces.

ANDREW: Chupaletas, caramelos ...

MANUEL: ¡*Whoo*! ¡No hombre! No hombre, no, no, no ...

ANDREW: Más dulces que eso no puede haber.

MANUEL: No digo esa clase de dulces, atascado. Te estoy diciendo de otra clase de ... , las palabras que te estoy diciendo yo ... , te digo, son palabras halagadoras.

ANDREW: ¿Cómo qué?

MANUEL: ¿No sabes lo que son palabras halagadoras?

ANDREW: Pues ... *halagadoras*, pues *halagadoras* ... , no sé que son *halagadoras* ...

MANUEL: ¡Váleme! Tú de veras estás muy iliterato, ¿verdad, mano? ¡Chihuahua! Mano, ¿no sabes ni cómo tratar a una mujer, verdad?

ANDREW: Pues ... pues, no más le hablas ...

MANUEL: No ... , tienes que ... , pues, darle por su lado todo el tiempo, y ... Mira, mira ¿no me has visto con la güerita esa que vive en la esquina?

ANDREW: ¿Cuál?

MANUEL: La que ahorita vive de la esquina, en la casa de la esquina, allí, al otro lado del apartamento primero, en el segundo apartamento. La güera del pelo ... , ésa que tiene un cuerpo como un ... como Coca-Cola.

ANDREW: Esa ... ¿Cómo se llama? ¿Tú la conoces?

MANUEL: ¡Cómo si la conozco! ¡*Whooo*! Sí, ésa es mi mera mera; yo soy el pachote de ella.

ANDREW: ¿Tú ... tú andas con ella?

MANUEL: Yo soy el mero mero que ... Pues no hay otro, ella no quiere a otro más que a mí. Yo soy el número "*number one*".

ANDREW: ¿Y andas con ella tú?

MANUEL: ¡Pues! ¿Para qué yo te diga? ¿Pues no me has visto?

ANDREW: ¿Y ella sabe?

MANUEL: ¿Cómo que si ella sabe? ¡Pues!

ANDREW: No, bueno, a lo mejor ella no sabe ...

MANUEL: Cómo no, que ella sabe; seguro que ella sí sabe. ¡Seguro que ella sí sabe!

ANDREW: Pues puede ser mentira . . .

MANUEL: Yo soy su dios para ella. Yo puedo tratarla de cualquier manera que me dé la gana y ella me obedece a mí, hombre, porque . . . ¡está enamorada de mí! ¡Está locamente, me entiendes, enamorada de mí!

ANDREW: ¿Y el marido sabe, también?

MANUEL: ¿Qué? ¿El marido? *Who?* ¿Aquél?

ANDREW: ¿El boxeador?

MANUEL: ¡¿Qué quién?!

ANDREW: El boxeador.

MANUEL: Oh, el boxeador. Oh, él, me viene guango ese boxeador. Ése está *"punch drunk"*.

ANDREW: ¿Está *"punch"* quién?

MANUEL: Está *"punch-drunk"*.

ANDREW: Pues, así te va a caer a ti cuando acabe contigo.

MANUEL: No, no, no te creas. No, no, no te creas. No, pero para que me pesque, ha de ser la buena.

ANDREW: A poco me vas a decir a mí que tú entras y sales allí cuando te da la gana.

MANUEL: Ah, mano, cuando me da a mí la gana yo llego ahí, yo me meto y de ahí me salgo.

ANDREW: Mira, mira, mano, algún día vas a entrar y no vas a salir, mano.

MANUEL: ¿Por qué?

ANDREW: Pues fíjate, ya verás, porque te va a pescar el boxeador, y te va a dar una rapiza. Te va a usar para un *"punching bag"*.

MANUEL: No, no, no, señor, mira ¿pero tú crees que yo voy a venir como un burro sin mecate, entrar ahí en el apartamento sin tener mis suertes de cómo hacerla para que no se dé cuenta? Yo sé . . . , mira, aquí sí hay esos, aquí sí hay esos. No soy como tú, mano. Tú eres un hombre que no sabe nada, ves. No sabes nada. Por eso no tienes chanza con las mujeres tú. Porque si tú tuvieras chanza, y si supieras hablarte a las mujeres, y cómo tratarlas, entonces te llevabas a cualquier mujer que quisieras.

ANDREW: ¿Cómo . . . cómo le haces?

MANUEL: Pues tienes que estudiar, como yo, de ser un hombre así, que tenga un poquito de inteligencia.

ANDREW: Oh, pero no te voy a creer.

MANUEL: ¿Cómo no vas a creer, hombre?

ANDREW: No, tú me estás echando mentiras ahí ... , no ...

MANUEL: ¡No hombre! Déjame ... , mira, mira, mira ...

ANDREW: No, soy como Santo Tomás, ver es creer.

MANUEL: Pues déjale así a un lado. Mira, mira, Chapulín, mira, te voy a contar ... , mira, yo a nadie le he contado mi secreto que tengo yo aquí en ése, cómo hacerle ... cómo conseguir a una muchacha, ves. Pero te voy a decir a ti, nomás para que aprendas tú, y para que cuando tú te encuentres a una que te guste, entonces es cuando tú azotas, así, mano. Pero tienes que ser como yo, no es andar ...

ANDREW: Que si me meto con algún boxeador, voy a ser azotado más pronto que la azoto ...

MANUEL: No, hombre, no. No empieces con eso. Hay que saberlo hacer, y así todo sale bien.

ANDREW: Pues tú ya tienes cuerpo, pero a mí, a un trompazo nomás me hallo desbaratado.

MANUEL: No, no, no te va a desbaratar, hombre. ¿Quién ... ? No va a darse cuenta nadie, ni hay quien sepa nada, hombre.

ANDREW: Ahora tengo yo los golpes que no me fallan.

MANUEL: ¿Cuáles son esos?

ANDREW: El que me da y cuando caiga yo.

MANUEL: Oh, órale, mira nomás, hombre. No hombre, pues no, nadie te va a pegar, ni te van a pescar tampoco.

ANDREW: Pues a ver. ¿Cómo lo haces tú, mano?

MANUEL: Pues mira, te voy a dar consejo, ves.

ANDREW: ¿Cuál es el secreto éste?

MANUEL: Pero el secreto, o el consejo, que te lo voy a dar a ti, no quiero que te lo vayas a pasar a nadie, nomás porque todos van a querer usarlo también.

ANDREW: Oh no, no, no, no ...

MANUEL: Es tuyo, de ahí nomás, hombre.

ANDREW: Oh, yo me callo. Yo me callo la boca.

MANUEL: Nomás que es tuyo, ¿verdad?

ANDREW: Yo soy un hombre muy *callao*, todo lo que digas, aquí se queda.

MANUEL: Ándale, así me gusta. ¡Pónla ahí!

ANDREW: Soy muy macho, muy ...

MANUEL: Anda ... , ¿más macho que las mujeres, verdad?

ANDREW: Más macho que las mujeres, sí . . .

MANUEL: Bueno, bueno, te voy a decir. Mira, bueno, sabes que cuando yo quiero venir a ver a esa muchacha, ves, yo, para saber si está el esposo allí, o no está, (voz baja) le hago como un gato, ¿ves?

ANDREW: ¿Como un cómo?

MANUEL: Como un gato.

ANDREW: ¿Cómo como un gato?

MANUEL: Pues sí, hombre, me paro en la puerta, me paro en la puerta, y le digo, "¡Miau!"

ANDREW: Uh huh.

MANUEL: Y si acaso la gata me contesta, entonces patas pa' arriba pa' entrar pa' adentro luego luego. No me detengo ni . . . ni a resollar, me meto luego luego, brinco a la ventana o a la puerta, lo que sea, pero me meto pa' adentro. Y ya está todo el asunto arreglado, y es que no está el marido allí.

ANDREW: En otras palabras, ¿si tú te paras, y le haces, "Miau," y ella te hace, "Miau" pa' atrás, tú, "Miau" pa' adentro, ¿verdá?

MANUEL: Ah, exactamente, exactamente, exactamente. Ése es el sistema.

ANDREW: ¿Pero cómo le haces si acaso está el marido allí?

MANUEL: Ah pues, entonces no. Mira, no me dejas terminar, déjame terminar primero. Cuando está el marido, entonces la muchacha ésta, ya no es gata.

ANDREW: ¿Ya no es gata?

MANUEL: No, por seguro, se vuelve perra.

ANDREW: ¿Cómo seguro que es perra?

MANUEL: Pues si me hace: "¡Guoof, guoof, guoof!"

ANDREW: Oh, ah, ya la pesqué. Entonces tú te paras allí, y si tú le haces así, le haces, "¡Miau!" ¿Y si no está el marido, te contestan, "¡Miau!" pa' atrás?

MANUEL: ¡*Right*!

ANDREW: ¿Pero si está el marido, te contesta, "Guau, guau, guau"?

MANUEL: Como un perro, sí, ándale. Y entonces cuando oigo el perro, ni me paro a resollar, me arranco a un lado para que no me vaya a pescar, pues. ¿Por qué crees tú que estoy yo todavía vivo?

ANDREW: Y tú, que dijiste, "¿Ya, ya se creyó éste?" No hombre.

MANUEL: ¿No me quieres creer, hombre?

ANDREW: Soy tapado, pero no tan tapado, mano.

MANUEL: ¡Mira! Te lo juro, mano.

ANDREW: Me lo jurarás, pero yo no tengo que creerte. Yo soy como Santo Tomás: ver es creer.

MANUEL: Mira, es un sistema bueno, éste, para ti. Mira, te voy a enseñar. ¿Quieres que te lo pruebe? ¿Quieres que te lo pruebe?

ANDREW: Pues sí.

MANUEL: Bueno, pues, fíjate, allí vamos. Pero fíjate, fíjate muy bien.

ANDREW: Espérate, espérate, espérate. ¿Te vas para allá a hacer como un gato?

MANUEL: Sí.

ANDREW: Pues espérame, yo acá te espero, mano.

MANUEL: Oye, ¿por qué me vas a esperar acá tan lejos?

ANDREW: ¿Pues cómo voy estar lejos?

MANUEL: ¿Pero no quieres aprender?

ANDREW: ¿Y si sale el perro?

MANUEL: ¡No hombre! ¡No hombre! No quieres aprender entonces?

ANDREW: ¡No! Acá te espero. Tú, hazle con el gato allá. Acá estoy listo yo para . . .

MANUEL: Entonces patas para qué son, ¿verdad?

ANDREW: Sí, sí.

MANUEL: Tú eres gallina tú, mano. Eres más gallina que . . . ¡Así nunca vas a llegar a nada, hombre . . . !

ANDREW: Soy hombre precavido; hombre precavido vale por dos.

MANUEL: Oh bueno, pues entonces, pero fíjate. Fíjate bien cómo lo voy a hacer. Y así quiero que cuando tú te conozcas a una . . . Pero no te vayas a tratar de hacerlo como yo, igual, a copiarme, nada de esto. Tú haces tu gato de tu clase, diferente.

ANDREW: No, sí, diferente manera.

MANUEL: Ahí voy yo. Fíjate bien, fíjate . . . allí vamos. . . . (Voz baja.) Bien . . . ahí vamos . . . juntito a la puerta, a ver . . . Miauuuu.

VOICE: Miauuu.

MANUEL: ¿Lo creíste? Bueno, con permiso, ahí voy. (Voz baja.) (Tac tac.) Con permiso . . . ahorita vengo.

ANDREW: ¡Sinvergüenza! ¡Mal amigo!

MANUEL: (Se oyen pitos bajos y labios besándose.)

ANDREW: Te he de detener, te he de detener ...

MANUEL: (Se oyen pitos bajos y labios besándose.)

ANDREW: Yo no, yo no, yo soy hombre honrado.

MANUEL: (Se oyen besos estrepitosos.)

ANDREW: ¡Qué bárbaro! No, no, no ...

MANUEL: ¡Ayyyyy *whooooo*! (Todavía se oyen los besos.)

ANDREW: Eso no, no está bien eso, hombre ...

MANUEL: ¡Ummmm *whoooo* hummmm! (Todavía se oyen los besos.) ¡Ahhhhhh!

ANDREW: Allí viene ...

MANUEL: ¡Hijo! ¿Qué tal ehhh? ¿Qué tal, manito? ¿Cómo te dejé en el ojo? ¿Pelón o flojo?

ANDREW: No hombre, ya no me hables tú.

MANUEL: ¿Cómo ya no? ¿No me lo creíste?

ANDREW: No, no ...

MANUEL: ¡Fíjate! Nada más que eso, quiero que sepas una cosa ...

ANDREW: A mí la casta mujer es todo en el mundo, ¿me entiendes? Con la casada, uno no se mete.

MANUEL: Oye, espérate una cosa, mano. Fíjate, mírate, yo andaba quebrado, también, y ella me dio uno de a veinte.

ANDREW: ¿Hasta dinero le sacaste?

MANUEL: Me dio veinte dólares para que fuera a traer algo que cenar.

ANDREW: ¡Qué bárbaro, mano!

MANUEL: Pues no, no hice nada todavía, mano. Voy a traer algo que cenar. Así es para que cuando tú te consigas algo, aprende, aprende, pero tú tienes que tratarlas como macho, nada de eso de que (Voz fementida.) " ... de que por favor ... " Lo pides: "Azótame con veinte!", y luego luego: o diez, quince, veinte dólares, y luego. Bueno, con permiso, ahorita vengo, voy aquí al restaurante de la esquina, eh. Ahi te miro.

ANDREW: Lárgate.

MANUEL: Vamos. (Se oyen pasos.)

ANDREW: ¡Mantenido! ¡Sinvergüenza! ¡Vas a ver cómo te va a ir! Ahorita yo aquí me voy a quedar. Cuando venga el marido de ella, te voy a rajar todo. ¡A ver cómo te va a ir! Yo no sé qué, qué puntadas de hombre, que pa' meterse con una mujer casada, hombre que ... que nomás se para, y como cualquier cosa, y le hace "¡Miauu!" y ya, se quedó todo *arreglao*.

VOICE: Miauuuu. (Voz femenina.)

ANDREW: No, no es cierto. No, no puedo, no. Además, yo soy novio, mano. No, no, ahí se para, luego diría el marido que ahí se para un individuo, que se para allí en la puerta y que hace "¡Miau!"

VOICE: ¡Miauuuu!

ANDREW: (Muy tímido.) Miau.

VOICE: Miau.

ANDREW: Voy pa' adentro *fiao*.

VOICE: (Muy baja.) Miau.

ANDREW: (Voz de tonto.) Ahorita vengo yo.

MANUEL: Ah, que el tonto ya se fue. Ah, que ése es más bruto que mandado hacer. Ese hombre nunca va a llegar a nada porque es muy tímido, muy tímido, y tiene miedo a todo. Bueno, aquél no ... , a veces que, por no hablar ¡*whooo*! A lo mejor se queda callado toda la tarde. Bueno ¿quién se lo manda?, si nunca va a tener la suerte que tengo yo. Que tiene que tener un poquito de acceso para poder operar como yo lo hago. ¡Chihuahua! Pues vale más usar el *code* porque a lo mejor ya llegó el marido. Hay que andar precavido. Vale más hablarle: ¡Miauuu! ... Ay ¡jijo! ¡Miauuuu! ¡Miauuuuuu!

ANDREW: ¡Guoof! ¡guoof! ¡guooooff!

MANUEL: ¡Ay! ¡Vámonos, vámonos! (Se oyen patas correr por las tablas.)

The Lover

Good afternoon, ladies and gentlemen. We are going to have the pleasure of presenting you a beautiful show which we hope will be pleasing to each and every one of you.

First we are going to present, before going on with the show, a cute skit between myself, your servant, Manuel Mendoza, and that fellow, the Grasshopper. We hope that it will please you, and if by chance we should make some mistake, we would like you to pardon us. And ... hopefully you will enjoy it. With your permission, eh, here we go.

ANDREW: Hey, Manolo! Manolo, I'm looking for you, man!

MANUEL: What do you mean, you're looking for me?

ANDREW: When are you going to ... to sell me that thing that you carry with you?

MANUEL: What do you mean? Sell what? Have they told you now that I'm going around stealing?

ANDREW: No, no, no, no, but, but you have something. I want to learn ... to see how to treat the girls.

MANUEL: Ohhhh! Get off it!

ANDREW: *Ay*, all the time you ... the girls all the time, they fall for you right away, and they don't want to fall for me.

MANUEL: No, look, brother, you better dig it, bro', look, your personality and looks, and mine, my personality and looks. How could you expect them to pay more attention to you than to me? Aren't I more charming than you?

ANDREW: Why? What do you have that I don't have? (Laughing.)

MANUEL: Ah, all right, all right. All right! Well, I'm better looking, isn't it true?

ANDREW: When I was real little didn't they tell me all the time that I was real cute ... ?

MANUEL: Didn't you tell me the other day that they used to use you for a Baby Jesus in the Christmas Nativity scenes?

ANDREW: Well, yes, also ...

MANUEL: And now?

ANDREW: Well now, I don't know why they don't ... , it's something that you carry. Do you carry something?

MANUEL: No man, it's nothing, it isn't anything ...

ANDREW: You carry some kind of thing, because ...

MANUEL: No, look, let me tell you, brother, look, all you have to know is ... how to treat women. Women like for you to flatter them. You have to ... treat them ... with a lot ... , how shall I say it? Tell them pretty words, sweet words. Do you know any sweet words?

ANDREW: Sure I do ... , of course ...

MANUEL: Let's see, toss me out a few sweet words.

ANDREW: Lollipops, caramels ...

MANUEL: Whoo! No man! No man, no, no, no ...

ANDREW: There can't be any sweeter than those.

MANUEL: I'm not talking about that kind of sweets, lunk-head. I'm telling you about another kind of ... , the words that I'm talking about ... , I'll tell you, they're flattering words.

ANDREW: Like what?

MANUEL: Don't you know what flattering words are?

ANDREW: Well ... *flattering* ... , well, *flattering* ... , I don't know what *flatterings* are ...

MANUEL: Bless me! You really are very illiterate, aren't you, bro'? *Chihuahua*! Bro', you don't even know how to treat a woman, right?

ANDREW: Well ... well, you just speak to her ...

MANUEL: No ... , you have to ... , well, let her have her way all the time, and ... Look, look, haven't you seen me with that blond that lives on the corner?

ANDREW: Which one?

MANUEL: The one that's been living right on the corner, in the corner house, there, on the other side of the first apartment, in the second apartment. The blond with the hair ... , that one that has a body like a Coca-Cola bottle.

ANDREW: That one ... , what's her name? Do you know her?

MANUEL: Do I know her! Whoo! Yes, she's my real deal; I'm her big daddy.

ANDREW: You ... you're going out with her?

MANUEL: I'm the real deal that ... Well, there isn't anyone else, she doesn't love anyone but me. I'm her "*number one.*"

ANDREW: And you are going with her?

MANUEL: Hey! What can I tell you? Look here, haven't you seen me?

ANDREW: And she knows about this?

MANUEL: What do you mean, does she know? Well!

ANDREW: No, well, she probably doesn't know ...

MANUEL: Of course she knows; for sure she knows. She knows for sure!

ANDREW: Well, it could be a lie ...

MANUEL: I'm a god for her. I can treat her any old way I feel like, and she'll obey me, man, because ... she is in love with me! She's crazy about me, you understand? She's so in love with me!

ANDREW: And her husband knows, too?

MANUEL: What? Her husband? Who, him?

ANDREW: The boxer?

MANUEL: Who?!

ANDREW: The boxer.

MANUEL: Oh, the boxer. Oh, him, he seems soft to me, that boxer. That guy's "*punch-drunk.*"

ANDREW: He's "*punch*" who?

MANUEL: He's "*punch-drunk.*"

ANDREW: Well, that's how you're going to end up when he's finished with you.

MANUEL: No, no, don't you believe it. No, don't you believe it. No, but he'd have to get real lucky to get hip to me.

ANDREW: Next you're going to tell me that you go in and out of there whenever you feel like it.

MANUEL: Ah, bro', when I feel like it, I go there, and I go in, and I come out of there.

ANDREW: Look, look, bro', some day you are going to go in, and you're not going to come out, bro'.

MANUEL: Why?

ANDREW: Come on, dig it, you'll see, because the boxer is going to get wise to you, and he's going to give you a licking. He's going to use you for a "*punching bag.*"

MANUEL: No, no, no, mister, look, but do you think that I'm going to go wandering in there like a donkey on the loose, go into the apartment without having my ways of doing it so that he won't find out? I know ... , look, there are ways, there are ways. I'm not like you, bro'. You're a man that doesn't know anything, see. You don't know anything. That's why you don't have a chance with women. Because if you were to have an opportunity, and if you knew how to talk to women and how to treat them, then you could have any woman that you wanted.

ANDREW: How ... how do you do it?

MANUEL: Well you have to study, like me, to be such a man, one who has a little intelligence.

ANDREW: Oh, but I'm not going to believe you.

MANUEL: What do you mean you're not going to believe?

ANDREW: No, you're just telling me lies ... , no ...

MANUEL: No man! Let me ... , look, look, look ...

ANDREW: No, I'm like Saint Thomas, seeing is believing.

MANUEL: Okay, let's leave him out of it. Look, look, Chapulín, look, I am going to tell you ... , look, I have never told anyone about my secret that I have about this ... , about how to get a girl, see. But I'm going to tell you, just so that when you run into one that you like, that'll be when you strike, just like that, bro'. But you have to be like me, you can't go around ...

ANDREW: If I mess around with some boxer, I'm going to be hit sooner than I make a hit with her.

MANUEL: No, man, no. Don't start out with that. You have to know how to do it, and that way everything will come out all right.

ANDREW: Well, you're a big guy, but me, one punch would flatten me.

MANUEL: No, no, you're not going to get flattened, man. Who ... ? No one is going to notice, nobody knows nothing, man.

ANDREW: Now, I have some punches that won't fail me.

MANUEL: Which ones are those?

ANDREW: The one that he hits me with and the one I'll get when I fall down and hit the ground.

MANUEL: Oh, come off it, man. No, man, nobody's going to hit you, and they're not going to find out about you, either.

ANDREW: Okay, we'll see. How do you do it, bro'?

MANUEL: Look, I'm going to give you advice, see.

ANDREW: What is this secret?

MANUEL: But the secret, or the advice, that I'm going to give you, I don't want you to pass it on to anybody, just because everybody is going to want to use it, too.

ANDREW: Oh no, no, no, no ...

MANUEL: It's for you and no one else, man.

ANDREW: Oh I'll shut up. I'll keep my mouth shut.

MANUEL: It's just for you, right?

ANDREW: I'm a very close-mouthed man, everything that you say, it all stays right here.

MANUEL: There you go, that's how I like it. Put it there!

ANDREW: I'm very *macho*, very ...

MANUEL: There you go, more *macho* than the women, right?

ANDREW: More *macho* than the women, yes ...

MANUEL: All right, all right, I'm going to tell you. Look, all right, you know when I want to come see that girl, see, I, in order to see if the husband is there or not, (whispering) I make like a cat, see?

ANDREW: Like a what?

MANUEL: Like a cat.

ANDREW: Well, yes, man, I stop by the door, I stand by the door, and I say, "Meow!"

ANDREW: Uh huh.

MANUEL: And if by chance the female cat answers me, so then it's up on my feet to go inside right away. I don't wait for anything, nor do I take a deep breath, I go in right away, I jump to the window or to the door, whatever, but I go inside. And then the whole deal is set up, and it's that her husband isn't there.

ANDREW: In other words, if you stop, and you go, "Meow", and she goes, "Meow" back, you, "Meow" on inside, right?

MANUEL: Ah, exactly, exactly, exactly. That's the system.

ANDREW: But how do you do it if by chance the husband is there?

MANUEL: Ah, well, then you don't. Look, you're not letting me finish, let me finish first. When the husband is there, then this girl, now she's not a cat.

ANDREW: Then she's not a cat?

MANUEL: No, for sure, she turns into a bitch.

ANDREW: What do you mean that for sure she's a bitch?

MANUEL: I know, if she goes, "Woof, woof, woof!"

ANDREW: Oh, ah, now I've figured it out. So you stand there, and if you go like this, you go, "Meow!" And if the husband isn't there, they answer you, "Meow!" back?

MANUEL: *Right!*

ANDREW: But if the husband is there, she answers you, "bow, wow, wow"?

MANUEL: Like a dog, yes, that's right. And so then when I hear the dog, I don't even stop to take a breath, I get out of there fast so that he won't get wise to me. Why do you think that I'm still alive?

ANDREW: And you, what do you think, do you think that I believe this? No, man.

MANUEL: You don't want to believe me, man?

ANDREW: I'm not too bright, but I'm not that stupid, bro'.

MANUEL: Look! I swear that it's true, bro'.

ANDREW: You can swear it to me, but I don't have to believe you. I'm like Saint Thomas: seeing is believing.

MANUEL: Look, it's a good system, that one, for you. Look, I'm going to show you. Do you want me to prove it to you? Do you want me to prove it?

ANDREW: Yes, sure.

MANUEL: All right, pay attention, we're going over there. But pay attention, pay real good attention.

ANDREW: Wait a minute, wait, wait a minute, you're going over there to make like a cat?

MANUEL: Yes.

ANDREW: Well, wait a minute, I'll wait for you here, bro'.

MANUEL: Listen, why are you going to wait for me here so far away?

ANDREW: How do you mean I'm going to be far away?

MANUEL: But don't you want to learn?

ANDREW: And if the dog comes out?

MANUEL: No man! No man! So then you don't want to learn?

ANDREW: No! I'll wait for you here. You make it with the cat over there. Here I'm ready to ...

MANUEL: So then what are feet for, right? [i.e. for running.]

ANDREW: Yes, yes.

MANUEL: You're chicken, bro'. You're more chicken than ... You're never going to get anywhere like that, man ... !

ANDREW: I'm a cautious man; a cautious man is worth two.

MANUEL: Oh, all right, but pay attention. Pay close attention to how I'm going to do it. And that's how I want you to do it when you meet one. But don't you go trying to do it like I do, the same way, to copy me, none of that. You do your cat in your own style, different.

ANDREW: No, yes, in a different way.

MANUEL: Here I go. Pay good attention, real good attention ... there we go (Whispering.) ... All right ... there we go ... right up next to the door, let's see ... Meowwwww.

VOICE: Meowww.

MANUEL: Didn't I tell you, do you believe it? All right, with your (Whispering.) permission, I'm going now. (Knock knock.) With your permission ... I'm coming right now.

ANDREW: Shameless one! False friend!

MANUEL: (Soft whistling, smacking kisses.)

ANDREW: I'm going to have to stop you, I'm going to have to stop you ...

MANUEL: (Soft whistling, smacking kisses.)

ANDREW: No, not me, not me, I'm an honorable man.

MANUEL: (Loud smooching.)

ANDREW: How awful! No, no, no ...

MANUEL: (Still smacking.) Ayyyyy whooooo!

ANDREW: Not this, this is no good, man ...

MANUEL: Ummmm whoooo hummmm! (Still smacking.) Ahhhhhh!

ANDREW: There he comes ...

MANUEL: Son of a ... ! What about that, ehhh? How about it, bro'? How'd that grab you?

ANDREW: No man, don't even talk to me now.

MANUEL: What do you mean, not now? Didn't you believe me?

ANDREW: No, no ...

MANUEL: Look! It's just this, I want you to know something ...

ANDREW: To me the chaste woman is everything in the world, understand? One doesn't mess around with a married woman.

MANUEL: Listen, wait just a minute, bro'. Look, I was broke, too, and she gave me a twenty.

ANDREW: You've even gotten money out of her?

MANUEL: She gave me twenty dollars so that I could go get something to bring back for dinner.

ANDREW: How awful, bro'.

MANUEL: Well, no, I still haven't done anything yet, bro'. I'm going to go bring something back for dinner. So when you get a woman for yourself, learn, learn; you have to treat them like a *macho*, none of this (effeminate voice.) " ... oh, please ... " You ask for it: "Hit me with twenty!"; and right away: or ten, fifteen, twenty dollars, and right away. All right, excuse me, I'll be right back, I'm going down to the restaurant on the corner, eh. I'll see you.

ANDREW: Get out of here.

MANUEL: I'm going. (Manuel heard walking away.)

ANDREW: Gigolo! Scoundrel! You'll see how it's going to come down for you! Right now I'm going to stay right here. When her husband comes, I'm going to spill everything. Just see how it's going to go for you! I don't know how a guy has the nerve to mess around with a married woman, a man that

... that he just goes up, just like any old thing, and he goes "Meoww!" and presto, everything is all arranged.

VOICE: Meowwww (Feminine voice from off-stage.)

ANDREW: This can't be happening. No, I can't do it, no. Besides, I'm engaged. No, no, if I go any closer, then her husband will say, "There's some guy hanging around here, he's standing there at the door, and he's going 'Meow!'"

VOICE: Meowwww!

ANDREW: (Hesitant, timid.) Meow.

VOICE: Meow.

ANDREW: I'm going inside.

VOICE: (Very low.) Meow.

ANDREW: (Foolish tone.) I'm coming right now.

MANUEL: Ah, the fool already left. Ah, he's such an idiot. That man is never going to amount to anything because he's very timid, real shy, and he's afraid of everything. Well, that guy ... , sometimes, by not speaking, whooo! He'll probably not say a word all afternoon. Well, who knows, he's never going to have luck like mine. You have to be a little bit forceful in order to operate like I do. Chihuahua! Well I had better use the code because her husband might have come home already. One has to be careful. I'd better call to her: Meowww! ... Ay, son of a ... ! Meoowwww! Meooowwwwww!

ANDREW: Woof! Woof! Woooff!

MANUEL: Ay! I'm getting the hell out of here! (Sound of running off stage.)

Manuel

That's the end of the skit. Of course the husband wasn't really home, it's just that Chapulín knew, you see, and he was barking like a dog.

Andrew

There was one skit that we originally had done during the Depression that was about the hard times, about how hard it was to eat or survive. Mamá was the one who made it up. It's called "El adivino," "The Fortuneteller."

El adivino[2]

ANDREW: Ándale, Juana, hombre ¿qué vamos a hacer? ¡Piensa! Porque yo tengo mucha hambre.

JUANITA: Yo no sé, yo no sé nada. Pero fíjate, fíjate una cosa, te sale si te buscas trabajo. ¿Qué vamos a hacer? Ya me muero de hambre, la mera verdad; ya no aguanto más.

ANDREW: Luego a mí, pero sigo buscando, y ... no hay nada.

JUANITA: ¿Fuiste a la Plaza?

ANDREW: Tú siquiera tienes algo de gordura, pero mira, yo voy desaparecer, mano ...

JUANITA: Pero tú me dijiste en la mañana que ibas allá a la Plaza.

ANDREW: Pues fui a la Plaza. Pues allí en la Plaza ¿qué hay en la Plaza?

JUANITA: Pues, yo no sé, pues pide limosna.

ANDREW: Pues, "pide limosna", pues ¿quién me va a dar limosna por esta ropa?

JUANITA: (Voz aturdida.) Ay, pues yo no sé, yo no sé ...

ANDREW: (Voz tonta.) Pues, todo el tiempo hay que salir a la calle bien vestido.

JUANITA: Pues ¡piensa algo! Tú nomás lo dejas a mí ...

ANDREW: No, pues, tú eres la cabeza, tú me dijiste que eres el *brain*.

JUANITA: Pues sí, pero tú tienes que comprender, tú tienes que ayudarme a mí también, yo sola no puedo hacer todo.

ANDREW: Pues piensa, piensa, piensa, tú dijiste que tú eres la cabeza, y tú vas a decir qué.

JUANITA: ¡Ah! ¡Ahhhh! Ya se me vino una idea. A ver, déjame verte ...

ANDREW: ¿Qué vas a hacer? Yo no voy a morir, oye, eso no ...

JUANITA: No, hombre, no, hombre, ... no, hombre. Date vuelta, vólteate, vólteate ... Oye, sí.

ANDREW: Tampoco me puedes vestir de mujer.

JUANITA: No, espérate, no te ... ¡espérate! Déjame, no sabes ni ...

ANDREW: De mujer yo no voy a vestir.

JUANITA: No te voy a ... , no más estoy viéndote, a ver si sirves para eso ...

ANDREW: ¿Pa' qué?

JUANITA: No, no, hombre. Mira, vamos a hacer una cosa. Estoy pensando que ... podemos decir que tú vienes de la India.

A como que, mira, tú tienes esta nariz, que te queda muy bien, el aspecto que tienes como del indio.

ANDREW: ¿Que los indios son narizones como yo? O ¿qué?

JUANITA: No indios de acá, es jindú, no indio.

ANDREW: Es una nariz de marca, no cualquiera la tiene, señora.

JUANITA: Bueno, pues sí, pero mira, podemos hacer una cosa. Yo puedo decir que te traje de la India, hombre . . .

ANDREW: ¿Que ahorita de la India . . .

JUANITA: De la India . . .

ANDREW: ¿Y soy yo indio? o ¿qué?

JUANITA: ¡Jindú! Indio no, hombre. Jindú. De esos que adivinan. Eres *Hindu*. un adivino.

ANDREW: Oh ¿yo soy adivino?

JUANITA: Ah hah.

ANDREW: Bueno.

JUANITA: Nomás, mira, espérame tantito, no más te traigo una sábana, y te tapo los ojos . . .

ANDREW: ¿Una sábana? ¿Pues qué . . . ?

JUANITA: Pos pa' enredarte la cabeza, pa' hacerte un turbante.

ANDREW: ¿Que me vas a vestir de papalote? O ¿qué?

JUANITA: No, mira, déjame, déjame traer la sábana, yo te explico. Mira, ves, y así: mira, a cualquier persona que venga, le podemos cobrar. Como que yo te traje, ves, y que tú adivinas todo lo que quiera saber, y todo; así les sacamos, y sí vamos a comer siquiera. Ay, mira, hay una fonda muy buena, y venden unos tamales, y todo, y ya me muero de hambre, eh?

ANDREW: ¿Y qué quieres? ¿Qué vamos a adivinar? Yo no sé adivinar nada.

JUANITA: Pues si salen mentiras, hombre ¿a cómo lo saben?

ANDREW: ¿Yo, mentiritas?

JUANITA: ¡Puras mentiras! Ahí, si dicen una cosa, tú diles lo contrario. Tú sabes, pura mentira. ¿Cómo se darán cuenta? Ya la cosa es que paguen.

ANDREW: Ah, bueno. Está bueno. Pa' mentiras no me digas a mí, tú sabes que yo soy bueno pa' mentiras. ¡Que bárbaro!

JUANITA: Bueno, nomás cuando ya paguen, entonces ahí diles . . . , antes no.

ANDREW: Pues todo el tiempo ando echando mentiras.

JUANITA: Ah bueno, está bueno. Entonces, espérame tantito. (Se oyen ruidos.) Mira, aquí está ya. Mira, déjame ponerte. ¡Pero no te la vayas a quitar!

ANDREW: No, hombre, no me la quito.

JUANITA: Mira, te miras muy bien.

ANDREW: ¿Me miro como un marajàn?

JUANITA: Como un maharajàn, ¡*maharajah*!

ANDREW: Pues yo nunca me he rajado, soy de Jalisco.

JUANITA: No, no te dije de nacionalidad. Ahorita tú eres marajà. No te vayas a decir eres de Jalisco, porque entonces eches tú todo a perder. Vienes de . . . , de Marajàn.

ANDREW: De guisa.

JUANITA: No, no, ¿qué de guisa? No de nada. ¡Mira! ¿Quieres comer?

ANDREW: Yo sí quiero.

JUANITA: ¿Entonces?

ANDREW: Bueno, soy marajà.

JUANITA: Bueno, eres marajà.

ANDREW: (Voz baja de resignación.) Soy marajà.

JUANITA: Y te voy a poner este turbante, y te voy a tener que tapar los ojos. Pa' que sí se vea mejor. Te adivinas con los ojos cerrados.

ANDREW: ¿Con los ojos cerraos?

JUANITA: Sí.

ANDREW: Pa' echar mucha mentira, sí, está bueno, sí.

JUANITA: Porque si adivinas con los ojos abiertos, luego te han de conocer.

ANDREW: Pues sí, es cierto.

JUANITA: Porque te pueden conocer, hombre. Tú siempre has sido muy bien conocido.

ANDREW: No, está bien.

JUANITA: Así es que, tapándote los ojos, y con éste . . . , según vienes, con lo que te puse, así ya. Ya pareces uno de esos jindús. Así es que . . . a la primera que cae.

ANDREW: ¿Cómo que parezco uno de esos otros? ¿Cómo es . . . ?

JUANITA: De esos jindús. ¿Cómo de esos otros? ¡Hombre! ¡De esos jindús!

ANDREW: Oh, bueno, pues cuídate de lo que estás hablando.

JUANITA: No, pero te pareces uno de esos jindús, dije.

ANDREW: Oh, bueno.

JUANITA: Jindús, ¿*okay*?

ANDREW: Jindús, ya sé.

JUANITA: Pero, pues, oh, sí, pues nadie pasa por aquí. ¡Ah! Allá viene una, espérate, parece que ni trae dinero la señora esa, pero ...

ANDREW: ¿Que me tape los ojos?

JUANITA: ¡Sí, hombre! ¡Pronto! ¡Ándale!

ANDREW: Espérate, espérate, tengo que ponérmela.

JUANITA: Pero acuérdate, ¡no te vayas a meter la pata!

ANDREW: No, no meto la pata.

JUANITA: ¡No hables tú nada!

ANDREW: No hablo nada.

JUANITA: Porque ya te conozco.

ANDREW: Bueno, pues ... uh ...

JUANITA: Acuérdate, tienes hambre ¿verdad?

ANDREW: Bueno, pues, pico cerrado.

JUANITA: *Okay.* ... Señora, señora ¿para dónde va Ud., señora?

MARÍA: Pues, aquí ando ... caminando dando la vuelta ... , sí.

JUANITA: Caminando, sí. Pues, mire señora, yo no más quiero decirle, mire, ¿ve Ud. a este hombre que está aquí?

MARÍA: Mire no más ...

JUANITA: Qué raro ¿verdad?

MARÍA: Sí, sí, se ve raro.

JUANITA: Fíjese bien qué raro. Muy raro.

MARÍA: Bastante raro.

JUANITA: Es un maharajá.

MARÍA: Oh, ¿es maharajá, adivino?

JUANITA: Es un jindú.

MARÍA: Ah, es jindú. Son los mejores.

JUANITA: Apenas lo traje.

MARÍA: Dicen que son los mejores adivinos.

JUANITA: ¿Verdad?

MARÍA: Sí.

JUANITA: Sí, y me costó mucho dinero traerlo.

MARÍA: ¿Y cobra mucho por adivinar, por decirme alguna cosa que yo quiero saber?

JUANITA: No, mire Ud., señora, como estamos comenzando ... no más puede darnos ... pos unos ... , bueno, por ser Ud. ¿Cómo anda de dinero? ¿No trae dinerito? ¿O no trae?

MARÍA: Pues, no traigo ni mucho ni poquito.

JUANITA: Bueno, mire, este marajá es muy, muy, muy caritativo.

MARÍA: Mire nomás.

JUANITA: No, mire, no nos entiende, ve. No habla.

MARÍA: ¿No habla?

JUANITA: No, *I mean*, sí habla, pero como está concentrando ahorita, no más con el puro pensamiento.

MARÍA: Ah, sí, ah ...

JUANITA: Así es que le cobramos ... así es que le cobramos cincuenta centavos.

MARÍA: Oh, oiga, pues está muy caro.

JUANITA: ¿Muy caro?

MARÍA: Oh, sí.

JUANITA: Porque no hemos comido ... , (Casi un susurro o lloriqueo.) ay ...

MARÍA: Oh ¿no han comido?

ANDREW: (Mascullando.) Por todo quieren un peso, ¿verdad?

JUANITA: Oh, no ... sí, quiero decir que ... porque no hemos conocido, conocido mucho aquí, no sé qué se me salió, pero no hemos conocido mucho aquí, y apenas llegamos en el barco. ¿En cuál llegamos, eh, tú?

MARÍA: Oh ¿vienen de la India?

JUANITA: ¡Ah! Espérese.

ANDREW: En el *Mississippi*.

JUANITA: Ándale, en el *Mississippi*.

MARÍA: Ohhh, el *Mississippi*.

JUANITA: Ándale, *on the Mississippi River*.

MARÍA: Oh, bueno.

JUANITA: Así es que, nomás que trabajamos los dos.

ANDREW: No más que se flateó en el camino, y ...

JUANITA: (Al Chapulín.) Ya, ¡está bueno, ya! (A María.) Sí, así es que si Ud. quiere ... ?

MARÍA: ¿Y ... se le pregunto ya?

JUANITA: Oh, sí, nomás, pero tengo que dormirlo primero.

MARÍA: Oh bueno, pos, que le espero pa' que lo duermas ...

JUANITA: Yo lo duermo a él. A ver ...

ANDREW: A lo mejor me dará un palo.

JUANITA: Ah ... ha ha, ya sabe Ud. que está medio ... está medio adormecido, no se fije de lo que está diciendo.

MARÍA: ¿Desvaría?

JUANITA: Ándale, sí, porque tiene que concentrar primero.

MARÍA: Ah, bueno.

JUANITA: A ver ... (Se oyen las manos raspándose.) ¿Shiva?

ANDREW: ¿Uh?

JUANITA: ¿Shiva?

ANDREW: Meeeeeee. (Se oye un balido como de chiva.)

JUANITA: (Riéndose.) Así ... así comenzamos.

MARÍA: Oh ¿es así? ¿De veras?

JUANITA: Así comenzamos. ¿Verdad que es raro? (Todavía se oyen las manos raspándose.)

MARÍA: Sí, sí, es raro.

JUANITA: ¿Maraján? ¿Maraján?

ANDREW: ¿Mahara *who*?

JUANITA: Ya, ya está, ya mero. Ya mero. ¿Ya te estás durmiendo?

ANDREW: (Voz sepulcral.) Ya me estoy durmiendo.

JUANITA: Calamalaya ...

ANDREW: ¿La hija de quién?

JUANITA: Ah, ah, así comienza. Baba Can ...

ANDREW: ¡Uyyy!

JUANITA: ¡Caramalaya!

ANDREW: Kalamazoo.

MARÍA: Oh ¿Kalamazoo ... ?

JUANITA: Ya está dormido. Ya está.

ANDREW: Detroit, Michigan.

MARÍA: Ya, ya se revolvió a la India con Michigan.

JUANITA: No eso, eso no. No, no, no. Sí, porque como él trabaja no tanto en eso, ve, así trabaja: tiene que revolverse así. A veces dice Detroit, a veces dice Mississippi, así. Pero no lo perturbo. ¿Ya estás dormido?

ANDREW: Ya mero.

JUANITA: ¿Bien dormido? ¡Ya estás bien dormido! ¡Ya quiero que estés bien dormido!

ANDREW: Ummm ummm.

JUANITA: ¡Ya!

ANDREW: Ya. Ya estoy dormido, hombre.

JUANITA: Ya, *okay*. Ya se durmió. Así. Con confianza . . . Ah, perdóneme, los cincuenta centavos primero. Gracias. Marajá, te va a preguntar.

ANDREW: A ver, señora, . . . a ver, señora ¿qué quiere Ud. saber?

MARÍA: Quiero saber exactamente . . . , porque voy a sacarme un boleto de lotería, y quiero saber . . .

ANDREW: Bueno. ¿Y eso a mí, qué me importa?

MARÍA: ¡Oiga! Pos entonces . . .

JUANITA: Espérese, espérese, espérese un poco, se desvarió un poco, espérese Ud. nomás.

MARÍA: Pero Ud. me dijo que . . .

JUANITA: Está concentrando. ¡Espérese . . . !

ANDREW: Uh upppp . . . uh . . . pregúntame, pregúntame.

JUANITA: Pregúntele pues. Es que desvaría de tanta presión que tiene ahorita, de tanta magia . . .

MARÍA: Ohhhh.

JUANITA: Se hace maje . . . , no, *I mean* magio, magio, no, es magio.

MARÍA: ¿Es magio, o maje?

JUANITA: Magio, magio.

MARÍA: Magio, voy a comprar un boleto de lotería, y quiero saber la hora, y el número, y a qué hora va a salir. Porque yo necesito saber rápidamente . . . del boleto de lotería. Primeramente la hora, los números . . . , y quiero saber también cuándo.

JUANITA: Cuándo sale. Uh huh, *okay*.

ANDREW: (Mascullando.) Y quiere saber cuándo.

JUANITA: ¿Tú sabes, maharajá? Contéstale a la señora lo que te está preguntando.

ANDREW: Muy bien.

JUANITA: (Voz amenazadora.) ¡No tengo que repetírtelo, porque ya lo sabes!

ANDREW: Ummmgh. Señora, se va Ud. a las ocho de la mañana.

MARÍA: Me voy a las ocho de la mañana.

JUANITA: A las ocho, acuérdese ¡a las ocho!

MARÍA: A las meras ocho.

ANDREW: Compra Ud. el número cinco cuatro, cuatro cinco ocho.

MARÍA: Cinco cuatro . . .

JUANITA: Cuatro cinco . . .

MARÍA: Cuatro cinco ocho.

JUANITA: ... Ocho. ¡Acuérdese!

ANDREW: Lo compra.

MARÍA: Lo compro.

ANDREW: Se lo lleva para la casa.

MARÍA: Me lo llevo para la casa.

ANDREW: Cuando llegue a la casa ...

MARÍA: Cuando llegue a la casa ...

ANDREW: ... Lo agarra ...

MARÍA: ... Lo agarro ...

ANDREW: Lo agarra en las manos.

MARÍA: Lo agarro en mis manos.

ANDREW: Lo hace Ud. una bolita.

MARÍA: Lo hago una bolita.

ANDREW: Se lo pone Ud. en la boca.

MARÍA: Me lo pongo en la boca.

ANDREW: Agarra Ud. un vaso de agua.

MARÍA: Agarro un vaso de agua.

ANDREW: Y se lo toma.

MARÍA: Me lo tomo.

ANDREW: Y mañana sale.

MARÍA: ¡Viejo majadero! ¡Hablador! ¡Mentiroso!

JUANITA: No, no, espérese, espérese tantito. No se enoje, es que ... , es que ... , hubo ... , espéreme, espéreme. ¡Oye, maharajá!

ANDREW: Ummm.

JUANITA: Mire, ¿sabe qué? Pregúntele otra pregunta, mejor.

MARÍA: Bueno ...

JUANITA: Es mejor que le pregunte otra, porque ... como no está completamente en sí ahorita. Se concentró ... , se concentró demasiado.

MARÍA: Pues, dígale que se concentre no tan demasiado.

JUANITA: Ah bueno, sí. Pero, pos, ay vale cincuenta centavos más.

MARÍA: Bueno, sí se los doy.

JUANITA: Pos démelos primero. (Al Chapulín.) ¡Oye!

ANDREW: Oigo.

JUANITA: Aquí está la señora. Es la misma señora, y quiere preguntarte algo. Te va a hacer unas preguntas ¡y vale más que las contestes bien!

ANDREW: Ah, bueno.

JUANITA: ¡Porque si no ... !

ANDREW: ¡Bueno!

JUANITA: ¡ ... Te va a ir muy bien!

ANDREW: ¡Uuuuyyy!

JUANITA: *Okay*, ya te dije.

ANDREW: ¿Qué es lo que quiere saber?

MARÍA: Este ...

JUANITA: ¡Eh! Él ... Ahora le voy a ... Eh! He ... decir una cosa. Ud. pregúntele a él ... algo de su vida ... que quiere saber. Así, mire, para que Ud ... ¿Ud. no le cree por lo que dijo ahorita, verdad?

MARÍA: No ...

JUANITA: Ah, bueno. Mire, le voy a demostrar que el Marajú, el Maharajú ...

MARÍA: Ah hah ...

JUANITA: Bueno, le digo Marajú y Marajá. ¿Verdad? Tiene dos nombres.

MARÍA: Sí.

JUANITA: Marajú y Marajá, las dos cosas.

ANDREW: (Cantando en voz baja.) El se fue a verla, y no me quiso llevar ... (Juanita le da un golpe en la espalda.)

JUANITA: Estás dormido. Acuérdate ¡estás dormido! ¿Sabe Ud. qué? Como se concentra en la Baba Cuba ...

MARÍA: ¿Y le puedo preguntar? ¿Cualquier otra pregunta que no sea la misma?

JUANITA: Sí, sí. Ah hah. Puede preguntarle. Dígale, fíjese, pregúntele Ud. si él sabe de su pasado, o su presente, o algo así.

MARÍA: Bueno, oh, ya le entendí. Pues, eso a mí me urge mucho, también.

JUANITA: Sí, pos sí. Pos sí ...

MARÍA: Bueno, quiero que me diga de mi pasado, y mi presente, y de mi futuro.

ANDREW: ¿Ud. quiere saber de su pasado, de su presente, y de su past, futuro?

MARÍA: Pero Ud. me tiene que contestar, porque Ud. me va adivinar a mí.

ANDREW: ¿Ud. quiere que yo le adivine algo de su vida, en otras palabras?

MARÍA: Sí.

ANDREW: Muy bien.

JUANITA: ¡Acuérdate! De su vida.

ANDREW: Señora, Ud. tiene una hija.

MARÍA: Sí, la tengo.

JUANITA: ¿Ud. tiene hija?

MARÍA: Sí.

JUANITA: Oooohhhh . . .

ANDREW: Esa hija . . . está casada.

MARÍA: Sí, está casada.

JUANITA: ¿Está casada . . . ?

MARÍA: Sí.

ANDREW: Tiene dos de familia.

MARÍA: Tiene dos de familia.

ANDREW: Un hombre y una mujer.

MARÍA: Tiene una mujer y un hombre.

ANDREW: Es lo mismo.

MARÍA: Bueno . . .

JUANITA: ¿De veras? ¿De veras, de veras?

MARÍA: Sí.

ANDREW: Esa hija dejó a su marido.

MARÍA: Sí, lo dejó.

JUANITA: (Con emoción.) ¿Lo dejó?

MARÍA: Lo dejó.

ANDREW: Lo dejó.

JUANITA: (Incrédula.) ¿Todo lo que está diciendo es cierto?

MARÍA: Es muy cierto. Está hablando con la verdad.

ANDREW: Lo dejó porque . . . Ud se metía mucho en la vida de su hija.

MARÍA: Es muy cierto.

ANDREW: Ud. decía que su yerno era un huevón, un mantenido, que no quería trabajar.

MARÍA: Es cierto, sí.

ANDREW: Lo que pasa con Ud., señora, es que Ud. ha sido una vieja muy metiche todo el tiempo, ¡oiga! Una vieja sinvergüenza que se mete en lo que no le importa.

MARÍA: (Molesta.) ¿Y Ud.? ¿Cómo lo sabe?

ANDREW: Pos . . . ¡yo soy el Marajá! ¡Vieja! ¡Vieja desgraciada! ¡Vieja metiche! ¡Vieja sinvergüenza!

JUANITA: ¡Oye! ¡Oye! ¡Oye! ¡Oye!

ANDREW: ¿Eh?

JUANITA: ¿Pos cómo? ¿Pero qué tienes tú? ¡Ya te echaste tú todo a perder! ¿Cómo te pones a insultar a esta señora?

ANDREW: (Rápido, con emoción.) Pos, ¿cómo la voy a insultar si es mi suegra? ¡Hombre!

The Fortuneteller

ANDREW: Come on, Juana, man, what are we going to do? Think! Because I'm very hungry.

JUANITA: I don't know, I don't know anything. But look, think about this, maybe you'll get something if you look for a job. What are we going to do? I'm dying of hunger; I really can't stand it anymore.

ANDREW: Me too, but I keep on looking, and ... there's nothing.

JUANITA: Did you go down to the Plaza?

ANDREW: You hardly have any fat on you, but look at me, I'm going to disappear, bro' ...

JUANITA: But you told me this morning that you were going down to the Plaza.

ANDREW: Well, I went down to the Plaza. Well down there in the Plaza? What's down in the Plaza?

JUANITA: Well, I don't know, you could beg for a handout.

ANDREW: Well, beg for handouts, who's going to give me a handout with these clothes?

JUANITA: (Distraught.) Ay, well I don't know, I don't know ...

ANDREW: (Stupid voice.) Hey, you always have to be well-dressed when you go out in public.

JUANITA: Well, think of something! You always just leave it up to me ...

ANDREW: No, you're the smart one, you told me that you're the *brain*.

JUANITA: Okay, yes, but you have to understand, you have to help me, too, I can't do everything by myself.

ANDREW: Okay, think, think, think, you said that you're the brain, and that you're going to be in charge.

JUANITA: Ah! Ahhhh! I just got an idea. Let's see, let me have a look at you ...

ANDREW: What are you going to do? I'm not going to die, you hear me, not that ...

JUANITA: No, man, no, man ... , no, man. Turn around, turn yourself around, turn around ... Listen, yes.

ANDREW: You can't dress me up like a woman, either.

JUANITA: No, wait a minute, don't ... wait! Let me ... you don't even know ...

ANDREW: I'm not going to dress up like a woman.

JUANITA: I'm not going to ... I'm just looking you over to see if you'll do for this ...

ANDREW: For what?

JUANITA: No, no, man. Look, we're going to do something. I'm thinking that ... we can say that you come from India. After all, look, you have this nose, that suits you very well, it makes you look like an Indian.

ANDREW: The Indians have big noses like me? Or what?

JUANITA: Not Indians from here, it's not American Indian.

ANDREW: It's a classy nose, not just anybody has one like it, madam.

JUANITA: All right, yes, but look, we can do something. I can say that I brought you from India, man ...

ANDREW: That just now from India ...

JUANITA: From India ...

ANDREW: And I'm an Indian, or what?

JUANITA: Hindu! Not an Indian, man. One of those that tells fortunes. You're a fortuneteller.

ANDREW: Oh, I'm a fortuneteller?

JUANITA: Ah huh.

ANDREW: All right.

JUANITA: Only, look, wait a minute, I just need to get you a sheet, and cover up your eyes ...

ANDREW: A sheet? What ... ?

JUANITA: Look, to wrap around your head, to make you a turban.

ANDREW: Are you going to dress me up like a kite? Or what?

JUANITA: No, look, just let me bring the sheet, and I'll explain it to you. Look, you see, it's like this: we'll be able to charge any person that comes along. Since I brought you over, see, and since you can tell them anything they might want to know, and all, we'll get something out of them, and we'll at least be able to eat. Ay, look, there's a real good food stand, and they're selling tamales, and everything, and I'm already dying of hunger, eh?

ANDREW: And what do you want? What are we going to foretell? I don't know how to foretell anything.

JUANITA: Well, if they turn out to be lies, man, how will they know?

ANDREW: Me? Tell them little lies?

JUANITA: Pure lies! If they say one thing, you tell them the opposite. You know, all lies. How will they know the difference? The thing now is that they pay.

ANDREW: Ah, all right. It's all right. You don't have to tell me about lies, you know that I'm real good at lying. Good grief!

JUANITA: All right, just when they've already paid, then you tell them . . . not before.

ANDREW: Well, I go around telling lies all the time.

JUANITA: Ah, all right, it's all right. So just wait for me a little bit. (Rattling or knocking noise.) Look, now it's ready. Look, let me put it on you. But don't you go taking it off!

ANDREW: No, man, I won't take it off.

JUANITA: Look, you look real good.

ANDREW: I look like a ma-raja?³ Like a coward?

JUANITA: Like a maharajah, a maharajah!

ANDREW: Well, I've never backed down, I'm from Jalisco.

JUANITA: No, I'm not talking about nationality. Right now you're a maharajah. Don't go saying that you're from Jalisco, because then you'll ruin everything. You come from . . . from Maharajan.

ANDREW: In disguise.

JUANITA: No, no, what about in disguise? No way. Look! Do you want to eat?

ANDREW: Yes, I do.

JUANITA: So then?

ANDREW: All right, I'm a maharajah.

JUANITA: All right, you're a maharajah.

ANDREW: (Defeated whisper.) I'm a maharajah.

JUANITA: And I'm going to put this on you, and I'm going to have to cover up your eyes. So that you will see better. You tell fortunes with your eyes closed.

ANDREW: With my eyes closed?

JUANITA: Yes.

ANDREW: For telling a lot of lies, yes, that's good, yes.

JUANITA: Because if you tell fortunes with your eyes open, then you'll be bound to be recognized.

ANDREW: Hey yes, that's true.

JUANITA: Because they could recognize you, man. You've always been real well known.

ANDREW: No, it's all right.

JUANITA: So we'll cover up your eyes, and with this . . . , and with what I put on you, there you are. Now you look like one of those Hindus. Now . . . for the first one that comes along.

ANDREW: What do you mean, I look like one of those other guys? What do you mean . . . ?⁴

JUANITA: One of those Hindus. What do you mean, one of those other guys? Man! One of those Hindus!

ANDREW: Oh, all right, but be careful about what you're talking about.

JUANITA: No, but you look like one of those Hindus, I said.

ANDREW: Oh, all right.

JUANITA: Hindus, *okay?*

ANDREW: Hindus, I know now.

JUANITA: But, look, oh, yes, but nobody passes by here. Ah! Here comes a woman, wait a minute, this lady doesn't look like she has any money, but . . .

ANDREW: Should I cover up my eyes?

JUANITA: Yes, man! Quick! Hurry up!

ANDREW: Wait a minute, wait, I have to put it on.

JUANITA: But remember! Don't go putting your foot in it!

ANDREW: No, I won't put my foot in it.

JUANITA: Don't you say anything!

ANDREW: I won't say anything.

JUANITA: Because I know how you are.

ANDREW: All right, well . . . uh . . .

JUANITA: Remember, you're hungry, right?

ANDREW: All right, I'll button my lips.

JUANITA: . . . Ma'am, ma'am, where are you going, ma'am?

MARÍA: Well, I'm just walking along here . . . going for a walk . . . , yes.

JUANITA: Walking along, yes. Hey, look, ma'am, I just want to tell you, look, do you see this man here?

MARÍA: Sure, just look at that . . .

JUANITA: Pretty strange, right?

MARÍA: Yes, yes, he looks strange.

JUANITA: Look carefully how strange. Very strange.

MARÍA: Pretty strange.

JUANITA: He's a maharajah.

MARÍA: Oh, he's a maharajah, a fortuneteller?

JUANITA: He's a Hindu.

MARÍA: Ah, he's a Hindu, they're the best.

JUANITA: I just brought him over.

MARÍA: They're supposed to be the best fortunetellers.

JUANITA: Really?

MARÍA: Yes.

JUANITA: Yes, and it cost me a lot of money to bring him over.

MARÍA: And would you charge a lot for fortunetelling, to tell me something that I want to know?

JUANITA: No, look, señora, since we're just starting out ... you could just give us ... well about ... , well, because it's you, how are you doing for money? Do you have a little money on you? Or don't you have any?

MARÍA: Well, I'm not carrying either a lot or very little.

JUANITA: All right, look, this maharajah is very charitable.

MARÍA: Just imagine.

JUANITA: No, look, he doesn't understand us, see. He doesn't speak.

MARÍA: He doesn't speak?

JUANITA: No, *I mean*, he does speak, but since he is concentrating right now, just with pure thought.

MARÍA: Ah, yes, ah ...

JUANITA: So we'll charge you .... so we'll charge you fifty cents.

MARÍA: Oh, listen, well, that's very expensive.

JUANITA: Very expensive?

MARÍA: Oh, yes.

JUANITA: Because we haven't eaten ... (Almost a whisper or a whimper.) ay ...

MARÍA: Oh, you haven't eaten?

ANDREW: (Mumbling.) Everything costs money, right?

JUANITA: Oh, no ... yes, I mean to say that ... because we haven't learned our way around here yet, I don't know what came out of me, but we don't know our way around here yet, we just got off the boat. Which one was it we came on, eh, you?

MARÍA: Oh, you come from India?

JUANITA: Ah! Wait a minute.

ANDREW: On the *Mississippi.*

JUANITA: That's right, on the *Mississippi.*

MARÍA: Ohhh, the *Mississippi.*

JUANITA: There you go, *on the Mississippi River.*

MARÍA: Oh, all right.

JUANITA: So it's just that ... just that the two of us work together.

ANDREW: It's just that we had a flat tire on the road, and ...

JUANITA: (To Chapulín.) Enough, it's all right, already! (To María.) Yes, so if you would like to ... ?

MARÍA: And ... I can ask him questions, now?

JUANITA: Oh, yes, but I just have to put him to sleep first.

MARÍA: Oh, all right, well, I'll wait for you to put him to sleep ...

JUANITA: I'll put him to sleep. Let's see ...

ANDREW: She's probably going to hit me over the head and knock me out.

JUANITA: Ah ... ha ha, you know, he's halfway ... he's halfway asleep, don't pay any attention to what he's saying.

MARÍA: He's delirious?

JUANITA: Right, yes, because he's got to concentrate first.

MARÍA: Oh, all right.

JUANITA: Let's see ... (Sound of hands rubbing together.) Shiva?

ANDREW: Uh?

JUANITA: Shiva?

ANDREW: Meeeeeee. (He bleats like a goat.)[5]

JUANITA: (Laughing.) That's ... that's how we begin.

MARÍA: Oh, like that? Really?

JUANITA: We begin like that. It's weird, isn't it? (Rubbing sound continues.)

MARÍA: Yes, yes, it's weird.

JUANITA: Maharajah? Maharajah?

ANDREW: Mahara who?

JUANITA: All right, now he's ready, right now. Are you falling asleep now?

ANDREW: (Sounds like a voice from the tomb.) I'm falling asleep now.

JUANITA: Kalamalaya ...

ANDREW: Whose daughter?[6]

JUANITA: Ah, ah, that's how he begins. Baba Khan ...

ANDREW: Uyyy!

JUANITA: Karamalaya!

ANDREW: Kalamazoo.

MARÍA: Oh, Kalamazoo ... ?

JUANITA: He's asleep now. He's ready now.

ANDREW: Detroit, Michigan.

MARÍA: Now, now he's mixed up India with Michigan.

JUANITA: Not that, no, not that. No, no, Yes, because he works at this so much, see, he works like this: he has to get mixed up like that. Sometimes he says Detroit; sometimes he says Mississippi; like that. But I don't disturb him. Are you asleep now?

ANDREW: Right now.

JUANITA: Sound asleep? You're sound asleep now! I want you to be sound asleep now!

ANDREW: Ummm ummm.

JUANITA: Right now!

ANDREW: Now. I'm asleep now, man.

JUANITA: Now, okay. He's in his trance now, so proceed with confidence ... Ah, excuse me, first, the fifty. Thanks. Maharajah, she's going to ask you something.

ANDREW: Let's see, ma'am, ... let's hear it, ma'am, what do you want to know?

MARÍA: I want to know exactly ... because I'm going to buy a lottery ticket, and I want to know ...

ANDREW: All right. So what? What's it to me?

MARÍA: Hey! Did you hear that! So!

JUANITA: Wait, wait, wait a minute, he's a little delirious, just wait a minute.

MARÍA: But you told me that ...

JUANITA: He's concentrating, just wait a minute ... !

ANDREW: Uh upppp ... uh ... ask me, ask me.

JUANITA: Go ahead and ask him. It's just that he gets delirious from all the pressure he's under right now, from all the magic ...

MARÍA: Ohhhh.

JUANITA: He makes a fool out of himself, *I mean*, a magician, magician, he's a magician.[7]

MARÍA: Is he a magician or a fool?

JUANITA: A magician, a magician.

MARÍA: Magician, I'm going to buy a lottery ticket, and I want to know the time, and the number, and what time it's going to come out. Because I need to know right away . . . about the lottery ticket. Mainly the time, the numbers . . . and I also want to know when.

JUANITA: When it will come out. Uh huh, *okay*.

ANDREW: (Mumbling.) And she wants to know when.

JUANITA: Do you know, Maharajah? Answer the lady's question.

ANDREW: Very well.

JUANITA: (Menacing tone.) I don't have to repeat myself, because you already know!

ANDREW: Ummmgh. Ma'am, you go out at eight o'clock in the morning.

MARÍA: I go at eight o'clock in the morning.

JUANITA: At eight, don't forget, at eight!

MARÍA: Right at eight o'clock.

ANDREW: You buy ticket number five, four, four, five, eight.

MARÍA: Five, four . . .

JUANITA: Four, five . . .

MARÍA: Four, five, eight.

JUANITA: . . . Eight. Remember!

ANDREW: You buy it.

MARÍA: I buy it.

ANDREW: You take it home.

MARÍA: I take it home.

ANDREW: When you get home . . .

MARÍA: When I get home . . .

ANDREW: . . . You take it . . .

MARÍA: . . . I take it . . .

ANDREW: You take it in your hands.

MARÍA: I take it in my hands.

ANDREW: And you roll it up into a little ball.

MARÍA: I roll it up into a little ball.

ANDREW: You put it into your mouth.

MARÍA: I put it into my mouth.

ANDREW: You grab a glass of water.

MARÍA: I grab a glass of water.

ANDREW: And you drink it.

MARÍA: I drink it.

ANDREW: And it will come out tomorrow.

MARÍA: Dirty old man! Big mouth! Liar!

JUANITA: No, no, wait, wait a minute. Don't get mad, it's that ... it's that ... there was ... wait a minute, wait a minute. Listen, Maharajah!

ANDREW: Ummm.

JUANITA: Look, you know what? Ask him another question, it'll be better.

MARÍA: All right ...

JUANITA: It would be better to ask him another question because ... he's not completely himself right now. He concentrated ... he concentrated too much.

MARÍA: Well, tell him not to concentrate so much.

JUANITA: Ah, all right, yes. But, well, that will cost fifty cents more.

MARÍA: All right, I'll give it to you.

JUANITA: Okay, give it to me first. (To Chapulín.) Listen you!

ANDREW: I'm listening.

JUANITA: Here is the lady. It's the same lady, and she wants to ask you something. She's going to ask you some questions, and you'd better answer them right!

ANDREW: Ah, all right.

JUANITA: Because if you don't ... !

ANDREW: All right!

JUANITA: You're going to get it good!

ANDREW: Uuuuyyy!

JUANITA: Okay, now I've warned you.

ANDREW: What is it that you want to know?

MARÍA: Well ...

JUANITA: Eh! Now I'm going to tell you something, ask him something ... about your life ... that you want to know. So that you'll ... You don't believe in him because of what he said just now, do you?

MARÍA: No ...

JUANITA: Ah, all right. Look, I'm going to show you that the Mahara-who, the Mahara-who ...

MARÍA: Ah hah ...

JUANITA: Look, I call him Mahara-who and Maharajah. Right? He's got two names.

MARÍA: Yes.

JUANITA: Mahara-who and Maharajah, both names.

ANDREW: (Singing in a low voice.) He went to see her, and he didn't want to take me along ... (Juanita slaps him on the back.)

JUANITA: You're asleep. Remember, you're asleep! You know what? Since he's concentrating in the Baba Kuba ...

MARÍA: And I can question him? Any other question as long as it's not the same?

JUANITA: Yes, yes. Ah hah. You can ask him. Ask him, go ahead, ask him. Ask him if he knows about your past, or your present life, or something like that.

MARÍA: All right, oh, now I understand. Well, this is also very important to me.

JUANITA: Yes, yes. Yes, sure ...

MARÍA: All right, I want you to tell me about my past, my present and my future.

ANDREW: You want to know about your past, your present and your future?

MARÍA: But you have to answer me, because you're going to read my mind.

ANDREW: So, in other words, you want me to divine something about your life?

MARÍA: Yes.

ANDREW: Very well.

JUANITA: Remember! About her life.

ANDREW: Ma'am, you have a daughter.

MARÍA: Yes, I do have one.

JUANITA: You do have a daughter?

MARÍA: Yes.

JUANITA: Oooohhhh ...

ANDREW: This daughter ... is married.

MARÍA: Yes, she's married.

JUANITA: She is married ... ?

MARÍA: Yes.

ANDREW: She has two children.

MARÍA: She does have two children.

ANDREW: One boy and one girl.

MARÍA: She has one girl and one boy.

ANDREW: It's the same.

MARÍA: All right ...

JUANITA: Really? She really does? For real?

MARÍA: Yes.

ANDREW: Your daughter left her husband.

MARÍA: Yes, she left him.

JUANITA: (With emotion.) She left him?

MARÍA: She did leave him.

ANDREW: She left him.

JUANITA: (Incredulous.) Everything that he is saying is true?

MARÍA: It's very true. He's telling the truth.

ANDREW: She left him because ... you used to interfere a lot in your daughter's life.

MARÍA: It's very true.

ANDREW: You used to say that your son-in-law was a lazy lout, a kept man, that he didn't want to work.

MARÍA: That's true, yes.

ANDREW: What's wrong with you, ma'am, is that you've been a busybody old woman all the time, you hear! A shameless old woman who interferes in what doesn't concern her.

MARÍA: (Angry.) And you? How do you know?

ANDREW: Well ... I'm the maharajah! Old wretched old woman! Old busybody! Shameless old woman!

JUANITA: Listen! Listen! Listen! Listen!

ANDREW: Eh?

JUANITA: Listen, what? What's the matter with you? You just ruined everything! What do you mean by going and insulting this lady?

ANDREW: (Fast, with feeling.) Look here, how am I going to insult her if she's my mother-in-law? Man!

Juanita

They used to have some of those skits in the Carpa García. They had some of them, but not all. I think Mamá invented some of the other ones herself. I'm pretty sure that she invented "El compadre." People really used to like that one. My brother and I did it by ourselves, just the two of us. Sometimes we'd take an hour, or even an hour and a half, with just that one skit.

Mamá had all of those skits, and all of those hundreds of songs that we used to do, in her head. She had them all memorized. She was a very intelligent woman.

Andrés and I worked real well together, because we both know how to act. We're both natural actors.

Andrew

Well, we were brother and sister, and so we would really click like that. We each knew what the other one was going to do. We improvised together real well. It was a family deal all the time. That's what made it special.

CHAPTER 8

The Show Goes On

Andrew

In 1947, we went on the road for the first time since the war began. We were booked up from San Antonio all the way to Los Angeles. So, by the time we hit Santa Fe, New Mexico, we had already made a little money.

After Doctor Nopal took his cut, Lydia and Mamá would split what was left half and half. But before they made the split, they would take out ten percent of the whole thing. Out of that ten percent they would give the rest of us all even money. They gave it to María, Juana, Manuel and Juan, Lydia's husband. Since I wasn't performing in the show yet, I only got a dollar fifty a week. I never asked for a raise. Well, I had room and board, what more do you want? I was just a teenager. Well, one time I did say something.

"Mamá," I said, "do you know that I'm growing up? That I'm becoming a man? That I only get one dollar and fifty cents a week? Don't you think that I'm going to have a girl someday, and then how am I going to take her to the movies or something ... ?"

"That's your problem, son," she replied.

When I started appearing on stage with the others, then we would all get even money out of that ten percent. So when we started out on the road, we began saving our money—all of us: me, Manuel, Juan, María and Juana. So when we got to Santa Fe, Juan, Lydia's husband, said, "Let's go buy a suit."

"Okay, we'll go with you," Manuel and I said.

We had the money. We had saved it. So we went into this fancy men's store. The salesman came over and said, "Yeah, can I help you?"

"Well, we're just looking around first," Juan said. "We want to see what you have."

"But I mean, is there anything I can show you?"

"Well," Juan said, "we're just looking around right now, but we're thinking of buying a suit. But we don't know yet."

And the salesman looked at us real funny and said, "You guys really need a suit?"

You can imagine what we were wearing.

"Man," he told Juan, "you look like you're wearing your cell suit right now."

"Hmmm, don't pay any attention, he's just telling us that because he wants to sell us a new suit," Juan told the rest of us.

You can just imagine what we must have looked like. Manuel had been in the Army, Juan hadn't been making good money for a long time and I'd never had any money. All that changed when we went back on the road.

There was a funny thing at that time. They didn't trust me to drive. We'd be out on the road, and sometimes we would have to go as much as five hundred miles from one job to the next. Manuel did all the driving, and he would have to go without stopping. Well sometimes, he had to go to sleep, so he would let Janie drive. Manuel wouldn't let me drive. He let her drive. He knew that Janie could drive.

Manuel had just gotten married, and his wife was expecting a baby. We were out on the road, and when we hit Walsenburg, Colorado, Manuel received a telegram from his wife. She was going to have the baby. Manuel had to leave the show and go back to San Antonio right away.

We had to keep on going all the way to Los Angeles, because that was the deal. We had a contract. But when Manuel said that he had to go, Mamá got very nervous. She didn't know what to do, because there was nobody to drive the car. So she said, "Well, Juana can drive it."

"Yeah, I'll drive it," Juana told her. She'd had a few drinks, and she said, "Yeah, I can drive it!"

"Well, there's nothing to it," Juan, Lydia's husband, told her, "just follow me. I've been driving all the time, all you have to do is just follow me. Follow me slow, and that's all you have to do."

"Oh yeah, I can do that, I'll follow you," Juana said.

So, Manuel got on the bus and headed back to San Antonio, and the next day, when we were leaving, because we had to keep on going, Juanita panicked. She couldn't drive—she just couldn't do it. So, I said, "Wait a minute, let me tell you something."

"Okay."

"I don't know how to shift gears, but you do. I'll drive the car, you shift my gears."

That's the way we got to California. Juanita was in the driver's seat, and I was right next to her. She was shifting and putting on the brake and the clutch, and I was just steering. We were following my brother-in-law. Juan was in front, driving Lydia's car, and he said, "All you've got to do is just follow me. Wherever I go, you go. You just follow me, don't lose me."

And I didn't lose him. I don't believe that a person that is driving has any time to be scared. I think it's a case of his being more concentrated on what he is doing. That's when I learned how to drive. I don't remember exactly how old I was, but I was very young.

* * *

When we appeared in those theaters, the announcer or master of cere-monies would start things off by going out in front of the audience, intro-ducing the show and telling a joke or two to get the people in the mood. In the original stage show, Manuel would tell the jokes, but after that night in Trinidad where I took Manuel's place in an emergency, I started telling the jokes most of the time. I would tell clean jokes. There was one that I used to tell about the turtle and the Bible. It goes something like this:

El arca de Noé[1]

Voy a decir un chiste mientras comienzan los arreglos los artistas para seguir el siguiente número. Y para que no estén Uds. tristes, ¿verdad? Voy a platicarles algo de la Biblia, ¿ver-dad? Del arca de Noé.

Platican que, según la historia, ¿verdad?, que a la arca de Noé subieron una pareja de cada animalito a la arca ¿verdad? Entonces, ya cuando estaban todos allá subidos, estaba llueve y llueve. Y entonces, uno de los animalitos, que fue el perro ¿verdad? se asomó y miró pa' afuera, y allá a lo lejos miró una lucecita chiquita.

Entonces, él vino y le dice al rey de la selva, que es el león, le dijo, "Oye, fíjate que allá se halla una lucecita chiquita muy lejos ¿qué será?"

Y dijo el león, "Pues, a ver". Y se asomó el león, y miró y, "Mira, verdad que está raro. ¿Qué será?"

Entonces vino el tigre, y le dijo, "Mira, fíjate, las lucecitas. Mira, allá muy lejos, a lo lejos, mira las lucecitas. ¿Qué será?"

Y dijo el tigre, "Pues ¿quién sabe?" Dijo, "¿Por qué no vas a ver?" le dijo el león. Dijo el tigre, "No, no, no voy. Está lloviendo muy fuerte. A lo mejor me ahogo".

Y dijo éste, "Pues ¿sabes qué? Mira ¿por qué no mandamos a la *cheetah*? Es más rápida. Ésa corre sesenta millas por hora, en un ratito allí viene".

"Bueno, pues, anda. Dile que venga". Y al llegar la *cheetah*, dijo la *cheetah*, "Pues, que no. No voy. Me ahogo".

Y bueno, le hablaron al leopardo, a la pantera, a los animales más rápidos. Al lobo. Y nadie quería ir. No querían ir porque tenían miedo, porque estaba llueve y llueve, y la arca estaba medio moviendo. Y dijeron no, porque: "si nos ahogamos . . . nos dejarán pa' atrás".

Y de repente sacó la cabeza la tortuga, y dijo: "Yo voy". Todos la miraron. Y la miró el tigre, la miró el león, y la pantera, y todos, y dijeron, ésta no mandes porque se va a ahogar. No lo hagas. ¡Camina muy despacio, hombre!"

Dijo el león, "Pues sí, pero nadie quiere ir. Es la única voluntaria. A ésta mandaré, no hay más". Bueno, pues, la cargaron de comida, verdad, le echaron bastante comida en la concha, verdad, y la mandaron. Y que se fue la tortuga.

Bueno, pues, pasó el primer día, el segundo día, el tercer día, el cuarto día . . . , el quinto día, y ya el arca empezaba a querer levantar. Y pues empezaron los animales a averiguar con el león, ¿verdad? "Pues, oye ¿no te dije que no la hubieras mandado? ¡Qué barbaridad! Que se va ahogando. Mira, pues ¿dónde se va en el agua ya? Y el arca va a subir. Y fíjate ¿cuándo va a llegar allá, ante la luz? No ¡caray! No la hubieras mandado".

Y estaban averigua y averigua cuando sacó la cabeza la tortuga, y dijo, "¡Si están averiguando tanto, no voy!"

Noah's Ark

I'm going to tell a joke while the artists begin their preparations for the next number. And so that you folks won't be sad, right? I'm going to tell you about something from the Bible, right? About Noah's ark.

They say that, according to the story, that one pair of each kind of animal went on board the Ark. So then, when they were all on board, it was raining and raining. And so then, one of the little animals, which was the dog, right, got up and looked outside, and there in the distance he saw a little light.

So then he went to the King of the Jungle, which is the lion, and he said, "Listen, there's a very little light very far off, what might it be?"

And the lion said, "Hey, let's see." And the lion looked out, and said, "Look, it really is very strange. What might it be?"

So then the tiger came, and he asked him, "Look, see the little light. Look out there very far away, off in the distance, look at those little light. What might it be?

And the tiger said, "Hey, who knows?" And the lion said, "Why don't you go and find out?" The tiger replied, "No, no, I'm not going. It's raining very hard. I'd probably drown."

And the tiger said, "Okay, you know what? Look, why don't we send the cheetah? She is faster. She can run sixty miles an hour, she'll get there in no time at all."

"All right, well, go and get her to come." Upon arriving, the cheetah said, "Oh, no, I'm not going. I'd drown, too."

And so, they spoke to the leopard, to the panther, to all of the fastest animals. To the wolf. And nobody wanted to go. Nobody wanted to go because they were afraid, because it was raining and raining, and the ark was starting to shift a little. And they said no because, "if we drown . . . we'll be left behind."

And suddenly the turtle stuck her head out and said, "I'll go." Everybody looked at her. And the tiger looked at her, the lion looked at her, and the panther, and everybody, and they said, "No, don't send this one because she'll drown. Don't do it. She moves very slowly, man!"

The lion said, "Yes, sure, but nobody else wants to go. She is the only volunteer. I'll have to send her, there's nobody else." All right, so they loaded her up with food, they put enough food into her shell, and they sent her off. And off went the turtle.

All right, now the first day went by, and then the second, the third, the fourth day, . . . the fifth day, and now the ark started to rise. And the animals started arguing with the lion, "Hey, listen, didn't I tell you that you shouldn't have sent her? How awful! She's out there drowning. Look, where out there in the water is she now? And the ark is rising. And just think, how long is it going to take her to get to the light? No, damn! You shouldn't have sent her."

And they were arguing and arguing when the turtle stuck her head out, and said, "If you're all going to argue about it so much, I won't go!"

Andrew

After I opened with a few jokes like that, the first act I would announce would be Juanita and Manolo, the comedians. They would do a comedy sketch that would last up to thirty minutes. For instance, they used to do one that was called "Los Compadres." Mamá and Antonio Montes originally had done it in our stage show during the '30s, and we kept on adapting it to the changing times. It was about two people who were *compadres* who hadn't seen each other for a long time.

Manuel

We never exactly rehearsed those things with Mamá, but we put them together piece by piece. Mamá just gave the orders. A lot of what we used to do in the skits was our own invention. We used to invent things. For instance, when Juanita and I were talking together, she would be my long lost *comadre*. So we would start talking to each other about the time that has passed. I keep on telling her: "Well, comadre, I've been over here, I've been over there, I've been all over the place. I've been across the border."

And then I mention this place in the red zone.[2] People would really laugh at that. But that was my own invention, that wasn't originally part of the skit. You'd be surprised how much of a kick some people would get out of that joke. We used to have one skit that lasted one hour and ten minutes between the two of us.

Juanita

I, Juanita, was the *coupletista*. Singing *couplets* is not like *ranchera* singing. It's different. I had to talk to the audience. I had to shine the little mirror at the men and at the boys, and I had to talk to the old men and to the young men. I would sing, too, songs like "Mírame, mírame," and another one that goes:[3]

> Todas las muchachas se quieren casar.
> Será por quitarse de trabajar.
> Pero ahora se casan, pues deben saber
> que buscan marido a quien mantener.
> Ay yiiie, ay yiie.
>
> Este mundo está al revés
> en cuestiones del amor.
> Ay yiiie, ay yiie. En cuestiones del amor
> no hay más.
>
> Allí veo a los novios,
> muy juntos están.
> Mirando hacia su lado,
> por lo que dirán.

La madre dormida,
ni cuenta se da
que su buena hijita,
vacilando está.
Ay yiiie, ay yiie.
Ay yiiie, ay yiie.

Este mundo está al revés
en cuestiones del amor.
Ay yiiie, ay yiie.
En cuestiones del amor
no hay más.

All the girls want to get married. Probably to get out of
working. But now they get married, they should know
that they look for a husband to support. Ay yiiie, ay yiie.

This world is all backwards in questions of love. Ay
yiiie, Ay yiie. In matters of love there is nothing more.

Over there I see the lovers, they are very close together.
Looking over their shoulders, they don't want any gos-
sip. The sleeping mother doesn't even notice that her
good little daughter is going on a spree. Ay yiiie, ay
yiie. Ay yiiie, ay yiie.

This world is all backwards in questions of love. Ay
yiiie, ay yiie. In matters of love there is nothing more.

Andrew

In between the parts of the song, Juanita would dance. She wouldn't be
singing straight through. She would sing a piece, and then she would dance.
And then she would sing another piece and so on. And María would play
the piano behind her. Later on, when they were the Dueto, María would
accompany her on the guitar, but for the stage show she used the piano
because it had a fuller sound.

María

I learned to play music strictly by ear. Nobody taught me. We learned
by watching each other in the family. We were always looking, and that's
how we learned. They didn't send us to a teacher. When I was a little girl,
they would have a piano somewhere in the houses where we went to play

private parties. I would go over there and sit down and play the piano. And the ladies would say, "Hey, she knows how to play."

I was just a little girl. And my mother and father would say, "She knows how to play everything."

And I was proud of myself. I would start to play, my fingers would just play almost by themselves. I was so little.

"How come she knows how to do it?" people would ask. "Well, I'm just doing it," I would reply. And then I started to learn more and more and more. Then I started to play in the orchestra, by ear. Because I would just hear the song that they were going to start to play, and I would follow them, and then I started to play the piano.

Once Mamá sent me to a teacher, because she wanted me to learn to read music, which is better. Mamá knew a lot about music. The teacher would put the sheet music in front of me, and I would just go play, play, play, along and I didn't look at the music. The teacher told Mamá, "It's no use. I'm wasting my time, and you're wasting your money."

I guess I just didn't understand; I just played it the way I wanted it. Then in the '40s, during the war, I believe it was '43, or '44, when the variety shows came here to the Zaragoza Theater and the National Theater, I was the pianist, and I couldn't read music, although I learned a lot more about the piano from Arturo Vásquez at the Club Bohemio. It was the same in our stage show: I played strictly by ear.

I really started the show, because I played a tune while they were announcing the show and everything. I would play "Juárez" and "Laredo," Spanish tunes. The people knew that the *variedad* was going to begin when I played "Juárez" and "La marcha de Zacatecas." When I finished playing those, the curtain would go up and the show would begin.

Manuel and Juanita would go out and dance—that was the first act of the *variedad*. I would keep on playing the piano while they danced and sang their number. They did strictly Mexican songs, like "Las espuelas de Amozoac" and "Viva Jalisco."

After they finished their dance numbers, then Juanita began her solo act. I would accompany her on the piano while she did Spanish dances. She had some castanets. She would dance, sing and play the castanets all at the same time. She was very good.

Juanita

When I finished my number, Manuel would sing a song, or Andrew would come out and tell a joke until I got dressed. We had to dress fast! For instance, when I finished one number, I'd be wearing a costume with some little ribbons on it. Then I'd have to change real fast into a different costume for the next number, the one where I went out to shine the mirror at the young men, the boys, and I wanted to look real pretty. Or I would have to go out and dance with my brother. I hated changing costumes so fast, but Mamá would be there ready to make sure that I did. I had to do it in the time it took María to play one song on the piano, or for Andrew to tell one joke.

Andrew

Sometimes I had to tell jokes in a series because I was announcing the *variedad.* I had to entertain the people while the girls were changing costumes or getting ready to go on. So I would tell the audience a few jokes. For instance, I would say:[4]

> Luego, ahorita, mientras que comenzamos, les voy a platicar lo que me pasó ahora que venía de San Antonio. Me venía en el *"bus"*, ¿verdad? Entonces, se asomó un señor, ¿verdad?, y lo vi yo que traía las manos así. Bueno, a lo mejor era un paralítico o algo. No, pues, seguimos el camino.
>
> Y vamos a ir en el restaurant pa' un descanso, tomarnos una taza de café, o un refresco, o algo, ¿verdad? Me bajé, se bajó el señor, y entonces me paré allí, y pedí una soda. Y el señor se paró allí donde estaba yo, y dijo, "Señor, haga Ud. el favor de que me den a mí una soda también".
>
> Ya dije, "Quiere el señor una soda aquí. Dénos una soda a él".
>
> Y luego me dice, "Mire, me hace el favor Ud. de darme una soda en la boca, ¿por favor?"
>
> Le dije, "Sí, cómo no".
>
> Luego luego, se lo di, ¿verdad? Lo tomó. Y le dije, "Permítame pagar".
>
> Y él dijo, "No, no, señor, yo pago".
>
> Le dije, "No, permítame Ud. pagar".
>
> Y dijo, "No ¡yo pago!"
>
> Le dije, "Bueno, muy bien".
>
> Me dijo, "Métale la mano en la bolsa y saque un dólar de allí".
>
> Metí la mano en la bolsa, saqué un dólar, y él pagó.
>
> Le dije, "¿Le puedo hacer una pregunta?"
>
> Y dijo, "A ver, dígame".
>
> Y le dije, "Está Ud. *parálisis* o ¿qué le pasa? ¿Por qué está así?"
>
> "Oh, no ¿Ud. es de acá?"

Le dije, "Sí".

Dijo, "No sabes que vengo pa' acá, de acá, voy pa' allá pa' el otro lado, ¿verdad? Y mi suegra me encargó unos zapatos, y me dio la medida, y pa' que no me la olvide, así se la trae".

Right now, then, while we're getting ready to begin the next act, I'm going to tell you about something that happened to me on my way here from San Antonio. I was coming on the bus, right? So then a man got on, and I noticed that he was holding his hands like so. Okay, he was probably a paralytic or something. Okay, we went on down the road.

Then we pulled into a place for a rest stop, to have a cup of coffee or a soda or something, right? I got off the bus, this man got out, and then I went up and asked for a soda. The man came up next to me and said, "Sir, please do me a favor and have them give me a soda, too."

So I said, "The gent here wants a soda. Give him one, too."

And then he says to me, "Look, do me a favor and pour the soda into my mouth for me."

"Sure, of course," I told him.

I gave it to him right away. So he drank it. And I told him, "Allow me to pay."

"No, no, mister, I'll pay," he said.

"No, allow me to pay," I told him.

And he told me, "No, I'll pay!"

"All right, okay," I said.

"Stick your hand in my pocket and take out a dollar," he told me.

I stuck my hand in his pocket, pulled out a dollar, and he paid.

"Can I ask you a question?" I said to him.

He said, "Go ahead, ask."

"Are you paralyzed, what's wrong with you? Why are you like that?"

"Oh, you're from around here?"

"Yes," I told him.

"Don't you know that I come here, I'm going over there to the other side, right? And my mother-in-law wants me to buy her some shoes and gave me the size, so I'm holding my arms like this so I won't forget it.

I had to come up with millions of little things like that to entertain the people while the girls were changing or dressing. Then after I did the jokes, when Juanita and María were ready to go on, I would announce them like this:

> Ahora, sí, respetado público, voy a tener el gusto de presentarles a Uds. nada menos que a Juanita y a María Mendoza, que van a cantar unas bonitas canciones. Vamos a recibirlas con un fuerte aplauso.

> Now, respected public, I am going to have the pleasure of introducing to you no less than Juanita and María Mendoza, who are going to sing some pretty songs for you. Let's receive them with a big applause.

And then Juanita and María would go on and sing.

Juanita

María and I started singing together before we ever made any records. We started singing together when we went to California before the war. When we sang at the Mason Theater they didn't pay any attention to us. We used to sing at least three or four songs together each performance. Depending on the audience, if they liked us, we might sing even more, sometimes as many as seven or eight, once in awhile even ten.

When María and I sang as a *dueto* on stage, one of our favorite numbers was a song called "Los casados," ("The Married Men"). Before we would sing "Los casados," I would always tell the audience, "Now we're going to sing a song that's going to say a few little things to the married men. But I don't want the married men to feel bad, because all of the things that I say in the song aren't really true, it's just a song, it's just for fun, just to have a good time."

And then María and I would go ahead and sing it to them while Mamá or Lydia helped out on the guitar.

Los casados[5]

> Voy a hablar de los casados,
> los que tienen sus quereres,
> que se salen a la calle
> nomás a buscar mujeres.
> Le dicen a la mujer:
> "Al final ya no me quieres."

Desque el hombre está en la casa
haciéndose el enojado,
está buscando salida,
que tiene que ir a un mandado.
Está buscando salida
para ir de enamorado.

Y se van a la cantina
presumiendo pesos dobles,
y en su casa al colector
le alcabalan con los pobres.
Pero la mujer no sabe
que los billetes se esconden.

Cuando están en la cantina
son retedisparadores.
Si les pide la mujer
ahí les dan retorcicones.
Si les pide la mujer
ahí les dan hasta torsones.

Y llegan a la cantina
y le dan vuelo a la hilacha,
besando a las cantineras
que hasta el pico les retacha.
Se les hacen retelindas
aunque tengan cara de hacha.

Cuando estiran su picote
para darle su tronado,
en su pensamiento dicen:
"¡Ah qué viejo tan volado!
Ahorita lo vuelvo loco,
y lo despacho quebrado".

Hay algunos tempranillos,
aunque estén recién casados,
no tienen otra ilusión
que bailar y jugar dados.
Y si van a trabajar
más pronto salen volados.

También hay otros más viejos,
de los treinta a los cuarenta,
que se gastan todo el cheque,
y no pagan ni su cuenta.
Que se gastan todo el cheque,
y no pagan ni la renta.

También hay otros viejitos
que apenas pueden andar,
pero al ver a una muchacha,
quisieran hasta volar.
Pero cuando ya se pasan,
luego empiezan a requejar.

Mujeres nos despedimos,
ya nos duelen los sentidos.
Estarán echando rayos
todititos sus maridos,
pero al cabo es la verdad,
ellos juntitos conmigo.

The Married Men

I'm going to talk about the married men,
those that have their love affairs,
who go out on the street
just to look for women.
They tell their wives:
"In the end you don't love me anymore."

As soon as the man gets home
acting angry,
he's looking for a way to go out,
that he has to go out on an errand.
He's looking for a way to get out
and go be a lover.

And they go out to the *cantina*
bragging that they have big bucks,
while at home they poormouth
the bill collector.
But his wife doesn't know

that he hides the big bills.

When they are in the *cantina*
they are real braggarts.
If their wives ask them for something
it gives them a bellyache.
If their wives ask them for something
it really makes their guts ache.

And they get to the *cantina*
and they really act their worst,
kissing the barmaids who
recoil from their pecking.
The barmaids seem real pretty
to them even if they're hatchet-faced.

When she stretches out her beak
to give him a kiss,
in her thoughts she says:
"Ah, what a fake old turkey!
Right now I'm going to drive him crazy
and then I'll send him off flat broke."

There are some young men,
who, although they've just wed,
don't think about anything but
dancing and shooting dice.
And if they do go to work
pretty soon they go off to party.

Also there are other, older men,
from thirty years old to forty,
they spend their whole paycheck
and don't even pay their bills.
They spend their whole paycheck
and don't even pay the rent.

Also there are even older ones
that can barely even walk anymore,
but when they see a girl,
they even might want to fly.
But when they are passed by,

then they start to really complain.

Women, we say goodbye,
now our feelings are really hurting.
All of your husbands will
probably be blowing their tops,
but when you get right down to it,
everything we say is the truth.

But when the men in the audience heard "Los casados," they would start getting really riled up, and when we finished the song, they would start to holler, "Now sing "Las casadas!" We want "Las casadas!" So we would always have to sing "Las casadas" ("The Married Women") after singing "Los casados."

Las casadas[6]

Voy a hablar de las casadas,
las que tienen sus maridos,
que al peso de medianoche
los dejan muy bien dormidos.

(Se repiten los últimos dos
renglones de cada estrofa.)

De que la mujer empieza a
mirar y mirar pa' fuera
es porque le están haciendo
señas de la nopalera.

Luego luego se le antoja
ir a traer pronto el mandado.
Es porque le están haciendo
señas por el otro lado.

De que la mujer empieza,
"Ya me voy pa' el mandado,"
es porque le están haciendo
señas por el otro lado.

Y si el marido, por desgracia,
en la calle se emborracha,
se encuentra con su rodilla,

lo lleva para su casa.

Luego la mujer le dice,
"¿Pa' qué traes a ese viejo?"
haciéndose de papeles
pa' poderlo hacer cangrejo.

Cuando el hombre le reclama,
le reclama sus deberes,
ahí le dice la mujer,
"¡Norieguito nomás tú eres!"

Y el marido le reclama
celos por otros quereres.
Luego la mujer le dice,
"¡Norieguito nomás tú eres!"

Después de haber platicado
y haber pasado el rato,
si tantito se descuida,
comen en el mismo plato.

Las muchachas que hoy se casan
hacen cariñitos tiernos
por enfrente del marido,
y por detrás les ponen cuernos.

Las mujeres de hoy en día,
muchas se visten de verde;
al paso de medianoche,
la que no es conejo, es liebre.

Las muchachas de El Paso, Tejas,
mucho les gusta dar al verde,
arriba del automóvil,
la que no pellizca, muerde.

Las mujeres son el Diablo,
parientes del alacrán,
nomás ven al hombre pobre,
paran la cola y se van.

Las mujeres son el Diablo,
parientes del Demonio,
con unas tijeras mochas
pelaron a San Antonio.

Las mujeres que han oído
dirán que soy hablador,
no le hace que me lo digan,
otras lo oirán mejor.

Todas las mujeres dicen,
"Mal haya ese cantador,
que no hay quien le dé en el hocico
ni le quite en lo hablador".

Ya con ésta me despido,
ay, riéndome a carcajadas.
Aquí se acaban cantando
los versos de las casadas.

Ya con ésta me despido,
cantando flores moradas.
Aquí se acaban cantando
los versos de las casadas.

The Married Women

I'm going to talk about the married women,
those that have their husbands,
who, in the dark of night,
sneak off and leave them sound asleep.

(The last two lines of each
stanza are repeated.)

The reason the wife starts
looking out the window all the time
is because her lovers are making
signals to her from the cactus patch.

Right away she desires to
quickly go and run some errands.
It's because her lovers are making

signals to her from outside.

The reason the wife starts saying,
"I'm going out on an errand,"
is because her lovers are
signaling to her from outside.

And if the husband, unfortunately,
gets drunk out in the street,
he'll run into his girl friend,
and she'll carry him on home.

Then the wife asks the girl friend,
"Why are you bringing me this old drunkard?"
putting on an act in order to
make him crawl like a crab.[7]

When the man reproaches her,
when he demands his rights,
then the woman tells him,
"You're just a nobody!"

And the husband reproaches his wife
for having other lovers,
but then the wife tells him,
"You're just a nobody!"

After having talked it over
and having been with her a while,
if he slips up just a little,
she'll be doing it to him all over again.

The girls who get married these days
are very affectionate
when with their husbands,
but behind their backs they are unfaithful.

The women nowadays,
many of them dress in green;[8]
and in the dark of night,
if she's not a rabbit, she's a hare.[9]

The girls of El Paso, Texas,
really like to fool around,
and as soon as they're in a car,[10]
the one that doesn't pinch, bites.[11]

Women are the Devil,
close relatives of the scorpion,
as soon as they see a man who's broke,
they raise up their tail and run away.

Women are the Devil,
close relatives of the Demon,
with some blunt scissors
they sheared San Antonio.[12]

The women who have heard me
will probably call me a liar,
it doesn't matter what they say to me,
other women will believe it.

All the women say,
"To hell with this singer,
there's no one to hit him in the mouth
or to stop him being a liar."

Now with this I say goodbye,
ay, laughing my head off.
This is where the verses about
married women come to an end.

And with that I say farewell,
singing "wilted flowers."
Here we finish singing
the verses about married women.

María

We recorded both "Las casadas" and "Los casados," which was written by a composer in Los Angeles. We just learned "Las casadas" because, when we were presenting the stage show, and we would sing "Los casados," after we finished the song everyone would yell, "Now sing 'Las casadas!'" So we had to learn it, too. The two songs went together very well in the stage show and would really get the crowd going.

Andrew

After Juanita and María sang their *duetos*, it would be either Manuel or Lydia. Manuel has a beautiful voice, a tremendous voice! María would play the piano, and Manuel would sing to the girls. He's still a lover, he's been a lover all his life. He had lots of charisma with women, you know. He would look around, and then he would look at a girl that he liked, and he would sing to her.

Juanita

And then when we went to another town, he would look at another girl, and he would sing the same song to that other girl.

Manuel

We used to play with movie stars, too. Did Lydia tell you? We used to play with Juan José Martínez Casado, he came out in a lot of movies. We were right there in Denver, we were putting on a show, and he came over to our dressing rooms. And there were these two young girls, and they started asking me to give them my autograph. As I was giving them my autograph, this man, that famous movie actor, came walking up and told those girls who he was. The girls didn't care, they wanted to get my autograph.

Then the movie star went and told Lydia, "Look, I'm the movie star around here, why is your brother giving them his autograph instead of me?"

The time that we went to California in 1939, we played with El Chaflán, Carlos López Chaflán. He was a Mexican movie star, a comedian. We played at the same theater with him, yeah, right there at the California Theater.

Andrew

Then after the war, Ramiro Cortés, el Doctor Nopal, had lots of movie stars with his shows—Pedro Infante, Emilio Tuero—he had big movie stars with him, and they went with us. So we would be appearing on the same stage with Pedro Infante, Tin Tan y Marcelo, and that lady that used to dance, Cati Cortez—she was a dancer. Fernando J. Mantequilla, he was with us, too. A lot of movie stars were on those tours we played for Ramiro Cortés.

We met Tin Tan out there in El Paso. He got his start out there. He was a radio announcer for a program in Ciudad Juárez. It was called Los Aficionados. It was sort of like the Gong Show. He used to ring a little bell when people struck out, to put them out of the contest or whatever. That's why they called him "Tin Tan," because of the sound of that bell. It was sort of a talent show, an amateur hour.

Manuel

When I was little, to tell you the truth, I wasn't too interested in music. I used to hate it! I used to hate being in show business. I like music now, but then I used to hate it. I like it more now than I used to then because Mamá used to force me to go out there and do this and that, and I just did it. I did it against my will, but I had to do it. Somebody had to do it, or else. ...

Juanita

Yes, and out in California at the Mason Opera House, Manuel and I used to get standing ovations. Manuel was so realistic that he even frightened the manager, Ramiro Cortés, because he would fall down, and it looked like he really fell.

Manuel

I'm telling you, hell man, we used to dance, and then I would jump up and land right on my back and bang! People would go crazy laughing. You know, I didn't even feel it then. I'd sure as hell feel it now.

Andrew

It was after the war that Juanita and I seriously developed our comedy routine where she would play the straight role to my comedian. That was our real time in show business. We didn't have anything else to do but think up and sing songs. So we would do a whole variety of comic material. We would make a lot of plays on words, word jokes and visual jokes and parodies of songs. We had to have a good variety. It all had to be different.

For instance, there's a very old, popular Mexican song called "Paloma blanca"; a lot of the big *ranchera* singers have recorded it over the years, and everybody in our audience would recognize it right away. The straight version goes something like this:

Paloma blanca[13]

Paloma blanca, blanca paloma,
quién tuviera tus alas,
tus alas quién tuviera,
para volar, y volar para
dónde están mis amores,
mis amores dónde están.

Tómale y llévale, llévale y tómale,
este ramo de flores, de flores este ramo,
para que se acuerde de este pobre corazón

Tuve un amor, un amor tuve,
lo quise y lo quiero
lo quiero y lo quise,
porque era fino, porque fino era,
fino como un diamante,
como un diamante fino.

Tómale y llévale, llévale y tómale,
este ramo de flores, de flores este ramo,
para que se acuerde de este pobre corazón.

White Dove

White dove, dove of white,
if I only had your wings,
your wings, if only I were to have them
in order to fly, in order to fly to
where my loves are,
my loves, where they are.

Take it to her, carry it to her, carry it to her, take it to her,
this bouquet of flowers, of flowers this bouquet,
to remind her of this poor heart of mine.

I had a love, a love I had,
I loved it and I love it now,
I love it and I did before,
because it was fine, so fine,
fine like a diamond,
like a diamond so fine.

Take it to her, carry it to her, carry it to her, take it to her,
this bouquet of flowers, of flowers this bouquet,
to remind her of this poor heart of mine.

That's the way everyone was familiar with that song, but Juanita and I had our own version. We would start off as if we were two *artistas*— not very bright ones, it was comedy, you see—who were trying to present a stage show.

Pelona linda[14]

ANDREW: ¿Qué vamos a cantar?

JUANITA: "Pelona linda".

ANDREW: ¿La anuncio yo? ¿O la anuncia Ud.? No, la anuncio yo, ¿verdad?

JUANITA: Anúnciela Ud.

ANDREW: Bueno. *Ladies and gentlemen* ...

JUANITA: Oiga, oiga, oiga ... espérese, espérese ¿qué está haciendo?

ANDREW: Pos, estoy anunciando.

JUANITA: Pero ¿cómo les decía: *"gentlemen"*? ¿Qué es eso?

ANDREW: Pos, estoy en inglés ... en inglés les estoy anunciando ...

JUANITA: Oh ¿Ud. sabe inglés?

ANDREW: Pos ...

JUANITA: ¿Pero que no mira Ud. que aquí es un lugar donde se habla puro español? Ud. sabe, pues, todo lo que estamos hablando en español porque ... porque ¿cómo se supone Ud.? No, oiga, ¿cómo se pone Ud. a anunciar en inglés?

ANDREW: ¿Por qué? ¿No ha llegado de oír de eso de *"bilingual"*?

JUANITA: ¿De quién?

ANDREW: Pos, que tiene que hablar uno en español y en inglés.

JUANITA: ¿*"Bilingual"*?

ANDREW: Ora ¿quién va a hablar en inglés? ¿Yo o Ud.? ¿Me va a dejar anunciar o no voy a anunciar?

JUANITA: Sí, pero sí, pero te voy a decir una cosa, pero dígalo correctamente, si ya me averigua ...

ANDREW: Pos voy a decirlo correctamente.

JUANITA: Bueno, ándale ...

ANDREW: *Ladies and gentlemen* ... *now* ...

JUANITA: ¿Nomás *"Ladies and gentlemen"* sólo? ¿Nomás, puros *"ladies"*?

ANDREW: No, les estoy diciendo a la gente que estamos comenzando, que estoy comenzando, no es que ...

JUANITA: No, no, no, *I'm sorry* ... No dispénseme, lo siento también.

ANDREW: *Ladies and gentlemen* ...

JUANITA: Ya lo dijo.

ANDREW: Ya lo ... pos, bueno, ¡déjeme comenzar, hombre!

JUANITA: ¿Pues, cuántas veces vas a repetir lo mismo?

ANDREW: Pos yo lo voy a repetir las veces que yo quiera. ¿Pero es que yo voy a anunciar o va a anunciar Ud.?

JUANITA: Ah bueno, está bueno, ándale ...

ANDREW: *Ladies and gentlemen* ...

JUANITA: Otra vez, oyyy ... (Suspirando.)

ANDREW: ... *Now* ... (Pausa larga.) no, espéreme, me falta algo, ¿verdad?

JUANITA: ¿Qué se le olvidó?

ANDREW: No, no, me falta algo.

JUANITA: Ah, bueno ...

ANDREW: (Pausa.) *Boys and "boyas" too* ...

JUANITA: Oooh ¿qué "*boys* y *boyas*"?

ANDREW: Pues sí, "muchachos y muchachas" ¿no?

JUANITA: ¡Ahhh! (Se oye un manazo.) ¡*Girls*!

ANDREW: Bueno, es lo mismo, "*boys* y *boyas*", ¿no?

JUANITA: No, no, ¿cómo dices "*boys* y *boyas*"?

ANDREW: Sí, es lo mismo. "*Boys* y *boyas*" *too, now we are* ... (Habla relentamente con acento muy artificial.)

JUANITA: Mire, sí sabe ... (Tono de admiración.)

ANDREW: *We are going to* cantar ...

JUANITA: Oiga, ahí le falló.

ANDREW: ¿Eh?

JUANITA: Así no se dice en inglés: "cantar".

ANDREW: ¿No? ¿Cómo se dice "cantar"?

JUANITA: "*Sing*".

ANDREW: ¿*Sing*?

JUANITA: Ah hah.

ANDREW: *Now we are going to sing* ...

JUANITA: "Pelona linda".

ANDREW: *No hair* ...

JUANITA: ¿Cómo que *No hair*?

ANDREW: ¿*No hair*?

JUANITA: Bueno, está bueno, *okay* ...

ANDREW: ¿ "Pelona linda"?

JUANITA: ... Bueno, está bueno ... pues ...

ANDREW: ¡No! "Beautiful No Hair".

JUANITA: *Okay*, bueno, entonces que ... vamos a comenzar, pero no se me vaya a equivocar, acuérdese bien de lo que estás haciendo.

ANDREW: Yo ... yo le sigo ...

JUANITA: Ud. me sigue, pero cuando … no, no, no, no cante conmigo.

ANDREW: ¿De qué me acuerdo?

JUANITA: Yo voy a comenzar, y Ud. me … Ud. me … Ud. cante después de mí. Yo comienzo, y Ud. me sigue.

ANDREW: ¿De qué … ? ¿Pero de qué me voy a … acordar de qué?

JUANITA: ¡De las palabras!

ANDREW: Oh … (Voz de mentecato.)

JUANITA: No se me vayan a olvidar porque siempre se alivia olvidando todo.

ANDREW: Yo pos sabía que la novia …

JUANITA: (Pausa.) Ah, pues sí, entonces ¿tú tienes una novia?

ANDREW: Sí, tengo una novia. Tuve muchas.

JUANITA: Tuvo muchas novias … ¡de veras! ¡Ay! Estás presumiendo …

ANDREW: Tuve … varias …

JUANITA: Estás presumiendo.

ANDREW: Déjame, la recargué, te … bueno, no me …

JUANITA: ¡Estás presumiendo!

ANDREW: … Un hombre bien parecido como yo, verdad …

JUANITA: Estás presumiendo. ¿Dónde estaba tu novia?

ANDREW: ¿Eh?

JUANITA: ¿Dónde está tu novia?

ANDREW: Y luego ¿con esta ropa que traigo … ?

JUANITA: No, pues sí … me gusta tu pantalón, qué bonito.

ANDREW: No, bueno, me la recargo …

JUANITA: Se mira muy bien, se mira …

ANDREW: Yo, siempre se me ha gustado éstos también …

JUANITA: El gorro también está así, está bonito su gorro.

ANDREW: … No, entonces, porque ésa es la última moda que salió.

JUANITA: De la última moda, mire …

ANDREW: Ése es el estilo de John Wayne.

JUANITA: Oh, de John Wayne …

ANDREW: Me lo regaló Jorge Negrete.

JUANITA: ¿Se lo regaló Jorge Negrete?

ANDREW: Jorge Negrete me lo regaló.

JUANITA: ¿De veras? ¿Y la camisa?

ANDREW: Cuando estaba haciendo la película esa *Ay Jalisco no te rajes.*

JUANITA: Pero está muy feo. No él, él no está, pero éste ...

ANDREW: Es que se rajó, por eso es feo ya, pues ... ¿Qué quieres que haga? Son cosas que pasan en el mundo.

JUANITA: Bueno, ya sabe, yo comienzo y Ud. me sigue ¿eh?

ANDREW: Bueno, yo le sigo.

JUANITA: Ton ta ra, ton ta ra, ton tan ...

ANDREW: Qué bonito toca la guitarra.

JUANITA: Pues ¿qué quiere que haga si no tenemos guitarra? ¡Ves! Si te burlas, no te ayudo.

ANDREW: No, no, bueno, se puede agarrar que es melódica, ya ...

JUANITA: (Cantando.) Ton ta ... Pelona linda ...

ANDREW: (Cantando.) Linda pelona ...

JUANITA: Quién tuviera tres mechas ...

ANDREW: Tres mechas quién tuviera

JUANITA: ... Para vacilar ...

ANDREW: ... Vacilar para ...

JUANITA: ¿Dónde están mis amores?

ANDREW: Por ahi están sentados.

JUANITA: Tómale, llévale ...

ANDREW: Llévale, tómale ...

JUANITA: ... Esta suave paleta ...

ANDREW: ... Esta paleta suave ...

JUANITA & ANDREW: Para que se acuerde de este suave vacilón, ti pi tin, ti pi ton, ti pi ti pi ton, ti pi ton, ti pi ton ...

ANDREW: ... ti pi tin, ti pi ton, ti pi ti pi ti pi ton, ti pi tin, ti pi ton, ti pi ...

JUANITA: ¡Eh! ¡Ya!

ANDREW: Ah, bueno ...

JUANITA: (Cantando.) Tuve un amor ...

ANDREW: Yo tuve muchos ...

JUANITA: ... Por allá por Tepic ...

ANDREW: (Hablando.) ¿Por dónde?

JUANITA: (Cantando.) Por allá por Tepic ...

ANDREW: ¿Por dónde dijo?

JUANITA: Por allá por Tepic.

ANDREW: Te pito por allá ...

JUANITA: ... Que vivía junto ...

ANDREW: Junto vivía ...

JUANITA: ... Junto de tu mamá ...

ANDREW: (Cantando.) Yo ya no estaba allá ...

JUANITA: (Cantando.) Tómale, llévale ...

ANDREW: Llévale, tómale ...

JUANITA: ... Este suave camote ...

ANDREW: ... Este camote suave ...

JUANITA & ANDREW: Para que se acuerde de este suave vacilón, ti pi tin, ti pi ton, ti pi ti pi ton, ti pi ton, ti pi ton ...

Pretty Flapper

ANDREW: What are we going to sing?

JUANITA: "Pretty Flapper."[15]

ANDREW: Shall I introduce it? Or you? No, I'll introduce it, right?

JUANITA: You do it.

ANDREW: All right. *Ladies and Gentlemen* ...

JUANITA: Listen here, wait a minute, what are you doing?

ANDREW: Well, I'm doing the introduction.

JUANITA: But why are you saying: "*gentlemen?*" Why are you doing that?

ANDREW: Well, in English ... I'm telling them in English ...

JUANITA: Oh, you know English?

ANDREW: Well ...

JUANITA: But don't you see that this is a place where everyone speaks Spanish? You know, we're saying everything in Spanish because ... because why do you suppose? No, listen, what do you think you're doing, announcing in English?

ANDREW: Why? Haven't you heard of "*bilingual?*"

JUANITA: Of who?

ANDREW: Well, that one has to speak in Spanish and in English.

JUANITA: "*Bilingual?*"

ANDREW: Okay, who's going to speak in English? You or me? Are you going to let me do the introduction, or am I not going to do it?

JUANITA: Yes, but I'm going to tell you something, just say it correctly, if you start arguing with me ...

ANDREW: I'm going to say it right.

JUANITA: All right, go ahead ...

ANDREW: *Ladies and gentlemen ... now ...*

JUANITA: Just: *"Ladies and gentlemen?"* Nothing else? Just *"ladies ... ?"*

ANDREW: No, I'm telling the people that we're going to begin, that I'm starting, it's not that ...

JUANITA: No, no, no, *I'm sorry* ... No, excuse me, I'm sorry also.

ANDREW: *Ladies and gentlemen ...*

JUANITA: You already said that.

ANDREW: I already ... all right man, just let me begin!

JUANITA: Hey, how many times are you going to repeat the same thing?

ANDREW: Hey, I'm going to repeat it as many times as I feel like, but let's get it straight, am I going do the announcing or are you?

JUANITA: Ah, all right, it's all right, go ahead ...

ANDREW: *Ladies and gentlemen ...*

JUANITA: Again, oyyy ... (Sighing.)

ANDREW: *Now ...* (Long pause.) No, wait a minute, I forgot something, right?

JUANITA: What did you forget?

ANDREW: No, no, something is missing.

JUANITA: Ah, all right ...

ANDREW: (Pause.) *Boys and "boyas" too ...*

JUANITA: Oooh, what do you mean, *"boys and boyas?"*

ANDREW: Well yes, "boys and girls," right?

JUANITA: Ahhh! (Slapping sound.) *Girls!*

ANDREW: Well, it's the same, *"boys and boyas,"* isn't it?

JUANITA: No, no, what do you mean saying *"boys y boyas?"*

ANDREW: Yes, it's the same. *"Boys and boyas" too, now we are ...* (Speaking very slowly with an artificial accent.)

JUANITA: Look, he does know how to do it. (Tone of admiration.)

ANDREW: *We are going to cantar ...*

JUANITA: Listen, you blew it there.

ANDREW: Eh?

JUANITA: You don't say *"cantar"* in English.

ANDREW: How do you say *"cantar"*?

JUANITA: *"Sing."*

ANDREW: *Sing?*

JUANITA: Ah hah.

ANDREW: Now we are going to sing ...

JUANITA: "Pelona linda."

ANDREW: *No hair ...*

JUANITA: What do you mean, *No hair?*

ANDREW: *No hair?*

JUANITA: All right, it's all right, okay ...

ANDREW: "Pelona linda"?

JUANITA: ... All right, it's all right, already.

ANDREW: No! "Beautiful No Hair."

JUANITA: Okay, all right, so then ... we are going to begin, but don't get me wrong, remember real well what you're doing.

ANDREW: I'll ... I'll follow you ...

JUANITA: You'll follow me, but when ... no, no, no, don't sing with me.

ANDREW: What am I supposed to remember?

JUANITA: I'm going to start, and you ... you sing after me. I'll start, and you'll follow me.

ANDREW: But what ... ? What am I supposed to remember?

JUANITA: The words!

ANDREW: Oh ... (Meek simpleton voice.)

JUANITA: Don't go forgetting them on me, because you always get off by forgetting everything.

ANDREW: Okay, I knew that my girl friend ...

JUANITA: (Pause.) Ah, okay, so then you have a girlfriend?

ANDREW: Yes, I have a girlfriend. I've had lots of them.

JUANITA: You've had lots of girlfriends ... really! Ay! You're putting on airs ...

ANDREW: I had ... several ...

JUANITA: You're putting on airs.

ANDREW: Give me a break, you're getting on my case ... all right, don't ...

JUANITA: You're putting on airs!

ANDREW: ... A good looking man like me, right ...

JUANITA: You're putting on airs. Where was your girlfriend?

ANDREW: Eh?

JUANITA: Where is your girlfriend?

ANDREW: And then, with these clothes that I'm wearing ... ?

JUANITA: No, well, yes, I like your pants, how cute.

ANDREW: No, all right, I really put on the dog.

JUANITA: You look real nice, you look ...

ANDREW: I've always liked them, too ...

JUANITA: The cap is also all right, it's cute too.

ANDREW: No, then, its the latest style that just came out.

JUANITA: Now, just look at that, the latest style ...

ANDREW: That is the style of John Wayne.

JUANITA: Oh, John Wayne's ... (Laughing.)

ANDREW: Jorge Negrete gave it to me.[16]

JUANITA: Jorge Negrete gave it to you?

ANDREW: Jorge Negrete gave it to me.

JUANITA: Really? And the shirt?

ANDREW: When he was making that movie *Ay Jalisco no te rajes.*[17]

JUANITA: But it's real ugly. He's not, no, but this hat ...

ANDREW: No, it's just that he ripped it, that's why it's ugly now. What do you want me to do? These things happen in the world.

JUANITA: All right, you've got it straight now? I begin and you follow me, right?

ANDREW: All right, I'll follow you.

JUANITA: Ton ta ra, ton ta ra, ton tan ...

ANDREW: How nicely she plays the guitar.

JUANITA: Well, what do you want me to do if we don't have a guitar? If you make fun of me, I won't help you.

ANDREW: No, no, all right, you can tell that it's melodic ...

JUANITA: (Singing.) Ton ta ... Pretty flapper ...

ANDREW: (Singing.) Pretty flapper ...

JUANITA: Oh, if I only had but three locks of hair ...

ANDREW: Three locks, if only I were so lucky as to have them ...

JUANITA: ... To have a good time with ...

ANDREW: ... A good time to have with ...

JUANITA: Where are my loves?

ANDREW: They are sitting over there.

JUANITA: Take it to her, carry it to her ...

ANDREW: Carry it to her, take it to her ...

JUANITA: ... This soft popsicle ...

ANDREW: ... This popsicle soft ...

JUANITA & ANDREW: To remind her of this smooth good time song, ti pi tin, ti pi ton, ti pi ti pi ton, ti pi ton, ti pi ton ...

ANDREW: ... Ti pi tin, ti pi ton, ti pi ti pi ti pi ton, ti pi tin, ti pi ton, ti pi ...

JUANITA: Eh! Enough already!

ANDREW: Ah, all right ...

JUANITA: (Singing.) I had a love ...

ANDREW: I had many ...

JUANITA: Over there near Tepic ...

ANDREW: (Speaking.) Over where?

JUANITA: (Singing.) Over there near Tepic ...

ANDREW: Over where did you say?

JUANITA: Over there near Tepic ...

ANDREW: I'll whistle at you over there.[18]

JUANITA: That used to live next door ...

ANDREW: Next door used to live ...

JUANITA: Next door to your momma.

ANDREW: (Singing.) I was no longer there ...

JUANITA: (Singing.) Take it to her, carry it to her ...

ANDREW: Carry it to her, take it to her ...

JUANITA: This soft sweet potato ...

ANDREW: This sweet potato soft ... [19]

JUANITA & ANDREW: To remind her of this smooth good time song, ti pi tin, ti pi ton, ti pi ti pi ton, ti pi ton, ti pi ton ...

Juanita

That's it. We used to dance while we sang the song. Andrés was really funny; he was called El Chapulín, The Grasshopper.

Andrew

See, when she's singing, she's insulting me, and I will find my way out. That's why I stop, and she keeps on saying it. And then I keep on thinking up the answers. I come out with good answers. In Spanish it comes out with a good answer.

They never really recorded too much of that kind of thing, which was amazing. But all that sort of went out back in the '30s. Comedians used to sing funny, comedic songs. A few of them were recorded, and then they stopped. I don't know what happened. They have come out lately with a lot of dirty jokes, but this was something different. The comedians would tell jokes and sing funny songs, but they were more of a family kind of thing.

We used to compose a lot of that type of thing for our stage show. We used to break our heads making them up. Actually, we were forced to invent them. Our mother used to force us to do something, and when she told you to do it, you had to do it. She used to say, "You have to make up something different. The same people might come back again, and they've already seen the show, so we have to give them something else."

What I had to do, it's not an easy thing to do, to be a comedian, because you have to break your brains to make people laugh. And it's not an easy thing to do. What are you going to say? How are you going to entertain for that person for five minutes so the next act can get dressed and all that. You have to get it out of your head, because if you don't, what are you going to do?

"Just go out and do something," my mother would say. So I would go out there and do something and say something, entertain the people. And it's not as easy as it looks. I guess that's why a lot of comedians have writers.

Juanita

You have to remember that some of those routines were real long. And when you finished you had to dance. As soon as we finished, we would start dancing. We had to come up with our own ideas. And sometimes Andrew would make me laugh, and Momma would get real mad at me. You see, when you're acting, you're not supposed to laugh, you ruined the act, but we were just children. Momma would raise hell if we laughed or messed up the act.

Andrew

For instance, in Lamesa, out in West Texas, we used to play the Capitán Theater, and then the tent that was next door. We would play out in the tent until the movie was over, and then we would jump over to the other side and play inside the theater. We would jump back and forth. Sometimes the audience would already have heard us out in the tent, so when we went into the theater we had to change. We'd give them something different.

Juanita

Some people liked us so much that they would follow us. If they knew that we were going to be in a little town not too far away, they would come to see us. We used to notice that we would see some of the same people in different places where we would play. They would travel pretty far just to get a chance to see more of the show.

Andrew

Lydia would end the *variedad*, and then she would say:

Para terminar esta variedad vamos a tener a todo el conjunto.

To end this variety show we're going to have the whole group.

And everybody would come out, and everybody would sing, and everybody, except Lydia and María, would dance. We would sing something like:

Qué malas son, qué malas son las mujeres.
Qué malas son, qué buenas son las mujeres.

How bad they are, how bad the women are.
How bad they are, how good the women are.

And then we would dance, and in the middle there would be some joking. Originally Juanita and Manuel would end the show, dancing and singing. Afterwards I would do it. They would sing, and I would dance, and Janie would dance. Then we used to sing "Doña Mariquita."

And then I would start dancing with Juanita. The people would be laughing because of the funny way that I danced. I would make all kinds of comical dances. Then Lydia would come out and end the show.

Juanita

In the late forties they would still show movies between our performances. Although, sometimes, they'd tell Mamá that we could make a little more money, not a lot, but a little, if we played two shows, a long one and short one, so they didn't have to show a movie. Mamá would always say okay, because that way we got more money. We would give them about two hours. Towards the end of that period—the early '50s—Lydia would go with us part of the time, but not always. We managed real well without her.

María

When we started out with the variety show like that after the war, people wanted to hear Juanita y María, Las Hermanas Mendoza. We were already stars, we had a name, and people wanted to hear us. We had made a lot of records. People knew that we were Lydia's sisters, but they came to hear us.

Standing: Juanita and Manuel. Seated: Lydia and María. (Courtesy of the Lydia Mendoza collection).

We played to full houses on the road with just the Hermanas Mendoza and the *variedad*.

CHAPTER 9

Life on the Road:
"No Dogs or Mexicans Allowed"

Lydia

We toured practically all over the United States during the late '40s and early '50s, but some of the places where we really used to draw in the most people were the tents that a man named Stout Jackson had down in South Texas. When Stout Jackson was still alive and we worked those *carpas*, we really pulled in the people. I was still in my prime, very popular, and you just imagine, especially with all the people that used to come to work around there, how well we did.

They used to give us a percentage. None of those places ever paid a fixed amount. For example, they might offer you thirty percent or at the most, forty percent of the gate. Those *carpas* were actually primarily for showing movies. Sometimes after the film, they would present a *variedad*. They would charge the audience a little bit more for the *variedad*, and so then they would give us forty percent and take care of all the other expenses. And we usually did very well there.

It was my *compadre*, El Doctor Nopal, Ramiro Cortés, who booked us into those South Texas *carpas*, and he knew Stout Jackson very well.

Ramiro Cortés

I didn't usually book my acts into *carpas*. We really specialized in movie theaters. The only *carpas* I played were in Robstown, Alice, Falfurrias and Kingsville. Those big, huge tents, they were owned by a man by the name of Stout Jackson, who used to be the strongest man in the whole, wide world. He was even in the *Believe It or Not* book. He would raise five bales of cotton on his back, which was twenty-five hundred pounds on his back. I mean ... he was strong. They called him "Stout." And, when I met him—a long time ago, when I was working with the motion pictures on the road, I met him in Corpus—he had a side show in a carnival. He would hold up an automobile with his back, doing a strongman. And he had this nice little tent ... a nice little tent which would hold about eight hundred seats, something like that. And I told him, "Hey, Stout, would you like to go into show business, into the motion picture business?"

"Hey, how can I do that?" he says.

"Well, you're maybe getting tired of lifting things," I asked, "and what you gonna do then with the tent?"

"Well, I don't know," he says.

"Well," I told him, "why don't you set your tent over here in Robstown, buy a couple of projectors and have somebody show movies in them. I'll give you the pictures. I'll send you the motion pictures on a percentage basis."

Stout took to the idea right away. He talked to his wife and to his son. They closed his show right away, because he was very tired of lifting things.

Stout Jackson was a man who would always have some of those big nails, number eight nails as wide as your finger, you know, in his pocket. When he would meet someone, he would wrap up his handkerchief around one of those nails, and—"Yeeeeeee!"—he'd twist it up like a pretzel and give it to you as a souvenir. He was getting tired of that. So the next time I was around, he already had his tent put up in Robstown, Texas, in an empty space he had found there. He had already gone to Dallas and bought these two projectors, which were very good at that time. They were portable, thirty-five millimeter movie projectors.

I gave him a picture to show, and he made so much money so fast! And he only was charging twenty-five cents admission price. They were all Mexican pictures that I supplied him with. That first one was *Chucho el Roto*, that was the title of the picture. Stout Jackson started doing really well, and I told him that I was only going to charge him thirty-five percent. Well, I believe that first night he made about a thousand dollars. That was two hundred and fifty dollars for the motion picture, and seven hundred and fifty dollars for him. He was so happy. He forgot about the nails, the horseshoes and holding back a train. He used to be very strong, very strong!

I went back to San Antonio, and I told my boss there, "Mr. Jiménez, I've already opened up another place."

My job in those days was to try to open up places where they would show the pictures. Because most of the theaters didn't care for the Mexican pictures. They didn't know what they were losing. You see, before I started working with Lydia, I was working for this man, Mr. Jiménez. He had the first distributing office for Mexican and Spanish language motion pictures in the United States; it was called the Latin American Film Agency. I still use that name for my company here in Hollywood today, because I'm now a distributor of pictures, myself. I sell pictures, I buy pictures, and I sell them to Mexico—not exactly a distributor, but a broker.

This man Jiménez was in San Antonio, Texas, with his office, which was a branch office. The main office was in El Paso, Texas, and was run by the Calderóns. The Calderón brothers, they used to be producers of these pictures, and they were also buyers from all of the independent producers in Mexico. In that time, they used to produce maybe three or four pictures a year in Mexico. These pictures were distributed out of San Antonio and El Paso for California, Texas and Arizona, where most of the Latin people, almost all the Mexican people, were living in those days.

I started with Mr. Jiménez, and I worked for him for a while. I learned where all these places were, all these little towns. I worked there one year before I went out on the road with Lydia. So when I went out, I quit this man, because I didn't like to be working for nobody, for nobody! So, I went to work as an impresario, as the manager for the Lydia group, for the Mendoza group. But I had made all my contacts with the theaters all over the Southwest while I was working for Mr. Jiménez and the Calderón brothers; and one of the people I had developed for them was Stout Jackson.

So then this guy Stout Jackson, he had some money saved already, and he bought another tent. He opened up a tent in Alice, and then another in Falfurrias and one in Kingsville. Kingsville, that was the big one. But as time went by, he had done so well that he made these tents into theaters. He made them into big theaters, like a tent, only the top was made out of asbestos and wood and everything, but it was in the form of a tent. And Stout Jackson was right. "The people," Stout used to say, "they like to go to a tent. They like to go to the circus. The people, the lower class people, you know, the cotton pickers and all those kind of people, they don't like to be in a nice theater. They like to go where they can spit and eat and everything."

And Stout was right, he was right. Because after that, a lot of people opened up big, nice theaters, for the Mexican people, but they didn't have any business. The people wanted a tent. They still do!

Stout Jackson passed away already. The *carpas* were still pretty popular then in those places. And in Mexico, a lot of *carpas* go around the country after the harvest time. They still have a lot of *carpas*, beautiful ones. I love those *carpas*, man. I wish I had one myself.

I would go with Lydia to Stout Jackson's tents not only every year, but every six months. Stout used to call me up, "Hey, Cortés, come on, bring Lydia, God damn it."

"All right," I'd say.

We used to make a lot of money in those tents, a lot of money. Lydia was never the only act. We always took the family. And when the family didn't want to go out, when they were going to school or something like that, I'd get somebody else. Like, another girl, you know, that would show her legs, like a ballet!

I used to tell my *comadre*, "Why don't you show something?" Just for fun, you know. We had a nice time. It was nice. It is a very beautiful episode in my life. I mean, I got a good living out of show business myself. I enjoyed it very much. Every day was a holiday for all of us. We used to have a good time going on the road.

I'm too old now, otherwise I'd be out on the road now with somebody. I liked it. I was on the road all the time. I used to put on a hundred thousand miles in six months on one station wagon. I used to buy two station wagons every year. That was my life; that was my tool to work with.

We never missed a day out on the road. Sometimes we even had to play three towns in one night. For instance, out here in California we used to play San Francisco, San Jose and Salinas all on the same night. Yeah, I used to travel. And at that time, it was harder to travel because there were no freeways like nowadays.

A lot of people ask me about those days because I'm the oldest impresario in the Mexican business—the oldest one. And sometimes they ask me about what it was like back then, and I make fun, and I say, "Ah, we used to have small, little narrow roads. We used to fight with Indians to get through. ... "

In my career in show business, I had some real bad nights—when just nobody showed up. But not with Lydia, but I had it with other people. Yeah, I had it with other people, but never with Lydia. I took care of all of the promotion. We would go to the radio stations, sometimes, not all the time. I would call, like, one week before. I arranged for my tour, and one week before we would arrive in each town, I would call the theater, and, "Hey, I'm coming with Lydia Mendoza next Wednesday. I'll see you next Wednesday," I would tell the manager of the theater.

"All right," he would say.

I had a printing shop in San Antonio which would make me some window cards and handbills. And then I would give this printing shop the order and say, for instance, "You send to the Granada Theater in Fresno, California, send them fifty window cards and send them a thousand handbills."

So the printer would do that. He already had the form made for the whole thing, see, only he would just have to print the head, the name of the theater, and the date, that's all; the rest of it was already made. They do it now with phototypesetting, they don't make no more cuts. They used to make lead cuts, remember, a long time ago? Now they don't do that, they just photograph everything. It's easier now and cheaper.

We usually just advertised the show by placards that would be put up in the windows, window cards. And then, when the theater manager received the printed stuff, he would start advertising on the radio programs that he ordinarily used himself. In his town, he would pay for the whole thing himself. The print shop would send him everything C.O.D., collect. But, a lot of times, we would get to the town in time to go on the radio program and help with the promotion. We would go to the radio station. I never let Lydia sing on the radio, only talk, say hello to the public, "I'll wait for you tonight at the theater. ... " and all of that. But they would play a record for her. We would talk on the radio; tell the public that we were going to be there.

Lydia Mendoza was quite a show. She was made for that, she was born for that. I understand that she's still performing for people, still bringing in the crowds somewhere. She can still sing.[1] She can sure play that big guitar. She lost a lot of guitars. They would steal the guitars from her. She's one of the few people that can play that type of guitar. Very few people can do it. I think she is the only one in the Mexican field that plays a twelve string guitar. It's hard just to tune that guitar.

Lydia

In those days all of those places in South Texas were very good for us because of all the workers that would concentrate there, but ever since the introduction of the harvesting machines for cotton, the work for the people has disappeared down there and the workers no longer congregate there like in the old days. But back then, Sinton, Corpus, Robstown, Alice, so many little towns, were all strictly cotton towns, and they would overflow with people during the harvest time. Stout Jackson set up those theaters, and they were overwhelmed with people. It was like that wherever you went down there during the '40s and '50s. But ever since the machines came in, all that is just a memory, it all came to an end with the machines. Even the theaters have disappeared. All through West Texas and the Valley, where there were once many theaters, now there are almost none. They no longer operate. In many places they were pulled down, and in others they have been converted into *salones de baile*, dance halls, but of movies and *variedades* like before, nothing remains.

Nowadays there are lots of *caravanas*, some of them very big, that bring lots of *artistas* from Mexico as well as local ones, but they do their shows in stadiums and auditoriums, not in theaters as in the old days. And then television came along, and everything went down hill. The crest of success of the artist who worked the theaters came to an end, principally of those artists who would tour around the theaters presenting variety shows. These *caravanas* they have nowadays are *un matadero de los demonios*, a demon's slaughterhouse. They really work you hard, they keep those *artistas* running. In the old days, it wasn't like that. You would arrive at the theater and present your two variety shows, or maybe just one, and that was it; you were finished for the night. Nowadays, no, you work over here and then over there and on and on. You might work four or five times in different locations on the same night—it's a slaughterhouse, a real killer. In the old days we were very tranquil and very happy.

When we were going on the tours out West, like around Lubbock, Amarillo, all that, we did experience some discrimination. They didn't serve Mexicans in those places. One time we went into a restaurant without knowing, and they didn't serve us. And there was a sign where it said "No Mexicans." My brothers and sisters remember some of those incidents very well.

Manuel

We used to run into some discrimination when we were out on the road. They used to think that Mamá was a gypsy. She used to wear great big earrings, those big round ones. And every time that we tried to rent a tourist court to stay in the places where we worked, they would look at us and say,"No, no vacancy."

There would be a sign outside which said "Vacancy," but when we asked for a room, there was "No vacancy."

The place that really took the cake, though, was over in West Texas, a town called Levelland. That place was so famous for its discrimination that Arturo Ortiz even wrote a *corrido* about it during the war. Something happened to us there when I came back from the Service. I don't even like to think about it. It's just something that happened, and I want to erase it out of my mind. I hate to think back about how they treated people in places like that. But it's part of our history, and I'll tell you what happened.

We used to go play around a lot of those little towns out in West Texas: Sweetwater, Levelland, Lamesa. There was a restaurant there in Levelland that had a sign right on the door: "No Dogs or Mexicans Allowed." It was the same way at the tourist camps: "No Mexicans Allowed."

Juanita

One time María and I went to Denver, Colorado, to sing at the Arapahoe Grill. The owner was white, really white. He was Spanish, but he was really white. He looked like an Anglo. One afternoon that we weren't working at the Arapahoe Grill, we went out to work in Greeley. On the way back, we stopped at a restaurant in Greeley. We all went inside and sat down. It was the owner of the Arapahoe, Mamá, María and I. The waitress came over and said, "We can serve him," she said, "but not the rest of you."

I really got mad. He was Spanish, too, only he was really white. I got so mad that I threw a glass. And then the owner of the Arapahoe, he really got mad, too.

"If you don't serve them," he said, "I won't eat either!"

"Well, we can serve you," the waitress replied, "and they can eat in the kitchen."

Then Mamá got real mad, she got really mad! And the owner of the Arapahoe talked to the owner of that restaurant: "You don't know who these girls are," he said. "They're singers, they're famous performers. You don't know what you're doing!"

We didn't eat at that restaurant. I guess that we weren't really hungry, anyhow. This happened in the early 1950s, when Mamá was still alive. María and I were making records, and we were starting to become real popular. We got a contract to go out and play in Denver. We worked at the Arapahoe Grill there and also at the Juárez Club.

Andrew

When we talk about discrimination, we have to talk reality. You see, what we have to understand is the difference that there was at the time for the Anglos and the Mexican Americans. If you don't try to understand the way it was, then there will be things that you won't understand. It was not a simple matter for a Negro to go into a restroom with a White man. It was the same thing with the Mexican American. I mean, the Mexican American was a gypsy. ...

María

Over there in Colorado they don't like Mexican people or Negroes or gypsies, just Americans.

Andrew

They were pretty bad over there in West Texas, too. One time we were touring over in that area and we happened to have Valerio Longoria, the accordion player and *conjunto* leader, along with us. Valerio went to Lubbock with us. We made the show, and then when we got out. "Let's go to a restaurant and buy some hamburgers or something," Valerio told me. "Okay," I said, "we're all hungry."

So we went into this restaurant, and we were standing there, and the waitress came over, and said, "What you want?"

"Well, we just want about six hamburgers to go," I told her.

And the waitress looked at me, and she said, "Is he with you?" pointing at Valerio.

"Yes, ma'am," I said, "he's with me."

"Well, I'll sell to you," she said, "but I won't sell to him."

"Well, okay, it doesn't matter," I replied, "sell to me."

"Well, you have to tell him to get out of here first," that waitress told me.

So I said, "Okay, Valerio, she says that she doesn't want you in here. She says for you to go out."

"Why?" Valerio asked me.

"Well, I mean, because she doesn't want to sell to you. That's the way it is here."

So Valerio went out and waited for me. I got the hamburgers, and we got out of there, and Valerio said, "I'm not a Negro. I'm not that dark, I'm white."

"Well, you're halfways," I said.

I'm not really sure what that woman was thinking, maybe she thought that Valerio was Black. I don't know, I think she thought that either he was a Negro or ... I don't know. But she didn't want him inside. She'd accept me, but she didn't accept him. That was in Lubbock, Texas in the fifties.

Valerio Longoria

I first met Juanita and María Mendoza about 1947 or 1948. I went out to West Texas with them about two times, two years, for the cotton harvest. I guess their mother had heard about me. They needed an accordion player, so she got in touch with me. I had already had some hits on Corona, so she must have heard them, and then she called me. We didn't go to pick cotton, we used to play at the theater in Lubbock. It was the Royal Theater. I went with Juanita and María Mendoza, and their mother, Lydia Mendoza's mother, was the one who booked them. They took me along to accompany them on the accordion. I was also the driver. The car belonged to Mrs. Mendoza, their mother, and Juanita and María, and Lydia. It was an old car, and they hired me to drive the car and work with them in the theater.

We would go directly to a motel, get ready for the show, and then we would go to the theater. First they would show a movie, American movies, and then, in the middle of the show, they would open up for the *variedad*, for Juanita and María Mendoza to sing. They had brothers, one was Manolo, I remember him very well, and the other, he was like a clown, a comic, Andrés, El Chapulín. He used to get up there first, and then Juanita, María and I would come on to play second. María Mendoza would play the guitar and I would accompany them on accordion. It was just the accordion and the guitar, no *bajo sexto*, no drums. Juanita and María sang very beautifully, and the people really liked it. They had good voices. And Lydia, well, I never went with Lydia. She was on the guitar also, playing, but I never accompanied Lydia. Lydia didn't go on those trips out to West Texas. It was just Las Hermanas Mendoza. The audience was all people who had come for *las pizcas*, the cotton harvest. A lot of people would go up there to pick cotton, really a lot of people.

One time they put me out to talk, to introduce the show to the theater. I was too young. Mrs. Mendoza got mad at me because I just went out there and said, "Well, ladies and gentlemen, now we have Juanita and María Mendoza," right away. I didn't say anthing like a comic or anything like that, because I didn't know, I didn't know how to do it.

She really got mad: "What're you doing? You're supposed to talk! You're supposed to talk and make the people laugh and make them feel happy, so that when Juanita and María came out, the people are already happy!"

What could I tell her? I didn't know how. She was in good health, maybe forty-five or fifty years old, and very strong. She was a big woman.

So we would play in Lubbock one night, and then the next night we would play in Big Spring, and then the next night in Lamesa—Friday, Saturday and Sunday. The rest of the week everybody would be out in the fields picking cotton all day. Sometimes I went to pick cotton, also. But I didn't pick cotton too much. Maybe fifty pounds a day, or something like that. People used to do lots more than that. I knew a guy that used to pick twelve hundred pounds a day! That was back in 1946 or '47, or maybe '48. Then the machines came in and put an end to all that. We would spend the whole cotton harvest up there, maybe a month or a month and a half, two months.

When we were on the road from San Antonio to Lubbock and Big Spring, they wouldn't let us use the restrooms. Like in Fredericksburg, and all those other little towns, they didn't want Hispanics in the restaurants. They wouldn't let you go into the restaurants. They had a little window to the outside, and they would sell you the hamburgers, or whatever, chili, to the outside through a little window. You had to buy your food on the outside, and they didn't let you use the restrooms. They didn't want you on the inside or in the restrooms.

Discrimination, there was a lot of it! Especially up until the Second World War. After the war, then some guys who came from the Army, they tried to tell them to stay out, but they went inside, balls up, right (*a huevo, eh*). They would be afraid to kick them out, because they would break everything in the place. In Fredericksburg, I saw something like that. Two Hispanics, they came from the Army, they were Hispanics, but they were dressed in uniforms. They went inside a restaurant, and the management kicked them out. So those two guys grabbed rocks and broke all the windows, they "made pieces" out of that restaurant, and then they ran. They ran, because there was still discrimination there. But nobody was going to take them on while they were doing it. Those two guys, Hispanic soldiers, came from the Army, but they still didn't want to sell to them.

Pretty soon, they started letting Hispanics in, because they were afraid of them. Now there's not so much of that. There's still places, like Fredericksburg and all these little towns, between Lubbock and San Antonio, there are still places where you can get in, but the people, the Anglo people, they look at you hard. They don't want to sit down with you or talk with you or anything like that. There's still discrimination in some parts of Texas. Even in San Antonio a lot of the restaurants, the big restaurants, if Hispanics go in there, well, if you're well-dressed, it's all right, but you know, average people, they don't wear a tie, and you can tell by the way the Anglos look at you, the way they act.

At that time, the Hispanics used to break up restaurants. When we went to West Texas to work, they didn't want you inside of restaurants, they would just sell to you through a little window. And if you went to a gas station, they wouldn't let you use the restroom. They'd say, "Hey, go outside to the pasture, my restroom is broke. No Mexicans allowed."

They used to put that sign on restaurants: "No Mexicans Allowed." These people used to eat in the kitchen in those days in Texas. Either outside, in the back or in the kitchen.

Ramiro Cortés

We used to tour in the West, we used to play West Texas, like Lubbock, San Angelo, those were the bad places. I used to take Lydia and the family show over there during the cotton-picking season; there were a lot of people, a lot of money. Not now, because now they pick cotton with machines. But then, it was all by hand. Especially, we used to stay about three weeks in Lubbock, Texas. And every night we would play a different town, and every night come back to sleep in Lubbock.

That was how we managed to avoid a lot of the discrimination that you could run into out there. Lydia would cook for all of us. She was a good cook. She used to make the finest flour tortillas I have ever tasted in my life. And, during the day we didn't do anything; we just stayed indoors in the tourist court or whatever and rested. We would go out at seven o'clock at night to certain towns around. ... Out to Amarillo, for instance, and then we would play in Colorado, too, Denver, Colorado. And, some places around Colorado, we used to play around all that too. But mostly, in Texas, in West Texas, and that's where they had a lot of discrimination. You would see restaurants where it would say: "No Mexicans Allowed," "No Negroes Allowed," "No Colored People and No Dogs," at that time. But I would make sure that we didn't have to go in those places. Nothing ever happened to us because I was pretty careful. I was pretty careful not to visit those places where I would see the signs in all of these towns. I used to put all of my people in a tourist court—in tourist courts where they had kitchenettes—and we used to cook our own meals. That way, we'd keep out of trouble.

For instance, there was a town out close to Eagle Pass, I forget the name of this town, oh, but it was bad. There was a president of the United States that was born in this little town. It's on the highway coming from San Antonio to Del Rio and to Eagle Pass. There was this town ... oh, it was bad. We used to go play there, but we used to come from San Antonio and go back to San Antonio the same night. That was how we generally managed to stay out of trouble: by being very careful about everything we did.

Just being around that kind of discrimination could make you feel pretty strange. I used to see a lot of things I didn't like, but, I mean, what could I do? There were a lot of people that used to go work out there in West Texas, a lot of movie stars; they were run out of restaurants, nice people. There was another fellow, by the name of Antonio Badú. He was a big movie star, big one, one of the biggest ones they ever had in Mexico. He is still living. We went into one of those restaurants, just because we wanted to go. We were in Lubbock, Texas—that was the worst of them all, Lubbock. Lamesa, San Angelo, all those places out there were pretty bad, but Lubbock was the worst.

Antonio and I stopped at the best hotel, the hotel was all right. Antonio was making personal appearances with me over there. I took him around. We saw a big sign right across the street from the hotel. The sign was in front of a big, nice, beautiful restaurant: "No Mexicans or Colored Admitted." See? This was in Lubbock.

So I told Antonio, "Let's go in there. Let's go and see how it is."

"All right, let's go," he said.

We were dressed up very nice, you know. So, we got in, we sat down at a table, we ordered a big steak, nice food. They served us, very nice, and everything. "Anything else?" the waiter asked us when we finished.

"No, no, no ... ," we told him.

We lingered over our coffee, and we talked, and we stayed there about an hour, and nothing happened. We got the bill, we left a tip, we got up and paid.

As we were going out, I told the cashier, "I thought you said 'No Mexicans allowed,' you know? Well, we're Mexicans." And we showed her our passports.

"My goodness!" she said, "you don't look like it." "Well," we said, "you're making a mistake. All the time you've been missing out. There's a lot of Mexicans ... "

So, we had a good time, you see, we had our laugh. It was just for fun, you know. But that was it. But, nowadays, no more of that.

Lydia

Despite some of the things that we had to endure out on the road, I'm very glad to be able to say that in every place that I have sung in my long career, I have never received any disappointment from any audience. All have treated me the same. Of course, some, like when I went to South America, have shown incredible enthusiasm, that tremendous emotion of the public. Another very great satisfaction was when I went the first time to Chihuahua. We entered the city, which is the state capital, on June 27, 1950. The people received me there like they would have received a king, a president. They put ... from corner to corner in all of the streets some banners saying, "Welcome Lydia Mendoza." For some three or four miles before entering the city there were people along the side of the road waiting for the car that I was riding in to pass by. They seated me in a convertible, and they filled it with flowers. I went passing through, and as I went by the people threw confetti and shouted, "¡Viva Lydia Mendoza!" And it was the same when I entered the city. That was a very great satisfaction when I went to Chihuahua.

They gave me the same type of welcome when I went to Cuidad Juárez. A truck went around throwing confetti with a mariachi playing music. I played strictly in theaters on that tour. The tour lasted about a week.

They presented me in Cuidad Juárez, then in Chihuahua, then in Camargo, and ... it was a week like that, just eight days as I recall. My *compadre*, El Doctor Nopal, Ramiro Cortés, arranged that first tour of ours to Mexico and remembers some of the details.

Ramiro Cortés

I used to bring big stars from Mexico for the tours that I put together, and I used to put Lydia together with the biggest stars from Mexico. And everybody was astonished. Everybody would admire her so much, because they liked the way she was singing. But I wasn't smart enough to take Lydia and the *variedad* to Mexico, and I didn't realize that we were really missing out on a great opportunity. Because Lydia was also extremely popular on the other side of the border, in Mexico, on the frontier of Mexico and the United States. She was even more popular there than in her own Texas, on this side. Like, for instance, in the State of Chihuahua, all the northern part of Mexico, she was so very popular because of her recordings and all the airplay that she was getting on those powerful border radio stations.

I finally became aware of all this in 1950 when I received a telegram from a fellow in Chihuahua City asking me if Lydia Mendoza was available to appear for a couple of days in Chihuahua and how much I wanted for her—just her, he didn't care about the group or nothing—just her. But I didn't even answer this guy because I thought, well, we ain't got no business in Mexico, you know, our business is here in the United States. I was a fool.

This guy kept on after me. One day he called me on the phone in San Antonio. He phoned me there. And he said, "Look, Señor Cortés, why don't you answer my telegrams?"

"Well," I said, "I don't care to take Lydia across the border; we've got plenty of work over here in the United States: more than I can do. She's got to go to Chicago and up to New York and all those places."

"Look," this guy tells me, "I'll give you five thousand dollars for two nights."

At that time, five thousand dollars, you had to break all of the banks to get five thousand dollars! That was a lot of money: it was a fortune. I thought the guy was playing with me. "Well, listen," I started to tell this fellow.

"No, you listen to me," he said, "I can send you a draft right now. I can send you a check. I can order the bank, the Commercial Bank in San Antonio, to pay you five thousand dollars any time you want. Just send me a telegram saying 'yes.'"

So then, I talked to Lydia, "Look, Lydia, this guy must be crazy. He's offering me five thousand dollars for two nights. Only for you, not to the rest of the show."

Lydia says, "Well, let's get the money," and then she thought for a minute, and she says, "All right, let's go."

"No, let's get the money first," I told her. Because I still didn't believe it.

So, I send the guy a telegram. And the next day, the very next day, they called me from the Commercial Bank, El Banco Comercial, in San Antonio: "Yeah, we got an order here to pay you five thousand dollars." So, I went and picked up the money.

At that time, I was working ... I always worked on a percentage basis with Lydia, see. We had a salary paid to the family, and then she and I would split the difference. We'd split the balance. We were making very good money. I made enough money to educate my big boy in colleges and everything. And Lydia made enough money, too, only her husband would just spend most of it all the time, you know.

So here came the day that we had to leave for Mexico, my goodness! Well, I drove Lydia all the way. I had a brand new station wagon, and I drove her down to Chihuahua.

You know, before you get to Chihuahua, the city of Chihuahua, you have to go through about 230 miles of the state of Chihuahua. They both have the same name, Chihuahua, and it's all desert. It must have been about fifteen kilometers before we got to Chihuahua City, we were stopped by the police out on the highway. I thought they were Immigration or something about papers, you know, so we stopped. "Pull over and get out of the car, come over here. Come to the side, get over to this side," they told us.

There were some policemen in uniform and some other men in civilian clothes there, and they had a little tent, a little tent set up off to the side of the highway. "Lydia Mendoza?" one of the officers asked us.

"Yeah, that's Lydia Mendoza," I told them.

"All right, this is the city mayor of Chihuahua, and I'm the chief of police, and these are two of my other colleagues, important politicians. We have a parade going, we have a parade fixed for Lydia, and we want her to get dressed here in the little tent—put on her costume, you know, for the parade."

I was astonished, myself. All right, so I told Lydia what it was all about, and she got dressed in that little tent. She changed into one of her costumes and everything. Then they put her in an open car, a brand-new Oldsmobile convertible, which was followed by a truck, a big, beautiful truck, all with ribbons and flowers, a full *mariachi* band and a big arch that says "Lydia Mendoza" riding on the flatbed.

I was in the automobile, myself, along with Lydia, the city mayor and a couple other big shots. God damn, I ... I'm telling you!

When we got right into the city, we were really surprised. All the main streets were jammed, so many people were waiting for Lydia. And they had arches and banners across the streets saying things like, "Welcome Lydia Mendoza, *Bienvenida a Lydia Mendoza*, Welcome Lydia Mendoza!"

So then, that's when I said,"My goodness! I think I made a mistake. I should've took ten thousand dollars instead of just five."

If I'd've asked that guy for ten thousand, he'd have probably given it to me without blinking an eye. He told me later on, "You don't know how to do business with this woman, Mr. Cortés," he says. "If you'd've asked me for ten thousand, I would've given it to you."

I'm telling you! The show was going to be in the bullring, because it was larger, had more seats, than any theater in Chihuahua. It was the biggest place they had. It wasn't big enough—the bullring was not big enough. They

Lydia Mendoza entering Chihuahua, June 27, 1950. Courtesy of the Lydia Mendoza collection.

must have had about twenty thousand people that night there that came to see that show. They had other people in the show, you know, other artists, local artists, and then, at the top of the bill, Lydia. The second night was the same as the first—really wild.

Then another guy came in from Torreón, Coahuila, a big town in the state of Coahuila. And this guy came over, and he says, "I want to present Lydia in Torreón, have you got any dates available for Lydia?"

"Yeah, yeah, she's available," I answered. "Well, I'll give you, I'll give you fifty percent of the gross," he tells me. "I'm going to put her two days in the bullring, too, in Torreón."

"No, you give me some guarantee," I told the guy. You see, what happened in Chihuahua had opened up my eyes, I learned pretty fast, myself. I said, "You give me a guarantee, so much money, a guarantee, and then, you give me fifty percent."

"All right," that promoter told me. I've forgotten how much guarantee he gave me, but we went over to Torreón for two days. I'm telling you, it was a big commotion; hordes of people came out to see Lydia in that town. I don't remember exactly how much money we made there in Torreón, but we must have made about ten thousand dollars, something like that. You have to realize that there must have been a lot of people, because they couldn't have charged too much at the door. Things were pretty cheap back then: I mean ten pesos or fifteen pesos, like that, one dollar at that time. It was about twelve and a half pesos to the dollar in those days.

But then, I opened my eyes, I didn't want to take any more chances on just improvising the shows down there. And promoters were coming over to see me from Saltillo, from Monterrey, from all the border towns. But I said, "No, no more business. We're going back home. We're going to organize something better than this."

It was great down there: very beautiful hotels, very nice, everything was very nice. Very nice, as good as in the United States, and, in a lot of places, much better. But, I didn't want to do it because I told Lydia, "I'm going to think about business now. If we're making so much money here, let's go back home and think about it and organize a tour, a real organized tour. Let's do it right. This is all we're going to do right now."

"No, we have to go to Saltillo."

"No, no, no, let's go back home," I insisted. "We're going back to San Antonio and organize a tour through Monterrey, Tampico ... *todito el norte*."

Which is exactly what we did, see. We went back and organized a regular tour. But, at that time, I was busy, myself, over here, and I didn't go with Lydia back down to Mexico. I just handled her over there, and she went by herself with the family. Her mother was very wise for business. Lydia's always been quiet, very quiet. She didn't know nothing about numbers, she didn't know nothing about dollars. Between her mother and her husband, Juan, they're the ones that got all the money. Lydia never even knew how much. She never knew nothing but singing and playing the guitar.

CHAPTER 10

"May She Rest in Peace"

Lydia

Up until 1952 we—the whole family—were going around united, and I was always helping out, giving a hand with everything without thinking or believing that I was the star, that I was any better or more important. Of course, the public, they looked at it that way, but I didn't. But in spite of the way I was with my brothers and sisters—so partial to them, just like their equal—one of them was a little jealous of me in everything!

If people would come up to meet us and say hello to us after we finished our show, they would come up to me. Well, of course, I was the best-known act. Naturally, and since my sister Juanita was there, I would introduce her. Juanita was the one who became very envious of me. But I don't want to hurt her, and I don't want her to be jealous of me. We never disparaged her or put her down. We were all equal there. We were all one family working together. María was never envious, and my brothers were even less so.

My mother had tremendous will power, and that was what really kept the family together. But like everything on this earth, she couldn't last forever. My mother had always been very healthy, and she never had any operations. But finally she had an attack in the shoulder, she got pleuresy ... and she let it go. She got sick. It's an illness that forms pus around the lungs. She got so that she was always sick and very weakened. We took her to the doctor, and he found this pleuresy. The doctor said that she had to be operated on, but she didn't want to. The disease became complicated and became ... pneumonia. She woke up one day very sick ... with intense pain. She was vomiting. We took her to the doctor. The symptoms that she had were of pneumonia. But the doctor didn't grasp that. He said that she had caught a cold and that she was sick and all. He was the same doctor who had been attending her and giving her medicine for the pleuresy. Then we asked the doctor—we had heard that ice was good for vomiting—if we should give her ice cubes. "Well, go ahead and give them to her," he said.

So we gave Mamá some ice cubes, and the pneumonia that she had affected the bronchial tubes . . . and it turned into bronchial pneumonia. She was suffocating herself . . . and they wanted to take her to the hospital, but she didn't want to go. "Well," the doctor said, "she's going to suffocate here."

"Well, doctor, isn't there some way to bring oxygen here?" we asked.

"If you all can afford it, yes," the doctor told us.

Right away we brought her a hospital bed, the tent to put over it and the oxygen tanks . . . with a lot of sacrifices.

Then after three days like this the doctor said that we'd have to take her out, but . . . she wouldn't permit it. She was suffocating. The doctor said that she couldn't stay under the oxygen; we'd have to take her to the hospital. Again, she didn't want to go—she refused. There she stayed and there she died: under the oxygen.[1]

I loved my mother very much. I worshipped my mother. Of course, there were times when she would punish me for something I would do. Even when she punished me, I never came to the point of hating her . . . of being angry at her. . . . I tried to behave myself well so as not to hurt her. I tried to help her to do . . . everything I could for her. I think all of us felt that way about her.

You have to remember, too, that over the years our family had never had very much to do with doctors. I had three daughters, and I never took them to the doctor. If they got chest colds, for instance, the remedy that I would give them was the one that my mother made for us when we were little. Mamá would take a fresh tomato (I can't help laughing when I remember this) and put it on top of the *comal*, the tortilla griddle, so that it would roast. Then when the tomato was roasted, Mamá would cool it a little and then split it in half. For this treatment she had a large scarf. She put one slice here and the other there, and she would wrap it tight with the scarf, and with that medicine we would sleep all night. And she would give us a little something to eat. Then she would tie the other half of the tomato to the bottom of our feet with another scarf, and we would sleep all night like that. The next day in the morning we wouldn't have the colds anymore.

The same for coughs, she would fill a little spoon with sugar and put in two drops of kerosene. Kerosene! With that I would get rid of the cough. That's what my mother made for us. And that's what I made for my daughters. I never went around taking them to doctors for colds. The same for these measles: I made remedies. Like when the youngest got chicken pox . . . these illnesses make you very thirsty, but Mamá wouldn't give us water. She would make us *agua de borraja*,[2] a tea made from an herb from

Mexico. In the same way my mother made all these things, I made them for my daughters.

I didn't take them to the doctor for these illnesses. Thank God they never got really sick on me, except for the one time that the oldest got diptheria. She started to come down with it. I don't know where she might have caught it, from school or . . . ? But that was the only time that . . . I could take her to the doctor, and he treated her for me. But from then on, no more. So you can see that as a family, we never had very much experience with doctors.

Manuel

We all felt we had an obligation to our mother to help her survive. We had to do something. I used to hate it, especially when I was still just a kid, like back before the war. I'm honestly telling you, I used to hate going around working with the family group like that, and watching other kids playing. I used to see kids playing with tops or playing with toy guns or other things while I couldn't do it because we had to go down to sing in the Plaza. They would be hanging around then, just getting out of school. And I used to see those kids coming from school with books, and I wasn't going to school. I used to be jealous of them. So I used to say: "God damn, why is life treating me this way?" So I'd say to myself, "Someday I'm gonna make something of myself. I don't know what the hell I'm gonna make, but I'm gonna be doing better than what I'm doing right now."

So I used to hate it, although, I guess, deep down inside me, I didn't hate it too much. After I got married, my wife used to say, sometimes when we'd have an argument—because I liked to hang around some guys and sing and have a good time and all that—she would say, "You know, I don't like that kind of thing, noise and all that. I don't think you're happy with me, because I don't like to do those things you like to do."

"No," I'd say, "it's not that I'm not happy with you. It's just, that if you don't say anything, don't get in my way when I'm having fun like that, going singing with the guys, I don't see anything wrong with our marriage."

"I don't know . . . ," she'd say, " . . . you should've married Estelle García."

María

Estelle García was from the Carpa García. She was in love with Manuel. Estelle loved him a lot, but he didn't love her. Mamá liked Estelle because she was a performing artist like us.

Manuel

Estelle wanted to marry me, that gal, but she was a . . . Well, she wasn't too bad, she wasn't so bad. What got me mad at her ... she tried to blame something on me. It happened to her so I could marry her, and that's for the birds. I wasn't that dumb. I was dumb, but not that dumb. She went and got in trouble with some guy, some radio announcer, and then she tried to blame it on me. And her brother Raimundo used to say that he was Juanita's boyfriend.

María

Mamá wanted other *artistas* for us, other performers.

Juanita

Mother didn't like any of the boys that we met. She slapped me! Once in the Bohemia Club, right in front of all the people, she slapped me because I liked this boy.

Andrew

She could see right through a man. She could tell if that man was going to be a success or not. And she would tell my sisters the truth: "This man ain't got nothing. How is he going to support you? The reason that he wants to marry you is because he wants you to support him."

Our mother was a very frank old lady.

Juanita

I used to have a boy friend, I had a lot of them, but she never would let me get married. I was engaged three times, and she didn't let me get married. For instance, there was a boy named Pancho, he wasn't bad, but Momma never liked him. And so where am I? By myself.

Valerio Longoria

Leonor Mendoza didn't like me, but she called me to work with Las Hermanas Mendoza. She didn't like me at all because she knew that I was after Juanita. The old lady was very jealous with Juanita and María. She was always watching them, and she was jealous even if you just looked at them. Even when I was touring with Las Hermanas, there was never a chance to talk to the girls. The old lady would go to sleep on the back seat of the car while we were on the way, but she wasn't asleep, she was watching all the time. Even at night, that woman didn't even sleep! If I, or any other guy, started to talk with one of the girls: "Let's go! Let's go! Goodbye! Be quiet, let's go!"

In a way I don't blame her. They were artists, and maybe she would lose them. Maybe they would fall in love, and go off with someone else. Then she wouldn't have had a show. She was a nice lady, but she was very jealous with the girls, with Juanita and María. Whenever I tried to talk to Juanita, the old lady would start talking to me. "You have to do this, you have to do that!" Bossing me around while she got in front of her daughter. She never gave me a chance to talk to her.

I used to be in love with the youngest, with Juanita. Juanita was a beautiful girl: she was short, with great, big eyes. I think she used to like me, she used to smile at me, she used to try to talk to me, but I never told her nothing. I never had the guts to tell her, "Hey, let's do something." You know, sometimes when you're young, you're kind of stupid. When we were in San Antonio, I went to see her at her house when her mother wasn't home. On the way to her house I was thinking that I was going to ask her to marry me, or at least to go out with me. She answered the door and said, "Come in, come in!"

She put out a chair for me, and I sat down. Then she sat down in the middle of the floor, you know how girls are, with that great, wide skirt that she used to wear spread out all around her. She was very beautiful, but I didn't have the guts to tell her anything. Daniel Garcés told her something, and she got a family from Daniel.

Andrew

The good man that Mother liked, Juanita didn't like. That's just what happened. Mother didn't want anything bad for them, she wanted the best.

María

You don't just see a man and decide that you're going to get married, and then see another one, and then get married again. No. Just one. And I found love, real, real love when Mamá passed away, because she didn't want me to get married.

Mamá didn't want Juanita to marry either, but I was the one she watched over the most. I feel sorry for Mamá. It was just me and her in the house, all of the others had already married. And since I was the oldest, if she bought something, all the time she would say, "Ask María, see if she likes it."

And Juanita got jealous because Mamá paid so much attention to me. And if she bought something, she would take me along to sign for it. And then I made all of the meals in the house, it was even imposed on me. And then when I told her once that I was going to get married... ¡Ay, Chihuahua!

I was going to marry a man from El Paso. His name was Johnny Navjar; I think he was an Arab. He was a good-looking man, and I was already grown-up. I wasn't a little girl anymore. So then he came over to my house because that was something that Mamá insisted upon. "Well, tell them to come to the house if they really like you," Mamá always used to say. And many wanted to come and many didn't.

This man Johnny Navjar had seen me playing there at the Club Bohemia. I was playing the guitar and the piano, because Arturo Vásquez had taught me to play the piano.

"Listen, have you been playing for long?" Johnny Navjar asked me.

"Yes," I told him.

"You didn't just learn?"

"No."

"You play the guitar very beautifully," Johnny said, "I think you play it very prettily. And you sing very prettily, too."

"Well," I told him, "well, thanks."

Then he started to give me money ... for songs. He started to throw it into the guitar. And he was carrying a lot of money. I don't know what he might have been—what he did for a living—just that he had been a gambler or something. He was very well mannered and also very good-looking.

Mamá didn't come with us to the Bohemia anymore because she was now very sick. But she still didn't let us go alone, because she never let us go by ourselves.

"Do you have a mamá?" Johnny asked me.

"Yes," I told him, "she's sick."

"Well, I'll go to your house, give me the address."

So then he went inside, and Mamá was in there lying on the bed.

"Mamá, he's here," I said, "I'm going to introduce you."

"Who are you going to introduce me to?" she asked.

"Well, a boy," I said, although he wasn't so very young. He was thirty-one years old. Well, he wasn't either old or young, just ... but he was good-looking. "Well, who's this guy?" Mamá asked me.

"Well, he's someone that I met ... there singing."

"He's married," she said.

"Mamá, he's not married," I told her.

"This one is strictly a married man, it'd be better if you didn't even go out with him," Mamá insisted.

"Why?" I asked, because Johnny had already asked me to go out to dinner, and he was going to take me dancing. I didn't even know how to dance, but I did want to go to hear the music.

So there it was. Johnny was sitting down, and he said, "Tell your Mamá that if she'll let you, that I'll take you ... " —it was Sunday— "... out for dinner or to the park or whatever. I'll bring you home early."

I didn't want to get Mamá mad because she was sick. "Well, right now," I said to myself, "if she gets mad, she'll die."

"My mamá will let me go," I told him.

"No, you're not going anywhere. You won't go," he predicted.

And she didn't let me, and he left. He came back to the Bohemia, but he didn't come back to the house. So then, well, that was it. Nothing happened.

Juanita

Something was wrong with me and my mother and my sister. We had boyfriends, because when we were working at the club there were a lot of nice boys, and when we were young we weren't bad looking. But Mamá never liked the men we picked. She thought that she was never going to pass away; she didn't want us to leave her.

I was twenty-eight when I had my son Danny. I should have married sooner. There were a lot of boys that wanted me, there was a doctor, there were a lot of them.

Once I ran away with my boyfriend. I ran away with the one that I loved. Believe it or not, I stayed with his mother, I slept with her. And then the next day we came together and tried to talk to Mamá. She was really mad. She was blaming us and everything. We asked her for forgiveness, and we prayed then for her permission to get married.

"Yes," Mamá told my boyfriend, "but I'm going to tell you one thing. Just let Juanita finish the recording she has to do first."

I was going to go and record in Encinal. Mamá went with us.

"Okay," I said, "that's all right."

When we came back from there, I was going to get married. When we came back from Encinal, all of a sudden I said, "I don't want to get married."

I don't know, just like magic, or I don't know what, I said I didn't want to do it, that I didn't want him. And he really got mad! Because, you know, he had come and asked for forgiveness, and his mother had helped us and everything.

When my mother died, that man, my former boyfriend, called me at my house and he said, "Now that your mother is dead, I'm already married to someone else. You didn't marry me when you had the chance, and you're going to feel sorry all of your life."

See? All of the boys came into my life, just for a little while, and then all of a sudden, the same thing. And when my mother passed away, I fell in love with a man that I shouldn't have. Well, I don't blame him, because he's the father of my son and my daughter.

Lydia

The group, *la variedad*, broke up in 1952. This began when Mamá died and María got married. María met her husband ... and got married.

Juanita was left alone. They went on recording for a while, but with a lot of difficulties. The two of them, *el dueto*, went to California because they had a commitment with Azteca. The two of them went out there alone, without me, after my mother had died. But afterwards, just as soon as they had done that, María came back to San Antonio and got married.

Then the difficulities began ... on account of María's husband. He opposed her career. He started to interject a lot of problems. He wanted María to be paid more because she was playing the guitar. He said that Juanita didn't play an instrument, that she only sang, and the discord began with that. And the difficulties became so great that the day came when ... well, María just folded her hands. And the *dueto* was wrecked. Juanita wanted to make a solo career; María, the same. But they didn't come to do it. They both tried recording on their own, but, well, it didn't work out.

María

When I met my husband, the one that I eventually divorced, I was crying too much, just crying all the time because Mamá was gone. I was by myself in the house, and I didn't know what I was doing because everything was closed for me.

Juanita

Mamá left us; we didn't leave her, she left us.

María

Then Arturo Vásquez, from the Bohemia Club, came and said, "Let's go! Start singing again."

I didn't want to sing anymore because I felt so bad on account of Mamá. She passed away. Juanita and I went away for a while: we went out to California. And then when I came back, and I went over there to the Bohemia Club—it'd only been three months since Mamá passed—I met my husband, and I got married.

I needed to have known him better. But I got so excited when he swore to me, when he promised me ... But no, well, I had in mind what Mamá told me, that he was probably married or something. Mamá told me that if I got married and then things went bad, he would leave me with family, with the children, or something like that. Because that's what Mamá always told Juanita and me: that they—the men who were interested in us—were going to leave us with a little boy or a little girl, whichever it might be, and they weren't going to come back.

The first few months, I didn't understand my husband, I couldn't. I was even afraid of him. He told me that everything I did was bad. Little by little

I started to understand him. And we lived a very happy life. Well, we had our disputes, our arguments, like everybody that gets married. But finally he changed, when my kids were grown up. I don't know what happened. After twenty-four years of marriage he suddenly turned to me. "You know what," he told me, "I want to divorce you, and I want you to give me a divorce."

That's when I fell sick, I got sick because of that. I didn't believe him—I didn't believe anything.

"You're going to receive some papers," he said. He left in November of 1979, and he didn't come back. We got married March 30, 1954. Then one after another all of my children have left home, and now I am alone.

Right after Mamá died and I got married, my husband, he didn't want me to go and sing with Juanita anymore.

"You can make a lot of money by yourself," he told me. "You don't need your sister, because you play the guitar, and she doesn't play anything."

He didn't want me to sing with her, he wanted me to stop.

"Oh, tell your sister that she has to pay you for strings for the guitar," he would tell me. He was always coming up with things like that.

"No," I told him, "I don't want to get money from Janie because she needs it more than I do. You and I have everything, and Jane, she doesn't have anything."

My husband wanted me to take more than half when we worked, he wanted me to make more than Juanita. It wasn't like that before. While Mamá was with us, we never had any problem about the money. If one of us wanted to buy something, we'd just say, "Sister, I want to buy this, I want to buy that," and we'd just buy it, and we managed. I'm the older sister, but I didn't like to buy a lot of things. Juanita's different. We used to go downtown together, and she'd always buy a whole pile of things.

"You didn't bring anything home," Mamá used to tell me, "why didn't you buy anything?"

Well, I laid money away at Woolco and at other stores. When I did buy things, I liked to get real nice ones, expensive ones. I like to have everything I own to be of good quality. Then when I got married, I didn't have anything. My husband had to buy me everything.

"Well, I don't like that," I would tell him. "I don't like a lot of cheap things."

I wanted nice things, and he made a lot of money. He could have afforded it. But he didn't want to give money to me or buy me quality things.

Juanita

What are you going to do with a man like that? The same sort of thing happened to me. My ex-husband was jealous of me because I could make more money than he could. He didn't like me making records, he didn't like it at all. He wanted me to stop singing. He was jealous about the money.

When Daniel, my husband, and I went to work—he, too, is a musician and we worked together for a while—he didn't want to give me my money. He wanted to keep it and pay the rent and everything. I wanted my money for myself, so I said, "To hell with you! I'm gonna stop, I don't want to sing with you anymore!"

Because it was my money! They paid it to him for me, but he wouldn't give it to me. So I sang with Lupita Vira without him, and I sang at La Casita—a club here in San Antonio—for a year and a half on my own.

Lydia

Juanita didn't get married to Daniel Garcés, she just lived with him. He was going to marry her, he promised to marry her, but he couldn't really do it. She found out afterwards that he was already married. He just deceived her. Juanita was left with two children by him. The boy, he's in New York now. He certainly turned out to be a very intelligent lad, very smart. He studied a lot, they gave him two scholarships. And the girl was the same. Both of Juanita's children are now married.

Juanita

My son sings, too; he sings real pretty. Daniel Garcés, the songwriter, is his father. Daniel's a very important songwriter. He dedicated many of his songs to me, songs like "Mujer paseada," "Te busqué," "Mi güerita Coca-Cola," beautiful songs, songs that were real popular.

Mujer paseada[3]

Así te quiero mujer,
no le hace que seas paseada.
Te quiero porque me nace
de las entrañas del alma.

Coro:

Tú no sabías querer
porque eras mujer paseada,
y te burlabas de mí
cuando de amores te hablaba.

Pero llegaste a saber
que con mi amor no jugabas,

y con el tiempo supiste
lo mucho que tú me amabas.

Tú despreciabas mi amor
cuando en tus brazos lloraba,
pero llegaste a quererme
así como yo deseaba.
(Esta estrofa se repite
después del coro final.)

Easy Woman

I love you just as you are, woman,
it doesn't matter that you've been around.
I love you because my feeling
comes from the depths of my soul.

Chorus:

You didn't know how to love
because you were an easy woman,
and you would make fun of me
whenever I would speak to you of love.

But you came to realize that
with my love you couldn't just play around,
and as time went by you found out
just how much you really loved me.

You used to scorn my love when
I would lie crying in your arms,
but you finally did fall in love
with me just the way I wanted.
(This stanza is repeated after
the final chorus.)

María
My sister and I even recorded an "answer," a *contestación* to that song.

Contestación a "Mujer paseada"[4]

Si fueras hombre formal

no andarías divulgando.
¿Si me quieres como dices
para qué lo andas contando?

Si he sido mujer paseada
es porque a mí me ha gustado.
Pero del hombre que es hombre
nunca jamás me he burlado.

Si yo te llegué a querer
fue porque nunca pensaba
que anduvieras difamando
a la mujer que te amaba.

A los hombres como tú
pronto les doy su cortada,
porque yo tengo palabra
aunque sea mujer paseada.

Answer from an Easy Woman

If you were an upright man,
you wouldn't go around making it all public.
If you love me like you say you do,
why do you go around telling stories?

If I've been an "easy woman,"
it's because I've enjoyed it.
But I've never tried to make a fool
of a man who's a real man.

If I ever came to love you,
it was because I never thought
you would ever go around ruining the reputation
of the woman who loved you.

Men like you,
I cut them off real quick,
because I keep my word, even though
I may be an "easy woman."

Juanita

Daniel Garcés was also part of a trio, Los Tres Reyes. I used to sing with them sometimes. Another song Daniel wrote for Los Tres Reyes, and which they recorded and was real popular was "Mi güerita Coca-Cola" ("My Girl with the Coca-Cola Body").

María

After I was married, and I was singing by myself, I mostly had to stay home because I had five kids. I couldn't go and leave my kids. My husband would be around, he liked to stay around, and he liked to listen to me sing. So, sometimes he would take me to Houston and to Corpus to sing in public by myself, not with Janie. When I sang at those places, I sang for him, my husband. I sang all the songs to him and for him, and he knew it. I put all my heart and soul into those songs for him.

When we got home he would laugh, and he would say, "I know what you're doing when you sing the songs, you're trying to tell me how you feel. Why don't you ever tell me in person?"

Juanita

María used to sing some songs that really represented how a woman felt. I've heard her sing some bad ones at parties. She'd get up there, and she'd say, "I'm going to sing you a *bolero* ... " or something like that. But she wouldn't sing what she said she was going to, she'd sing some bad ones, some real nasty songs. For instance, she used to sing a song called "Leña y lodo," "Mud and Firewood." This is how it goes:

Leña y lodo[5]

Para hacer leña y lodo conmigo
ya las trampas tenías bien armadas.
Al quererme salir de tu infierno
ya la trampa tenías remachada.

Me enseñaste a tragar el veneno
de tu boca maldita y salada.
No apreciaste lo bueno del mundo,
lo mejor de la vida te daba.

¿Qué pecado tan grande debía
cuando tú te cruzaste conmigo?
Mucha gente dirá que te quiero
sin saber que yo soy tu enemigo.

Ves mi vida arrastrando en el suelo
y me quieres echar tierra encima.
Cuando tengas los mismos errores,
verás que de veras lastimas.

¿Qué pecado tan grande debía
cuando tú te cruzaste conmigo?
Mucha gente dirá que te quiero
sin saber que yo soy tu enemigo.

Firewood and Mud

To make firewood and mud out of me
you already had the traps all set up.
And when I wanted to get out of your hell,
you already had the door locked.

You taught me to drink the poison
from your damn salty mouth.
You didn't appreciate the good things of this world,
I gave you the best of my life.

What sin so great did I owe for
when you crossed my path?
A lot of people will say that I love you
without knowing that I am your enemy.

You see my life dragging on the ground,
and you want to throw dirt on top of me.
When you have made the same mistakes,
you'll see that it really hurts.

What sin so great did I owe for
when you crossed my path?
A lot of people will say that I love you
Without knowing that I am your enemy.

María
    I always liked that song, but I never recorded it. I only recorded once
on my own after Janie and I stopped working together, and I never had the
chance to do "Leña y lodo" in a studio. I wanted to record it, but they
wouldn't let me, so I recorded something else instead. It's not too old of

a song. Back in the days when we were recording for Azteca, they didn't have songs like that. This song is newer.

Juanita

It never really bothered us that most of the songs we sang were written from the point of view of a man singing to a woman. They were songs, and that's how they went. We just sang the songs with all of the emotion that we felt, but we sang them the way that they were written. They are made by real life people, they're about real life.

Some songs I don't like to sing, myself, because I just don't like them. Other songs, I like a lot. For instance, one song that I like very much is "Por mala suerte." I love that song. I haven't heard it for a long time.

Andrew

If Juanita and María would have kept on singing together, they would have kept on making it big. Right now they would be making it, right now, like Lydia, because they had as much popularity, in fact more popularity, than Lydia.

Still, right now, once in awhile KCOR plays one of Juanita and María's records, and every time they do, they get a lot of letters and phone calls asking, "What happened with Juanita and María Mendoza?"

"We cannot tell you anything about them because they retired," the station always answers. "The only information we have is that they haven't been recording since their mother died. As far as we know they have retired."

People loved the way they sang. But after our mother died back in 1952, they split up. They didn't want to sing together again. And that was the biggest mistake they made in their lives. María got married, and then her husband didn't want her to sing with Janie. Then María wanted to make a record, and they told her, "No, we cannot make any record with just you. We'll make one with both of you, but not just one."

Juanita

María didn't make it alone, and I didn't make it alone. I have a few records, but they would always say to me, "Where is María?"

Lydia

When Mamá died, the group was ruined. I stayed on alone. Dr. Nopal, Ramiro Cortés, he said to me, "Well, Lydia, even if your sisters don't want to work anymore, if you still want to go to work, I will get you contracts, because people are asking for you."

So, then I put together a new *variedad*. I added a couple of numbers to fill out the show, and I presented myself like that in the theaters. I continued to work, but I stopped playing the violin when my mother died. When she was living, we always put on a quartet at the end of the variety show, the whole family: Mamá on guitar, my sisters, and me on the violin, the mandolin and everything. It was a "*finale*." But when my mother died, I stopped playing the violin because I was traveling alone and there was no one else to play the guitar.

An impresario from California even got me a contract to go to Mexico. I went to Mexico City and appeared at the Teatro Esperanza Iris. I believe this was around 1952. This gentleman got me an engagement there for two weeks. Well, I went for two weeks and stayed six months. But not just in the capital. I only worked two weeks in Mexico City, and then an impresario who took performers all over Mexico contacted me, and that's how I went touring. I didn't tour as a solo act down there, but in a big road show with lots of Mexican celebrities. A recording artist like me has to make a lot of personal appearances and tours to promote her records. My work is known in Mexico, to be sure, but not as universally as here.

I'll tell you a story that happened to me the first time I appeared at El Teatro Iris. They gave us a rehearsal call. Well, we were all there at 10:00 a.m., and I told the stage manager that I hardly ever went to rehearsals because I did my own accompaniment and knew all my numbers. "No, but it's different here in Mexico," the stage manager told me, "all the artists have to show up for rehearsals here."

Well, fine, so we got there, and everyone showed up—dancers and singers and all. And after a while it was "Lydia Mendoza on stage," to do my turn. Well, I came in with my guitar, and the stage manager stood looking at me.

"And you, what are you going to do?"

I thought he didn't recognize me. "Why, I'm going to sing," I told him.

"To sing with what?" he asked me.

"Why, with my guitar," I replied.

"If you think," says he, "that I'm going to present a singer here with just a guitar—why, they'd throw tomatoes!"

"Well, *señor*," I said, "I'm Lydia Mendoza, and that's my act. This isn't the first theater that I've worked in. I've been to New York, to California, to the big cities."

"Oh, no, you don't understand," the stage manager said, "but these audiences here are different. Here they're demanding. And we're not about to put an artist on stage here, even a star, with just one instrument."

"Well, that's the way my contract reads," I said.

"No, we'll have to put you on with a *mariachi*," he said. "You'll be in front, but the *mariachi* will be there with you, too."

"Fine, just as you please," I said.

They went right out and got a Mexico City *mariachi* group. And the boys there arrived at the Teatro Iris with their instruments and said, "What are you going to sing, Lydia?"

Well, "Besando la cruz" was the first number, and there were two or three others they knew already. Opening night the show went on, and finally it came time for Lydia Mendoza. Well, the *mariachi* band was at the rear of the stage, and I stood behind the curtain. As soon as the *mariachi* started playing our first number, the curtains opened up and I came out with my guitar, singing. Oh, the audience gave me a nice round of applause. Well, to make a long story short, the *mariachi* just accompanied me on that one song, "Besando la cruz." Because after that, the audience started yelling and hollering: " 'Mal hombre.' Sing 'Mal hombre' for us, Lydia!"

Of course those *mariachis* hadn't practiced "Mal hombre" or anything, and furthermore, they didn't even know it. Well, the audience started off, "Play 'Mal hombre,' Lydia Mendoza! Play 'Pajarito herido' . . . " and all the other songs from my records. And the *mariachi* just stood there watching me. They were standing behind me, and I was playing my guitar alone, and the audience was loving it all, no flying tomatoes or anything of what the stage manager had been talking about. Well then, that's the way the week went. Just the first number with the accompaniment, and from then on those *mariachis* just stood there silently behind me on the stage. Well, at the end of the week, the stage manager finally said, "Why are we paying all of these expenses for nothing? The boys aren't working."

"Well, what do you want?" I replied. "You said you needed a *mariachi*—pay them."

"No, I guess we'll stick with just the guitar," he told me, "you really can do it alone."

So the second week I went up alone with my guitar. I showed that stage manager, that, well, I have my fans, and he just couldn't imagine it, that the audience would accept me with just my guitar. After those two weeks at the Teatro Iris, I went all over Mexico with just the guitar. And everywhere I was just as well received.

While I was in Mexico City, I dropped in to say hello to Mr. Rivera Conde of Victor Records, whom I knew quite well. I went to see him first to say hello, and then to ask him about a record I had made, a composition of mine; I don't recall the name. They had never reported the sales to me or whatever had happened. And I just went to ask him that question. Señor Rivera Conde sent me to the department . . . where they have all their accounts and records and all. Sure enough, I had some money there: royalties for ... like composer's rights. I don't recall how much it was ... but they gave me a check there. And then I went back and thanked Mr. Rivera.

"No, Lydia, before you go," he said to me, "let's record two little songs." "Of course," I told him, "let's do it, but how?"

"Well, right now!" Rivera Conde replied.

"Ummm, well, I didn't exactly come prepared ... ," I stammered out.

"Oh, don't worry about a thing, just come on over here!"

Señor Rivera Conde grabbed me by the arm and practically pulled me down through the hallways to the recording studio. I recorded "Mal hombre" and "Tengo a mi Lupe"—songs I originally had recorded on Blue Bird—just like that, right away. Rivera Conde just put an accordion and piano with me. He recorded me in a style—of course with the guitar—but in a halfway *gaucho* style with the accordion, like a tango, an Argentine style. It was very pretty; the recording came out very well.[6] I also recorded with Columbia during that same visit to Mexico.

In the period that followed my appearance at the Teatro Iris, I recorded for a number of years with Columbia of Mexico. I would go to Mexico City to record for them, and they would pay my fare. I would go about twice a year. Since I didn't have a contract with Columbia, I just recorded without one. I would just go and record, I didn't usually make any appearances.

I did perform in a Mexican film during one of those visits, somewhere around 1958. They made the picture in two parts. I sang one song in the first and another in the second. The movie was called *Relámpago* while it was being filmed, but I believe the name was changed afterwards.

The funny thing is that I happened to see the first part of it by chance one Mother's Day here in Houston at the Ritz Theater. They hired me to sing, and there were lots of artists and prizes there. But they also showed a movie, and it was mine. And I hadn't even noticed. I believe that nobody even knew. And all of sudden, there I was on the screen, singing there in the movie. I never did get to see the second part of the film. I sang "La guía" and "Por qué te vas," another song I also have recorded, in the first part.[7]

La guía[8]

Soñaba anoche que me querías,
y que en tus brazos me adormecía.
Pero con otro tú me engañabas
y yo tan tonto te lo creía.

En una palma nació otra palma,
sembré una higuera y nació otra higuera.

Si quieres, chata, que otro te quiera,
pídele, negra, a Dios que me muera.

En una parra nació otra parra,
sembré una higuera y nació una guía,
y de la guía nació un letrero
en el que decía: tú eres María.

Tus juramentos salieron falsos,
tú me juraste un dichoso día,
y desde entonces yo te aborrezco
años y meses y eternos días.

Sembré una fruta y nació difunta,
sembré un elote y nació un camote,
y como tengo tantos sembrados,
de ahí nacieron los diputados.

The Sprout

I dreamt last night that you loved me,
and that I was lying half-awake in your arms.
But you were deceiving me with another,
and I, such a fool, believed in you.

In a palm tree, another palm sprung forth;
I planted a fig tree, and another fig tree sprouted up.
If you want, honey, that another man love you,
pray to God, beloved,[9] that I die.

In a grapevine, another vine sprung forth;
I planted a fig tree, and a shoot sprouted up,
and from the sprout a sign, on
which it said: you are Mary.[10]

Your promises came out false;
you swore to me one confounded day,
and from then on I have detested you:
years and months and endless days.

I planted a fruit and it came up dead;
I planted an ear of corn, and up sprouted a sweet potato,[11]
and since I have planted so many

from there were born the politicians.

My brother also recorded that song for Decca. It was Manuel and Juanita. You can even tell from their voices that they were just children. They recorded it in San Antonio in 1937, so they were both still very young. The other song, "Por qué te vas," is a *ranchera*.

Many different artists appeared in that movie. Among them was Luis Pérez Meza, and of course, he, along with several of the other *artistas*, sang in the film. I don't remember exactly what the movie was about—*rurales* or *hacendados*, something like that. I think that even Cruz Alvarado was in it—there were quite a few artists involved. The scene where I appear in the first part of the film is set in a cantina, a very large one. There is a high balcony up above, and there are a lot of girls sitting around some tables with men, and I come out and sing "La guía."

On that same occasion I recorded an LP for Victor of Mexico called *Adiós mi México lindo*.[12] I recorded with the Mariachi Vargas de Tecalitlán on one side, and Los Mexicanos accompanied me on some boleros or something on the other.

One time during those years, I went down to Tampico to sing, and then from there I went on to Mexico City to make some records. That was the first time I ever flew in an airplane. It was when I was recording for Columbia Records, sometime around the mid-fifties. It was on a Mexican airline, it was a very small airplane and I was very frightened. It just went *brinque y brinque*, bump and jump. I am horrified by those little airplanes. It really scared me. Now of course, I'm no longer afraid of flying. I think it's all the same; death is the same up above as below. On the earth ... I don't have any fear.

During the time I was recording for Columbia of Mexico, on some occasions I would go all the way to Mexico City, and at other times they would come up to Monterrey to make a series of recordings. Then I would just go down to Monterrey, and we would record there. But without a contract, see. They just paid me for the series that I made with them. I recorded for Columbia with Los Montañeses del Álamo and also with Los Alegres de Terán up there in Monterrey. When I was recording for Columbia, I recorded for royalties and I made good money. Every three months they sent me a report of what had been sold and of how much they had advanced me, and they continued to send me money.

In the years after the war, a lot of small, independent record companies started up all over the Southwest, even out in California, like Azteca, but especially in Texas. There were, and still are, a lot of little labels in South Texas, and over the years my sisters and I have recorded with almost all of them.

One Texas label I have recorded for practically from the start is Discos Falcón. My sisters and I have recorded hundreds of songs for Discos Falcón over the years. I recorded a bunch of seventy-eights with them. I believe it was about 1949 or 1950, they called me then to come and record. Then I stopped recording with them for a while, but went back to them again during the 1960s and '70s. For instance, I made an LP of Christmas songs for Falcón, and on it I recorded a song of mine that's called "Llorando en Navidad" ("Crying on Christmas")—I wrote that song. I did another LP of songs for Mother's Day, and on it I sang "Perdón yo pido" ("I Beg For Forgiveness")—also a composition of mine. And just a few years ago they put out a very big line of LPs in Mexico with all of those recordings I made for them back in the early '50s.

Arnaldo Ramírez

When I first brought Lydia to record for Falcón, it wasn't a question of running into her by accident or anything like that. Lydia Mendoza was pretty well known. I went looking for her—I didn't just run into her. I remember when I was a youngster, before I ever thought about making records, the song "Mal hombre" was heard all over. "Mal hombre" was the first record she made, and it's also her biggest hit. Then over the years she has had many other big records, like "Celosa" ("Jealous") and some of those others. She was an institution. I mean, I had a lot of respect and admiration for her long before I even thought of getting into the record business. So when I had a chance to touch base with her and approach her on the possibilty of recording for my company, for me, it was really something—an opportunity.

And Lydia didn't defraud me; she didn't disappoint us one bit, because the very first release—number ninety-seven, I can't forget that number— was a real big hit record. It was "Besando la cruz" ("Kissing the Cross"), a song by the composer Chucho Monge, and the other side, the flip side, "Ángel de mis anhelos" ("Angel of My Desires"), which was written by a composer from San Antonio. But anyway, "Besando la cruz"[13] was the big hit.

And I remember, in Ciudad Juárez, in Mexico, boy! That's where most of the success of that record started, right in that area, in that region. Of course, then it became my standard with us in our catalog—I mean for a long time. And later, many years afterwards, when I recorded Lydia again, I recorded that number again with her. You will probably find it in one of her later LPs.

Lydia Mendoza made her first numbers for Falcón on August 17, 1950, when she recorded four songs including "Besando la cruz." Others followed.

Up through 1962, all her recordings were not on a royalty but on a fixed pay basis. We started paying her $25.00 per record and then upped it to $35.00. While this amount appears to be null now, it was a substantial sum then. In 1968 we had an agreement with Lydia to record on a royalty basis with an advance of $150.00 per LP. Later on we increased the amount to $200.00 and $400.00 for both her recordings and compositions.

Lydia's first recordings were mostly released on 78s. We later released ten LPs containing 120 songs—plus we made four more LPs that Falcón never released. We also put out one LP with ten songs by Juanita and María.

Most of the songs Lydia recorded for me at Falcón, I gave her. But I was also suprised at the number of songs she had from way back. I mean, she would remember all the words and the melody, everything. Lydia'd know just about any song that you could think of. She knew all those old songs, but then she was also very fast in learning new songs. I found that out because I gave her a lot of original material. Lydia was quick; sometimes she would come in and learn the new songs right here in the studio. Yes, Lydia Mendoza was quite an institution within the recording industry.

Lydia

Actually, back in the early '50s, there was another record company down in South Texas that was even bigger than Falcón at that time; it was called Ideal. The recording side of Ideal was run by a man from Alice, Texas, named Armando Marroquín.[14] When Marroquín first came to look for me, I was still recording for Falcón Records. Then I started to make some recordings with Marroquín and Ideal Records. After a while Falcón called me back. Since I didn't have a contract with Marroquín, I resumed recording with Falcón as well—I would go back and forth. I recorded for both of them without a contract. The difference was that Marroquín put groups—mostly *conjuntos*—with me. I got to record with Tony de la Rosa, with Narciso Martínez, with all of those artists. And there with Falcón: just with their orchestra and the guitar, nothing else.

Because of the experiences that I've had with a few of the smaller Texas recording companies, I usually prefer to record for a set price in advance and not worry about royalties. For instance, back in 1978 I recorded an LP in Corpus for a composer that has a little company down there—Discos Gaviota. His name is Johnny Herrera, and they were all songs of his. It was the same old thing: "Well, Lydia, I'll give you so much in royalties." "No, I don't want to do it that way," I said, "just pay me a set price, and that will be the end of it." Because some of these local companies never report anything to the *artista*.

Johnny Herrera

I remember meeting Lydia Mendoza for the first time very well. I had just gotten out of the Army, and I was about, oh, nineteen years old. It must have been around 1952, the latter part of '52. I had hitchhiked back and forth from one end of Texas to the other, trying to get everybody to publish or record my songs, and then ... Lydia happened to be playing here in Corpus Christi. She was going to be at one of the radio stations—I forget what it was called in those days—and then she was to appear at the Avalon Theater here in Corpus, over on Brownlee Street. I really remember her ... just like an idol. And I remember her beautiful gown, her guitar, everything. I think she was the only attraction, and she had a full house there.

Everybody told me, "You're crazy to even try to approach her, because she's a big RCA recording star." "No," I said, "I don't care, I've got to give it a try."

So I went over there, and Lydia performed, and then I very meekly walked up there to her and said, "Look, my name is Johnny Herrera, and I write songs ... and I've got a new label, Gaviota. And I know that you are a very famous star, but ... "

And before I knew it, she hugged me—gave me an *abrazo*, you know.

"Calm down ... now," she said, "I'm just another person, just take it easy."

And I just shook ... I didn't know what to say. Back there when I used to live in the Valley, when I was just a kid growing up, I had some of her recordings: some on Columbia, some on Blue Bird. So, like I told you, when I got that hug, I'll never forget it. She is an authority.

So then I said, "Well, I'd like for you to listen to my *boleros*, and maybe you'd be interested in recording. Like I said, it's not a big recording company, and I figured, well, if you can, let me know if ... "

Lydia hugged me again. I wanted to cry. She was so simple, so nice, so ... just down-to-earth.

So then, Lydia said, "Well, okay. I'm going to do a performance tomorrow. I'll be at your house in the afternoon before I have to go to the theater."

We had one of those simple recording machines. So, I said to myself, "Well, maybe she's just saying it, just to get rid of me." After the performance I walked home and waited there; I couldn't even sleep. And what do you know? Here comes Lydia exactly when she said she would.

I introduced my family to Lydia. "This is my mother," I said, "this is my father. ... " and they gave Lydia a cup of coffee.

"We haven't discussed it yet, but ... " I started to say.

"Don't you worry about the price ... " Lydia said.

I had two songs ready, and then, of course, the musicians were there. And, right away, Lydia started learning the songs. I ran to the other room, and I started writing two more, because Lydia told me when I started to talk about the money, "I'll tell you what I'm going to do, I'm only going to charge you one hundred dollars for four recordings."

"God ... !" I said," I've only got two songs!"

So then, while Lydia was recording the first two songs, while they were there singing and playing in ... we can't even call it a studio, because that's not what it was ... I finally finished the other two songs. Then Lydia came in and said, "I'm through with it." And it didn't take her twenty minutes ... or thirty minutes, at the most. She had just learned the songs, recorded them, and she said, "Okay, let me see what you got there?" So then, she had another cup of coffee, she learned the new songs and she said "Okay."

Well, we had started about nine o'clock; I think by about twelve o'clock, Lydia had already done the four songs ... on the Gaviota records, and to this day, I am so elated, I owe so much to that woman. Because of that *abrazo*. Just a simple hug, here I felt, Lord! Here I am, a nobody ... and that, to me, is what Lydia represents: beauty. She's our pioneer, of course, in this music, and over all, she is here to stay forever. And what more can I say? That is Lydia Mendoza to me. She also recorded an album for me of my songs many years later, around 1978. Someday I'm going to get around to it, and get her to record another one.

Lydia

Throughout the '50s I kept on working, appearing in theaters all over and recording for all the different companies. My first husband, Juan Alvarado, and I never separated. Juan worked as a shoe and boot maker until the day of his death in 1961. He worked for a company there in San Antonio called the Lucchese Boot Company. Lucchese made boots, of course, but even more, they specialized in making footwear for people with deformed feet: special shoes. My husband was an expert at this. He was a very good shoemaker. And the boss liked him a lot. To the extent that when my husband passed away, he took Mr. Lucchese with him. Lucchese died when we gave him the news of my husband's death.

Juan was well and healthy: nothing was wrong with him. And I went out on a contract in California. My guitar had been stolen on a tour, and I could only get those guitars in Los Angeles. But when they called me for that contract, I didn't really want to go. "Why don't you go? Go on!" my husband told me. "You'll be able to buy your guitar out there—one of those guitars that you can only get in Los Angeles."

So I went to work, and Juan stayed behind, very happy and all. The week of my engagement in Los Angeles ended on a Wednesday. As soon as I finished the week there, I spoke to Juan right away on the phone that night. "I just finished," I told my husband, "but I'm going to stay until the weekend because I got a contract in another club. I'm going to work on Friday at noon. Since I'm already here, I might as well take advantage of it. So if I leave on Sunday, I'll call you and let you know."

"Good," Juan replied, "call me so I can pick you up."

And we left it like that. Well, Friday I got up and went to my job—the club where I was playing. I had finished giving my show when they called me from San Antonio. One of my daughters spoke to me: "Mamá, come immediately because Papá just went into the hospital!"

"Well, how could this be?" I said to her, "I just spoke to him a few days ago."

"Well, he was going to go to work," she said, "but then he said no, that he wanted to vomit. We thought that dinner might have sat badly with him. He threw up a lot of blood. The doctor says that if the vomiting continues, he won't last the night."

Ay, well, right away I dropped everything and told my daughter, "I'm coming right away."

The owner of the club got mad, and he said, "I'm not going to pay you."

"Don't pay me!" I told him. "I'm going now. My husband needs me."

Well, "No, no, no ... it's okay," they say to me. And they took me to the airport. It was about ten thirty, and the airport was real far away. We got there just as the last plane was taking off. There wasn't another flight until seven o'clock in the morning. And there I stayed. Finally I managed to communicate with San Antonio again.

"He's still not very well," they told me. "Mamá, come home!"

When I arrived, they had already taken Juan from where they had him—the hospital. He was back in his room, and the vomiting had stopped. I was very pleased to find him well and all.

"No," Juan says to me, "I don't know why you came. There's nothing wrong with me."

"No," I told him, "I want to be here with you."

On Monday the vomiting returned. It ripped him apart. It was because he drank a lot. And there was no remedy. He died. But I reached him in time, thank God.

Juan died at five o'clock in the morning. At that hour my daughter called to tell Mr. Lucchese, because he wanted to be kept informed of my husband's condition. His wife said that when she got the call, he asked, "Who's that?"

"They're calling from Alvarado's house," Lucchese's wife told him.

"What happened?" Mr. Lucchese asked her.

Well, then his wife told him that Juan had died. And Lucchese just turned over and, apparently, went back to sleep. His wife got up and started to get ready to go to the shoe shop, and she saw that Mr. Lucchese didn't get up. When she went to speak to him, he was dead. He died as soon as they gave him the news that Juan had died. That same day we were mourning two corpses: the owner's and my husband's.

My husband Juan wasn't a drinker back in the days before the war when the family was touring. He didn't start drinking heavily until after we stopped touring and he went back to shoe making. He and Mamá usually got along real well. For instance, in later years when Mamá was ill, I had to let things go at my own house so that I could be with Mamá and help her out, and Juan didn't mind at all. Juanita and María weren't able to help her then because they were working at a night club.

Juan died in 1961. Since my three daughters were already married by the time he passed away, I wrote some letters to the enterprises I had worked for before. I wrote one to New Mexico, another to California—to the impresarios. And still another to Denver. And ... I said to myself, "the first one that answers, well, I'm going to go and work for them ... "because I wasn't left with any way of making a living. In my life I earned a lot of money ... on all of my tours. But not really so much, because the impresarios who had contracted for me ended up with the major part of my money. They would ask for one week ... a thousand dollars or fifteen hundred, and they wouldn't give me more than five hundred. So when I was left alone, the only thing that was left for me was an insurance policy of five thousand dollars. Five thousand dollars, well, that's not much money anymore. I didn't have property. I didn't have anything.

So I wrote those letters from San Antonio where I was still living, and I told myself that I'd go to work for the first one to answer. Of course, my daughters didn't want for me to go, but I didn't feel capable of sitting myself down in some corner or being there taking care of grandchildren and all that. I still felt full of life and vigor for pushing on ahead, right! So then, well, within my sorrow, the loss of my husband, well I wasn't going to stay stuck there. Well, what would I have done?

So the first one to answer me didn't write, he called me on the phone. It was Mr. Paco Sánchez of Denver. He has already passed away now. Paco Sánchez had a very large ballroom where they gave dances every weekend. It was a very beautiful place, very pretty. "Lydia, you have a job here for as long as you want," he says to me. "Come ... immediately. If you want, I'll send you money so that you can come." And he did send me the money so that I could go. "Come on, you and your guitar!" he urged me.

I went to Denver and stayed there for two years. That was where I met

Lydia and husband Fred Martínez. Courtesy of the Lydia Mendoza collection.

my present husband. I'd been up there for about a year, working for Paco Sánchez, before we met. When we thought we were going to get married, I told my present husband that I didn't want to stay there in Denver. We got married in 1964, and I brought him to Texas. My first husband was a bootmaker, and this one is also a shoemaker. For some reason it just happened that both of my husbands were shoemakers.

CHAPTER 11

"Ay, Mamá, Why Do You Like
that Silly Song?"

Lydia

It's more difficult to build a career like I did for a woman than for a man. Now, of course, the luck one has also counts a lot. I, thank God, had a lot of luck. Everybody liked me and praised my voice and predicted great things for me. Nonetheless, I made my career by way of pure sacrifice.

At the time that I began my career, I didn't have any rivals because there weren't any other female singers that sang *en el estilo popular*, in the style of the people. There wasn't anybody that could rival me because, well, there were very few other women singers. When Manuel J. Cortez organized those two contests that I appeared in back in the early '30s in San Antonio, then more female singers came up. Some of them sang fairly well, and others were not so good. Of those that took part, none of them did anything. They didn't come to make any career.

The only one that also rose out of that scene in San Antonio, in the time that I began, was Eva Garza. Eva Garza even recorded for the same company that I did, Blue Bird. Another woman, Rosita Fernández, made something of a name for herself with the American audience, but that wasn't until around the beginning of the war. She started to get big, singing on the radio. Rosita Fernández and her sister even recorded as a duet, but they never went anywhere.

As for Eva Garza, she recorded, but she didn't achieve much fame on account of her voice there in San Antonio. Success came to Eva Garza when she went on tour with a dancer, Sally Rand: an American woman that danced with fans. Sally Rand came through San Antonio with a variety show, and she met Eva Garza and took her on as a dancer . . . and singer. When they arrived in New York, Eva Garza went to see El Charro Gil y sus Caporales—one of the most popular Mexican groups in the city at that time. I think Eva Garza just went to say hello to them, but the thing is they met, and El Charro Gil fell in love with Eva Garza. When El Charro Gil fell in love with Eva, he split off from the Caporales. There had been three Caporales plus El Charro Gil. Afterwards the three Caporales who remained became the Trio Los Panchos. They stayed in New York, but Eva Garza and El Charro Gil went to Cuba, to Puerto Rico; they traveled around. They went to South America, all over. They went roaming around, just the two of them, but they finally ended up in Mexico. El Charro Gil was very well known in Mexico, and Eva Garza was able to make a name for herself there.

El Charro Gil helped her career quite a bit. Eva Garza started singing in Mexico on the strength of El Charro Gil's name, and that was how she got on the radio station, XEW, of Mexico City. And she made a lot of recordings for Columbia, and I believe that she even made some films. But she made her career in Mexico, not here, not in San Antonio. She started out here, but I guess she just didn't have good luck. And Eva Garza was one of the other most well known female singers of that epoch.

Now, lately, there is another one. They call the two of us *las dos grandes de Tejas*, "the two Texas greats." She is Chelo Silva, who is a singer with a large audience who mainly sings *boleros* and is very well-liked. She still has a big name—principally in Mexico. She is well known because she records for Columbia. Columbia also has very good distribution here in the United States. All over, you'll find Chelo Silva's records because she records for Columbia. So wherever she is presented, they already know her. You could say that Chelo Silva and I are the two best known women singers from Texas. Because most of those that have come up just pass by like a gust of wind. Today there is an infinity of women singers there in San Antonio, but they don't go on from there. They don't achieve anything.

Many people have gotten me mixed up with another very well known singer whose last name is the same as mine: Amalia Mendoza. They often wonder if we're related or connected in any sort of way. Well, we ran into her and her family on a tour once, and my brothers and sisters talked to them about that.

Manuel

There's a singer from Mexico, her name is Amalia Mendoza, and her story is very similar to ours. She came from a real poor family. Her father's name was Pancho Mendoza. That is to say that a man named Francisco Mendoza was Amalia's father, but not the same Francisco Mendoza who was our *papá*. When Amalia Mendoza was young, her family used to sing in a little park in Mexico City, where they come from, just like we used to sing in the Plaza in San Antonio. Some people have said that they must be relatives of ours, but I don't really think we're related to them.

Juanita

No, Amalia said no, that there isn't any relation. But one time when we were up in Lubbock, and we saw the Trio Tariácuri, Juan Mendoza, Amalia's brother, said they were related to Lydia. But Amalia said no.

Lydia

So there's probably no truth to the stories about my being related to Amalia Mendoza. Nonetheless, I'm probably one of the two or three artists from the South Texas music scene to have achieved a truly international reputation. I didn't even realize myself how well-known I was outside of the United States and Mexico until I went to Colombia for the first time in 1982. That trip to Colombia was something very big for me. I didn't expect that I would have such a big audience there. They received me there with so much enthusiasm and affection! People there had heard me back in the years when I was recording for Blue Bird, but they had almost lost all hope of ever meeting their favorite artist.

The people down there in Colombia are very fanatical for the old-time music, for all of the artists like Agustín Lara, Toña la Negra, Las Hermanas Águila, Juan Arvizu, Margarita Cueto, Juan Pulido, Pilar Arcos, myself . . . in short, of that epoch. The Colombian fans have all of the records; from the first record a particular artist made, they have them. And they have transfered a lot of those old recordings to cassettes. Even some business enterprises there have done this, and they play them for the public so the old music can be heard.

Back in 1941 on the last tour we made before we had to stop because of the war, we were in Chicago—the whole family—and some promoters wanted to send me to South America. They were impresarios from down there and they told me, "We want you to come and appear on the radio and in theaters and to make some recordings."

But they were only interested in my act. They didn't want to take the whole family down there.

"If you like, I'll go with the whole group," I told them, "but if they don't go, I won't go either."

I couldn't go off and leave the family like that. What could they have done? That's why I didn't accept the contract.

Then in 1973, I went to Chicago with a big caravan of *artistas*—they had hired me for four days. There were some newspaper reporters from Medellín, Colombia, up there doing stories, and I got to know them during

the show. They brought over a tape-recorder and recorded an interview with me. "Oh, Lydia," they told me, "it's such a surprise to run into you up here. You really have a lot of fans back in Colombia. Why haven't you ever gone there?"

"No, no," I told them, "it never occurred to me. I've always been so busy working around here in the United States."

"Oh, well, you've got tons of fans in South America," they told me. "Please let us record a couple of songs to take back."

So I sang some songs for them, and also recorded a *saludo*, a message for my public there. Those reporters left very happy, and I went back to Houston. Well, a few weeks later, I started getting piles of letters from down there in Colombia. Lots of people had read the interview and the *saludo* because they were published in *El Colombiano*, a very big newspaper down there.[1]

CHICAGO. (Por José Calle Restrepo).—Se presentó recientemente en los teatros Atlantic y Congress de Chicago, una caravana de artistas latinos y entre ellos la simpática e inconfundible Lydia Mendoza. Sí, la Mendoza, que llenó todos los traganíqueles y las cantinas de Medellín y de los pueblos de Antioquía en tantos años, a partir de los años treinta hasta se puede decir hoy día.

Yo recuerdo mucho aquella época en que se oía siempre el rasgueo de su guitarra y su voz delgada y alta, cantando aquellas canciones de la más profunda raíz popular.

Ella estaba en su apogeo y en la voz del pueblo. Era el folklor popular y eran las canciones de las gentes sencillas hechas vivas por su incomparable y su inconfundible estilo. Lydia Mendoza ha sido única. No sabíamos quién era y de ella se tejieron muchas leyendas y cada uno inventaba de dónde era: Que argentina porque cantaba el tango; que mexicana, que había muerto, etc.

CHICAGO. (By José Calle Restrepo).—Recently a line-up of Latin performers appeared in the Atlantic and Congress Theaters in Chicago, and among them was the congenial and unmistakable Lydia Mendoza. Yes, Mendoza, the one who filled all the jukeboxes and bars of Medellín and the other towns of Antioquia for so many years, beginning in the '30s up until today.

I remember that epoch very well when her delicate, high

voice and the strumming of her guitar were always heard, singing those songs that came from the deepest roots of the common people.

She was at her peak and was the voice of the people. "Popular" folklore and the songs of the common people were brought to life by her incomparable and unmistakable style. Lydia Mendoza has been unique. We didn't know who she was, and we would invent many legends about her, and each person would make up where she was from: that she was an Argentine because she sang tangos, that she was Mexican, that she had died, etc.

Many people wrote to me and told me they thought I had died. They all wanted to know why I had never come to sing in their country. I wrote back to them and said, "Well, let's see if some impresario wants to set something up." Because, in reality, I had a very great desire to go there.

One of those impresarios didn't waste any time in getting hold of me. And so finally the project was arranged, and due to those reporters who came to interview me, I was finally able to visit Medellín for the first time in 1982.

About two years later, I went back down there again. I appeared in Medellín, Río Negro and Barranquilla—lots of places there, I don't even recall them all. I can't complain, I was received very well, the public went crazy trying to meet me. But always ... I couldn't really relax or get into the spirit of my songs there. It's very frightening there—it's a real rough situation. You can't even go out in the street because if you're wearing a gold chain, for instance, somebody will pull it off you, or your watch, they'll drag it right off your wrist. Every morning they find bodies that have been beheaded, and kidnappings are an everyday occurrence. A person can't really go out in the street with the confidence that they won't be assaulted or done wrong. There's always something horrible happening.

The last show I did there, they presented me in a big stadium—like a big bullring, it was immense—and it filled up with people. I did my songs, and just as I was finishing my last number, the lights went out. Down there, the electricity goes out all the time, it's a regular occurrence. The lights just went out, all over, just like that, and you can imagine what happened that night. The electricity didn't come back on until about midnight. How did all those people get out of the stadium? Families, little children that were up in the stands? All you could hear was the shouting, the pandemonium, it was the only way that you could follow the people as they tried to get out. And the lights never came back on while they were trying to leave. And that kind of thing happens all the time down there. It's very disorganized there, and for that reason I didn't go back this year [1985] when they invited me.

But when I went there the first time, it was incredible! Good grief! I didn't expect that kind of reception from the public. I didn't realize that they still remembered that music. The people were crying when they looked at me. They would come up and touch me to see if I was really Lydia Mendoza. It was a marvel, the reception that they gave me there. It even got to the point that they were asking for public prayers to be said for my return.

I also recorded an album of Colombian songs for Falcón Records. Arnaldo Ramírez brought me a disk Luciano Ramírez had sent him with all of the songs I was to record on it. When Arnaldo played it for me, I told him, "The music is very pretty, but I don't sing that way. I'm not going to be able to sing them like they are on this disk. I'll have to change them."

"It doesn't matter," Arnaldo said, "it's what they want. You go ahead and record those songs in your own style."

And that's how I recorded them, and Falcón paid for all of that work. The album that resulted from all this is called *Un canto a Colombia.* They put together some good arrangements ... an orchestra and a *mariachi* and all.

Arnaldo Ramírez

I used to go to South America at least once a year. We had quite a number of releases of ours in Colombia, Venezuela, Ecuador and Central America. And Lydia Mendoza—I was really very pleasantly suprised when I found that Lydia Mendoza was pretty well-known in Colombia.

I got this particular friend of mine, who is an old, old-timer within the record industry. I told him to see if he couldn't provide me with some of the authentic Colombian music, the oldies. Most of these songs he got for me, which I gave to Lydia. This record was specially made for our Colombian market.

Throughout the years, Lydia would go and sing and record all over the place. I guess she was recording for everybody, she was in demand. And I still have about three LPs of her material, good material I haven't released. The time has not been right. It's hard to sell records right now [1984]. Three years ago, maybe we could have taken a chance, but right now it's real tough; we've got to be very cautious.

Lydia's music is international. She had this particular sound that nobody else had. As soon as she started hitting on those strings, you knew it was Lydia Mendoza. And there's always these particular songs that would cater to any audience. That's how she was popular in South America, in Colombia.

Actually, Colombia has a lot of similarity in their songs to the Mexican songs, the romantic songs. But anyway, Lydia was an international artist, as far as I'm concerned. She didn't just appeal to the audience here in Texas, the Southwest. She would say in one of her songs, she says: "I'm *la cancionera de los pobres, cancionera, nada más*" ("the songstress of the poor, I'm just a songstress, that's all").[2]

Lidya (Guapango)

Ni muy alta, ni bajita,
soy de un cuerpo regular;
soy sencilla, visto humilde,
y mi trato es siempre igual.

Soy de rango muy humilde,
mas alegre en mi cantar,
y yo canto a todo mundo
la canción del arrabal.

"Mal hombre, que no tiene ... "
Todos dicen: —¿Quién es Lidya?
Todos hablan: —¿Quién será?
Mas yo digo: —¡No soy nadie,
no presumo y nada más!

Cancionera de los pobres,
cancionera, nada más,
mi guitarra, compañera
de mis cantos de arrabal.

"¡Mal hombre!"
Mi voz no es de lo más linda,
ni estudié a cantar con nadie;
sólo canto porque quiero
expresar lo que yo siento.

Mi madre me dio la vida,
y por ella es por quien canto,
con sonrisas o con llanto,
¡con sonrisas o con llanto!

Cancionera de los pobres,
cancionera, nada más,
mi guitarra, compañera
de mis cantos de arrabal.

"Mal hombre. ... "

Me despido sin recelos,
me despido con amor,
y el aplauso más sincero,
lo guardo en mi corazón.

Lidya (Guapango)

Neither very tall nor short,
I am of regular build;
I'm unpretentious, I dress simply,
and I treat everyone the same.

I'm of humble birth,
but my singing is very merry,
and I sing the song of the poor
outskirts of town to everyone.

"Cold-hearted man, has no ... "
Everyone says: "Who is Lydia?"
Everyone is talking: "Who might she be?
But I say: "I am nobody,
I don't put on airs, and that's that!"

Songstress of the poor,
a songstress, nothing more,
my guitar, companion of my songs
from the poor outskirts of town.

"Cold-hearted man!"
My voice isn't the prettiest,
nor did I study singing with anyone;
I only sing because I want
to express what I feel.

My mother gave me life,
and it is for her I sing,
with smiles or with weeping,
with smiles or with weeping!

Songstress of the poor,
a songstress, nothing more,

my guitar, companion of my songs
from the poor outskirts of town.
"Cold-hearted man. ... "

I bid farewell without reservations,
I bid farewell with love,
and the most sincere applause,
I save it in my heart.

Arnaldo

Well, heck, she catered to more people than just the poor. I can assure
you of that. Her records are sold all over the Spanish-speaking world. All
over, seriously, I mean it. When you get to selling something to the Puerto
Ricans, you're really going over the fence, you know, because that's a different type of music completely. The feelings are different in their music.
But then, all of the Spanish-speaking go to the basics. Once you get to
that common denominator, and Lydia Mendoza had this talent to reach the
common denominator, then she would sell to the Puerto Ricans, and sell all
over the world.

Lydia

I have also appeared in Canada and Alaska. Those were "cultural programs" that were presented at schools and colleges to audiences that were
predominately non-Latin, non-Spanish-speaking. The first time I went to
Canada was to a big festival they had up there, the Smithsonian Festival of
American Folk Life in Montreal, Canada. They invited an artist from each
nation. There was a great big dome all made of glass, and each nation had
a pavilion inside the dome where they would present their artists. Well, the
Mexican pavilion had to present a Mexican number, and I felt very honored
that they had chosen me when they could have brought someone like Amalia
Mendoza or Lola Beltrán or some artist like that from Mexico. That must
have been around 1971.

After I appeared at that festival, I started to get a lot of job offers. In 1976
I appeared at the Tucson Meet Yourself Festival, organized by Jim Griffith,
a Tucson folklorist. In January 1977 the American Folk Life Center had
a meeting at the Library of Congress in Washington, D.C. on the subject
"Ethnic Recordings in America: A Neglected Heritage." The conference
included an evening concert in the Library's Coolidge Auditorium. The
first half featured the Polish Highlanders from Chicago, and the second half
featured me, Lydia Mendoza. I not only performed, but also participated in

Lydia Mendoza and friends in front of the White House during her appearance at the Smithsonian Festival, 1982. Courtesy of the Smithsonian Institution.

the conference with Jim Griffith, who served as my interpreter and asked me questions. I spoke in a round-table discussion with other recording artists on the second day of the conference. I was invited to Toronto, Canada, and Quebec, Canada. Then they sent me to Alaska in 1979. And in September of 1984, I was also in Puerto Rico. It was the same there, I was received very well by the public. After singing for so many years, people there have gotten to know me. They may not have known of me before, but they do now. John and Irene Ullman helped organize some of those tours.

John

Lydia probably had first come to our attention through Chris Strachwitz, possibly by Chris talking to Mike Seeger. We first worked with Lydia Mendoza around 1978 when we brought her to the West Coast to be part of a traveling folk festival called the American Old Time Music Festival. It was put together by Mike Seeger and myself, and funded, in part, by the National Endowment for the Arts.

Irene

A year or two before that we went to Houston and we visited two people: Lightning Hopkins and Lydia Mendoza. We flew in, did that, and left. We wanted to introduce ourselves to her so that she would associate flesh and blood people with the voices over the phone, and to explain to her what we were doing. We were working largely with grants from the Endowment, bringing folk artists to a more general audience than just a small folk audience.

John

Each of these tours hit about a dozen venues; some of them were festivals and some were halls. We did the Great American Music Hall in San Francisco often, which was a commercial venue, but a lot of them were colleges and universities, and we tried to throw in some public school performances wherever we could. We concentrated on the Western United States and Canada.

When we first visited Lydia in Houston, we had some difficulty in communicating directly because our Spanish isn't so great and neither is her English. But her husband was there and we communicated. She wanted to go on the road; she was very enthusiastic about touring: she's a trouper. She wanted to get out there and do it, and she wanted to reach as many people as possible.

The idea of the tour was to reach as wide, as general, an audience as possible. We frequently got artists videotaped or broadcast, so the performances themselves were often not as effective as the media attention we got for the tour. Since it was a mixture of colleges and festivals, we knew it would be a fairly general audience, an audience interested in folk music and a curious audience. But we also made a real attempt to do outreach into the community, the Hispanic community. In Portland, Oregon, for example, where it was somewhat easier for us because we lived there, we did a mailing to something like one hundred-fifty either Hispanic organizations or radio stations or interested people or politically active people. From that mailing, the first time Lydia came to Portland, people drove from one hundred-fifty miles away, they came back-stage and embraced her. . . .

Irene

It was incredible, it was a really charged audience—they were shouting things back and forth between the stage and the audience in Spanish. Those of us who didn't speak Spanish couldn't really understand what was going on, but we could feel the energy. It was really emotional.

John

People came back-stage later and explained to us that they had been listening to her records for thirty-five or forty years and never thought they would live to see the day they would see her in person. They had simply not seen that as a possibility. There were around four hundred or four hundred and fifty people that came to see the show. The hall, the Portland Art Museum, was full. It was very exciting.

Irene

Lydia and her sidemen were also really, really emotional that night because it was a reunion.

John

Lydia came up with two sidemen, probably because Chris Strachwitz told us we needed to do that. We got an accordion player, Leo Garza, and a *bajo sexto* to back her up. Unfortunately the *bajo* player's name has slipped my mind. In any case, they were people Lydia had picked up and brought with her. The tour took them through Utah up into Canada, where they did Edmonton and Calgary and then came back through Vancouver. When they were crossing the border in Vancouver, one of these sidemen was not allowed to come back into the country. The reason was that he was evidently under indictment for a manslaughter or murder charge—he had actually killed someone in a fight or something back in Texas. The papers he had allowed him to leave the country but didn't allow him to come back in. He had some sort of green card. I've heard of this happening before. It's very bizarre. It's part of the real Orwellian, big brother garbage that goes on in Immigration.

Irene

They didn't explain to him the consequences of his leaving.

John

None of us understood. We didn't know he had committed this crime or had any problem at all. These musicians knew what the itinerary was, but they had paid very little attention to it or, characteristic of musicians in general, had thought, "Okay, we'll do it and it'll work itself out, what the hell." So all of a sudden, we were minus one of these guys, and he was in Canada. His options were to go to the Mexican Consul in Vancouver and get flown back to Mexico City, or to sit there. But it turned out there was a third option. The upshot was that he was smuggled back into the United States. Not, of course, by us. I wound up the Friday morning of that concert we've been talking about, picking him up at the Greyhound bus station at 3:00 a.m. He was very glad to see me; we were glad to have him back.

The Canadian people that engineered this, two of them put him in between them on the front seat, so he was sitting in the middle. They coached him on what to say and how to say it, and they drove him across to Point Roberts—a peninsula that sticks out into Puget Sound from Canada below the fifty-fourth parallel, so it's technically in the United States. The town of Point Roberts is an American town even though you have to go up through Canada to get there. Because of this sort of technically weirdly located place, he was able to drive in fairly easily, and once he got in there, they put him on a boat, a power boat, that took him to Bellingham. Then another person put him on a bus in Bellingham.

Irene

Because of the location of this Point Roberts area, people were crossing back and forth across the border there all the time and they were fairly loose about it there.

Lydia had played one date in Seattle without this guy, so it was a very emotional evening down in Portland.

John

As far as the things that happened with Lydia, we weren't prepared for her having that much effect on the Hispanic population of Oregon.

Irene

She is such a strong performer that even people who knew nothing about that kind of music were moved. When she performed there in Portland, she played just that one night. We were moving each night to a new venue. Of course, she was not the only act, it was part of a traveling festival.

It was obvious in watching Lydia operate that she was a real pro—her presence, the way she prepared for her performances, the costumes that she wore. The costumes were just incredible, and she was often asked about how she made them.

John

That tour had Sweet Honey in the Rock, Tracey and Elouise Schwartz, and Lydia, and maybe Louis Budreau.

Irene

We tried to combine at least three different elements, like a Cajun musician, some Appalachian musician or group, and a Blues act or something. On the tours we would stay generally in motels. Sometimes people we knew would stay with us, or with other people they knew, but in general people stayed in motels. We would usually drive two station wagon loads of people around.

There in Portland we had a large, large house, so everybody could stay with us. We'd get up early, like 8:00 a.m., and we'd go down to the kitchen, and Lydia was already cooking up a storm. Shortly after she arrived, she walked two blocks up to the grocery and came back with all these groceries. I think it was the opportunity to cook after being on the road. She cooked up all this food—they were there several days. She prepared this one dish that had vermicelli and some kind of meat, and other things as well. But the thing that was really amazing was that early in the morning she already had a big stack of tortillas made! We had this old-fashioned, combination wood/electric stove, and Lydia took one of the heavy iron lids off the wood part and put it over on to the electric burner, and she had made these tortillas from scratch using that as a griddle. She was cooking all this food for her sidemen.

John

A lot of performers just hang out, and when it's time to go on stage, they go on stage. But Lydia would want to, essentially, get away from what was happening a couple of hours before. She took a fairly long time to dress, make herself up, make sure her hair was right. No mystic ritual or anything, just basic professionalism.

Irene

I think people who are real high-energy performers do recognize they need to do that. Especially in the folk circuit you get a different kind of attitude where the way they perform in your living room is the same as on stage. They just move from one scene to another: this wasn't true of Lydia!

John

On that first tour we hit about a dozen places. Subsequently, we did a tour with Lydia and Flaco Jiménez in New Mexico and up into Colorado and Utah. That was around 1981. We had Western States Arts Foundation money for that. This was all organized by the State of Texas, and the Western States Arts Foundation—Texas still doesn't belong to it and California didn't back then either—who made some money available to do this sort of "cultural trade." Some group from the western states, it was possibly even an Oregon group, went to Texas and toured in Texas, and in turn Texas sent a group into the western states to tour. I think as part of that someone took Lydia and Flaco up into Oregon and Washington.

Irene

We heard reports about the audience being really highly charged in those areas, too. The presenters still talk about wanting to recreate that tour.

John

Except not quite the same way—we had a lot of vehicle breakdowns on that tour. Lydia was very stoic. I don't think it was very comfortable for her driving a couple of hundred miles a day in a van, but she did it, and she didn't complain about it. One thing that was quite striking, especially for someone who has been around Flaco and his *conjunto* very much, they're different people around Lydia! She really mellows them out. They're very respectful of her and they like her a lot. Occasionally, they would bring her on stage to do a song with them.

Irene

It also, I think, made their repetoire a lot better, too!

John

She would usually sing one or two numbers with Flaco and his band. They did that because it made it a better show. She mainly would work as a solo artist on those shows, which I think was at least as effective as having people with her. In the festival we wanted her to have an accompaniment because we wanted people to hear an accordion sound. Before that there hadn't been much accordion in these traveling festivals or on the folk circuit at all. We also had Lydia up at the Vancouver Folk Festival once or twice, and that worked very well.

As far as presenting Mexican music to a largely Anglo audience, well, the people that heard it, liked it. Because it wasn't faddish—it's getting to be faddish now with Los Lobos; it's possible that more can be done—, it was never as marketable as, say, blues. It probably still isn't from the point of view of just going into commerical venues. From the point of view of what fine arts presenters want, there's an incredible vacuum where someone could create a sort of Boys of the Loch of Hispanic music and come in and clean up. There's a Mexican group, Los Folkloristas, that's attempting to do that this year [1988-89]. The Western States Arts Foundation has a touring program, and they've had on the program, to my mind, some fairly weak Spanish-speaking musicians, simply because they're so hungry to get that and incorporate it. So there's an audience there. There's also a feeling amongst arts administrators that with or without an audience, it's a necessary thing to do.

One year, Lydia played at the San Diego Folk Festival and quite a number of Mexican Americans came to that. If people are invited in a way that makes them feel welcome, they'll come. When we got people to come to the Portland Art Museum, we did it by doing this mailing. We also did a Spanish press release and a Spanish public service announcement to the radio stations. So it was not only announced, it was announced in Spanish.

Irene

There is a fair amount of Spanish-language radio activity in the Portland area. I remember one day around Christmas when I was throwing pots like crazy in the basement, I caught one of these shows, and they played an hour of Christmas-related music, and it seemed a large majority of the stuff they were playing was Lydia's music. So people were familiar with her name.

As far as any prejudice against Mexican or Mexican-American performers, it's probably stronger here in California, compared to the Northwest. I don't think it's something you notice so much up north.

John

There's probably a bunch of components to it. There's probably out-and-out ethnic prejudice—I mean, every ethnic music has its sort of tacky analogue. People often aren't prepared for the integrity of someone like Lydia Mendoza from all this stereotyped music in the same way they aren't prepared for the integrity of someone like Tommy Jarrell in the face of "Hee Haw" and this sort of bowdlerized Appalachian music. So I don't think it's just Hispanic music that suffers from that, I think all ethnic music has this problem.

In general, non-English language music doesn't attract as big of an audience. I once did a radio show where this fellow in Portland said, "Okay, I'm going to invite you to do this radio show and you can bring your favorite records." So, I brought a lot of Tex-Mex music, and finally, in the middle of the show, he basically whispered in my ear, and he said, "You can't do more of this, because they'll listen to so much non-English language stuff and then tune out. There's a phenomenon." Now, I don't know if that's really true. I don't know how true that phenomenon is, but this guy was not a racist, he was anything but. He was somewhat of a radical and he was an iconoclast. I wouldn't have been on the radio otherwise; he got fired soon after anyway. So, he wasn't doing it from the point of view of personal prejudice, I'm quite certain. But when we had something that was French, then something that was Spanish, etc. it was a little much. So, I think just non-English is a problem. So, Hispanic music then has several strikes against it as far as meeting a general audience's criterion.

Lydia

I have always liked American music, and I would have liked to have sung in English. But, well, as I don't know the language ... I've worried about it sometimes, especially when I've played for audiences who mostly didn't speak Spanish. I'm afraid they won't understand me. For instance, when I played for the San Diego State University Folk Festival in 1975 there were a lot of kids there that couldn't really understand my songs, but they told me they loved the music, anyway, especially the *corridos*. Both the kids who spoke Spanish, and those who didn't, seemed very eager to understand Mexican music. The American music I like the most is country and western.

When I was young, I listened a lot to Caruso, Enrico Caruso. My father was a fanatical fan of Caruso. Papá had his entire collection ... recorded on some great big records, bigger than standard 78s. The records were the size of an LP, but they were actually acoustically recorded twelve-inch 78s.

Now Pilar Arcos, I met her about five years ago when I was in California ... [3] I also listened to her music, I enjoyed it very much. She sang "El pajarillo barranqueño," and ... lots of Mexican music. I listened to her a lot in 1931. I also had many of Margarita Cueto's records, and many of Juan Pulido's as well. I was very devoted to the old-time music. I liked that style of music, Juan Pulido's style. I liked his songs very much, that voice of his was so beautiful. I felt the same way about Pilar Arcos and also Margarita Cueto.[4]

Even nowadays, many families and persons of the public have come up

to ask me why I sing all my songs with so much feeling. They ask me if I
have passed through what I'm singing about in some part of my hard life.
Well, thank God, no. God has given me peace of mind, and I have had
happiness. But when I am singing a song, it seems like I live that moment.
It seems like I went through what that song or *corrido* says: I feel them.

For instance, sometimes my daughter makes fun of me, and she says:
"Aw, Mamá, why do you like that silly song?" "I don't know!" I tell her.
We're talking about a *corrido* about a horse, "El potro *lobo gatiado*."[5]

El potro lobo gatiado

En una manada vide
un potro que me gustaba;
me fui con el hacendado:
—Señor, traigo una tratada,
quiero que me dé un caballo
por mi yegua colorada.

—Ese caballo que quieres,
yo pensaba echarlo al carro;
por tu yegua doy quinientos,
y el potro te lo regalo;
a vaqueros y a caporales,
a todos los ha tumbado.

Y luego que ya trataron,
el charro le echó una hablada:
—Este caballo le juega
a su yegua colorada
por dos mil quinientos pesos,
ya se acerca la tratada.

Le contestó el hacendado:
—No pienses que tengo miedo;
nos vamos pa' la oficina
a depositar el dinero;
esta carrera se juega
para el veintitrés de febrero.

Por fin se llegó la fecha
de la carrera afamada;
volaban pesos tronchados

a la yegua colorada;
al potro *lobo gatiado*
ni quien le apostara nada.

Y dieron la voz de arranque
la yegua se abalanzó,
y el potro lobo gatiado
al disparo se paró,
pero al llegar al cabresto
con dos cuerpos les ganó.

Ya con ésta me despido,
dispensen lo mal trovado;
aquí termina el corrido
de un charro y un hacendado
y la yegua colorada
y el potro lobo gatiado.

The Striped Colt

Among a herd of horses I saw
a colt that I liked;
I went to the ranch owner:
"Sir, I'd like to make a deal,
I want you to trade me a horse
for my red mare."

"That horse you want,
I was thinking about putting it on the cart;
I'll give 500 for your mare,
and I'll give you the colt for free;
cowboys and foremen,
it has thrown them all."

And as soon as they made the deal,
the cowboy made the ranch owner a bet:
"I'll race this horse
against your red mare
for 2,500 pesos;
the deal will go down soon."

The ranch owner answered him:

"Don't think I'm afraid;
let's go to the office
to deposit the money;
this race will be run
on the twenty-third of February."

Finally the day came
of the famous race;
sure-thing *pesos* went flying
to the red mare;
there was no one who would
bet on the striped colt.

When they yelled to start,
the mare took off running,
and the striped colt
stood still at the sound of the shot,
but after it caught up with the mare,
it beat them all by two lengths.

Now with this I bid farewell,
excuse the poor composition;
here ends the *corrido*
about a cowboy and a ranch owner
and the red mare
and the striped colt.

What does this have to do with anything in particular? Nothing. Nevertheless, it's a *corrido* that really affects me a lot. I don't know why I like it so much, but I feel it deep down in my soul. Like "Mal hombre," many people tell me that song must be about something that happened to me personally. Well, nothing like what it says ever happened to me.

When I want to learn, to memorize, some songs, I do it in the quiet, so nobody disturbs me. I take advantage of the very early morning hours when there isn't any noise or any disturbances, when the telephone isn't going to ring or anything like that. I take my guitar and start to practice. In one morning I can learn very well three or four songs that I have never sung before. I just sing them two or three times ... and they stick in my head. And they don't go away. I don't forget either the melody or the words.

When there is a new record, and I want to learn a song from it, I play it and listen to it. The best way for me is on a little cassette. I start to play it, and the first thing that I write down is the words: first one verse, then the next. And then when I have the words, I go over the words following the music. So then, after doing that two or three times, it's stuck with me. Now I've learned it.

I do forget, of course, some songs that I haven't sung for years and years. For songs like that I have to give them a run through. But after a little run through, they come out all right. I was in Austin recently, for instance, and at one of the concerts the audience asked me for "No puedo dejar de quererte," "Deliciosa," "Tranquila es mi vida," and they asked me for "Lejos" and "Marimba"—all songs I had recorded. Impossible. I need a list of songs before I go on if I'm going to sing something I haven't done for a long time.

It's like now, that I'm getting ready to return to South America. The gentleman down there has sent me a list of my songs that the public there has heard and will ask for, and I have to learn them. If they ask for them all of a sudden, it's just impossible. But with just a little run through, they're right there again.

I don't know where I stick a song so it doesn't go away. I don't forget the music or anything. I can sing songs from memory for hours. I don't have to be looking at them. I have them here in my head. I believe I inherited something from my mother, her memory, the music . . . Mamá remembered a lot of songs—she carried them around in her head. I inherited some of that from her: her voice, her talent, her comprehension, some of all of that . . .

The piano, I also play it a little. I never forgot how to play the guitar. And the mandolin, well I still have my mandolin. Once in a while I play along with some of the records Chris Strachwitz has sent me, like those of the Trio San Antonio, and all. I record on a cassette—the mandolin with the records. I always practice more on the mandolin. I also want to buy a violin, just to have it. I haven't played one for many years. But I haven't forgotten how. When I have gone recently to do these programs—when I was in Washington, when I was in Fresno, at the colleges—people have occasionally brought me a violin so that I might play them some piece. I always struggle a little; it's been years since I have played the violin regularly. But the mandolin, yes, I can still play.

A painter that paints has to have a scene for inspiration. Let's say there is a tree there. He's not going to paint that tree like he is seeing it, really. But he has to have an imagination, an image, an idea, of what he wants to paint. So then he is going to paint that tree not like it is, but different, distinct in the way that he sees it. It is like that for those who compose. For example, we have "Amor bonito," a song that has become very well known because I recorded it. And it has been listened to, and many people now know it is my song. There is a reason I wrote it. I composed this song when I married my second husband. As fate would have it, he is from Denver. He had his business there, everything. He couldn't sell it quickly, just like that, in order to move to Texas. But he came here; we got married in Houston. About three or four days later, he had to go take care of his business. I stayed in Houston; then about two months later my new husband returned and was here with me for a month, two months, and then he went again. I love him a lot and missed him very much.

So then one of those times he went away, I went to Corpus, enthused that they were going to do a program there, and that I was going to teach a lot of students. I got everyone together, and I went with my kids to Corpus, and I was there for a while. And one night while I was there, I was inspired to compose that song: "Amor bonito."

Amor bonito[6]

El mundo estará muy lleno
de amores y de querencias,
pero pa' mí hay uno solo
que da luz a mi existencia.

Mi amor es retebonito,
brillante como un lucero;
en las tristezas de mi alma
me alegro con su recuerdo.

Coro
Doy gracias a mi Diosito
por lo bueno que es conmigo;
que siempre oye mis plegarias
a todo lo que le pido.

Amor bonito, bonito,
cariño, mi cariñito,
te quiero porque te quiero,
porque eres mi amor bonito.
(Esta estrofa se repite.)

Tu amor es retebonito,
radiante como una estrella;
que pensando en tu cariño,
se acaban todas mis penas.

Coro

Beautiful Love

The world might be full
of lovers and affairs,
but for me there is only one
that brings light to my existence.

My love is extra beautiful,
brilliant like a bright, unblinking star;
in the sadness of my soul
I cheer up with memories of him.

Chorus
I give thanks to my Dear Lord
for being so good to me;
He always hears my prayers
for everything I ask of Him.

Beautiful love, so beautiful,
beloved, my sweet, dear beloved,
I love you because I love you,
because you are my beautiful love.
(This stanza is repeated.)

Your love is extra beautiful,
radiant like a star;
just thinking about your affection,
all my troubles come to an end.

Chorus

Everything I say in "Amor bonito" is inspired by my husband. That song came to me ... because he was gone, and I was remembering him, and everything that referred to him. That's why I composed that song.[7]

I had already composed others before that, and after "Amor bonito" come other songs I have written. It hasn't really been my strong point: being a composer. Once in a while one comes to me. Like on one occasion when I was making a record of Christmas songs for Falcón. They told me, "If you have some song of your own, well, we'll record it. We'll put it on there." So I was inspired to compose a song, and I wrote one that is called "Llorando en Navidad." For Mother's Day, the same. I composed another that is called "Perdón yo pido." But that one was based on things that haven't really happened to me, but I had to think about something in order to compose it. It's like an inspiration.

My favorite song is the one called "Acércame a tu vida." It's just a little old *bolero*, but it is very pretty. And that's the one I like because it concerns my present situation. This is how it goes:

Acércame a tu vida[8]

Acércame a tu vida.
Dame algo de lo tuyo.
Y déjame saber la realidad
cómo se vive en ti.

Acércame a tu vida,
y llévame a tu mundo.
Enséñame el camino
que nos da la dicha de existir.

Tú sabes que no tengo
ni un secreto que provoque tus enojos.
Tú sabes que en tus brazos he encontrado
la razón de mi vivir.

Acércame a tu vida,
y llévame a tu mundo.
Enséñame el camino,
que nos da la dicha de vivir.

Tú sabes que no tengo
ni un secreto que provoque tus enojos.
Tú sabes que en tus brazos yo he encontrado
la razón de mi vivir.

Acércame a tu vida,
y llévame a tu mundo.
Enséñame el camino
que nos da la dicha de vivir.

Bring Me into Your Life

Bring me nearer to your life.
Give me something of yourself.
And let me know the reality,

how it is lived in you.

Bring me nearer to your life,
and take me to your world.
Show me the road
that gives us the joy of existing.

You know that I don't have
not even one secret that might provoke your anger.
You know that in your arms I have found
my reason for living.

Bring me nearer to your life,
and take me to your world.
Show me the road,
that gives us the joy of living.

You know that I don't have
even a single secret that might provoke your anger.
You know that in your arms I have found
the meaning of my life.

Bring me nearer to your life,
and take me to your world.
Show me the road
that gives us the joy of living.

It's an old song. I imagine it isn't even Mexican. It seems to me it's from somewhere around there like South America or Puerto Rico, but it's an old song.

Of course, there are also a lot of songs . . . like for instance, the one called "El Bootlegger." Oh, there's a lot of those! I don't sing many of them. They have them about the marijuana and all that, like the *corrido* about "Camelia," and all the others of that type. But those songs and *corridos* about the bootleggers and the smugglers and the marijuana . . . , well, that isn't really my kind of music.

I don't like the songs that insult, either, the real cheap ones that hurt the person. Like there are some *canciones de desprecio* [songs of disparagement] that are real heavy; I don't like that type of music. But I do like some of the insulting songs—the ones with good humor— and the romantic songs. I also like many of the *corridos* very much, I enjoy singing them very much.

Recently they have been composing a lot of *corridos* on this side of the border, mainly in San Antonio. We have José Morante, who is the owner of the Norteño, Sombrero and Lira record labels. He is a composer, and each event that happens—like if someone is killed in a *cantina* or if they shot somebody or whatever—right away, José composes a *corrido*. For instance, he wrote a corrido about President Kennedy. José Morante also composed a *corrido*, "Tragedia en Yuba City, California" (Trágico fin de 24 hombres), about what happened in California, there in Yuba City.[9]

Everything that happens ... when Eva Garza died, Morante wrote a *corrido* about her. Other people also write them. Just recently a *corrido*, "José Campos Torres," was written about the policemen here in Houston that threw that boy into the bayou: Torres.[10] The *corrido* came out right after they killed him and people found out. I thought it was a good *corrido*—very timely and to the point—but I didn't learn it to sing.

When I was growing up, I felt very Mexican, (laughs) of course. Although I would have liked to have lived in Mexico, well, I was born here, and my parents brought me here. We came here when we were very little, my brothers and sisters, so I got used to it. It put the environment of here on me. And I didn't feel like I was out of place anywhere, and I was happy just as I was. Although I was born here, and my parents were from Mexico, well ... for me it would have been the same if I had stayed here, or if I were to have stayed in Mexico.

I have always liked the music from both sides of the border, just that I have preferred the old-time music, especially, also, the instruments. I like very much a *conjunto* ... well, of course, the *norteño* music is very nice, but if I'm having a party, or something, I don't like a lot of wind instruments, whistles, saxophones, and all of that. I just like string instruments like violins, mandolins, *bajo sextos*, *contrabajos*, but those great big ones, not those electric basses, no. That's the music I prefer. It always has been and it always will. Only, now, it's difficult to find a string *conjunto* like that. There aren't any. Like recently, my birthday was coming up, my daughters in San Antonio told me, "Mamá, we're going to give you a big birthday party. We want to hold a dance for you, to get the whole family together and all your friends, in San Antonio, Texas."

"Yes," I said, "but what kind of music are you going to get? You're not going to get some orchestra that's going to play *cumbias* for me or anything like that. I don't like those."

"Mamá," they said, "where are we going to get the kind of group you like? There isn't any music any more, almost, of the kind you like. Well, we don't know, we'll just see what we come up with."

But they did just fine. They had a *conjunto* for dancing and earlier in the evening they got José Morante and some of his *mariachis* to play the old-time music I love. Everyone ended up having a great time.

I recorded another song that really expresses the woman's point of view: "Dime, mal hombre." It doesn't have any similarity to "Mal hombre," it's very different, but in some ways it talks about the same story. It's a woman speaking in that song, and it is also a *tango*.

Dime, mal hombre[11]

La noche que juraste que eras mío,
ser tuya para siempre yo juré.
Cegada por mis locos desvaríos,
la honra y el cariño te entregué.

Perdida entre las redes de tu engaño,
sintiendo un beso tuyo me dormí,
mas luego al despertar, el desengaño mató la ilusión,
pues, ya no te vi.

Dime, mal hombre: ¿Por qué me abandonaste?
Sola me dejaste, llorando tu traición.
Dime, mal hombre: ¿Por qué en mi labio impreso
dejaste aquel beso que fue mi perdición?

Gozaste tu traición, y entre la gente
tu infamia mi deshonra pregonó;
al verme sin honor bajé la frente
y el mundo sin piedad me señaló.

Juré vengar la afrenta recibida,
ahogando con tu sangre mi dolor,
y vine aquí a matarte decidida,
y al verte ante mí me faltó el valor.

Quiero mirarte y tenerte muy cerquita
ya que por ti palpita mi pobre corazón.
¿Por qué en mis labios aún vive prisionero
el beso traicionero que fue mi perdición?

Tell Me, Evil Man

The night you swore you were mine,
I swore to be yours forever.
Blinded by my crazy whims,
I gave over to you my honor and my love.

Lost in the nets of your deceit,
feeling your kiss, I fell asleep,
but later, upon awakening, the hard truth slaughtered
all my false dreams; you were no longer there.

Tell me, evil man: Why did you abandon me?
You left me all alone, bewailing your betrayal.
Tell me, evil man: Why did you leave impressed
on my lips the kiss that was my ruin?

You enjoyed your betrayal,
and your infamy advertised my dishonor among the people;
finding myself dishonored I bowed my head
and the world pitilessly marked me out.

I swore to avenge the wrong I had received,
drowning my pain in your blood,
and I came here determined to kill you,
but seeing you before me, my courage failed me.

I want to look at you and hold you close
now that my poor heart throbs for you.
Why upon my lips still lives, a prisoner,
the treacherous kiss that was my undoing?

I first recorded that song on Blue Bird. Unlike "Mal hombre," I have only recorded it twice. I believe those are the only two songs I recorded that are really written from the woman's perspective. Nowadays, if the lyrics to a song speak from a man's point of view, but a woman is singing it, they switch the names and everything around so that it's as if it were a woman's song. But in those years when I was recording, that wasn't done. The song would always be sung just as it was. If it was a *danza*, for instance, of a man for a woman or of a woman for a man, it would be sung like that, regardless of who was singing. And now it wouldn't. Now the music would probably be all turned around, too. Each singer sings however they feel like. Right now, if it's a *ranchera*, they make it a *bolero*. In the old days that kind of thing just wasn't done. Even me, I've recorded lots of songs of that type . . . like some of those Colombian songs, *danza* type songs, and that's how I recorded them: just as they were. Recently a singer from Mexico recorded "Pero ay qué triste" as a *bolero*; instead of singing the song like it really is, they changed its rhythm completely!

Nowadays, when we get together, the brothers and sisters, we make a remembrance of our times together when we were going around working, and back when we started singing. My sisters sing, or I sing with them. Mainly at New Years and at Christmas, we all get together, and the whole family has a party.

I've even tried to get them to record again, mainly my brother Manuel, who has a very pretty voice; he sings like ... when Jorge Negrete sang, he has a voice that is very ... not like Jorge Negrete, but of that timbre. Manuel sings beautifully. I've wanted to take him along to record, but as soon as I make the date, he doesn't go. He says, "No, no, I can't sing anymore."

But he does like to sing. When I go to San Antonio, Manuel always takes me to his house, or he takes me with his friends, and he introduces me, and I always take the guitar along, and we sing, and all. He sings with me ... but not by himself. Manuel has also written some very pretty songs:

Manuel
"Esa güerita" is a song I wrote and really like.[12]

Esa güerita

Qué bonitos ojos tiene,
y su cara redondita.
Cada vez que yo la miro
me sonríe y todo me agita.

Ay, Diosito de mi vida,
cómo quiero a esa güerita.
A todos trae dando vueltas
esa güera condenada.

Si le digo que la quiero,
ella tira una carcajada.
Ay, Diosito de mi vida,
Ah, qué güerita malcriada.

Ooh yoo yoooui. ...
¿Pues qué le vamos a hacer?
Ooh yoo yoooui. ...
¡Cómo quiero a esa mujer!

Y a todos trae dando vueltas
esa güera condenada.
Si le digo que la quiero,
ella me tira una carcajada.

Ay, Diosito de mi vida,
esa güerita malcriada.

This Darn Little Blonde

What pretty eyes she has,
and her round little face.
Each time I look at her,
she smiles at me and drives me crazy.

Oh, dear God,
how I love that *güerita*.
She has everyone going in circles,
this darn *güera*.

If I tell her that I love her,
she laughs in my face.
Ah, what a spoiled little *güerita*.

Ooh yoo yoooui. ...
Well what are we going to do?
Ooh yoo yoooui. ...
How I love that woman!

She has everyone going in circles,
this damn *güera*.
If I tell her that I love her,
she laughs in my face.

Ay, dear God,
this spoiled little *güera*.

Manuel
Lydia made that record, and I wrote the song. She recorded three of my songs, and that was one of them.

Por una mujer[13]

Por una mujer yo me he
vuelto muy perdido.
Me engañó con su querer,
me dejó el corazón herido.

Ya no me importa la vida,
pues ¿qué le vamos a hacer?
Yo me creía muy vivo;
me ha engañado una mujer.

Por esa mujer ingrata
ahora vivo en las cantinas,
por los juramentos falsos
que me hacía la muy ladina.

Because of a Woman

Because of a woman I have
become a lost man.
She deceived me with her love,
she left me with a wounded heart.

Life doesn't matter to me anymore,
but what are we going to do?
I thought I was real clever;
a woman has deceived me.

Because of this cruel woman
I live now in the barrooms,
because of the false promises
the deceitful woman made to me.

Manuel

I wrote these songs when we were out in California. I'd just pick up some piece of paper and start making the words rhyme.

As for myself, I got married in 1947 and didn't stay with the family's traveling *variedad* for long afterward. My wife didn't care too much for me to be traveling around, so I decided to call it quits and start working. I worked for a while in a furniture store and in a place where they were making trailers. From there I decided to drive a bus, so, in 1951, I started with Trailways. Since then, that's the only job I've ever had: bus driver. Then my wife started working, and my kids started going to school and everything, and they got educated.

My wife and I have three children: Manuel, Jr., Pearl and Roberta. Manuel is an architect, Pearl is an interior designer and Bobby is a school teacher. They all have degrees. Pearl likes to play a little piano, but not professionally, just when we get together sometimes at our house. They're all married. I don't know who they take after; I don't think they take after me, especially my boy. You know, he's going on his own now. He's getting together with some architects here, and he's going to open his own firm. He's going to Greece. In July, he and his wife are going to Greece [1984]. My youngest daughter, Roberta, she's in Pakistan right now. She's married to this major in the Army, and he was sent over there, so she went with him. She's teaching some Pakistanis how to speak basic English so they can come over here to study or something.

My family's religion, my mother and father's religion is Catholic. It was mine; it's not anymore, though. I've made my vows in the Protestant religion. But all my family, my brother and sisters, they're all considered Catholic. I don't know whether they still go to church or not. I think I go to church more now that I'm a Protestant.

Even though I went to a Catholic school, it wasn't put in my head to be a devoted Catholic. So, when I married my wife, she was a Presbyterian, so I got married by that church. Now I sing in church, I sing at weddings and all the funerals. And I even sing at the Hall, you know, classic music—not the kind of music I used to sing with the family show. On Easter Sunday and all those days, I usually sing in church. I'm not ashamed that I was a Catholic, though. I just believe that now, the way I believe now, I devote myself more to the church than I used to when I was a Catholic.

As for those faith healers, well, you know, those things are for people, that, you know, that ... it's up to the individual to believe in that. You know, just like Pedro Jaramillo, El Niño Perdido, El Niño Fidencio, La Señora de los Milagros, right here. My mother used to believe in this Señora de los Milagros. I used to go with her. Even when I came back from the Service, we went to San Juan de los Lagos, that's a big shrine over there in Mexico. Mamá had made a vow to take me when I came back from the Army. But, you know, deep inside of me, my belief was different. I never had read the Bible, and I think I read the Bible now more than I used to. And they didn't used to sing in the Catholic churches. I enjoy singing those hymns, that really hits me right here whenever I sing them, when I sing "How Great Thou Art." There's so many: "Open the Gates to the Temple," "The Holy City" and all those.

Maybe one reason why some of these Pentecostal churches are making pretty good headway amongst Mexican Americans is that they sing. But they're different, they operate different from the Presbyterian Church. You know, the Presbyterians and the Methodists are about the same, similar to each other. When I joined this Presbyterian Church, when I married my wife, I got involved in the witness. At first I was a deacon, then I was made an elder. Then we opened up a church over on Thirty-Sixth Street, and I was the ruling elder. Now I'm not, I'm just an elder. Once an elder, you're always an elder. Religion, it's nice, you know. Now I go to church more than my wife does.

María

Juanita and my brother went to school here, but I didn't. I went for a little while in Monterrey, but not for very long. Lydia didn't either. Well, at that time, they didn't require you to go to school here. Now they do. I learned English later when I got married. I learned it from my husband. I just barely learned it when I got married, and that was in 1954.

Now my children speak mostly in English, because they used nothing but English when they went to school. They speak Spanish, but they don't pronounce it well, they just speak it any old way. The one who speaks the best Spanish is my son William because he is involved in politics. My daughter, she speaks a little. And George, if you speak to him in Spanish, he doesn't understand you. He'll answer you if you say a word in English. My other son, who was in the Army, he knows both English and Spanish very well.

I would have liked to have gone to night school or to regular school to get some education, but I had a lot of children. I had little ones, one right after the other. I had five. The ladies in the neighborhood were all going to night classes over there at the school or someplace that they went, and they invited me to go with them. But I didn't have anyone to look after my children, and I wouldn't leave them alone. But I learned something from my husband. I was hearing all the words. I know that I still don't speak English very well, but I do understand it. I used to be pretty sharp, because they would say something to me, and I would just end up staring, because I didn't know what they were talking about and wouldn't know what to answer.

There are several female singers that still work around here in San Antonio, like La Paloma del Norte. And then there is Rosita Fernández who sings over there at Paseo del Río. And Laura Canales, they're working her so hard she's going to be dead pretty soon. She's a good singer, but they're going to kill her working her like that.

Juanita and I still sing every once in awhile [1984]. We sang together for the Virgin of Guadalupe a while back. A lot of people came to see us, and it was very cold.

I remember that I sure liked that life when I was little. Because you're happy, you don't care about nothing, and now, when you grow up and get married, you start thinking and have lots of troubles. You know, if my mother was alive, I wouldn't have gotten married. Mamá would never have let me get married. I got married when I was thirty.

My mother was very religious, but my father didn't believe in the church. He didn't believe in all of those rituals ... where you put some candles, he just had a big *Cristo grande* in his room and that's all. Papá didn't believe in anything, not in the Church. And he didn't believe in Baptism or Communion; my mother did.

Myself, well, I'm not so religious as to go every day to the church, but I burn my candles and pray for Heaven, for everybody, for my kids. And I go to church and pray. All of my kids made their Communion, Confirmation and Baptism, all in the church. I also believed in the healer, Pedrito Jaramillo. I believed in him too much—I had the prayer and I had the picture. He used to be a man that helped you when you were sick. I believe in Pedrito Jaramillo. I also believe in Niño Fidencio. He's over there in Espinazos, Nuevo León or Coahuila, over there near Piedras Negras. El Niño Fidencio has a little church over there with the Virgin of Guadalupe and San Juan, and I believe in him.

All my kids went to church while they were growing up, but not anymore, because, you know, they grow, and they like to be around young people. When they were little kids they would go with me. My husband doesn't believe in anything about the church. He didn't want to go with me, no way, to church, but I went with the kids. The church is over here, just one block. I have five children, three boys and two girls, and now I have some grandchildren, too.

Andrew

My mother was into religion. Mamá was a Rosicrucian, and as a Rosicrucian, she was realistic, and I have to follow in her footsteps. So, the basis that she left, and that basis hasn't been lost to this person that stands right here right now, was that we have to understand, we have to separate two things: one is what belongs to God, and the other is what belongs to the earth. Mamá taught me on that basis. She was very sincere and very specific when she talked about anything out of the Bible. And all of the teachings that she gave me out of the Bible, all of the understandings of the Bible that she gave me, and that I go by, are not what religion usually talks about.

I remember many times waking up during the night and going to the bathroom, and I would see her sitting down at two, three, four, five o'clock in the morning, sitting in bed. And sometimes I would find her outside in the yard. I wouldn't talk to her, but I would see her, and I would ask a question in my mind, like: "What is she doing?" Now I know what she was doing. You see, the only way that she could support us was by going out and working. She had to go out and play in different towns. And what she was doing, she was asking God, the Divine Providence, to find us work.

So when you ask us about religion, I don't think she had any religion. I think that her religion was the Divine Providence. Because she never specified, to us, God, in a name, like God, like Jehovah, or ... no, she wouldn't. I will never forget that, to her, God was the Divine Providence. Because, she would say the Divine Providence is everything. And if you don't understand it, you will never understand anything.

Lydia

Some of the people I know have told me all about Don Pedrito Jaramillo. If they have their belief, I respect that. But I just don't believe in this, and I have never seen the need to go consult one of those healers. Thank God, I have never been sick, never. God has protected me. The only thing that I have is arthritis, this ailment that hurts my bones and all [1984].

Real happiness and gaiety didn't come to us—my family and me—until I made my first Blue Bird recordings, and we started to live a less suffocated life. But before that, let's say from 1927 until 1933, we didn't have any novelties; we were just striving for life and working to make a living: sometimes better, sometimes worse. Encountering a lot of calamities, that was our life. And I say that it was my life, because I didn't know what parties ... or friends were. There was nothing to make my years happy. I didn't have clothes. We didn't have anything, and as I was growing up, reaching a certain age, well, I would look at the other girls, all so neat, and I didn't have anything like that. I didn't rebel against my situation, but it did give me sadness that I couldn't enjoy life like the other girls. But it was impossible. It was nothing but working in order to live. That is the reason that I had so little gaiety in my youth, just bitterness and sadness.

But all of what has happened doesn't bother me, because after all the years, in the autumn of my life, I can say that I have had many satisfactions. Everything that I desired was granted to me. The first desire I had was, well, to improve our life when I was still at home with my parents, and God granted it to me. Then when I married, when I had my daughters, my desire was ... I asked God to let me see them grown-up. And Christ granted that to me. And then, after they got married, I didn't want to die without knowing the grandchildren. In the end, everything that I have desired has been granted to me.

Notes

Introduction

[1]Early recordings by the Mariachi Marmolejo can be heard on ARH/FL CD/C 7011.

Chapter One

[1]In Mexico and other Spanish speaking countries it is customary to put the father's last name first, followed by the mother's. When a woman marries, she joins her father's name to that of her husband. Thus Lydia's grandmother became Teófila Reyna de Zamarripa when she married Refugio Zamarripa.

[2]Monterrey was finally captured by the Constitutionalist forces between April 22 and 28, 1914.

[3]Manuel is probably refering to the Head Tax established by the Immigration Act of 1917. Before 1917 there had been virtually no legal obstacle whatsoever to Mexican immigration. The Act imposed a literacy requirement and charged an $8.00 head tax, but even these requirements were suspended due to the labor shortage brought about by World War I, only to be reinstated in 1920. The Immigration Act of 1924 added a $10.00 fee to the $8.00 Head Tax. The resulting upsurge in illegal crossing gave rise to the creation of the Border Patrol. During the 1920s there were no real controls or limits on Mexicans entering the United States other than the payment of this tax. The tax stubs—proof of payment—served to distinguish legal immigrants from the illegals.

[4]Possibly it was Elisa Berumen, who recorded "Mal hombre" for Victor (Vi 78788–B) in Los Angeles, California, on May 11, 1926, with piano accompaniment by Leroy Shield and two guitars. It is probably the earliest recorded version of this song and was apparently quite a success for Elisa Berumen, although she never made another record. The lyrics were also printed in Mauricio Calderón's Fall 1928 catalogue under the listing for that disk. A number of people have expressed the opinion that the *couplet* or tango "Mal hombre" originated in Argentina.

[5]Lydia Mendoza first recorded "Mal hombre" at the Texas Hotel in San Antonio on March 27, 1934 for the Blue Bird label (Bb B 2200). This historic recording can be heard on ARH/FL CD/C 7002. The following text has been transcribed from Lydia's 1934 performance. The translation is ours.

Chapter Two

[1]The Mendoza version can be heard on Az 339, Azteca LP 8004(33).

[2]The text below was transcribed from Falcón 091, recorded by Las Hermanas Mendoza, Juanita y María. Composer credit is given to Leonor Mendoza. Another version of this song, recorded in San Antonio in 1929 by Pedro Rocha and Lupe Martínez, can be heard on Folklyric 9016(33).

[3]"Pero ay qué triste" can be heard on ARH/FL CD 7002. The lyrics can be seen in Chapter 4.

Chapter Three

[1] For Lydia's first guitar and her style of playing, see Dale Miller, "Lydia Mendoza: The Lark of the Border," *Guitar Player* 22.8.224 (August, 1988): 38-41, and Carlos B. Gil, "Lydia Mendoza: Houstonian and First Lady of Mexican American Song," *Houston Review* 3 (1981): 258, and James F. Griffith, "Lydia Mendoza: An Enduring Mexican-American Singer," *Ethnic Recordings in America: A Neglected Heritage*, Studies in American Folklife 1 (Washington: American Folklife Center, Library of Congress, 1982): 113, 126.

[2] Manuel J. Cortez was the father of Raúl Cortez. Raúl Cortez has the distinction of having started one of the very first full time Spanish-language radio stations in the United States: KCOR in San Antonio, Texas. KCOR did not go on the air until February 15, 1946. Before that time all Spanish language radio in San Antonio, and in the U.S. generally, was of the "block programming" type represented by the "Voz latina" organized by Manuel Cortez. An entrepreneur would purchase a "block" of time on an otherwise all English-language station, sell his own Hispanic advertising and provide his own Spanish-language programming. For details on the creation of KCOR, see: Jorge Reina Schement and Ricardo Flores, "The Origins of Spanish-Language Radio: The Case of San Antonio, Texas," *Journalism History* 4.2 (1977): 56-61.

[3] María Mendoza said that the station was KABC. According to Reina Schement and Flores (56), Raúl Cortez had two hours a day of Spanish programming on a station called KEBC in 1940. Since Spanish "e" is pronounced like the English name for the letter "a" it is probable that Reina Schement and Flores really are referring to KABC. Richard García, "Class, Consciousness, and Ideology—The Mexican Community of San Antonio, Texas: 1930-1940," *Aztlán* 9 (1978): 55, asserts that a man named René Capistrán Garza had a half hour daily show called "La voz de la raza" on KABC in the early 1930s. There are frequent advertisements for this show in *La prensa* from those years. KABC broadcast at 1420 kilocycles, and the "Voz de la raza" came on at 10:00 (in 1931).

Chapter Four

[1] This is the way Lydia remembers her first Blue Bird session. According to the Blue Bird session logs, however, the whole family group as it was then constituted went to the studio that day and recorded six sides. Lydia then recorded another six solo numbers. See *Discography* for details.

[2] This historic recording can be heard on ARH/FL CD 7002. The transcription and translation are those of Professor Guillermo Hernández and Yolanda Zepeda as they appear in the notes on the jacket of Folklyric 9023.

[3] Some of Lydia's brothers and sisters did record for Decca. See *Discography*.

[4] Lydia first recorded "Pero ay qué triste" for Blue Bird at the Texas Hotel in San Antonio on August 10, 1934. That recording can be heard on ARH/FL CD 7002. The transcription and translation are ours.

[5]Lydia also recorded "Los besos de mi negra" at the Texas Hotel on August 10, 1934 for Blue Bird. It can be heard on ARH/FL CD 7002. The transcription and translation have been adapted from those by Professor Guillermo Hernández and Yolanda Zepeda with some corrections by Zack Salem.

[6]The text of "Las cuarenta cartas" has been transcribed from the version by Lupe Posada y Regim Pérez, Rec. Victor 46994, 2 pts., Hollywood, Ca., May 13, 1930. The translation is ours.

[7]María Conesa was a famous Spanish singer who toured Mexico in 1908-09.

[8]The text of "Mírame, mírame" has been transcribed and translated from a performance by Juanita Mendoza delivered during the course of a tape-recorded interview conducted by Chris Strachwitz and Dan Dickey, San Antonio, Texas, June 1, 1983.

[9]Juanita and Manuel can be heard singing "La guía" on Folklyric 9035. The original recording was made in San Antonio for Decca, 2/8/37, about the same time as the events they are describing.

[10]The text of "Las jícaras de Michoacán" has been transcribed and translated from a performance by Juanita and María Mendoza delivered during the course of a tape-recorded interview conducted by Chris Strachwitz and Dan Dickey, San Antonio, Texas, June 1, 1983.

[11]The text of "Mariquita" has been transcribed and translated from a performance by Juanita and María Mendoza delivered during the course of a tape-recorded interview conducted by Chris Strachwitz and Dan Dickey, San Antonio, Texas, June 1, 1983.

[12]A *chinaco* suit is a variant of the *charro* outfit traditionally worn by *ranchera* singers.

Chapter Five

[1]Ramiro Cortés comments on this: "Yeah, Lydia Mendoza, *La Alondra*. ... I named her *La Alondra de la Frontera*. I gave her that name for advertising purposes. I called her that because the *alondra*, the meadowlark, is a bird that sings so beautifully. Have you ever heard an *alondra* sing? So that's why I called her *La Alondra de la Frontera*: the singing bird from the Border." This is, however, improbable, since Lydia was already using this name in the period 1936-37.

[2]It is very common to give bird names to Mexican female singers. For example, one of the most popular female duets of the 1970s and 80s is Las jilguerillas. The *jilguero* is a goldfinch. Rosa Domínguez, another Mexican singer, is "Mexico's Nightingale."

[3]This man was related to Mauricio Calderón, the record merchant of Los Angeles. Ramiro Cortés, Doctor Nopal, has this to say about the Calderón family:

"Before the war, I was working for the Calderóns. I was in New York, and they sent me to open up theaters in the Middle West. That's the film distributing company, they were related to the Calderóns who had this record shop here in Los Angeles. There were three brothers: Rafael, José and the one who was here in Los Angeles and had a furniture store and record shop—Mauricio Calderón. He was the one all right, Mauricio was the uncle of the famous Calderón boys, and he was the brother of

Don Rafael and Don Pepe—they're both dead, everybody has already died. But one of their sons, Perico Calderón, he's the oldest of the boys, and he's in Cuernavaca now. He's living retired in Cuernavaca with lots of money, lots of money. They own one hundred and twenty-five theaters in the state of Chihuahua.

They weren't always in the film business. No, when they got started, both of them, Pepe and Don Rafael, they were working for the railroad in Chihuahua. They were conductors on the train that ran from Juárez to Chihuahua City, and Mauricio was a telegraph operator. Then Mauricio came over here to Los Angeles. He was the one that came over here and opened up a little furniture store on South Main, only it didn't stay so little, later on it grew to be pretty big. I mean, he sold almost every Spanish language record that was sold in Los Angeles during the 1930s. Mauricio Calderón was the one who furnished the money for the other two brothers to get started in show business. Rafael and Pepe opened up a little theater in Juárez called—they still own it, it's still open—called the Alcázar: Cine Alcázar. It's downtown, right there near the Cine Plaza, which also belongs to them. The Alcázar was the first of the chain which they founded, and which gave the whole operation its name: *Circuito Alcázar*—the Alcázar Circuit. It includes one hundred and twenty-five theaters, and stretches all the way from Juárez to Parral. All of the theaters belong to them. Now the surviving members of the Calderón family have rented all those theaters to another outfit, but they still receive a lot of money for the rent of those places. The Calderóns are very rich people."

[4]The group was called the Compañía Arte Mexicano and their show was entitled "El amparo de los pobres."

[5]The newspaper ads began appearing December 1, 1937. Frank Fouce Jr. recalls, "We had, of course, a Spanish daily paper, which still exists, *La Opinión*, and we had some radio programs. On KMTR, for instance, there was Tony Zane and there was David Orozco, there was Ramón Arnaiz and there was Rodolfo Salinas, whose wife succeeded him when he passed away—Elena Salinas. These were probably the four most popular programs. They were really at KMTR, which is now KLAC.... And, in fact, we had a booth on stage. We had an early morning radio show from the stage of the California Theater every morning at dawn. I think it went from six to eight o'clock, something like that ... ; it was free. Anyone could just walk in off the street, and, unfortunately, most of the people were working. It wasn't really an hour when you drew huge crowds; you didn't, but there were always a few dozen people around watching the show. And, in those days, the radio programs not only sold advertising, but they also sold requests, and I think that somebody would pay twenty-five cents for a request. Well: 'This is a request by Juanito for María,' or something like that. And they would pay a quarter to have 'their' song played on the radio."

[6]On December 2, the day before the opening of the show, for example, an article appeared that said among other things "Lydia Mendoza is considered by the critics to be the best female Mexican singer to have arrived on the scene since the songs of our people assumed their present form."

[7]On Monday, December 13, 1937. There was even talk of extending the en-

gagement, and an announcement appeared to that effect in *La Opinión*, Thursday, December 9, 1937, but was retracted the following day, pleading prior arrangements. It is interesting to speculate about what may have been behind all this. The first of these notices reads: "A petición del público de esta ciudad, que ha quedado satisfecho de la manera en que Lydia Mendoza y su compañía despliegan su talento, la empresa del teatro 'Mason', donde se encuentra la conocida cancionera, ha decidido prolongar por poco tiempo más la estancia de la compañía Mendoza, en dicho sitio. Pocas han sido las veces en que se recibe una agrupación artística de la manera en que fue recibida la compañía Lydia Mendoza. A juzgar por la forma en que han acudido los de habla española en esta ciudad, dicha compañía se llevará de aquí los más gratos recuerdos de una buena temporada". (By request of the people of this city, who have been delighted by the way Lydia Mendoza and her show have presented their talent, the management of the Mason Theater, where the well-known singer has been appearing, has decided to prolong the engagement of the Mendoza company for a little while longer in the aforementioned venue. Very rarely has a group of artists been as well received as Lydia Mendoza's has been. Judging from the way the Spanish-speaking population of this city has flocked to see it, the aforementioned group will leave here with the fondest memories of a successful engagement.)

On the following day this notice appeared in the same space:

"La empresa que regentea el teatro 'Mason', situado en la Broadway entre las calles Primera y Segunda, nos manifiesta que compromisos contraídos con anterioridad por 'La Alondra de la Frontera', Lydia Mendoza, le impiden prolongar su temporada como se había dicho ayer. En consecuencia, Lydia y su compañía se despedirán el lunes próximo con una función de gala a beneficio de la estrella del cuadro, y en homenaje a sus méritos. Todavía no conocemos el programa para esa función, pero a juzgar por los preparativos que se están haciendo, y por la importancia del evento en sí, es de creerse que será muy escogido". (The company that runs the Mason Theater, located on Broadway between First and Second streets, informs us that previously contracted obligations will prevent the prolongation of the engagement of the 'Lark of the Border,' Lydia Mendoza, which we had reported yesterday. Consequently, Lydia and her revue will say farewell next Monday with a special 'Gala' performance in honor of the star of the show to render homage to her great talent. We still don't know exactly what will be on the program for this performance, but judging from the preparations being made, and by the importance of the event itself, we can be sure that it will be very special indeed.)

The advertisment that appeared on Monday, December 13, had this to say: "Teniendo que cumplir previos compromisos que había contraído—y que la obligan a transladarse violentamente a CAMDEN, N. J., para grabar nuevos discos—HOY LUNES dará por terminada su corta y brillante temporada, en este Teatro de la Colonia—la genial cancionera y guitarrista mexicana". (Having to fulfill previous commitments which she had contracted—and which oblige her to go immediately to Camden, N.J. in order to cut new records—TODAY, MONDAY, the inspired Mexican singer and guitarist will conclude her short but brilliant engagement at this theater of the Mexican Colony.)

The accompanying article concluded with the words "Lydia Mendoza deja un recuerdo imperecedero en el alma del pueblo mexicano de Los Angeles, por su sencillez, por el arte de sus canciones rancheras y por el éxito que fue su actuación desde el primer día". (Lydia Mendoza, because of her down-to-earth simplicity, the artistry of her *ranchera* style songs, and the great success of her appearance from the very first day, leaves a never-to-be-forgotten impression on the soul of the Mexican public of Los Angeles.)

[8]On April 8, 1938.

[9]Tuesday, August 2, 1938, Section B, p. 1.

[10]The documented date is: Tuesday, August 1, 1939.

[11]See photo, article and ad in *La opinión*, Sunday, July 30, 1939, Section #2, pg. 3, for details, including Lydia's "$10,000 favorite guitar." The article states that it was her first appearance in "more than a year," or in other words, since 1937. The article also states that Lydia's appearance would be very brief, since she was only "passing through on her way to contracts in the North." Reviewing the record in *La Opinión*, it seems probable that Lydia and the family show based themselves in Los Angeles for the summer, but made frequent sorties to other parts of the state, thus avoiding the pitfall of continuous over-exposure to their prime audience in Fouce's theaters. The ad that appeared on Wednesday, August 2, was the first to bring attention to her Blue Bird recordings. In this ad she is referred to as the "Mexican Nightingale" or "Ruiseñor Mexicano." The article also stresses that Lydia represents the "popular" or "vernacular" style of music. It is also worth noting that the article refers to the whole show as "un cuadro de variedades populares" or "ensemble of *popular* variety acts," with special emphasis on the Spanish meaning of *popular*, which we might render more accurately in English as "folk" or "working class" in contrast with "high-brow" or "culturally elitist."

[12]August 6, 1939.

[13]It is striking how much Señor Fouce's enterprise had prospered since the Mendoza's first visit to Los Angeles in 1937. Now, at the same time Lydia and the family were appearing at the Teatro California, Fouce had the Padilla Sisters and a singer named Adelina García in a *variedad* that also alternated with films at one of his other theaters, the Arrow. Although they had already become very popular through their recordings, Las Hermanas Padilla didn't receive anything like the billing that Lydia and her *variedad* did at this time, as one can plainly see from the ads that Señor Fouce ran in *La Opinión*.

Lydia's return to Los Angeles was heralded by an immense, half-page ad in *La Opinión* on Sunday, August 20, and her engagement began on Tuesday, August 29. This time she shared the top billing with the very well-known Mexican comedian and movie actor, Carlos López Chaflán. The show also included several other variety acts as well as the Mendoza family *variedad*. The press described it as a "mano a mano" or "hand to hand" competition between the two *variedades*. As had become usual, Lydia shared the California Theater (the flagship of Fouce's operation) with a couple of first-run films: one in Spanish, the other in English. According to *La Opinión*, August 31, 1939, Lydia and the family sold out every show. As was the custom at the Teatro California, every Friday Señor Fouce spiced up the proceedings by raffling off a brand-new stove.

Once again the performance was for one week, ending on Monday, September 4, 1939, although the Mendozas also appeared, along with the Hermanas Padilla and many other acts, in the great *homenaje* that was given for El Chaflán on the September 11. Lydia received her own "homage and farewell" presentation at the California Theater on the September 18. For Lydia's *homenaje* there were no less than twenty different acts on the bill. In between those two dates, the Mendozas also appeared for Fouce at the Arrow Theater on September 15, 16 and 17 to help celebrate Mexican Independence Day.

Blue Bird also seems to have taken advantage of the Mendoza family's presence in the Los Angeles area by recording them in Hollywood. They went into the studio on September 8, 12 and 19. In 1939, Blue Bird stopped going to San Antonio to record. The next year, 1940, Lydia recorded for Blue Bird in Mexico.

Chapter Six

[1]The following skit has been transcribed and translated from a performance delivered by Juanita and Andrew Mendoza during the course of a tape-recorded interview conducted by Chris Strachwitz and Dan Dickey in San Antonio, Texas, June 1, 1983.

[2]The word for both cloves and nails is *clavos*; thus two kinds must be distinguished: of for eating and for nailing.

[3]The following text was transcribed from Alamo 073. The side was recorded at KCOR Studios in San Antonio ca. 1953 by Las Hermanas Mendoza, Juanita y María con el conjunto Alamo. The translation is ours.

[4]This version of "El Güero Polvos" was recorded by Las Hermanas Mendoza, Juanita y María, con el conjunto Alamo at KCOR Studios in San Antonio ca. 1953, and released on Alamo 077B; it can be heard on Folklyric LP 9035. The following transcription and translation have been adapted from the text printed in the pamphlet accompanying Folklyric LP 9035 prepared by Enrique Ramírez and Philip Sonnichsen.

[5]María is probably refering to the sides she and Juanita recorded for Columbia de México in Monterrey during the early 50s. See Discography for details.

Chapter Seven

[1]The following skit has been transcribed and translated from a performance by Manuel and Andrew Mendoza given in the course of a tape-recorded interview conducted by Chris Strachwitz and Dan Dickey, San Antonio, Texas, June 1, 1983.

[2]The following skit has been transcribed and translated from a performance by Juanita, María and Andrew Mendoza given in the course of a tape-recorded interview conducted by Chris Strachwitz and Dan Dickey, San Antonio, Texas, June 1, 1983.

[3]El Chapulín is playing on words here. The /raja/ in "maharajah" sounds like /raja/ from the verb *rajarse*, "to back down or run away," often used to indicate cowardice. Chapulín pretends that he hears "ma raja" as "me rajo."

[4]Andrew probably means "homosexuals" by "other guys" here.

[5]Chapulín is pretending to confuse the sound of the name of the Hindu god, Shiva, with the Spanish word *chiva* = female goat.

[6]Chapulín affects to hear the nonsense mumbo jumbo word /kalamalaya/ as the Spanish: *mal haya*, which means to "damn" someone.

[7]Play on words. Juanita slips and says "*maje*," "fool," instead of "*mágico*," "magician."

Chapter Eight

[1]The following text has been transcribed and translated from a tape-recorded interview with Andrew Mendoza conducted by Chris Strachwitz and Dan Dickey, San Antonio, Texas, May 31, 1983.

[2]Many Mexican cities, particularily along the border, have an officially tolerated red light district that is usually referred to in Spanish as *la zona roja*, which is to say "the red zone."

[3]The following text has been transcribed and translated from a tape-recorded interview with Juanita and Andrew Mendoza conducted by Chris Strachwitz and Dan Dickey, San Antonio, Texas, May 31, 1983.

[4]The following text has been transcribed and translated from a tape-recorded interview with Andrew Mendoza conducted by Chris Strachwitz and Dan Dickey, San Antonio, Texas, June 1, 1983.

[5]The following text has been adapted from "Los casados" as sung by Las Hermanas Mendoza, Juanita y María, on Victor 23-5315A, recorded in San Antonio in 1951 and the same title sung by Juanita and Lydia on Sombrero LP 2012, recorded in San Antonio in August of 1967. The translation is ours.

[6]The following text has been adapted from the two-part recording of "Las casadas" by Guzmán y Hernández on Brunswick 41261 made in San Antonio on December 13, 1930, and the version recorded by Las Hermanas Mendoza, Juanita y María, on Victor 23-5543B, made in San Antonio in 1951. The translation is ours. The Guzmán y Hernández variant is both the earliest and the longest known to us.

[7]*Cangrejo* is also Mexican slang for "homosexual." The verse could then well indicate that the wife is emasculating her husband by her behavior, a meaning not inconsistent with the general tone of the song.

[8]The color green traditionally represents sexual impropriety in Hispanic culture.

[9]This last verse, consistent with the pervasive tone of *doble entendre* of the song, is open to several interpretations. One interpretation might be: " ... she that's not a prostitute, is at least very experienced at what she's doing." Another: " ... she that's not doing it for free, is charging money."

[10]This verse, of course, refers to the infamous reputation of the automobile, inherited from that of the carriage, as the ideal means of carrying on illicit sexual adventures.

[11]The verb *morder* in colloquial Mexican Spanish often means steal or take money, as in a bribe or other type of illicit transaction. The possibilities here beyond the simply sexual should be obvious.

[12]Here again the verse is rich in double meaning. Saint Anthony is "scalped" by women in hagiographic legend, but also the town of San Antonio is "fleeced" by mercenary women of easy virtue.

[13]The following text is from *Cancionero mexicano*, 2: 277. The translation is ours.

[14]The following text has been transcribed and translated from a tape-recorded interview with Juanita and Andrew Mendoza conducted by Chris Strachwitz and Dan Dickey, San Antonio, Texas, May 31, 1983. This skit, like so many others that the Mendozas worked into their stage show and still others that were performed by border comedians, such as Netty and Jesús Rodríguez, takes full advantage of all the comedic possibilities offered by widespread bilingualism in the Mexican-American community.

[15]A literal translation would be something like "good-looking baldheaded woman," but, of course, it really means "pretty flapper." In the 1920s, short, bobbed haircuts were an important feature of the "flapper" style so popular among young women. This style was particularily evident amongst the dancers in stage shows and *carpas*.

[16]Jorge Negrete, along with Pedro Infante, was one of the very first and most enduringly famous of the "singing cowboys" of the Mexican movies. His records continue to sell and his name is still a household word.

[17]Translation: *Ay, Jalisco, don't back down*. This film was one of the first "talking" pictures made in Mexico in the 1930s. It is an early example of the "singing cowboy" genre. The title song of the same name is still extremely popular and continues to be recorded by a multitude of artists. The Spanish verb *rajar* can mean a variety of things. The standard meaning is "to split or cut into strips," but in Mexico the reflexive form can also mean to "back down, chicken out," which is the meaning of the song title. El Chapulín, however, exploits the other possibilities here to achieve a comic effect.

[18]Andrew is playing on the similarity in the sounds of the words "Tepic," a city in the state of Nayarit in western central Mexico, and "*Te pito*": "I'll whistle for you."

[19]*Camote* has many slang meanings, including both something slippery, false or deceitful and the male organ.

Chapter Nine

[1]Mr. Cortés was speaking in July 1984.

Chapter Ten

[1]Leonor Mendoza died December 20, 1952 at the age of 63.

[2]*Borraja*: Borage. An edible plant of European origin. The flowers have long been used as a sleep-inducing soother and to cause sweat.

[3]The text of "Mujer paseada" as sung by Los Tres Reyes has been transcribed from Falcón 469. The vocal is by Daniel Garcés. The translation is ours.

[4]The text of "Contestación a 'Mujer paseada' " as sung by Las Hermanas Mendoza has been transcribed from Rio 341, recorded in San Antonio c. 1950-51. The composer credits on the disc say Garcés-Valdez. The translation is ours.

[5]The text of "Leña y lodo" has been transcribed from an informal performance delivered by María Mendoza during the taping of an interview conducted by Chris Strachwitz and Dan Dickey in San Antonio, Texas, June 1, 1983. The translation is ours.

[6]This was apparently June 24, 1952, when Lydia recorded four songs for RCA Víctor de México in Mexico City. See *Discography* for details.

[7]"Por qué te vas" can be heard on Paloma 1011(33), Ideal 1076, and along with "La guía" on Falcón 1091(45), LP 149(33), LP 1013(M)(33).

[8]Manuel and Juanita Mendoza, Rec. Decca 10186, San Antonio, Texas, February 8, 1937. This version of "La guía" can now be heard on Folklyric LP 9035. The text and translation of "La guía" have been adapted from those in the pamphlet accompanying Folklyric LP 9035, originally prepared by Enrique Ramírez and Philip Sonnichsen.

[9]Both *chata* (flat-nosed) and *negra* (black or dark-skinned woman) are used in Mexico as terms of endearment that transcend their dictionary entry meanings.

[10]The Virgin Mary is a symbol of Purity.

[11]*El camote* (the Mexican wild sweet potato) is often used to denote deceitfulness.

[12]This LP was recorded on March 11, 1958. See *Discography* for details.

[13]Lydia recorded "Besando la Cruz" on Falcón 097 in McAllen, Texas on August 17, 1950. Other renditions by Lydia of this classic can be heard on Zarape LP 1055 and Arhoolie LP 3012.

[14]Armando Marroquín was the Artist and Repertoire man for Ideal Records. The label was owned by Paco Betancourt.

Chapter Eleven

[1]The following is a partial transcription and translation of the article that appeared Sunday, October 14, 1973. The section appearing here was followed by a physical description of Lydia and a brief interview.

[2]The song is "Lydia Huapango," composed in Lydia's honor by Agustín Mendoza (no relation), musical director of the Cuarteto Michoacano. A reproduction of a broadside of this song appears in James F. Griffith, "Lydia Mendoza: An Enduring Mexican-American Singer," *Ethnic Recordings In America: A Neglected Heritage*, Studies in American Folklife 1 (Washington: American Folklife Center, Library of Congress, 1982) 102. The following text is taken from the broadside. The translation is ours. Lydia recorded this song for Blue Bird (Bb B-2249) at the Texas Hotel in San Antonio, August 10, 1934.

[3]Lydia is speaking in ca. 1984, so she probably means ca. 1979.

[4]Pilar Arcos, Margarita Cueto and Juan Pulido were all early concert performers and recording artists who sang in a very cultured, semi-operatic style. Before the introduction of the portable electrical recording process in 1926, this type of artist dominated the Spanish-language repertoire of the big recording companies. In fact,

Leonor and Lydia Mendoza were probably the first women recording artists to sing in a more "popular," country style.

[5]The following text is taken from the version recorded by Lydia on Norteño Cass & 8 TR 822. Many other versions can be found either recorded in various formats or printed in *cancioneros* (songbooks). Another interesting variant of the same *corrido* by the Mariachi México del Norte (recorded in Los Angeles, Calif. ca. 1948) which tells the story in a significantly different way can be heard on Folklyric LP 9041 and ARH/FL CD 7022/23/24 (Corridos of the Mexican Revolution).

[6]The text of "Amor bonito" has been transcribed from Lydia's April, 1964, San Benito, Texas performance on Ideal 2179. Lydia also recorded this song on May 13, 1975, in San Antonio for Arhoolie LP 3012. The translation is ours.

[7]Fred Martínez, Lydia's husband, says: "I don't go along when she sings very much. At first, right after we got married, I used to drive her. Like when she went to Ohio, I drove her over there, but it's tiresome, you know. You get tired of sleeping in motels and eating in restaurants and traveling; all that moving back and forth all the time. I really didn't care for it, so I told Lydia, 'If you want to keep on singing, go ahead. I'm going to be looking for a job.' And that's what I did. And I worked up until the time I retired. I don't particularily enjoy all that so much anymore, especially now that ... I used to kind of enjoy it all when I used to drink. Now I don't drink; I don't even care to go out."

[8]The text of "Acércame a tu vida" has been transcribed from Lydias's performance on DLB Cassette 1113, recorded in San Antonio on August 20, 1983. The translation is ours.

[9]Lydia is referring to the infamous Juan Corona mass murder case. Juan Corona was accused of murdering more than thirty migrant farm workers and then burying their remains. The *corrido* as performed by Los Conquistadores, José Morante y José Fidel with Flaco Jiménez on accordion, can be heard on Norteño 336.

[10]On May 6, 1977, Houston police arrested a young ex-Green Beret and karate expert during a disturbance at a bar. Joe Campos Torres was taken by six policemen to Buffalo Bayou where he was beaten, then thrown into the water and left to drown. Two were tried by a state court jury in Huntsville, convicted of negligent homicide and given a year's probation. The outcry in the Mexican-American community was intense, and the Carter administration's Justice Department filed federal charges of violating Campos Torres' civil rights against the four officers. Three of the policemen were later convicted of felony conspiracy in February of 1978. One example of a *corrido* about this outrage is "José Campos Torres," attributed to René Matamoros, performed by Los Príncipes Negros de René Matamoros, *Para nuestros amigos*, Discos Diana 1002, Baytown, Texas, 1978.

[11]The text of "Dime, mal hombre" has been transcribed from Lydia's performance on DLB Cassette 1094, recorded in San Antonio on February 15, 1983. The translation is ours.

[12]The following text of "Esa güerita" has been transcribed from the performance by the Dueto Monterrey, Lydia y María Mendoza, on Azteca 5055, recorded in Los Angeles, Calif., 1949. The translation is ours.

[13]The text of "Por una mujer" has been transcribed from Lydia's performance on Azteca 339, probably recorded in Hollywood, California in late 1947. The translation is ours.

Discography

Introduction and Guide

This discography is a listing of all known master recordings made by Lydia Mendoza and members of the Mendoza family. It is a catalog of their commercially recorded work and at least a partial overview of the artists' repertoire. In the pre-tape era (before the 1950s), each such recorded performance constitutes a roughly three-minute-long untampered audio snapshot of the artist, frozen in time, and preserved on a record. Three minutes was the usual length for popular material, since that was the maximum time which would fit easily on a 10" 78 rpm record. However, 45 rpm records, which began to be produced by the mid 1950s, were often shorter than 78s, not because the format could not hold as much music (the 45 could actually hold more), but because radio stations were losing income if they played that much music without a commercial! With the introduction of the 33 1/3 rpm Long Play record in the early 1950s, the playing time of a commercial record expanded to over 20 minutes per side and today's CD (compact disc) can easily hold 78 minutes of music. The records, or artifacts, manufactured from the master recordings are available to anyone to purchase or collect.

The only sure identification of each recorded performance, prior to the introduction of tape recording around 1950, is to note the matrix number which was assigned to each wax master from which pressings were eventually made after processing. This all important matrix number is given to the left of each song title. Following the title of the selection, you will note the type of song followed by the composer's name (if given on the record label). To the right, you find the abbreviated name of the record company which produced the recording and the catalog, or the release number not only of the original release but of subsequent re-issues. Most items listed as (33) LP releases are probably also available on cassettes, if the item is still in print. After the artist's name under which the record was released, you will note (if available) the names of other musicians who played on the recording, followed by when and where the recording was made.

A discography also gives you at least some clue as to which songs were the most popular or successful by the frequency with which the performer recorded them or by how many releases were issued from the same master. Unfortunately, a discography will not tell you how many copies of a record were sold! That information is generally carefully guarded by the record company and is considered a private matter between them and the artists.

As a life-long collector of vernacular music on records, I have been able to acquire about seventy percent of the recordings made by members of the Mendoza family. I am however keenly searching for the first recording made by the Mendoza family (as Cuarteto Carta Blanca) of "Delgadina" on OKeh or Vocalion and am willing to pay a handsome price or trade other recordings for a copy in excellent condition! I would further like to hear from anyone who has records which are not listed in this discography, including foreign releases of masters already included, in order that I may update this discography in case this book is reprinted at some future date. Please submit additions to: Chris Strachwitz, 10341 San Pablo Avenue, El Cerrito, CA 94530.

Compilation of this Discography

The completeness of a discography depends upon the data available. There is no magic single source for this information, especially for the post-1942 recordings. I have listed the recordings in more or less chronological order, but the fact that the Mendoza family members recorded for various labels simultaneously, plus the lack of recording data for many of the post-1945 recording sessions made this task difficult. I have tried to contact almost every company or recording director involved, and I checked all the label catalogs and actual discs in my collection. For the pre-1942 entries, I wish to thank fellow collector and discographer, Richard K. Spottswood, who spent years with the help of a small grant cataloging all foreign-language recordings made by American record companies within the territorial United States between the beginning of recorded music (before 1900) and 1942, when a musicians union strike just about brought recorded music to a halt. Dick Spottswood went to each of the record companies and painstakingly copied the ledgers and label copies and whatever documents were made available to him. Thanks to him, we can assume that this discography of the Mendoza family through 1942 is fairly complete, except for releases of these masters in South America. A mystery still remains as to which song was first recorded for Blue Bird. Lydia Mendoza insists that her solo material was recorded first and that "Mal hombre" was the first item recorded. She further insists that the recording director was mainly interested in her solo performances and that the family was only recorded upon her insistence. The Victor matrix numbers and ledgers, however, show a different story, according to Spottswood's seven volume *Ethnic Music On Records* (Urbana: University of Illinois Press, 1990).

For the information about recordings made for Mexican Victor/RCA in Mexico, Los Angeles and San Antonio, I wish to thank Philip Sonnichsen, who assisted me on a trip to Mexico City where he introduced me to Eduardo Magayénez of RCA. We were told that the plant in Mexico had burned down in the 1940s and all information and masters from before were destroyed. Mr. Magayénez introduced us to Carlos Castillo, who had been an engineer with Victor in Mexico for a long time, and Mr. Castillo showed us the ledger books from which I copied the information pertaining to the Mendoza family. On the same trip to Mexico, we also visited the CBS office in Mexico and Philip Sonnichsen's friend, singer and A&R director Federico Méndez, who was very helpful and showed me the matrix cards which pertained to the Columbia Mendoza sessions.

Almost nothing is known about Globe Records, except that this Los Angeles-based label operated from the mid-1940s to the early '50s and recorded the Mendoza material at a radio station in San Antonio. Discos Aguila was also a Los Angeles based firm and most of their 78 rpm records seem to date from the mid 1950s, and their LPs were distributed by Azteca. Rio Records in San Antonio produced about

400 releases between 1948 and 1954 under the ownership of Mr. Hymie Wolf, who with his wife Genie also operated the Rio Record Shop on West Commerce Street.

Azteca Records, founded by T. Peláez in the 1940s, belongs today to Al Sherman of Alshire Records in Burbank, California. Dick Ceja, who worked for both Azteca and as an independent producer for RCA and others, supplied me with the catalog of titles recorded by the Mendoza family along with matrix and release numbers, but was unable to find any other details.

Imperial Records of Los Angeles was owned by Lew Chudd, who started recording folk dance material in the late 1940s. This soon led him to record Mexican music, which the label recorded both in Texas and in Los Angeles, before he entered the Rhythm and Blues and Country fields in the early and mid-1950s. Imperial was sold to Capitol Records in the 1970s, and few documents remain. Thanks again to Philip Sonnichsen for obtaining for me copies of the Imperial Mexican catalog which showed matrix and release numbers, but may not be complete.

Ideal Records was founded by Paco Betancourt of San Benito, Texas in 1946, but the actual recordings were made in Alice, Texas by Armando S. Marroquín, who operated juke boxes and sensed a great demand for local music after World War II when the major U. S. labels stopped recording regional music. The musicians were paid a flat fee per record, which in the late 1940s was about $15 to the leader and $3 to $5 to each of the sidemen. Sales figures are hard to come by, but were probably modest; Ideal's biggest hit supposedly sold around 60,000 copies ("La Rosita" on Ideal #149, a *vals* by Beto Villa and his *orquesta* with Narciso Martínez on accordion, now available on Arhoolie CD/C 364). Ideal's initial pressing orders per record were generally for 500 copies in addition to unknown quantities pressed from duplicate metal parts in Mexico for distribution in Northern Mexico. Ideal was the first major Tejano-owned and -operated record company in south Texas. All Ideal masters were purchased in 1990 by Arhoolie Productions, which is in the process of re-issuing many of the best selections.

Falcón Records was started in 1948 in Mission, Texas, by Arnaldo Ramírez, who had long admired Lydia Mendoza and was well aware of what a popular artist she was. Lydia and her sisters began to record for the label in 1950 and, as Falcón became the major company for Tejano music in the late 1950s and 60s, Lydia continued to record for Falcón into the 1970s. Thanks to Mr. Ramírez's generosity in spending many hours with me digging up his well maintained files, the Falcón data is pretty complete with matrix numbers, dates and Falcón session numbers. Other musicians or people who came with the Mendozas to the sessions were sometimes only identified by first name, and were apparently listed if they were to be paid. After the sale or lease of the Falcón catalog to Royalco in 1970, session details were apparently no longer available or kept. Unfortunately, Mr. Ramírez did not want to divulge the titles of unissued material, but enough exists for at least two albums. A few years ago, all masters produced by Falcón/ARV/Royalco, etc., were apparently sold to EMI of Mexico.

Corona Records was started in 1947 by Mr. Manuel Rangel, Sr. who operated the Rangel Music Co. in San Antonio and whose son Manuel Rangel, Jr. is today the proprietor of Rangel Distributing, one of the main wholesalers of Spanish-language recordings. Corona recorded many San Antonio based artists, including Valerio Longoria, Santiago Jiménez and Lydia Mendoza. Apparently, no recording details were kept. Alamo, Sargento, Acme, Gaviota, Pegaso and Del Valle were other smaller South Texas companies in the 1950s. Del Valle (McAllen, Texas) became an important label in the 1960s, presenting mostly artists from Northern Mexico including Los Gavilanes.

José Morante, a singer, guitarist and composer, began his own recording career in San Antonio in 1937, when he recorded his first 78s for the Blue Bird label as part of a vocal duet with José Arellano. After service during World War II, Morante formed Los Conquistadores, who recorded for various South Texas labels in the late 1940s and early 50s and became a popular trio-styled group, appearing on local radio and television. In 1956, Morante started his own record label, Sombrero, and the Mendoza sisters were one of his first acts. He continued to record Lydia and her sisters for his Sombrero, Norteño and other labels until well into the 1980s. Morante kept no ledgers and no information was available beyond what appears on the record labels. I eventually located the year of the first release inside the master tape box which had been sent to the processing plant and which contained a dated note to the engineer! No other tape boxes contained any dates or information except label copy. José Morante leased or sold many of his recordings to various Los Angeles-based labels for wider distribution, and some of his masters were also pressed in Mexico.

Arhoolie Records is my own record label, begun in 1960 in Los Gatos, California. The Folklyric label has been used by Arhoolie Productions to present re-releases of older recordings (mainly from 78 rpm discs) of various regional and ethnic traditions, including many Mexican-American singers and musicians from the late 1920s to the 1950s.

Lydia Mendoza's most recent recording activities have been for Salomé Gutiérrez's DLB label in San Antonio. Mr. Gutiérrez is a prolific composer who has authored over 600 songs, many of which have become popular via recordings by a variety of artists both in Texas and in Mexico. Besides recording and composing, Mr. Gutiérrez also operates the Del Bravo Record Shop, and in recent years has devoted much of his time to SAMP (San Antonio Music Publishers) which represents not only many of his own songs, but those of other Tejano composers.

Chris Strachwitz—January, 1991—Arhoolie Productions Inc.
10341 San Pablo Avenue—El Cerrito, CA 94530

MENDOZA FAMILY DISCOGRAPHY: SECTION 1
Okeh, Blue Bird & RCA-Victor, Decca
Note: (C), (CD) or (CD/C) after catalog release numbers means cassette, compact disc and/or both.

(33) after catalog release number means LP record release.

Abbreviations: md=mandolin, vo=vocal, g=guitar, vln=violin,
FL=Arhoolie/Folklyric

OKEH RECORDS

CUARTETO CARTA BLANCA.
Leonora Mendoza-vocals & guitar, Francisco Mendoza-vocals & tambourine, Lydia Mendoza-vocals & mandolin, Francisca (Panchita) Mendoza-vocals & triangle. (OK/OD means release on both OKeh and Odeon labels; VO = Vocalion; FL = Folklyric LP.) San Antonio, TX, March, 8, 1928.

400425-B ★ JULIA ★ OK/OD 16266

400426-B ★ MONTERREY ★ OK/OD 16314, VO 8676, FL 9023(33), ARH/FL 7002(CD)

400427-B ★ CANCION DE AMOR ★ OK 16269

400428-A ★ AMORCITO CONSENTIDO ★ OK 16269, FL 7002(CD)

400429-B ★ LAS QUATRO MILPAS ★ OK/OD 16314, VO 8676, FL 9023(33), FL 7002(CD)

400430-B ★ EL TECOLOTE DE GUANDANA ★ OK Reject

Personnel same as last. San Antonio, TX, March 10, 1928.

400457-B ★ DELGADINA ★ OK 16324, VO 8677

400458-B ★ NO QUIERO SER CASADO ★ OK/OD 16278, FL 7002(CD)

400459-A ★ A MI JUANA ★ OK/OD 16278

400460-B ★ EN EL RANCHO GRANDE ★ OK 16324, VO 8677

400461-B ★ EL HIJO PRODIGO ★ OK/OD 16266

BLUE BIRD RECORDS

LYDIA MENDOZA.
Artist plays guitar on all the following issued under her name, except as noted. Her first name is consistently spelled "Lidya" on all 1930s releases.
Bb = Blue Bird; Vi = Victor; (M) = Mexican release; (C) = Colombian release; MW = Montgomery Ward; FL = Folklyric LP.

CUARTETO MONTERREY por la familia Mendoza.
Leonor Mendoza-vo/g, Lydia Mendoza-vo/vln, María Mendoza-vo/md, Francisco D. Mendoza-vo/pandero. Texas Hotel, San Antonio, TX, March 27, 1934.

BVE 82636-1 ★ OJITOS DE MI CHATA-Canción (Mendoza) ★ Bb B-2238, FL 9023(33)

BVE 82637-1 ★ POR TUS AMORES-Canción (Mendoza) ★ Bb B-2208

BVE 82638-1 ★ OJITOS CHINOS Y NEGROS-Canción ★ Bb B-2208

BVE 82639-1 ★ LA CHINA-Canción Costeña ★ Bb B-2238, FL 9023(33)

BVE 82640-1 ★ PARA QUE NESILIS A MI AMOR-Canción ★ Bb B-2293, Vi 32422

BVE 82641-1 ★ CASTOS SUEÑOS-Vals Canción ★ Bb B-2293, Vi 32422

LYDIA MENDOZA. Texas Hotel, San Antonio, TX, March 27, 1934.

BVE 82642-1 ★ MAL HOMBRE-Canción ★ Bb B-2200, MW M-4865, Vi 32148, Vi 75079(M), FL 9023(33), FL 7002(CD)

BVE 82643-1 ★ AL PIE DE TU REJA-Serenata ★ B-2200, MW M-4865, FL 9023(33), FL 7002(CD)

BVE 82644-1 ★ NO PUEDO DEJAR DE QUERERTE-Canción ★ B-2218, Vi 32148, Vi 75079(M), RCA (C) 05(0131) 00868(33)

BVE 82645-1 ★ LEJOS-Tango ★ Bb B-2218, Vi 32217

BVE 82646-1 ★ LA ULTIMA COPA-Tango ★ Bb B-2240, Vi 32217

BVE 82647-1 ★ LAMENTO BORINCANO-Danzón ★ Bb B-2240, Vi 32514

LYDIA MENDOZA. Texas Hotel, San Antonio, TX, August 10, 1934.

BVE 83919-1 ★ SIGUE ADELANTE-Bolero Canción ★ Bb B-2274, Vi 32343, FL 9023(33), FL 7002(CD)

BVE 83919-1 ★ LIDYA-Guapango ★ Bb B-2249, Vi 32935

BVE 83920-1 ★ VIVIRE PARA TI-Bolero Canción ★ Bb B-2249, Vi 32935

BVE 83921-1 ★ PERO AY QUE TRISTE-Canción ★ Bb B-2263, Vi 32297, FL 9003(33), FL 7002(CD)

BVE 83922-1 ★ LOS BESOS DE MI NEGRA-Canción ★ Bb B-2263, Vi 32297, FL 9023(33), FL 7002(CD)

BVE 83923-1 ★ MUNDO ENGAÑOSO-Canción ★ Bb B-2274, Vi 32343, Vi 75540(M), FL 9023(33), FL 7002(CD)

LIDYA MENDOZA Y CUARTETO MENDOZA.
Same personnel as for first session March 27, 1934. Texas Hotel, San Antonio, TX, August 10, 1934.

BVE 83924-1 ★ NO ME ANUNCIAS-Canción ★ Bb B-2269

BVE 83925-1 ★ TOMA ESTE PUÑAL-Canción ★ Bb B-2256, Vi 32922

BVE 83926-1 ★ CHINA DE LOS OJOS NEGROS-Canción ★ Bb B-2285, Vi 32376, Vi (M) 75110A

BVE 83927-1 ★ SI ESTAS DORMIDA-Canción ★ Bb B-2269

BVE 83928-1 ★ MARIA, MARIA-Canción ★ Bb B-2256, Vi 32922, LC LBC-2(33)

BVE 83929-1 ★ UNA RANCHERITA-Canción ★ Bb B-2285, Vi 32376, Vi (M) 75110A

LIDYA MENDOZA.
With María Mendoza on mandolin on some selections. Texas Hotel, San Antonio, TX, January 31, 1935.

BVE 87815-1 ★ SIEMPRE TE VAS-Canción (Lara) ★ Bb B-2310, Vi 32434

BVE 87816-1 ★ LA MUJER DEL PUERTO-Canción ★ Bb B-2310, Vi 32434

BVE 87816-2 ★ LA MUJER DEL PUERTO-Canción ★ Bb rejected

BVE 87817-1 ★ AS DE CORAZONES-Canción ★ Bb B-2320, VI 32502

BVE 87818-1 ★ LA CUMBANCHA-Canción ★ Bb B-2339, Vi 32512

BVE 87819-1 ★ TEMO-Canción ★ Bb B-2320, Vi 32502, Vi 75540(M)

BVE 87820-1 ★ LA COSTEÑITA-Canción ★ Bb B-2329, Vi 32543, Vi 75542(M), RCA (C) 05(0131)00868(33), FL 9023(33), FL 7002(CD)

BVE 87821-1 ★ EL LIRIO-Canción ★ Bb B-2329, Vi 32543, Vi 75542(M), RCA (C) 05(0131)00868(33), FL 9023(33), FL 7002(CD)

BVE 87822-1 ★ DELICIOSA-Canción ★ Bb B-2339, Vi 32512

LIDYA MENDOZA AND FAMILY.

Same personnel as for first session March 27, 1934. Texas Hotel, San Antonio, TX, February 1, 1935.

BVE 87861-1 ★ PANCHITA-Canción Abajeña ★ Bb B-2347, Vi 32560, FL 9007(33)

BVE 87862-1 ★ EL MUCHACHO ALEGRE-Canción ★ Bb B-2347, Vi 32514

BVE 87863-1 ★ TRAJE MI CABALLO PRIETO-Canción ★ Bb rejected

BVE 87864-1 ★ DIOS BENDIGA-Canción ★ Bb B-2356, Vi 32560

LIDYA MENDOZA vocal and guitar.

With María Mendoza-mandolin. San Antonio, TX, August 13, 1935.

BS 94464-1 ★ DIME MAL HOMBRE-Canción ★ Bb B-2368, Vi 32578

BS 94465-1 ★ LIMOSNA-Canción ★ Bb rejected

BS 94466-1 ★ OLVIDARTE JAMAS-Canción ★ Bb B-2379, MW M-4866, Vi 32582, Vi 75544(M)

BS 94467-1 ★ PAJARITO HERIDO-Canción ★ Bb B-2387, Vi 32624, Vi 75544(M), FL 9024(33), FL 7002(CD)

BS 94468-1 ★ POBRECITA DE MI ALMA-Canción ★ Bb B-2387, Vi 32624

BS 94469-1 ★ MARIMBA-Canción ★ Bb B-2379, MW M-4866, Vi 32582

BS 94470-1 ★ SOLA-Canción ★ Bb B-2401, Vi 32638, FL 9024(33), FL 7002(CD)

BS 94471-1 ★ CAPRICHO-Canción ★ Bb B-2392, Vi 32612

BS 94472-1 ★ PALIDA LUNA-Canción ★ Bb B-2392, Vi 32612, FL 9024(33), FL 7002(CD)

BS 94473-1 ★ ARRANCAME LA VIDA-Canción ★ Bb B-2401, Vi 32638

BS 94474-1 ★ BOHEMIOS-Canción ★ Bb B-2368, Vi 32578

LIDYA MENDOZA Y FAMILIA.

Same personnel as for first session March 27, 1934. San Antonio, TX, August 16, 1935.

BS 94611-1 ★ A ORILLAS DE UNA FUENTE-Canción ★ Bb B-2414, Vi 32656, FL 9023(33)

BS 94612-1 ★ EL HIJO PRODIGO-Canción ★ Bb B-2414, Vi 32656, FL 9023(33)

BS 94613-1 ★ VALENTINA-Canción ★ Bb B-2395, Vi 32645

BS 94614-1 ★ YO NO ESPERO-Canción ★ Bb B-2395, Vi 32645, FL 9013(33)

LIDYA MENDOZA vocal and guitar.

With María Mendoza-mandolin on (*) selections. San Antonio, TX, February 22, 1936.

BS 99259-1 ★ CUESTA ABAJO-Canción Tango ★ Bb B-2440, Vi 32714

BS 99260-1 ★ TU PARTIDA-Canción Fox* ★ Bb B-2453, MW M-4867, Vi 32724, FL 9024(33), FL 7002(CD)

BS 99261-1 ★ PIENSA EN MI-Bolero ★ Bb B-2443, MW M-4871, Vi 32689

BS 99262-1 ★ INOLVIDABLE-Canción Fox* ★ Bb B-2459, MW M-4868, Vi 32742

BS 99263-1 ★ POR QUE TE QUIERO TANTO-Danza ★ Bb B-2440, Vi 32689

BS 99264-1 ★ LADRILLO-Tango ★ Bb B-2459, MW M-4868, Vi 32742

BS 99265-1 ★ TE AMO, ME DIJISTE-Bolero ★ Bb B-2453, MW M-4867, Vi 32724

BS 99266-1 ★ CUANDO TU ME QUIERAS-Canción ★ Bb B-2484, Vi 32795, 32963

BS 99267-1 ★ IMPOSIBLE-Canción ★ Bb B-2469, Vi 32769, 32820

BS 99268-1 ★ OJOS TRISTES-Canción ★ Bb B-2484, Vi 32795

BS 99269-1 ★ DICES BIEN MIO-Vals ★ Bb B-2443, Vi 32714

BS 99270-1 ★ TODO PARA TI-Canción ★ Bb B-2469, Vi 32769

LIDYA MENDOZA CON FAMILIA.
Same personnel as for first session March 27, 1934. San Antonio, TX, February 22, 1936.

BS 99271-1 ★ LA RIELERA-Corrido ★ Bb B-2492, Vi 32852

BS 99272-1 ★ LLANO Y LAGUNA (MEXICO EN UNA LAGUNA)-Canción ★ Bb B-2492, Vi 32852

BS 99273-1 ★ MARGARITA, MARGARITA-Canción ★ Bb B-2474, Vi 32797, FL 9024(33)

BS 99274-1 ★ EL COCO-Canción ★ Bb B-2474, Vi 32797, NW 264(33)

LIDYA MENDOZA vocal and guitar.
María Mendoza-mandolin or guitar. San Antonio, TX, October 19, 1936.

BS 02682-1 ★ JURAME-Tango ★ Bb B-2943, MW M-7117, Vi 32984, FL 7002(CD)

BS 02683-1 ★ SORTILEGIO-Fox Canción ★ Bb B-2904, Vi 32854

BS 02684-1 ★ SI REGRESAS-Canción ★ Bb B-2912, Vi 32869, 32938

BS 02685-1 ★ MUJER SIN CORAZON-Canción ★ Bb B-2912, Vi 32869, 32936

BS 02686-1 ★ AMOR SIN ESPERANZA-Danza ★ Bb B-2901, Vi 32865, 32936, 32951

BS 02687-1 ★ COSAS QUE SUCEDEN-Fox Canción ★ Bb B-2943, MW M-7117, Vi 32984

BS 02688-1 ★ TU-Fox Canción ★ Bb B-2904, Vi 32854, 32951

BS 02689-1 ★ EL NOVILLERO-Paso Doble ★ Bb B-2901, Vi 32937, 32865

BS 02690-1 ★ VEN, DEJA DE LLORAR-Danza ★ Bb B-2907, Vi 32868, 32938

BS 02691-1 ★ TU ME HACES FALTA-Bolero ★ Bb B-2948, Vi 82014

Personnel same as last. San Antonio, TX, October 20, 1936.

BS 02708-1 ★ LLEGASTE-Fox Canción (A. Luis del Castillo y Narciso Delgado ★ Bb B-2918, MW M-7118, Vi 32895

BS 02709-1 ★ LA BAMBA-Rumba ★ Bb B-2907, Vi 32868, 32937

BS 02710-1 ★ LEJOS DE TI-Vals Canción ★ Bb B-2953, Vi 82003

BS 02711-1 ★ DONDE ESTAS CORAZON-Canción ★ Bb B-3017, Vi 82126

BS 02712-1 ★ PRINCIPE-Canción Vals ★ Bb B-2918, MW M-7118, Vi 32895

BS 02713-1 ★ LA BODA NEGRA-Tango Canción ★ Bb B-3017, Vi 82126, FL 9024(33), FL 7002(CD)

Personnel same as last. San Antonio, TX, October 22, 1936.

BS 02811-1 ★ ESPERANZA-Tango Canción ★ Bb B-2934, MW M-7115, Vi 32949

BS 02812-1 ★ LA JAIBERA-Son ★ Bb B-2923, MW M-7116, Vi 32904, FL 7002(CD)

BS 02813-1 ★ CARAMELO-Son ★ Bb B-2953, Vi 82003

BS 02814-1 ★ PLEGARIA-Vals ★ Bb B-2934, MW M-7115, Vi 32949

BS 02815-1 ★ DESVELO DE AMOR-Bolero ★ Bb B-2948

BS 02816-1 ★ NO ES IGUAL-Fox ★ Bb B-2923, MW M-7116, Vi 32904

BS 02817-1 ★ TODOS DICEN QUE NUNCA-Danza ★ Bb B-2940, Vi 32961

BS 02818-1 ★ NUNCA-Canción Yucateca ★ Bb B-2940, Vi 32961, FL 7002(CD)

LIDYA MENDOZA Y GRUPO.
Same personnel as for first session March 27, 1934. San Antonio, TX, October 22, 1936.

BS 02819-1 ★ TENGO A MI LUPE-Canción ★ Bb B-2928, MW M-7252, Vi 32905, FL 9024(33), Preludio(C) 11056(33)

BS 02820-1 ★ ELIZA-Canción ★ Bb B-2928, MW M-7252, Vi 32905

BS 02821-1 ★ CUATRO VICIOS-Canción ★ Bb B-2952, FL 9024(33), Preludio(C) 11056(33)

BS 02822-1 ★ NOCHE TENEBROSA Y FRIA-Canción ★ Bb B-3004, Vi 82061, FL 9024(33)

BS 02823-1 ★ UNA NOCHE SERENA Y OBSCURA-Canción ★ Bb B-3004, Vi 82061, FL 9024(33)

BS 02824-1 ★ EL VENADITO-Canción ★ Bb B-2952

LIDYA MENDOZA vocal and guitar.
María Mendoza-mandolin. Texas Hotel, San Antonio, TX, February 24, 1937.

BS 07251-1 ★ NOCHE DE RONDA-Canción ★ Bb B-2958, Vi 32964, 32987
BS 07252-1 ★ UNA MANCHA MAS-Tango ★ Bb B-2962, Vi 32795, 82081, 23-0487, RCA (C) 05(0131)00868(33)
BS 07253-1 ★ AQUEL AMIGO-Tango ★ Bb B-2975, Vi 82042, 82081, 23-0487, RCA (C) 05(0131)00868(33)
BS 07254-1 ★ AMOR DE MIS AMORES-Canción Bolero ★ Bb B-2958, MW M-7254, Vi 32964, 32987
BS 07255-1 ★ YO TE PERDONO-Canción ★ Bb B-2993, Vi 82060
BS 07256-1 ★ LAGRIMAS DE VINO-Vals Canción ★ Bb B-3009, Vi 82068
BS 07257-1 ★ OJOS NEGROS (Romanza Rusa)-Canción ★ Bb B-2962, Vi 32963
BS 07258-1 ★ ROSARIO-Tango [De la película del mismo nombre] (Jorge M. D da) ★ Bb B-3029, Vi 82143
BS 07259-1 ★ MUCHOS BESOS-Canción ★ Bb B-2993, Vi 82060
BS 07259-2 ★ MUCHOS BESOS-Canción ★ Bb rejected
BS 07260-1 ★ SI PUDIERA-Canción ★ Bb B-3012, Vi 82086
BS 07261-1 ★ SE ME HIZO FACIL-Canción ★ Bb B-3029, Vi 82143
BS 07262-1 ★ TU VANIDAD-Canción ★ Bb B-2982, Vi 82054

Same personnel as last. Texas Hotel, San Antonio, TX, February 25, 1937.

BS 07275-1 ★ UN DIA SOÑE-Canción ★ Bb B-2975, MW M-7253, Vi 82042
BS 07276-1 ★ SI-Canción Bolero ★ Bb B-2968, Vi 82030
BS 07277-1 ★ LEGADO DE AMOR-Canción ★ Bb B-2968, MW M-7253, Vi 82030
BS 07278-1 ★ PUÑALADA-Canción ★ Bb B-3009, Vi 82068, FL 7002(CD)
BS 07279-1 ★ INUTIL-Canción ★ Bb B-3012, Vi 82068
BS 07280-1 ★ ARRULLO-Canción ★ Bb B-2982, Vi 82054

LIDYA MENDOZA y su grupo.
Same personnel as for first session March 27, 1934. Texas Hotel, San Antonio, TX, February 25, 1937.

BS 07281-1 ★ DELGADINA-Canción ★ Bb B-2989, Vi 82143, FL 9016(33), FL 7002(CD)
BS 07282-1 ★ LOS BARANDALES DEL PUENTE-Canción ★ Bb B-2966
BS 07283-1 ★ TODA MI VIDA LA PASO BORRACHO-Canción ★ Bb B-2977
BS 07284-1 ★ RELUCIENTE ESTRELLA-Vals Canción ★ Bb B-2966
BS 07285-1 ★ CELIA-Canción ★ Bb B-2977, FL 7002(CD)
BS 07286-1 ★ EL DESTERRADO-Canción ★ Bb B-2989, Vi 82215

LIDYA MENDOZA vocal and guitar.
María Mendoza-mandolin. Blue Bonnet Hotel, San Antonio, TX, September 14, 1937.

BS 014159-1 ★ VIAJERA-Canción ★ Bb B-3078, Vi 82153
BS 014160-1 ★ DESESPERANZA-Canción Fox ★ Bb B-3044, MW M-7409, Vi 82150
BS 014161-1 ★ JANITZIO-Vals Canción ★ Bb B-3044, Vi 82150
BS 014162-1 ★ ADREDE-Canción (Juan S. Garrido) ★ Bb B-3078, Vi 82215, 82592
BS 014163-1 ★ CREI-Canción ★ Bb rejected, wax master broken upon receipt
BS 014164-1 ★ ENTRE TU Y YO-Canción Fox ★ Bb B-3071, Vi 82189
BS 014165-1 ★ ADIOS MUCHACHOS-Tango ★ Bb B-3071, MW M-7408, Vi 82152, Vi 75716(M), RCA (C) 05(0131)00868(33)

BS 014166-1 ★ A UNA OLA-Vals Canción (María Grever) ★ Bb B-3194, Vi 82153, 82521

BS 014167-1 ★ MAÑANA QUE LA AUSENCIA-Canción ★ Bb B-3062, MW M-7408, Vi 82152, Vi 75716(M)

BS 014168-1 ★ SOÑE QUE ME JURABAS-Vals Canción ★ Bb B-3052, MW M-7409, Vi 82189

BS 014169-1 ★ DEJAME LLORAR-Bolero Canción ★ Bb B-3062, Vi 82154

BS 014170-1 ★ FLORES NEGRAS-Canción (Sergio de Negras) ★ Bb B-3052, Vi 82154

MENDOZA FAMILIA.
Same personnel as for first session March 27, 1934. Blue Bonnet Hotel, San Antonio, TX, September 14, 1937.

BS 014171-1 ★ TU YA NO SOPLAS-Canción ★ Bb B-3046, MW M-7406, Vi 82151, FL 9024(33)

BS 014172-1 ★ LA PALOMITA-Canción ★ Bb B-3046, Vi 82151

BS 014173-1 ★ AQUELLAS CARICIAS-Canción ★ Bb B-3056, MW M-7406, Vi 82171

BS 014174-1 ★ DESENGAÑAME-Canción ★ Bb B-3056, Vi 82171

BS 014175-1 ★ LAS VIOLETAS-Polka ★ Bb B-3064, MW M-7407, Vi 82213

BS 014176-1 ★ AUNQUE MILES CALLES VIVAS-Canción ★ Bb B-3064, MW M-7407, Vi 82213

BS 014177-1 ★ SOY DESDICHADO-Canción ★ Bb B-3066, Vi 82199

BS 014178-1 ★ QUE BELLA ES LA VIDA-Canción ★ Bb B-3066, Vi 82199

BS 014179-1 ★ LETRAS DE TU NOMBRE-Canción ★ Bb B-3074, Vi 82214

BS 014180-1 ★ SU MAMA TUVO LA CULPA-Canción ★ Bb B-3074, Vi 82214

LIDYA MENDOZA Y GRUPO.
Lydia Mendoza-vocal and guitar, María Mendoza-mandolin, unknown string bass. Blue Bonnet Hotel, San Antonio, TX, April 8, 1938.

BS 022288-1 ★ FLOR DE DALIA-Canción ★ Bb B-3165, Vi 82477, Vi 75880(M)

BS 022289-1 ★ LAS ALTAS TORRES-Canción ★ Bb B-3156, Vi 82468

BS 022290-1 ★ MIRA LUISA-Canción ★ Bb B-3141

BS 022291-1 ★ EN TAMPICO ESTA LLOVIENDO-Canción ★ Bb B-3165, Vi 82477, Vi 75880(M), FL 9024(33)

BS 022292-1 ★ CORRIDO DE RIVERA ★ Bb B-3156, Vi 82468

BS 022293-1 ★ PERO PALOMA-Canción ★ Bb B-3141

LIDYA MENDOZA.
Personnel same as last. * = string bass out, maracas added, ** = violin, guitar only. Blue Bonnet Hotel, San Antonio, TX, October 24, 1938.

BS 028521-1 ★ MIA NO MAS-Bolero* (Agustín Lara) ★ Bb B-3216, MW M-7641, Vi 82522, Vi(M) 75921

BS 028522-1 ★ NUNCA VOLVERE A BESARTE-Colombiana ★ Bb 3216, MW M-7641, Vi 82522, LP 05(33), Vi(M) 75921

BS 028523-3 ★ ME JURASTE-Bolero* ★ Bb B-3249, MW M-7642, Vi 76112(M), Vi 82606

BS 028524-1 ★ VUELVEME A QUERER-Vals ★ Bb B-3270, MW M-7643, Vi 76098, Vi 76112(M), Vi 82606

BS 028525-1 ★ ARREPENTIDO-Tango** (Rodolfo Sciamarella) ★ Bb B-3232, Vi 82565

BS 028526-1 ★ NO ME ABANDONES-Canción ★ Bb B-3249, MW M-7642, Vi 76098(M), 82606

BS 028527-1 ★ RINCONCITO-Fox Canción ★ Bb B-3232, MW M-7648, Vi 82565

BS 028528-1 ★ VENGANZA-Bolero ★ Bb B-3270, MW M-7643, Vi 76098(M), 82719

BS 028529-1 ★ ADIOS, ADIOS-Canción ★ Bb B-3257, MW M-7644, Vi 75934

BS 028530-1 ★ YA NO ME IMPORTAN TUS CITAS-Tango ★ Bb B-3277, MW M-7982, Vi 76085(M)

BS 028531-1 ★ CUANDO MAS TE QUERIA-Canción ★ Bb B-3284, MW M-7983, Vi 76124(M), 82773

BS 028532-1 ★ EL SCHOTTIS ★ Bb B-3257, MW M-7644, Vi 75934

LIDYA MENDOZA y su grupo.
Same personnel as April 8, 1938. San Antonio, TX, October 25, 1938.

BS 028617-1 ★ COPITAS DE VINO-Corrido ★ Bb B-3289, MW M-7984, Vi 75960(M)

BS 028618-1 ★ PERO OYES, ANTONIA-Canción ★ Bb B-3289, Vi 75990(M)

BS 028619-1 ★ SE MURIO LA CUCARACHA ★ Bb B-3299, Vi 76138(M), 82762, FL 9007(33)

BS 028620-1 ★ MIENTRAS QUE DUERMAS-Canción ★ Bb B-3299, Vi 82762, Vi 76085(M), RCA (C) 05(0131)00868(33)

BS 028621-1 ★ SALI DE PUEBLA-Canción ★ Bb B-3305, Vi 76124(M)

BS 028622-1 ★ BLANCA ROSA-Canción ★ Bb B-3305, Vi 75990(M), 82701

BS 028623-1 ★ FEDERICO EL PELAO-Canción ★ Bb B-3307, Vi 76138(M), FL 9035(33)

BS 028624-1 ★ EL JARRITO-Canción ★ Bb B-3228, MW M-7647, Vi 82566

BS 028625-1 ★ ABORREZCO LA VIDA-Canción ★ Bb B-3307, Vi 82750, Vi 76075(M), RCA (C) 05(0131)00868(33), FL 9035(33)

BS 028626-1 ★ LOS MAGUEYES-Canción ★ Bb B-3228, MW M-7647, Vi 82566

BS 028627-1 ★ LA PASION DE ESA MUJER-Canción ★ Bb B-3313, MW M-7985, Vi 82773, Vi 76075(M)

BS 028628-1 ★ MUJER INVENCIBLE-Canción ★ Bb B-3313, MW M-7985, Vi 76046(M), 82750

BS 028629-1 ★ UNA CRUZ-Bolero [with maracas] ★ Bb B-3293, MW M-7982, Vi 76049(M)

BS 028630-1 ★ CANCION DEL ALMA-Vals ★ Bb B-3293, MW M-7982, Vi 76049(M)

BS 028631-1 ★ EL QUE A HIERRO MATA-Canción ★ Bb B-3284, MW M-7983, Vi 75960(M), 82701

BS 028632-1 ★ TU DIRAS-Canción ★ Bb B-3277, MW M-7648, Vi 76046(M), FL 9024(33), FL 7002(CD)

LYDIA MENDOZA vocal and guitar.
María Mendoza-mandolin. San Antonio, TX, October 28, 1938.

BS 028737-1 ★ CANTANDO-Tango (Mercedes Simón) ★ Bb B-3220, MW M-7645, Vi 75936, 82543, Vi(M) 75936

BS 028738-1 ★ MOCOSITA-Tango ★ Bb B-3244, MW M-7645, Vi 75986, 82581

BS 028739-1 ★ MALA ENTRAÑA-Canción ★ Bb B-3244, MW M-7646*, Vi 75986, 82581

BS 028740-1 ★ MI VIEJO AMOR-Canción (Alfonso Esparza Oteo) ★ Bb B-3220, MW M-7646, Vi 75936, 82543

(*The master of MALA ENTRAÑA was by mistake used for MW M-7649-A and labeled SONRISAS-Fox Canción by Cuquita y Regino (released by Blue Bird as Los Cardinales) who are heard on the B side of M-7649.)

LIDYA MENDOZA con su guitarra.
Probably María Mendoza-2nd guitar. Hollywood, CA, September 8, 1939.

PBS 036470-1 ★ MI JACA-Paso Doble Canción (R. Perelló-J. Mostazo) ★ Bb B-3367, MW M-8588, Vi 82970

PBS 036471-1 ★ LA CABAÑA-Vals ★ Bb B-3367, MW M-8588, Vi 82983

PBS 036472-1 ★ CANTA GUITARRA MIA-Paso Doble Canción ★ MW M-8589, Vi 82983

PBS 036473-1 ★ PARECE MENTIRA-Tango (Rodolfo Sciamerella y Antonio Rodio) ★ Bb B-3395, MW M-8589, Vi 82922

PBS 036474-1 ★ QUE TE IMPORTA-Canción Bolero (R H) ★ MW M-8590, Vi 82970

PBS 036475-3 ★ VIDA MIA-Canción ★ Bb B-3395, MW M-8590, Vi 82922

PBS 036476-2 ★ MIS OJOS ME DENUNCIAN-Canción ★ Bb B-3373, MW M-8591, Vi 82954

PBS 036477-2 ★ MORENA LINDA-Canción (Gonzalo Curiel) ★ Bb B-3373, MW M-8591, Vi 82954

PBS 036478-2 ★ AHORA SEREMOS FELICES ★ Bb B-3329, MW M-8601, Vi 82815

PBS 036479-1 ★ CUANTO TE QUIERO-Vals ★ Bb B-3401, MW M-8592, Vi 82923

PBS 036480-3 ★ TALISMAN-Fox ★ Bb B-3329, MW M-8601, Vi 82815

PBS 036481-1 ★ MENTIROSA-Canción (A. Esparza Oteo) ★ Bb B-3401, MW M-8592, Vi 82923

LYDIA Y MARIA MENDOZA vocal duets with guitars. Hollywood, CA, September 12, 1939.

PBS 036492-3 ★ HAY QUE SUERTE-Canción ★ Bb B-3350, Vi 82816

PBS 036493-1 ★ EL JARDINERO ★ MW M-8593, Vi 82890

PBS 036494-4 ★ POBRE DE MI CORAZON-Canción Fox (Manuel S. Acuña) ★ Bb B-3350, MW M-8602, Vi 82816

PBS 036495-4 ★ COMO ME HACES SUFRIR (Manuel S. Acuña) ★ MW M-8596, Vi 82889

PBS 036496-1 ★ SEPULTURERO-Canción* (Rubén Uquillas) ★ Bb B-3361, MW M-8595, Vi 82836

PBS 036497- ★ LOS MIRASOLES-Canción (Felipe Valdés Leal) ★ Bb B-3361, MW M-8595, Vi 82836

PBS 036498-1 ★ QUIERO UN AMOR (Rubén Uquillas) ★ MW M-8593, Vi 82888

PBS 036499-1 ★ LA MUJER PAGADA-Canción (J. Rodríguez) ★ Bb B-3339, MW M-8600, Vi 82837

PBS 042100-1 ★ VUELE BAILES-Vals ★ MW M-8597, Vi 82889

PBS 042101-1 ★ INCERTIDUMBRE-Canción (Curiel) ★ Bb rejected

Personnel same as last. Hollywood, CA, September 19, 1939.

PBS 042101-3 ★ INCERTIDUMBRE (Curiel) ★ Bb B-3379, MW M-8594, Vi 82868

PBS 042136-1 ★ TIEMPO AQUEL-Vals Canción ★ Bb B-3385, MW M-8598, Vi 82869

PBS 042137-1 ★ PREGUNTA-Canción Bolero ★ Bb B-3385, MW M-8598, Vi 82869

PBS 042138-1 ★ HAY QUE OLVIDAR-Canción Bolero ★ Bb B-3389, MW M-8599, Vi 82870

PBS 042139-1 ★ SOSPECHA-Canción Bolero ★ Bb B-3379, MW M-8594, Vi 82868

PBS 042140-2 ★ NO SE PORQUE TE QUIERO-Canción Vals (Manuel S. Acuña) ★ MW M-8596, Vi 82890

PBS 042141-1(2 R) ★ DESDICHADA DE TI-Canción ★ Vi 82888

PBS 042142-2 ★ NO SABES COMPRENDER-Tango Canción (Juan D. Montes) ★ Bb B-3339, MW M-8600, Vi 82837

PBS 042143-1 ★ LA POLLITA-Canción Chilena [Tonada] ★ Bb B-3389, MW M-8599, Vi 82870

(Many of the items from the previous three sessions were also released in Mexico on the Victor 75/76000 series, but the release numbers are unknown to us. Since we do not have many of the items from the last three sessions, we are unable to identify which items are sung by Lydia Mendoza solo and which are sung by Lydia and María as vocal duets.)

RCA VICTOR RECORDS OF MEXICO

The following sessions were produced by the Mexican division of RCA and issued as indicated.

LYDIA MENDOZA vocal and guitar.
María Mendoza probably second guitar and unknown bass. Monterrey, N.L., México, 1940.

MBS O45452 ★ VEN ACA ★ Bb B-3438, Vi 83362

MBS 045453 ★ LEJOS DE TI ★ Bb B-3438, Vi 83362

MBS 045454 ★ DEJALO VENIR ★ Bb B-3462

MBS 045455 ★ OYELO BIEN ★ Bb B-3462

MBS 045456 ★ FRAGILIDAD-Bolero (Miguel Prado) ★ Bb B-3439

MBS 045457 ★ Unknown title ★ Bb unissued

MBS 045458 ★ ANGUSTIA-Bolero (M. Alvarez y R. de Paz) ★ Bb B-3439

MBS 045459 ★ Unknown title ★ Bb unissued

MBS 045460 ★ Unknown title ★ Bb unissued

MBS 045461 ★ Unknown title ★ Bb unissued

MARIA y LYDIA MENDOZA vocal duet.

MBS 045462 ★ DEVUELVEME TU AMOR ★ Bb B-3440

MBS 045467 ★ SI SEÑOR, SOY RANCHERO-Huapango ★ Bb B-3473

MBS 045468 ★ MI PANDILLA ★ Bb B-3440

MBS 045469 ★ DESENGAÑO-Canción Ranchera (Alejandro G. Rosas) ★ Bb B-3473

(Note: Matrix #'s 463–466 are by Trio Nuevo León)

LYDIA MENDOZA con guitarra y mandolina.
Probably Lorenzo Caballero-guitar and María Mendoza-mandolin.

MBS 045481 ★ Unknown title ★ Bb unissued

MBS 045482 ★ OJITOS DE MI VIDA-(Alejandro Rosas) ★ Bb B-3441, Vi 83470

MBS 045483 ★ PARA ADORARTE A TI-Vals (arr. L. Mendoza) ★ Bb B-3441, Vi 83470

MBS 045484 ★ Unknown title ★ Bb unissued

(Note: For U.S. RCA release numbers, the prefix 23 indicates release as 78 rpm, while the prefix 51 indicates release as a 45 rpm disc.)

LYDIA MENDOZA con Lorenzo Caballero (guitar) y su conjunto (including accordion, saxophone and Juan Viesca on string bass). Monterrey, Nuevo León, México, May 22, 1950.

(Note: There was a pressing order in RCA's Mexico City files for 3,000 of each item for this and the May 1951 session.)

MBS 092188 ★ NOCHE TENEBROSA-Ranchera (Manuel Garza V.) ★ RCA(M) 70-8406-B, RCA 23/51-5229B

MBS 092189 ★ LA GUIA-Ranchera (Manuel Garza V.) ★ RCA(M) 70-8428-B, RCA 23/51-5229A, RCA(M) PCS-9949(33)

MBS 092190 ★ AY, QUE BONITO-Ranchera (Lorenzo Caballero) ★ RCA(M) 70-8489-A, RCA 23/51-5192B

MBS 092191 ★ TODO ES FALSO-Ranchera (Francisco Cantú) ★ RCA(M) 70-8428-A, RCA 23/51-5192A, RCA(M) PCS-9949(33)

MBS 092192 ★ AY, QUE SUERTE-Ranchera (L. Mendoza) ★ RCA(M) 70-8489-B, RCA 23/51-5172B

MBS 092193 ★ ELLA ME DIJO QUE NO-Ranchera (Santiago Jiménez) ★ RCA(M) 70-8406-B, RCA 23/51-5172A

LYDIA MENDOZA con el conjunto de Emilio Martínez. San Antonio, TX, May 9-11, 1951.

(Note: The last letter of the matrix (or in this case also stamper) number's prefix indicates whether 78 rpm (B) or 45 rpm (W) release. E prefix #s denotes stamper numbers.)

MBS 092996 (E1XB-3307) ★ LA MULITA-Ranchera (Manuel Martínez) ★ RCA 23/51-5527, RCA(M) 70-8607-A

MBS 092997 (E1XB-0998) ★ LA JULIA-Corrido (Manuel Martínez) ★ RCA 23/51-5589, RCA(M) 70-9024-A

MBS 092998 (E1XB-3308) ★ NO PUEDE UN CORAZON-Canción Ranchera (Manuel Martínez) ★ RCA 23/51-5527, RCA(M) 70-8607-B, Otra(M) LP 17(33)

MBS 092999 (E1XB-3379) ★ MUJER DE LA CALLE-Ranchera (Manuel Martínez) ★ RCA 23-5550, RCA(M) 70-8804-B

MBS 093000 (E1XB-3360) ★ PARA QUE ME ANDAS BUSCANDO-Ranchera (Lydia Mendoza) ★ RCA 51-5550, RCA(M) 70-8804-A, Otra(M) LP 17(33)

MBS 093001 (E1XB-0997) ★ QUIERO SER LIBRE-Ranchera (Emilio Martínez) ★ RCA 23/51-5589, RCA(M) 70-9546-A

MBS 093002 (E1XB-4434) ★ LA AGUILILLA (YO TE PREGUNTO)-Canción Ranchera (Juan Garza) ★ RCA 23/51-5622, RCA(M) 70-9546-A

MBS 093003 (E1XB-4433) ★ NOCHE DE ESTRELLAS-Canción Ranchera (Trad) ★ RCA 23/51-5622, RCA(M) 70-9024-B

HERMANAS MENDOZA Juanita y María.

MBS 093004 (E1XB-3348) ★ LA ZENAIDA-Canción Ranchera (Juan Garza) ★ RCA 23-5543, RCA(M) 70-8652-A

MBS 093005 ★ AUSENCIA-Canción Ranchera (Juan Garza) ★ RCA 23-5515, RCA(M) 70-8596-B

MBS 093006 ★ LOS CASADOS-Corrido ★ RCA 23-5515, RCA(M) 70-8596-A

MBS 093007 (E1XB-3347) ★ LAS CASADAS-Corrido (Tradicional) ★ RCA 23-5543, RCA(M) 70-8652-B

LYDIA MENDOZA y conjunto (with studio group). México, D.F., México, June 24, 1952.

M-093487 (E2XB-6760) ★ MAL HOMBRE-Tango ★ RCA(M) 70-8820-A, RCA 23-5818, Otra(M) LP 17(33)

M-093488 (E2XB-6761) ★ MI LUPITA-Canción Ranchera (NC) ★ RCA(M) 70-8820-B, RCA 23-5818, LP 05(33)(0131) 00868(33)

M-093489 ★ OLVIDARTE JAMAS-Blues (Gonzalo Curiel) ★ RCA(M) 70-8953A, Otra(M) LP 17(33)

M-093490 ★ PALOMITA DE ALAS BLANCAS-Canción Ranchera ★ RCA(M) 70-8953B

LYDIA MENDOZA con el Conjunto de Memo Mata.
Bass and arrangements by Guillermo "Memo" Mata. Los Angeles, CA; ca 1954-55.

G2TB-3242 ★ CORAZON HERIDO-Bolero (Manuel Valdez) ★ RCA 23/51-7016

G2TW-3243 ★ TU QUE SABES-Canción Ranchera (José Luz Alaniz) ★ RCA 23/51-7001

G2TW-3244 ★ MALA MOVIDA-Canción Polka (Manuel Valdez) ★ RCA 23/51-6975

G2TW-3245 ★ SUFRO POR TI-Canción Ranchera (Andrés Huesca) ★ RCA 23/51-6975

G2TB-3246 ★ MOCOSITA-Canción Tango (V. Solino-G.H. Matos) ★ RCA 23/51-7016

G2TB-3247 ★ LA ULTIMA COPA-Canción Tango (Canaro-Paul-Caruso) ★ RCA 23/51-6971

G2TW-3248 ★ FELIZ CUMPLEAÑOS-Vals (NC) ★ RCA 23/51-7001

G2TB-3249 ★ MUJER SIN CORAZON-Bolero (Memo Mata) ★ RCA 23/51-6971, RCA (C) 05(0131)00868(33)

G2TB-4746 ★ LEJOS-Bolero (Gene Luján) ★ RCA 23/51-7173, RCA (C) 05(0131)00868(33)

G2TW-4747 ★ MALDITA DISTANCIA-Canción Ranchera (A. Ortiz-R. Ortiz-S. Ortiz) ★ RCA 23/51-7082

G2TB-4748 ★ AMOR COMO EL QUE PERDI-Canción Ranchera (José Luis Alaniz) ★ RCA 23/51-7134

G2TB-4749 ★ ME HACES FALTA-Canción (José Luis Alaniz) ★ RCA 23/51-7134

G2TB-4939 ★ HORAS FELICES-Canción Ranchera (Manuel Valdez) ★ RCA 23/51-7173

G2TW-4940 ★ VEINTE PRIMAVERAS-Canción Ranchera (Sandra Ortiz) ★ RCA 23/51-7082

LYDIA MENDOZA con el Mariachi Vargas de Tecalitlán
(Note: On Mexican RCA single releases, prefix 71 denotes a 78 rpm release and prefix 76 denotes a 45 rpm release.) México, D.F., México; March 11, 1958.

MB-097058 ★ MADRECITA ADORADA-Ranchera (Salvador Núñez) ★ RCA(M) 71-343, RCA(M) LP 1132(33)

MB-097059 ★ TRES PUÑALADAS DE MUERTE-Ranchera (Norberto Jiménez) ★ RCA(M) LP 1132(33)

MB-097060 ★ BANDERA MEXICANA-Marcha (Víctor Cordero) ★ RCA(M) LP 1132

MB-097061 ★ ADIOS MI MEXICO LINDO ★ RCA(M) 71-343, RCA(M) LP 1132

MB-097062 ★ HOMBRE MALO-Ranchera (Norberto A. Jiménez) ★ RCA(M) LP 1132

MB-097063 ★ SIGUE VAGANDO MUJER-Ranchera (Salomé Tenorio Flores) ★ RCA(M) LP 1132

LA GUIA ★ RCA (M) film recording

POR QUE TE VAS ★ RCA (M) film recording

(Note: RCA(M) LP 1132 title: ADIOS MI MEXICO LINDO; Side 2: LYDIA MENDOZA con el trío Los Mexicanos (see next session). LA GUIA and POR QUE TE VAS were recorded for a film. These two selections were not commercially issued and I doubt if matrix #s were assigned.)

LYDIA MENDOZA con trío y ritmos. México, D.F., México, April 22, 1958.

M-097167 ★ MI CORAZON TE LO HE DADO-Bolero (Gene Luján) ★ Vik(M) 45-551, Otra(M) LP 17(33), RCA(M) LP 1132(33)

M-097168 ★ ESTOY DESESPERADA-Bolero Rítmico (Norberto A. Jiménez) ★ Vik(M) 45-551, Otra(M) LP 17(33), RCA(M) LP 1132(33)

M-097169 ★ JUSTICIA-Bolero (Carmen Rello) ★ RCA(M) 71/76-402-B, Otra(M) LP 17(33), RCA(M) LP 1132(33)

M-097170 ★ HUMILLADA-Bolero (Víctor Cordero) ★ RCA(M) 71/76-449, Otra(M) LP 17(33), RCA(M) LP 1132(33)

M-097171 ★ DULCE VENGANZA-Bolero (Nico Jiménez) ★ RCA(M) 71/76-402-A, Otra(M) LP 17(33), RCA(M) LP 1132(33)

M-097172 ★ QUE LINDO BESAS MUJER (Gene Luján) ★ RCA(M) 71/76-449, Otra(M) LP 17(33), RCA(M) LP 1132(33)

(Note: Vik 45 gives Víctor Cordero as composer of ESTOY DESESPERADA.
All preceding masters made by Mexican RCA between 1950 and 1958 may appear on other RCA releases in Mexico, Colombia, etc., but are not known to us.)

DECCA RECORDS

MARIA MENDOZA vocal and guitar. San Antonio, TX, February 8, 1937.

61682-A ★ TE QUIERO CON LA VIDA-Canción ★ Decca rejected

61683-A ★ ME PIDEN-Canción ★ Decca rejected

61684-A ★ EN VANO QUIERAS-Canción ★ Decca rejected

61685-A ★ CAPRICHO-Canción ★ Decca rejected

61686-A ★ SOLA-Canción ★ De 10185

61687-A ★ EL NOVILLERO-Paso Doble (Agustín Lara) ★ De 10185

PAQUITA Y MANOLO MENDOZA (10 y 12 años de edad)
Juanita and Manuel Mendoza vocal duet with mandolin and guitar, probably by Lydia and María.

61688-A ★ EL MARIACHE-Huapango ★ De 10186

61689-A ★ LA GUIA-Canción ★ De 10186, FL 9035(33)

MENDOZA FAMILY DISCOGRAPHY: SECTION 2

DISCOS AZTECA

Many Azteca recordings were also released in Mexico on the Peerless (Peer) label (one example is master number 509), but most Peerless release numbers are not known to us. Some Azteca releases were pressed and distributed in Mexico on the Azteca label using the same release numbers as the U.S. Aztecas. One example is Master number 442 and 444 (Az 5125). The Mexican pressing plant used stampers derived from the original mothers with the words "Hecho en México" added to the plates. On the labels of the Mexican pressings the words "Los Angeles, Calif." after

"Azteca" are replaced with "de México."
ARH indicates Arhoolie release licensed from Azteca.

LYDIA MENDOZA con su guitarra. Vocals with guitar. Radio Recorders, Hollywood, CA. Probably August or September, 1947.

187-2 ★ EL MUNDO ENGAÑOSO-Canción ★ Az 289, LP 8012(33)

188-2 ★ DEJAME EN PAZ-Bolero (Luciano Miral) ★ Az 289, LP 8012(33)

189-2 ★ SABOR DE ENGAÑO-Bolero (Mario Alvarez ★ Az 290, LP 8012(33)

190-1 ★ PARA QUE NECESITAS MI AMOR-Canción ★ Az 290, LP 8012(33)

191-3 ★ PAJARITO HERIDO-Canción ★ Az 291

192-4 ★ HOMBRE INFIEL-Canción (Juan Leonardo) ★ Az 291

193-1 ★ YA NO PUEDO DEJAR DE QUERERTE-Canción ★ Az 292

194-1 ★ FALSA-Canción ★ Az 292

195-1 ★ SI O NO-Canción ★ Az 293, LP 8017(33)

196-2 ★ CUANDO ESCUCHES ESTE VALS-Canción ★ Az 293

197-2 ★ CELOSA-Canción (Paulo Rodríguez) ★ Az 294

198-2 ★ PARA QUE MENTIR-Canción (Manuel Mendoza) ★ Az 294, LP 8030(33)

JUANITA Y MARIA MENDOZA con guitarras.

199-1 ★ CORRIDO DE LAREDO ★ Az 5007

200-3 ★ MORENA MORENITA-Canción Ranchera (Santiago Jiménez) ★ Az 5007

201-1 ★ ANDO TOMANDO MIS COPAS-Canción Ranchera (Francisco Cantú) ★ Az 5008

202-4 ★ LA DANZA BONITA-Canción ★ Az 5008

207-2 ★ CARLOS CORONADO-Corrido (Leonor Mendoza) ★ Az 5009

208-1 ★ LA BARCA MARINA-Canción ★ Az 5009

209-2 ★ LAS ISABELES-Canción Ranchera ★ Az 5010

210-2 ★ AMORCITO CONSENTIDO-Ranchera ★ Az 5010

LYDIA MENDOZA con su guitarra.

211-1 ★ LA FERIA DE LAS FLORES-Canción (Chucho Monge) ★ Az 299

212-4 ★ LA BORRACHITA-Canción (Tata Nacho) ★ Az 299

213-3 ★ AMOR DE MADRE-Canción ★ Az 300, LP 8012(33)

214-1 ★ SE ME HIZO FACIL ★ Az 300, LP 8012(33)

215-1 ★ EL HIJO PRODIGO-Corrido ★ Az 301, LP 8012(33)

216-1 ★ NUNCA CREAS-Canción ★ Az 301, LP 8012(33)

217-1 ★ NO ME VUELVO A ENAMORAR-Bolero (Chucho Monge) ★ Az 302, LP 8012(33)

218-2 ★ NOCHE DE RONDA-Canción (Agustín Lara) ★ Az 302, LP 8012(33)

JUANITA Y MARIA MENDOZA con guitarras. Probably Hollywood, CA, late 1947.

277-1 ★ CORRIDO DE SANTOS MEDINA (Víctor Cordero) ★ Az 5019

278-1 ★ CORAZON MEXICANO-Canción (Cuates Castilla) ★ Az 5019

279-1 ★ EL SOLDADO MARIHUANO-Corrido (V. Cordero) ★ Az 5020

280-1 ★ MARIA ISABEL-Canción Vals (Frank Cantú) ★ Az 5020

LYDIA MENDOZA con su guitarra.

281-1 ★ PAJARILLO BARRANQUEÑO-Ranchera ★ Az 358

282-1 ★ LA TORCACITA-Ranchera ★ Az 357, LP 8004(33)

283-3 ★ TANGO NEGRO-Tango ★ Az 353, 402

284-3 ★ NOVILLERO-Paso Doble (Agustín Lara) ★ Az 353, 407

285-1 ★ TIERRAS LEJANAS-Canción (Víctor Cordero) ★ Az 373

286-2 ★ MALA MUJER ★ Az 381

287-1 ★ YA NO JUEGUES CON MI AMOR-Canción (R. Elizondo) ★ Az 366

288-1 ★ JAMAS LA OLVIDARE-Canción Ranchera (Víctor Cordero) ★ Az 365, LP 8004(33)

289-1 ★ LOS BESOS DE MI NEGRA-Canción ★ Az 357, LP 8004(33)

290-A-2 ★ CONFESONARIO-Canción ★ Az 358, LP 8004(33)

291A-1 ★ OLVIDA QUE ME AMASTE-Canción (Leonor Mendoza) ★ Az 372

292-A-3 ★ TEMO SABER-Bolero (R. Elizondo) ★ Az 372

JUANITA Y MARIA MENDOZA con guitarras.

289-2-BL ★ EL RANCHERO ATRAVANCADO-Corrido (V. Cordero) ★ Az 5027

290-1 ★ LASTIMA QUE SEAS TAN LOCA-Canción (L.M. Moreno or Elmo López) ★ Az 5027

291-1 ★ ME IMPORTA POCO-Canción (Elmo López) ★ Az 5028

292-2 ★ NO SE TE VAYA A OLVIDAR-Ranchera (V. Cordero) ★ Az 5028

293-2 ★ MI QUERIDA VALENTINA-Ranchera (Luis Moreno) ★ Az 5011

294-1 ★ ARREJUNTESE MI PRIETA-Ranchera (Miguel García) ★ Az 5011

295-2 ★ CORRAL VIEJO-Corrido (V. Cordero) ★ Az 5012

296-4 ★ CHINA DE LOS OJOS NEGROS-Ranchera ★ Az 5012

LYDIA MENDOZA con su guitarra.

297-2 ★ TEMO QUE NO ME QUIERAS ★ Az 381

298-1 ★ MI PENSAMIENTO-Canción (Eusebio Rosas) ★ Az 366, LP 8027(33)

299-1 ★ HAY QUE SABER PERDER-Bolero (Abel Domínguez) ★ Az 365, LP 8004(33)

300-2 ★ NADA ME IMPORTA-Canción ★ Az 373

JUANITA Y MARIA MENDOZA con guitarras.

301-2 ★ EL CONTRABANDO DEL PASO-Corrido (Vda. de Jara) ★ Az 5023, LP 8048(33)

302-2 ★ PARA QUE FINGIR-Ranchera (Isabel Estrada) ★ Az 5023, LP 8048(33)

303-4 ★ SIEMPRE EN AMARTE PIENSO-Canción Ranchera (Leonor Mendoza) ★ Az 5024, LP 8048(33)

304-1 ★ OJITOS CHINOS Y NEGROS-Ranchera ★ Az 5024, LP 8048(33)

LYDIA MENDOZA con su guitarra.

305-2 ★ CON MI CANCION-Canción (Eusebio Rosas) ★ Az 332, LP 8030(33)

306-2 ★ MAL HOMBRE-Tango ★ Az 333, LP 8004(33)

307-3 ★ EL PUÑAL DE TU DESDEN-Canción ★ Az 332

308-2 ★ SERENATA TAPATIA-Serenata (Esperón y Cortázar) ★ Az 333

JUANITA Y MARIA MENDOZA con guitarras.

309-1 ★ TODOS LOS DIAS QUE AMANECE-Canción Ranchera (Leonor Mendoza) ★ Az 5029, LP 8048(33)

310-1 ★ INDITA MIA-Canción ★ Az 5029, LP 8048(33)

311-4 ★ EL MUCHACHO ALEGRE-Corrido ★ Az 5030, LP 8048(33)

312-2 ★ AY DE MI (Eusebio Rosas) ★ Az 5030, LP 8048(33)

LYDIA MENDOZA con su guitarra.

313-1 ★ NO LO NIEGO-Canción (Víctor Cordero) ★ Az 348

314-1 ★ DICEN-Bolero (E. Rosas) ★ Az 348

315-3 ★ LYDIA-Canción Blues (N. Delgado) ★ Az 349

316-1 ★ SEREMOS AMIGOS-Canción (Leonor Mendoza) ★ Az 349, LP 8030(33)

JUANITA Y MARIA MENDOZA con el Mariachi Azteca.
317-4 ★ POR TI APRENDI A QUERER-Canción Vals (Lorenzo Barcelata) ★ Az 326, LP 8037(33)

318-1 ★ ESA ROSITA-Canción (Luis Moreno) ★ Az 326, LP 8037(33)

319-2 ★ MARIA ELENA-Canción Vals (Lorenzo Barcelata) ★ Az 327

320-2 ★ ESO ES JALISCO-Canción Ranchera (Eusebio Rosas) ★ Az 327

LYDIA MENDOZA con su guitarra.
321-3 ★ QUIERO ESTAR CONTIGO ★ Az 338, LP 8004(33)

322-1 ★ AMOR PENDIENTE ★ Az 338, LP 8004(33)

323-2 ★ POR UNA MUJER ★ Az 339, LP 8004(33)

324-2 ★ EL INGRATO ★ Az 339, LP 8004(33)

369-2 ★ TE HE DE QUERER-Canción ★ Az 5154

370-1 ★ QUE HARE TAN SOLA-Canción ★ Az 5095, LP 8017(33)

371-1 ★ ANDO VAGANDO-Canción (L. Mendoza) ★ Az 5154

372-1 ★ TU PARTIDA-Canción ★ Az 5095

373-2 ★ CELIA-Canción (Leonor Mendoza) ★ Az 5170, LP 8030(33)

374-3 ★ SOLA-Canción (Agustín Lara) ★ Az 5142

JUANITA Y MARIA MENDOZA con guitarras.
375-3 ★ NO TENGO LA CULPA-Canción Blues (F. Cantú) ★ Az 5043

376-1 ★ POR ULTIMA VEZ-Canción Ranchera ★ Az 5031

377-3 ★ MIS PENSAMIENTOS-Canción (Luis Moreno) ★ Az 5043, ARH 3017(33)

378-2 ★ LA LIMA-Canción Ranchera (Luis Moreno) ★ Az 5031

LYDIA MENDOZA con su guitarra.
379-2 ★ VETE NO VUELVAS-Canción ★ Az 5096, LP 8017(33)

380-1 ★ A MARIA-Canción (L. Mendoza) ★ Az 5170, LP 8030(33)

381-1 ★ CUANDO MAS TE QUERIA-Canción (L. Mendoza) ★ Az 5148, LP 8017(33)

382-2 ★ AGUASCALIENTES-Corrido (L. Mendoza) ★ Az 5235, LP 8030(33)

383-1 ★ TE HAS ALEJADO-Canción (Lydia Mendoza) ★ Az 5142

384-1 ★ PORQUE TE QUIERO TANTO-Ranchera ★ Az 5183

JUANITA Y MARIA MENDOZA con guitarras.
385-2 ★ LA CHUPARROSA-Canción Ranchera (Luis Moreno) ★ Az 5040

386-1 ★ SI TOMO MIS COPAS-Ranchera (Luis Moreno) ★ Az 5040

387-1 ★ MIENTRAS TENGA CORAZON-Ranchera (Rafael Villareal) ★ Az 5042

388-2 ★ VALE MAS QUE TE LA CORTES-Canción (Rafael Villareal) ★ Az 5041, LP 8048(33)

389-2 ★ LOS VERSOS DEL CASAMIENTO-Corrido (C.L. Alvarado) ★ Az 5041, LP 8048(33)

390-2 ★ DELGADINA-Corrido (Leonor Mendoza) ★ Az 5042

LYDIA MENDOZA con su guitarra.
391-3 ★ AL PIE DE TU REJA-Ranchera ★ Az 5081, LP 8030(33)

392-3 ★ YA VA CAYENDO LA TARDE-Canción (L. Mendoza) ★ Az 5148, LP 8017(33)

393-2　★　QUE PRONTO HAS OLVIDADO-Canción (L. Mendoza)　★　Az 5193, LP 8017(33)

394-2　★　LOS HOMBRES "ASINA" SON-Canción　★　Az 5081, LP 8030(33)

395-1　★　AL CONTEMPLARTE-Canción　★　Az 5161, LP 8017(33)

396-1　★　DELICIOSA-Ranchera　★　Az 5161

JUANITA Y MARIA MENDOZA con guitarras.
397-2　★　CORRIDO DE ARNULFO GONZALEZ (Narciso Delgado)　★　Az 5047

398-1　★　JESUSITA-Vals (Miguel Salas)　★　Az 5047, LP 8027(33)

399-1　★　VALENTIN DE LA SIERRA-Corrido (L. Pérez Meza)　★　Az 5048

400-1　★　YA ME VOY PA' CALIFORNIA-Corrido (Narciso Delgado y R. Elizondo)　★　Az 5048

401-2　★　QUE CHULA PRIETA-Ranchera　★　Az 5058, ARH 3017(33)

402-1　★　NO LLORES PANCHA-Ranchera　★　Az 5057

LYDIA MENDOZA con su guitarra.
403-1　★　POR QUE INSISTES-Canción (Rafael Ramírez)　★　Az 5193

404-1　★　TE AMO ME DIJISTE-Canción　★　Az 5230

405-2　★　OLVIDARTE JAMAS-Canción　★　Az 5235

406-1　★　PERO AY QUE TRISTE-Canción (Leonor Mendoza)　★　Az 5230, LP 8030(33)

407-1　★　DIME QUE SI-Canción (arr. L. Alvarado)　★　Az 5277

408-3　★　FLORES NEGRAS-Canción　★　Az 5096

JUANITA Y MARIA MENDOZA con guitarras.
409-2　★　LA HIJA DESOBEDIENTE-Corrido (Manuel Gómez)　★　Az 5051, Az 9001(45)

410-2　★　EL CUARTELAZO-Corrido (Leonor Mendoza)　★　Az 5052

411-1　★　ME IMPORTA MADRE-Canción　★　Az 5052

412-1　★　ELISA-CanciónRanchera (Juan Mendoza)　★　Az 5051, Az 9001(45)

413-2　★　AQUELLAS CARICIAS-Canción (Leonor Mendoza)　★　Az 5057

414-1　★　YA ME VOY LEJOS MUY LEJOS-Canción (Lydia Mendoza)　★　Az 5058

"CONJUNTO ESTRELLA."
Lydia Mendoza-guitar only, no vocal (Her name is prominently featured on the label), Lorenzo Caballero-guitar, Leandro Guerrero-accordion, Juan Viesca-contrabajo. All selections by Conjunto Estrella are instrumentals with no vocals by Lydia. Los Angeles, CA, 1948.

415-2　★　PASE UD-Schottis (Luis Moreno)　★　Az 5032

416-2　★　JUAN CHARRASQUEADO-Polka (Víctor Cordero)　★　Az 5032

417-2　★　VENGAN COPAS-Polka　★　Az 5033

418-2　★　BONITO NUEVO LEON-Vals (Luis Moreno)　★　Az 5033

419-2　★　LA TROTONA-Polka (L.Moreno)　★　Az 5034

420-2　★　CUANDO TU QUIERAS-Polka (L. Moreno)　★　Az 5034

JUANITA Y MARIA MENDOZA y guitarras.
421-2　★　MUJERES FALSARIAS-Canción Ranchera　★　Az 5071

422-1　★　EL GALAN ENAMORADO-Corrido (Luis Moreno)　★　Az 5071

423-1　★　LOS PICONES-Canción Ranchera (Luis Moreno)　★　Az 5072, ARH 3017(33)

424-1　★　LINDA MORENITA-Canción (R. Rodríguez and A. Carranza)　★　Az 5072, ARH 3017(33)

425-3　★　SE QUERER DE CORAZON-Ranchera (R. Rodríguez and A. Carranza)　★　Az 5091

426-3 ★ TU MAMA TUVO LA CULPA-Ranchera ★ Az 5092

CONJUNTO ESTRELLA.

427-3 ★ MI LUPITA-Polka (L. Moreno) ★ Az 5037

428-1 ★ MONTERREY-Polka ★ Az 5037

429-1 ★ ROSITA-Vals ★ Az 5035

430-2 ★ CHICO'S-Polka (Leandro Guerrero) ★ Az 5035

431-1 ★ SAN JOSE-Schottis (Leandro Guerrero) ★ Az 5046

432-1 ★ CARMELA-Polka (Luis Moreno) ★ Az 5046

(Note: Masters 433-438 are by Conjunto Estrella accompanying María Padilla and Memo.)

LYDIA MENDOZA con su guitarra.

439-1 ★ HOMBRE CRUEL ★ Az 354, LP 8017(33), LP 8027(33)

440-1 ★ AGUILA O SOL-Ranchera ★ Az 354

441-2 ★ NO PRESUMO DE MATON-Ranchera (Lydia Mendoza) ★ Az 5277, Az 5277(45), LP 8030(33)

442-2 ★ JURASTE-Canción (Lydia Mendoza) ★ Az 5125, LP 8017(33)

443-2 ★ EN VANO-Canción (L. Mendoza) ★ Az 5183, LP 8017(33)

444-1 ★ MORENA-Paso Doble (Jorge del Moral) ★ Az 5125

CONJUNTO ESTRELLA.

Personnel same as for previous Conjunto Estrella. We do not know the matrix numbers for four of the following. We assume they use matrix numbers 445–448.

LA COQUETA-Polka ★ Az 5036

SILVIA-Vals ★ Az 5036

VIVA CHIHUAHUA-Polka ★ Az 5053

LA COSTEÑA-Polka ★ Az 5053

449-2 ★ EL CABALLO NEGRO-Schottis (Leandro Guerrero) ★ Az 5054

450-1 ★ MI DESGRACIA-Polka (Luis Moreno) ★ Az 5054

(Note: Possibly other selections were recorded by Conjunto Estrella, who also accompanied Las Hermanas Padilla).

JUANITA Y MARIA MENDOZA con guitarras. Los Angeles, CA, 1949.

503-3 ★ CUAL DE LOS DOS AMANTES-Canción ★ Az 5059

504-2 ★ DIGAN LO QUE DIGAN-Canción Ranchera (Jesús Favella) ★ Az 5060

505-6 ★ TAMPICO HERMOSO-Corrido ★ Az 5059

506-1 ★ ADIOS MORENITA LINDA-Canción (Jesús Favella) ★ Az 5060

DUETO MONTERREY con guitarras. Lydia and María Mendoza.

507-2 ★ SIGUE TU CAMINO-Canción ★ Az 5055, LP 8038(33)

508-3 ★ ESA GÜERITA-Ranchera ★ Az 5055

509-1 ★ CORAZON MARCHITO-Canción (L. Mendoza) ★ Az 5056, LP 8038(33), Peer(M) 5418

510-2 ★ NUESTRA SEPARACION-Canción ★ Az 5080, LP 8038(33)

JUANITA Y MARIA MENDOZA con guitarras.

511-1 ★ PARA ADORARTE A TI-Canción (Leonor Mendoza) ★ Az 5079

512-3 ★ LOS CASADOS MODERNOS-Corrido ★ Az 5139

513-1 ★ LO ADORO CON LOCURA-Canción Ranchera (Lydia Mendoza) ★ Az 5204

514-3 ★ POQUITO QUE ME QUIERAS-Canción Ranchera (Jesús Favella) ★ Az 5204

DUETO MONTERREY con guitarras. Lydia and María Mendoza.

515-3 ★ LA MANCORNADORA-Canción (M.B. Valle) ★ Az 5061

516-1 ★ TERESITA-Canción (Lydia Mendoza) ★ Az 5067, LP 8038(33)

517-3 ★ LAS CUATRO MILPAS-Ranchera (M. V. de Campo) ★ Az 5028, LP 8011(33)

518-4 ★ LAS VIOLETAS-Canción (Leonor Mendoza) ★ Az 5061, LP 8038(33)

JUANITA Y MARIA MENDOZA con guitarras.

519-1 ★ UNA MUJER DE ESTE BARRIO-Ranchera (Enrique Vela) ★ Az 5250

520-2 ★ MADRECITA LINDA-Canción (Jesús Favella) ★ Az 5104

521-2 ★ ANTONIA-Canción (Leonor Mendoza) ★ Az 5105

522-2 ★ ELENA POR QUE ESTAS TRISTE-Canción Ranchera (Jesús Favella) ★ Az 5079

DUETO MONTERREY con guitarras. Lydia and María Mendoza.

523-1 ★ PALOMA ERRANTE-Ranchera ★ Az 5062

524-2 ★ ALICIA-Canción (Leonor Mendoza) ★ Az 5062, LP 8038(33)

525-2 ★ LA NOCHE DE MAYO ★ Az 5194, LP 8011(33)

526-1 ★ MI CHATA-Ranchera (Manuel Mendoza) ★ Az 5080, LP 8038(33)

JUANITA Y MARIA MENDOZA con guitarras.

527-3 ★ SOÑE QUE ME JURABAS-Canción (Leonor Mendoza) ★ Az 5156, ARH 3017(33)

528-1 ★ CUQUITA-Ranchera (Tony García) ★ Az 5104

529-1 ★ QUISIERA SER COMO EL VIENTO-Canción Ranchera (Luis Moreno) ★ Az 5105

530-2 ★ PERDI UN AMOR-Canción (Rodríguez-Carranza) ★ Az 5184

DUETO MONTERREY con guitarras. Lydia and María Mendoza.

531-3 ★ MAÑANITAS TEXANAS-Serenata (Juan Gaitán) ★ Az 5056, Peer(M) 5418

532-1 ★ JOSEFINA-Canción (L. Mendoza) ★ Az 5093, LP 8040(33)

533-1 ★ LA PARRANDA-Ranchera (Manuel Mendoza) ★ Az 5066, LP 8038(33)

534-1 ★ ROSARIO NOCTURNO-Canción (Letra de M. Acuña; arr: L. Mendoza) ★ Az 5066

JUANITA Y MARIA MENDOZA con guitarras.

535-1 ★ TU POR ALLA YO POR ACA-Canción Ranchera (Jesús Favella) ★ Az 5250

536-1 ★ POR QUERERTE-Ranchera (Tony García) ★ Az 5156

537-1 ★ VALE MAS QUE TE ALEJES-Canción Ranchera (Leonor Mendoza) ★ Az 5198, FL 9035(33)

538-2 ★ DOS SERES QUE SE AMAN-Ranchera (P.J. González) ★ Az 5149, ARH 3017(33)

DUETO MONTERREY con guitarras. Lydia and María Mendoza.

539-2 ★ TRAIGANME OTRAS-Polka (L. Mendoza) ★ Az 5049, LP 8038(33)

540-3 ★ UN SENTIMIENTO DE AMOR-Canción ★ Az 5050

541-1 ★ PARA QUE-Canción ★ Az 5050, LP 8038(33)

542-4 ★ NO ME IMPORTA LO QUE HAS HECHO-Canción (arr: L. Alvarado) ★ Az 5049

JUANITA Y MARIA MENDOZA con guitarras.

543-2 ★ MORENITA DE OJOS NEGROS-Ranchera (Rodríguez-Carranza) ★ Az 5191

544-2 ★ CHAPARRITA DE MI VIDA-Ranchera (Felix Borrayo) ★ Az 5191

545-2 ★ VICIO INFELIZ-Canción (Leonor Mendoza) ★ Az 5149

546-2 ★ ESTE MUNDO INGRATO-Ranchera (Manuel Mendoza) ★ Az 5198

547-2 ★ YO VIVO EN LA PARRANDA-Canción Ranchera (Jesús Favella) ★ Az 5177, ARH 3017(33)

548-1 ★ MANUELITA-Canción (Félix Borrayo) ★ Az 5166, ARH 3017(33)

549-2 ★ PERO LUPITA-Canción (Leonor Mendoza) ★ Az 5177, ARH 3017(33)

550-2 ★ CHAPARRITA PRETENCIOSA-Ranchera (Lydia Mendoza) ★ Az 5166

DUETO MONTERREY con guitarras. Lydia and María Mendoza.
551-1 ★ DESDICHADA DE TI-Canción Ranchera (Leonor Mendoza) ★ Az 5199, LP 8011(33), FL 9035(33)

552-1 ★ AMELIA-Canción (arr.: L. Alvarado) ★ Az 5114

553-3 ★ UNA PLEGARIA A MI MADRE-Canción ★ Az 5194, LP 8011(33)

554-2 ★ ES TANTO LO QUE TE AMO-Canción (arr: L. Alvarado) ★ Az 5067

555-1 ★ TENGO UN AMOR-Ranchera (Luis Moreno) ★ Az 5114

556-3 ★ ANDA DILE A TU MAMA-Ranchera ★ Az 5208, LP 8011(33)

557-2 ★ POR QUE ERES ASI-Canción (Luis Moreno) ★ Az 5094

558-2 ★ MI RIVAL-Ranchera (Luis Moreno) ★ Az 5199, LP 8011(33)

JUANITA Y MARIA MENDOZA con guitarras.
559-2 ★ TRAGEDIA DE SEVERITA-Corrido ★ Az 5113

560-2 ★ YO SIEMPRE TE QUIERO-Canción (Luis Moreno) ★ Az 5113

561-3 ★ AY QUE SIENTO EN MI-Canción (Leonor Mendoza) ★ Az 5092

562-2 ★ CADA VEZ QUE ME ACUERDO-Canción (Luis Moreno) ★ Az 5091, ARH 3017(33)

DUETO MONTERREY con guitarras. Lydia and María Mendoza.
563-3 ★ PERLITA-Canción (C. Carrión y M. Lugo) ★ Az 5094

564-3 ★ VIVIRE FELIZ-Canción (Manuel Mendoza) ★ Az 5093, LP 8040(33)

565-1 ★ MUJER, MUJER-Canción (L. Mendoza) ★ Az 5225, LP 8011(33)

566-2 ★ sev BESOS Y CERVEZAS-Canción ★ Az 5225, LP 8011(33)

JUANITA Y MARIA MENDOZA con guitarras. Los Angeles, CA, 1952.
643-1 ★ QUIEN SERA-Canción Ranchera (Jesús Favella) ★ Az 5119

644-1 ★ LUKY LUKY-Corrido (Manuel B. Gómez) ★ Az 5119

645-2 ★ AY QUE LINDO ES TU MIRAR-Ranchera (A.R. Aragón) ★ Az 5120

646-1 ★ YA ME CANSE DE ESPERAR-Canción Ranchera (Jesús Favella) ★ Az 5120

DUETO MONTERREY con guitarras. Lydia and María Mendoza.
651-3 ★ TUS OJITOS CHAPARRITA-Canción ★ Az 5167

652-1 ★ DOS PAJARITOS-Ranchera ★ Az 5118

653-3 ★ SOY DE MONTERREY-Corrido ★ Az 5118

654-1 ★ TE VENGO A DECIR ADIOS-Ranchera (R. Rodríguez y A. Carranza) ★ Az 5157

JUANITA Y MARIA MENDOZA con guitarras.
655-3 ★ EL DESQUITE-Canción (Rodríguez-Carranza) ★ Az 5159, ARH 3017(33)

656-3 ★ TU SENTENCIA-Ranchera (Luis Moreno) ★ Az 5159, ARH 3017(33)

657-2 ★ YA ME VOY DE VACILON-Ranchera ★ Az 5139

658-2 ★ EL RESBALOSO-Canción Ranchera (Miguel Salas) ★ Az 5144, ARH 3017(33)

DUETO MONTERREY con guitarras. Lydia and María Mendoza.
659-2 ★ AQUELLAS NOCHES FELICES-Ranchera ★ Az 5167

660-1 ★ HIJO INGRATO-Corrido ★ Az 5151

661-1 ★ MAS VALE QUE NO-Canción Ranchera (Lorenzo Hernández) ★ Az 5157

662-3 ★ JUNTITOS TU Y YO-Ranchera ★ Az 5151

JUANITA Y MARIA MENDOZA con guitarras.

663-1 ★ LOS PACHUCOS-Corrido (R. Rodríguez y A. Carranza) ★ Az 5184, FL 9035(33)

664-1 ★ POR AHI SE DICE-Ranchera (Luis Moreno) ★ Az 5140, ARH 3017(33), Peer(M) 5440

665-1 ★ CONSENTIDA-Ranchera (Luis Moreno) ★ Az 5133

666-2 ★ LA RANCHERITA-Corrido (Miguel Salas) ★ Az 5133

DUETO MONTERREY con guitarras. Lydia and María Mendoza.

667-1 ★ VENTE CONMIGO-Canción ★ Az 5160

668-2 ★ TRIGUEÑA DEL ALMA-Ranchera ★ Az 5160

669-1 ★ ME VOY PA'L NORTE-Ranchera (Lorenzo Hernández) ★ Az 5134, LP 8011(33)

670-3 ★ NACHO BERNAL-Corrido (Luis Moreno) ★ Az 5134, LP 8011(33)

JUANITA Y MARIA MENDOZA con guitarras.

671-2 ★ UNA CARTA A ROSITA-Ranchera (Jacinto Gómez) ★ Az 5132

672-1 ★ ALGUN DIA-Ranchera (Rafael Villarreal) ★ Az 5132, ARH 3017(33)

673-2 ★ BELLAS MORENAS-Ranchera (Jesús Favella) ★ Az 5140, Peer(M) 5440

674-2 ★ ME CAES PESETA-Ranchera (Rafael Villarreal) ★ Az 5144

DUETO MONTERREY con guitarras. Lydia and María Mendoza.

675-1 ★ AYER SE ENOJO MI AMOR-Ranchera ★ Az 5189

676-1 ★ SIEMPRE SUFRIENDO ★ Az 5189

677-1 ★ HAZTE MAS PA'CA-Canción ★ Az 5145

678-1 ★ SI QUIERES SI PUEDES-Ranchera ★ Az 5145

JUANITA Y MARIA MENDOZA con el Conjunto Sánchez. Los Angeles, CA, early 1953.

(Note: During this period 78 rpm records were being phased out and 45 rpm records were becoming the main medium for singles. I suspect most releases from the following session were issued in both formats.)

767-3 ★ DE SOLDADO A GENERAL-Corrido (Víctor Cordero) ★ Az 5211

768-3 ★ ASI SOY YO-Ranchera (Víctor Cordero) ★ Az 5211

769-1 ★ MI VIDA SI TIENES-Corrido ★ Az 5218

770-4 ★ ERRANTE Y PERDIDO-Ranchera (Rafael Villareal) ★ Az 5245, LP 8008(33)

771-5 ★ BUENA SUERTE-Ranchera (Manuel B. Gómez) ★ Az 5222

772-5 ★ MUCHOS DIAS DE ESTOS-Ranchera ★ Az 5229

773-6 ★ SIN RUMBO-Canción (Víctor Cordero) ★ Az 5245, LP 8008(33)

774-5 ★ CORRIDO DE JUAN VASQUEZ (Víctor Cordero) ★ Az 5222, FL 9043(33)

775-6 ★ NO PIERDO LAS ESPERANZAS-Ranchera (Miguel Salas) ★ Az 5266, LP 8008(33)

776-7 ★ YO VOY POR EL CAMINO ★ Az 5229

777-4 ★ JUANITA QUERIDA-Ranchera ★ Az 5274, LP 8008(33)

778-6 ★ ESTOY PRISIONERO-Corrido (Víctor Cordero) ★ Az 5266, LP 8008(33)

779-7 ★ JUGUE Y PERDI-Ranchera (Alfredo Parra) ★ Az 5233

780-7 ★ SECRETOS DEL AMOR-Canción Ranchera (Víctor Cordero) ★ Az 5240, LP 8008(33)

781-9 ★ ARREPENTIDA-Ranchera (Alfredo Parra) ★ Az 5240, LP 8008(33)

782-6 ★ ESPERAR-Ranchera ★ Az 5274, LP 8008(33)

783-7 ★ FLORIDO MICHOACAN-Canción Vals (Víctor Cordero) ★ Az 5218

784-8 ★ EL ATRAVESADO-Corrido ★ Az 5260, LP 8008(33)

785-9 ★ SI ALGUN DIA-Canción Ranchera ★ Az 5260, LP 8008(33)

786-8 ★ EN DONDE ESTARAS-Ranchera (Luis Moreno) ★ Az 5233

(Note: Azteca LP collections 8035 and 8039 by various artists do include selections by Lydia Mendoza (8035) and Las Hermanas Mendoza (8039). We do not have these LPs and, consequently, do not know the titles of the selections.)

MENDOZA FAMILY DISCOGRAPHY: SECTION 3
Acme, Aguila, Alamo, Colonial,
Columbia of México, Corona,
Globe, Imperial, Río, Sargento

ACME RECORDS

JUANITA Y MARIA MENDOZA con Armando San Miguel y conjunto. San Antonio, TX, ca. 1956

QUE SUERTE LA MIA-Ranchera (J.A. Jiménez) ★ Acme 103(45)

COMADRES CHISMOLERAS-Ranchera (M.C. Valdéz-Daniel Garzes) ★ Acme 103(45)

AGUILA RECORDS

(Note: The Paloma LP jacket lists the last two titles below but they are, in fact, not included on the disk. Paloma LP 1011 was manufactured by Azteca Records and listed in the Azteca catalog.)

LYDIA MENDOZA con el Mariachi Aguila. Los Angeles, CA, ca. late 1950s.

LAGRIMAS DE VINO ★ Paloma 1011(33)

MUCHOS BESOS ★ Aguila 5036B, Paloma 1011(33)

FLOR DE MEXICALI ★ Paloma 1011(33)

PORQUE TE VAS (listed incorrectly on the disk as: POR QUE SERA.) ★ Paloma 1011(33)

MIRA MIRA ★ Aguila 5035, Paloma 1011(33)

EL QUELITE ★ Paloma 1011(33)

SOLDADO RAZO ★ Paloma 1011(33)

POR QUE ME ENGAÑASTE ★ Aguila 5036A, Paloma 1011(33)

(Note: On the label of LP 1011 title is given as "Porque te quiero")

HORAS FELICES ★ Aguila 5035

CELOSA ★ Aguila unknown release

NO TE VAYAS GOLONDRINA ★ Aguila unknown release

ALAMO RECORDS

HERMANAS MENDOZA: Juanita y María con el conjunto Alamo.
Leandro Guerrero-accordion; with probably: Willy Gonzáles-bajo sexto and Frank Corrales-guitar. Recorded at KCOR Studios. San Antonio, TX, ca. 1953.

R 073A ★ UNA CARTA PARA COREA-Canción (Rudy Guerrero) ★ Alamo 073-A

R 073B ★ QUE SUERTE LA MIA-Canción (J.A. Jiménez) ★ Alamo 073-B

R 076A ★ CONTESTACION A QUE SUERTE LA MIA (Jiménez-Cipriano) ★ Alamo 076-A

R O76B ★ EL CHISME (Juan Gaytán) ★ Alamo 076-B

R 077A ★ NO VOLVERE (Perón-Cortázar) ★ Alamo 077-A, FL 9035(33)

R 077B ★ EL GÜERO POLVOS (Juan Gaytán) ★ Alamo 077-B, FL 9035(33)

R 078A ★ LA PRISION DE COLORADO-Corrido ★ Alamo 078-A

R 078B ★ AMIGOS DE MI CAMADA ★ Alamo 078-B

(Note: Alamo 074 and 075 are not by the Mendozas.)

COLONIAL RECORDS

HERMANAS MENDOZA: Juanita y María con el Conjunto Norteño.
Including piano, accordion, etc. Los Angeles, CA, ca. 1952.

CR 105 ★ RESBALOSA-Polka (E. Navarrete) ★ Colonial 103-A

CR 106 ★ YA NO LLORES-Ranchera (Arturo Mosqueda) ★ Colonial 103-B

CR 107 ★ AHORA SOY YO-Polka (A. Mosqueda) ★ Colonial 119(45/78)

CR 108 ★ DERROTADA-Ranchera (Esteban Navarrete) ★ Colonial 119(45/78), Colonial 361(45)

CR 109 ★ JAMAS TE OLVIDO-Ranchera (Esteban Navarrete) ★ Colonial 107, Colonial 361(45)

CR 110 ★ EL ESTIBADOR-Corrido (Chato Beltrán) ★ Colonial 107

LYDIA MENDOZA y su guitarra con el Conjunto Norteño.

CR 258 ★ COMO UN PERRO-Bolero (S. Mirón) ★ Colonial 172

CR 259 ★ NO SEAS TONTA-Ranchera (NC) ★ Colonial 172, 538(45)

CR 260 ★ NO TE VAYAS-Ranchera (Cuco Sánchez) ★ Colonial 178, 538(45)

CR 261 ★ TU DI QUE SI-Ranchera (M.H. Miramontes) ★ Colonial 178

CR 262 ★ FUE MENTIRA-Bolero (A.E. Oteo) ★ Colonial 199(45)

CR 263 ★ SUFRO POR TI-Ranchera (Manuel Miramontes) ★ Colonial 199(45)

COLUMBIA RECORDS of MEXICO

LYDIA MENDOZA con el Conjunto Los Parachicos
With unknown accordion, guitar and string bass. Monterrey, N.L., México, October 12, 1951.

Mex-1716 ★ NOCHES DE ANGUSTIA-Ranchera (Arturo Mosqueda) ★ Co (M) 2133-C

Mex-1717 ★ UN HOMBRE CASADO-(José Morante) ★ Co (M) 2249-C, CBS(M)(33) TC-0668

Mex-1718 ★ EL CHISME-Corrido (Juan Gaytán) ★ Co (M) 2133-C, OK(M)LP 10254(33)

Mex-1719 ★ NO ME ABANDONES-Tango Canción (M.S. Acuña) ★ Co (M) 2301-C

LYDIA MENDOZA con Los Montañeses del Alamo.
Pedro, Jaime and Nicandro Mier. With alto sax, flute, guitar and string bass. Monterrey, N. L., Mexico, October 12, 1951.

Mex-1720 ★ FIGURACION (Aveline Alanis) ★ Co (M) 2203, OK(M)LP 10254(33)

Mex-1723 ★ LLANTO PERDIDO-Blues Ranchera (José Morante) ★ Co (M) 2301-C

Mex 1724 ★ PARA QUE SON PASIONES-Ranchera Popular ★ Co (M) 2249, OK(M)LP 10254(33)

Mex 1725 ★ LA TRAIDORA (José A. Jiménez) ★ Co (M) 2203

(Note: Mex-1721/22 are by Los Montañeses del Alamo.)

LYDIA MENDOZA con el Mariachi Jalisciense de Rubén Fuentes
With one trumpet, violins, guitarrón, and others. México, D.F., México, June 23, 1952.

Mex-2047 ★ ASI ES EL MUNDO ★ Co (M) 2936-C

Mex-2048 ★ ESPERO TU REGRESO-Bolero (Daniel Garzes) ★ Co (M) 2378-C, CBS(M)(33) TC-0668

Mex-2049 ★ DESTINO CRUEL-Ranchera (Jesús Cabral) ★ Co (M) 2433-C

Mex-2050 ★ BELLA ILUSION-Canción Vals (Víctor Cordero) ★ Co (M) 2378-C

Mex-2051 ★ NUNCA TE CREAS-Ranchera (P.J. Gonzales) ★ Co (M) 2433-C

Mex-2052 ★ LLORANDO EN SILENCIO ★ Co (M) 2936-C

Mex-2053 ★ NI AMOR NI DINERO (José A. Morante) ★ Co (M) 2506-C, OK(M)LP 10254(33)

Mex-2054 ★ ESTARAS CONMIGO-Bolero (José Morante) ★ Co (M) 2565-C

Mex-2055 ★ OLVIDA TODO AQUELLO-Ranchera (Ramón Ortega Contreras) ★ Co (M) 2565-C

LYDIA MENDOZA con guitarra and bajo sexto. Same session as last.

Mex-2056 ★ BODA NEGRA-Canción Colombiana (Popular) ★ Co (M) 2433-C, OK(M)LP 10254(33)

JUANITA Y MARIA MENDOZA con Los Montañeses del Alamo. Monterrey, N.L., or México City, México, January 16, 1953.

Mex-2320 ★ YO BIEN QUISIERA-Ranchera ★ Co (M) 2587-C

Mex-2321 ★ POR NINGUN MOTIVO-Ranchera (Johnny Herrera) ★ Co (M) 2587-C

LYDIA MENDOZA con los Montañeses del Alamo.

Mex-2322 ★ QUE HARIA USTED-Ranchera (Víctor Cordero) ★ Co (M) 2593

Mex-2323 ★ SOLO QUE LA MAR SE SEQUE-Ranchera (NC) ★ Co (M) 2593, CBS(M)(33)TC-0668

HERMANAS MENDOZA: Juanita y María con los Montañeses del Alamo. February 25, 1953.

Mex-2396 ★ EN LA MONTAÑA AZUL-Ranchera (Víctor Cordero) ★ Co (M) 2624-C

Mex-2397 ★ RAYANDO EL SOL-Ranchera (NC) ★ Co (M) 2624-C

JUANITA Y MARIA MENDOZA con Los Montañeses del Alamo. April 10, 1953.

Mex-2450 ★ LA YEDRA-Corrido (M.V. Elizondo) ★ Co (M) 2650-C

Mex-2451 ★ EL CELOSO-Corrido (arr. F. Valdez Leal) ★ Co (M) 2650-C

LYDIA MENDOZA con el conjunto de Toño Zepeda.
With piano, trumpet, string bass, conga or bongo drums. April 10, 1953.

Mex-2456 ★ CON TODO EL CORAZON-Bolero (Daniel Garcés) ★ Co (M) 2663-C

Mex-2457 ★ A MI NO ME INTERESA-Bolero (Víctor Cordero) ★ Co (M) 2663-C

LYDIA MENDOZA. July 23, 1953.

Mex-2693 ★ QUE PASO, POS QUE PASO ★ Co (M) 2795-C

Mex-2694 ★ MI AVENTURA ★ Co (M) 2795-C

JUANITA Y MARIA MENDOZA con los Montañeses del Alamo.

Mex-2879-1 ★ SOLO Y TRISTE-Ranchera (Nicandro Mier) ★ Co (M) 2937-C

Mex-2880-1 ★ EL DIA QUE TE CASES-Corrido (F. Valdez Leal) ★ Co (M) 2937-C

HERMANAS MENDOZA: Juanita y María con el conjunto de Humberto Reyes. With accordion, guitar and string bass. November 24, 1953.

Mex-3153-1 ★ PORDIOSERA DE AMOR-Ranchera (Jesús Rodríguez M.) ★ Co (M) 3079-C

Mex-3154-1 ★ AMOR COMPRADO-Ranchera (Jesús Ramos) ★ Co (M) 3079-C

LYDIA MENDOZA con Los Alegres de Terán. Monterrey, N.L., México, August 22, 1954.

Mex-3499-1 ★ VIDITA MIA-Ranchera (Manuel Valdez) ★ Co (M) 3410-C, Seeco 78-12024B & 45-12024B, OK(M)LP 10254(33)

Mex-3500-1 ★ SAQUEN PAÑUELOS-Ranchera (Federico Curiel) ★ Co (M) 3545-C, OK(M)LP 10254(33)

Mex-3501-1 ★ ADIOS SIN LLANTO-Fox Blues (José Morante) ★ Co (M) 3366-C

Mex-3502-1 ★ COMO DE QUE NO-Bolero Ranchera (Nicolás G. Curiel) ★ Co (M) 3254-C

Mex-3503-1 ★ LOCA, LOCA, LOCA-Ranchera (Federico Curiel) ★ Co (M) 3410-C, Seeco 78-12024A & 45-12024A, OK(M)LP 10254(33)

Mex-3504-1 ★ AVE DE PASO-Bolero (Federico Curiel) ★ Co (M) 3366-C, OK(M)LP 10254(33)

Mex-3505-1 ★ SIN TEMOR-Bolero (José Morante) ★ Co (M) 3545-C

Mex-3506-1 ★ CORAZON DE CERA-(José Morante) ★ Co (M) 3254-C, OK(M)LP 10254(33)

(Note: Title of OK(M) LP 10254: LA INCOMPARABLE LYDIA MENDOZA.)

JUANITA Y MARIA MENDOZA con el conjunto de Humberto Reyes. September 14, 1954.

Mex-3549-1 ★ MALDITA HERMOSURA-Ranchera (R. Cardona Jr.) ★ Co (M) 3290-C, Seeco 12019

Mex-3550-1 ★ NO ME VENGAS PRESUMIENDO-Canción Ranchera (Esteban Navarrete) ★ Co (M) 3290-C, Seeco 12019

MARIA MENDOZA con Los Rurales de Gilberto Parra. With accordion, bajo sexto and string bass. Probably Monterrey, N.L., México, November 21, 1956.

Mex-4900-1 ★ NI QUE AGRADECERTE-Ranchera (José Morante) ★ Co (M) 3923-C

Mex-4901-1 ★ TORMENTO Y CASTIGO-Ranchera (José Morante) ★ Co (M) 3923-C

CORONA RECORDS

MARIA MENDOZA. San Antonio, TX. ca. 1955

LOS QUE SE QUIEREN SE QUIEREN ★ Corona 2103

POR ELLA ★ Corona 2103

LYDIA MENDOZA con su guitarra.
Juan Viesca-bass. San Antonio, TX, ca. 1960s.

5201 ★ MADRECITA ADORADA-Canción (NC) ★ Corona 2332(45), LP 3003(33), Big Star C-7089

5202 ★ EN TU DIA-Canción (Leonor Mendoza) ★ Corona 2332(45), LP 3003(33), Big Star C-7089

5215 ★ EL QUELITE-Ranchera (NC) ★ Corona 2339(45), LP 3003(33), Big Star C-7089

5216 ★ AQUELLAS CARICIAS-Canción (NC) ★ Corona 2339(45), LP 3003(33), Big Star C-7089

5229 ★ PAJARILLO BARRANQUEÑO-Canción (NC) ★ Corona 2346(45), LP 3003(33), Big Star C-7089

5230 ★ CUANDO ESCUCHES ESTE VALS-Vals (NC) ★ Corona 2346(45), LP 3003(33), Big Star C-7089

5239 ★ EL ABANDONADO-Ranchera (NC) ★ Corona 2351(45), LP 3003(33), Big Star C-7089

5240 ★ LA VALENTINA-Ranchera (NC) ★ Corona 2351(45), LP 3003(33), Big Star C-7089

5289 ★ LOS BESOS DE MI NEGRA-Ranchera (L. Mendoza) ★ Corona 2374(45), LP 3003(33), Big Star C-7089

5290 ★ MUNDO ENGAÑOSO-Ranchera (NC) ★ Corona 2374(45), LP 3003(33), Big Star C-7089

(*Note: The title of Corona LP 3003 is: EN TU DIA.)

LYDIA MENDOZA con conjunto.

(Note: Santiago Jiménez, Jr.-accordion on #s 5325, 5326, and 5364. ca. 1966.

5325 ★ CORAZON YA NO LLORES-Ranchera* (NC) ★ Corona 2393(45)

5326 ★ TU FALSIA-Ranchera* (L. Mendoza) ★ Corona 2393(45)

5351 ★ CELOSA-(NC) ★ Corona 2403(45)

5352 ★ CARGA BLANCA-(M.C. Valdez) ★ Corona 2403(45)

5363 ★ MAL HOMBRE-Ranchera (NC) ★ Corona 2410(45)

5364 ★ AQUEL AMOR QUE YO JAMAS-Canción* (Linda Almanza) ★ Corona 2410(45)

FELIZ CUMPLEAÑOS ★ LP 3003(33), Big Star C-7089

LAS MAÑANITAS ★ LP 3003(33), Big Star C-7089

GLOBE RECORDS

LYDIA MENDOZA con guitarras. San Antonio, TX, ca. late 1945 or early 1946.

APP 18 A ★ SOMOS DIFERENTES-Bolero (B. Ruiz) ★ Globe 2001

APP 18 B ★ TEQUILA CON LIMON-Canción (M. Esperón) ★ Globe 2001

APP 19 A ★ NOCHECITA-Bolero (N. Delgado-F. Fernández) ★ Globe 2002

APP 19 B ★ TANTO COMO TE AME-Vals Canción (NC) ★ Globe 2002

HERMANITAS MENDOZA: Juanita y María con Lydia Mendoza (guitar).

APP 20 A ★ CLETO RODRIGUEZ-Corrido (A. Vásquez) ★ Globe 2003

APP 20 B ★ LA BARCA DE ORO-Canción (NC) ★ Globe 2003

LYDIA MENDOZA con guitarras.

APP 36 A ★ TRAIGO UN AMOR-Canción (NC) ★ Globe 2008

APP 36 B ★ LA PALOMA MENSAJERA-Canción (NC) ★ Globe 2008

IMPERIAL RECORDS

LYDIA MENDOZA y conjunto.

Although Lydia Mendoza's name appears on the labels of all releases of the first two selections, apparently to capitalize on her name, masters 287 and 288 are actually sung by Las Hermanas Mendoza, Juanita and María Mendoza.

Lydia Mendoza-12-string guitar; possibly María Mendoza-second guitar; unknown string bass. Probably San Antonio, TX, ca. 1947.

DI 287 ★ POR ULTIMA VEZ-Corrido (Frank Cantú) ★ Imp 230, Colony 113, Anfión (M) 20-005

DI 288 ★ PETRITA ★ Imp 230, Colony 113, Anfión (M) 20-005

LYDIA MENDOZA vocals and guitar. Probably San Antonio, TX, ca. 1948.

DI 381 ★ ENGAÑO DE AMOR (Manuel Mendoza or Pablo Sánchez) ★ Imp 288

DI 382 ★ EL ARBOLITO ★ Imp 331

DI 383 ★ MAL HOMBRE (José Rodríguez) ★ Imp 279, Anfión (M) 20-038A

DI 384 ★ AGUILA O SOL (P. Sánchez) ★ Imp 331

DI 385 ★ LLEGASTE-Canción (A. Villareal) ★ Imp 258

DI 386 ★ FALSARIA (José Rodríguez) ★ Imp 403

DI 387 ★ EL BUQUE DE MAS POTENCIA-Corrido (C. Cuevas) ★ Imp 279, Anfión (M) 20-038A

DI 388 ★ VIDITA MIA (José Rodríguez) ★ Imp 258

LYDIA MENDOZA vocals and guitar. Probably San Antonio, TX, ca. 1949-50.

DI 465 ★ AMOR CON AMOR SE PAGA-Corrido (Tradicional) ★ Imp 288

DI 466 ★ Unknown Title ★ Imp Unissued

HERMANAS MENDOZA (Lydia and María)
Con el Mariachi Imperial: one trumpet, violins, etc. Probably Los Angeles, CA, ca. 1950-51.

DI 559 ★ EL JARDINERO-Canción Polka (Tony García) ★ Imp 366

DI 560 ★ ME ENGAÑASTE-Canción Polka (Rubén Escamilla) ★ Imp 354

DI 561 ★ A MANOS-Canción Polka (Jesús Ramos) ★ Imp 354

DI 562 ★ NI CELOS NI RENCOR-Canción Polka (Jesús Ramos) ★ Imp 366

HERMANAS MENDOZA (Juanita and María Mendoza)
Con José Rodríguez y su conjunto: piano, accordion, guitar and bass. Probably Los Angeles, CA, ca. 1950-51.

DI 595 ★ ESTER, POR DIOS-Polka (Eusebio Rosas) ★ Imp 391

DI 596 ★ QUE BONITOS OJOS TIENES-Polka (Luis Moreno) ★ Imp 439

DI 597 ★ EL DESGRACIADO-Canción (Valente Ramírez) ★ Imp 403

DI 598 ★ CUANDO MAÑANA-Canción (Víctor Cordero) ★ Imp 391

HERMANAS MENDOZA con el Mariachi del Norte.

DI 599 ★ NO QUIERO VERTE LLORAR-Canción (Víctor Cordero) ★ Imp 377, Co (M) 1878-C

DI 600 ★ MORENA DE MI VIDA-Polka (Eusebio Rosas) ★ Imp 377, Co (M) 1878-C

DI 601 ★ NO ESTES CREYENDO-Canción (Eusebio Rosas) ★ Imp 383, Co (M) 1689-C

DI 602 ★ MUJER CANTINERA-Polka (Víctor Cordero) ★ Imp 383, Co (M) 1689-C

HERMANAS MENDOZA con El Mariachi El Prado. Probably Los Angeles, CA, ca. 1952.

DI 703 ★ EL AFORTUNADO-Canción Ranchera (Jesús Ramos) ★ Imp 460

DI 704 ★ TE HAS DE ACORDAR-Canción Ranchera (Jesús Ramos) ★ Imp 537

DI 705 ★ DE QUE TE SIRVE-Polka Canción (Víctor Cordero) ★ Imp 429

DI 706 ★ NO TE MOLESTES-Polka Canción (Jesús Ramos) ★ Imp 487

DI 707 ★ QUE BONITO ES EL QUERER-Polka Canción (Luis Moreno) ★ Imp 537

DI 708 ★ ESTA PASION-Canción Ranchera (Luis Moreno) ★ Imp 487

DI 709 ★ ISABELITA (Víctor Cordero) ★ Imp 439

DI 710 ★ BORRACHO ALEGRE-Polka Canción (Luis Moreno) ★ Imp 460

DI 711 ★ FLOR MARCHITA-Canción Ranchera (Luis Moreno) ★ Imp 429

LYDIA MENDOZA con el Conjunto de Aurelio García B.
Saxophone, accordion, bass and guitar. Probably Los Angeles, CA, ca. 1954.

DI 1142 ★ HASTA CUANDO CHAPARRITA (Arturo Mosqueda) ★ Imp 662(45)

DI 1143 ★ MANO A MANO-Polka (arr. de A. Mosqueda) ★ Imp 662(45)

DI 1144 ★ NO ME QUEJO-Ranchera (E. Navarrete) ★ Imp 654, Imp 654(45), Co (M) 2979-C

DI 1145 ★ PRISIONERO DEL RECUERDO-Ranchera (Mariano Peña) ★ Imp 654, Imp 654(45), Co (M) 2979-C

VI PASAR ★ Imp 1066 (?)

MEDALLA DE DIOS ★ Imp 1066 (?)

RIO RECORDS

HERMANAS MENDOZA con el conjunto de Ruco Villarreal.
Accordion, bajo sexto and string bass. San Antonio, TX, ca.1950-51.

R-1129 ★ TU ERES CULPABLE-Ranchera (Daniel Garcés) ★ Rio 341

R-1130 ★ CONTESTACION A MUJER PASEADA-Ranchera (Garcés-Valdez) ★ Rio 341

SARGENTO RECORDS

HERMANAS MENDOZA: Juanita y María con el conjunto Los Tres Sargentos y Don Tacho.
(Probably Rubén Galván-accordion; René Hinojosa-bajo sexto; probably Don Tacho-bass.) Houston, TX, ca. 1952.

ACA 1001A ★ YO TRAIGO UN SENTIMENTO-Canción Polka (Daniel Garcés) ★ Sargento 1001

ACA 1001B ★ NO TE PUEDO OLVIDAR-Canción Ranchera (Daniel Garcés) ★ Sargento 1001

MENDOZA FAMILY DISCOGRAPHY: SECTION 4

IDEAL RECORDS

Ideal used no matrix numbers and apparently issued everything more or less in sequence. The Fony label issued some Ideal masters in Mexico. Many Ideal masters, if not all, were pressed and distributed on the Ideal label in Mexico by Muebles Modernos in Monterrey, Nuevo León. All recordings by the Mendoza family, unless noted, were recorded in Alice, Texas by Armando Marroquín for the Rio Grande Music Company in San Benito, Texas owned by Paco Betancourt. The dates noted as recording dates show the month when the order for the plating of the discs was placed and the label was ordered.

LYDIA MENDOZA vocal and guitar.
David González-second vocal, Narciso Martínez-accordion, Reynaldo Barrera-bajo, Lorenzo Caballero-contrabajo. Alice, TX, January, 1950.
BELLA JOVENCITA-Canción ★ Ideal 418

VOLVER A VIVIR-Canción (Lorenzo Caballero) ★ Ideal 418

ANGEL DE MIS ENSUEÑOS-Canción ★ Ideal 424

RECUERDOS DE UNA INGRATA-Canción ★ Ideal 424

JUANITA Y MARIA MENDOZA con la orquesta de Beto Villa. August, 1950.
YO-Canción (Marcos Jiménez) ★ Ideal 476

EL BORRACHALES-Corrido ★ Ideal 476

PONTE ALERTA-Canción (NC) ★ Ideal 484

TRES CONSEJOS-Canción (José Morante) ★ Ideal 484, ARH CD/C 341

LYDIA MENDOZA con la orquesta de Beto Villa. August, 1950.
FELIZ SIN TI-Bolero (José Morante) ★ Ideal 480, ILP 120(33), Fony 114(33), ARH CD/C 341

TE QUIERES IR-Bolero (José Morante) ★ Ideal 480, ILP 120(33), Fony 114(33)

EL DEBER DE LOS DOS-Canción (Lorenzo Caballero) ★ Ideal 593

MI SENDERO DE AMOR-Canción (Ed. Vela) ★ Ideal 593

LYDIA MENDOZA con el Mariachi Ideal.
(Note: José Morante sings second voice on last two sides of this section.) October, 1950.
AMOR CON AMOR SE PAGA-Canción (M. Esperón & E. Cortázar) ★ Ideal 513, ILP 120(33), Fony 114(M)(33)

SOY REBELDE-Canción (José Morante) ★ Ideal 513, ILP 120(33), Fony 114(M)(33)

ESPINA DE TU DOLOR-Canción (José Morante) ★ Ideal 519

SEGUIRE TUS PASOS-Canción Rédova (Lorenzo Caballero) ★ Ideal 519

EN CADA COPA-Corrido (José Morante) ★ Ideal 525

DESDICHADOS SEREMOS-Canción (José Morante) ★ Ideal 525

JUANITA Y MARIA MENDOZA con el Mariachi Ideal. October, 1950.
UN CHAVO DE LA PALOMA-Canción (Manuel Valdez) ★ Ideal 512

RIFLE Y MANGO-Canción (NC) ★ Ideal 512

A NADIE LE IMPORTA-Canción (M.C. Valdez) ★ Ideal 523

TORMENTO INGRATO-Canción (M.C. Valdéz) (as by: Juanita Mendoza) ★ Ideal 523

SI NO TE GUSTA-Schottische (M.C. Valdez) ★ Ideal 529

MARCANDO VAS-Canción (José Morante) ★ Ideal 529

CUANDO JUEGUE EL ALBUR (José A. Jiménez) ★ Ideal 538

ANGEL DE MI ADORACION (M. Valdéz) ★ Ideal 538

TE QUIERO TANTO-Canción (NC) ★ Ideal 549

DOS AMORES COMPRENDIDOS (M.C. Valdez) ★ Ideal 549

LYDIA MENDOZA con el conjunto de Narciso Martínez. January, 1951.
A TI MADRE-Canción ★ Ideal 553, ILP 120(33), Fony 114(M)(33)

EL QUE A HIERRO MATA-Canción ★ Ideal 553, ILP 120(33)

JUANITA Y MARIA MENDOZA con el Conjunto de Narciso Martínez.
AMORCITO ENCANTADOR-Vals (José V. Franco) ★ Ideal 560

NO TE ME AQUERENCIES-Canción (María Alma) ★ Ideal 560

HOMBRE DE LA CALLE-Canción (Juan Gaytán) ★ Ideal 576

VEN LINDA MORENA (NC) ★ Ideal 576

ARRANCAME EL CORAZON-Canción (Raul Díaz) ★ Ideal 584, FL 9055(33)(C), ARH CD 361

SE FUE LA INGRATA-Canción (Jorge Tapia) ★ Ideal 584

YERBA MALA-Canción (F. Valdez Leal) ★ Ideal 623

DATE GUSTO VIDA MIA-Canción ★ Ideal 623

LYDIA (MENDOZA) Y LAURA (HERNANDEZ-CANTÚ) con el conjunto de Narciso Martínez.

POR NO HABERME QUERIDO-Canción Fox ★ Ideal 593

TRES GOTAS DE ROCIO-Danza ★ Ideal 561

JUANITA Y MARIA MENDOZA con el Conjunto Ideal. May, 1951.

TENDRAS QUE ARREPENTIRTE-Canción (M. Ortiz Villacarta) ★ Ideal 595

DICES QUE TE VAS-Canción Schottis ★ Ideal 595

AMOR ESCONDIDO-Canción (Rubén Fuentes) ★ Ideal 606

AQUI ME TIENES-Canción (M.C. Valdez) ★ Ideal 606

NO ME IMPORTA EL PASADO-Canción (M.C. Valdez) ★ Ideal 614

LEJOS, LEJOS-Canción ★ Ideal 614

ES MEJOR SEPARARNOS-Canción (M.C. Valdez) ★ Ideal 634

JUAN JOSE MALDONADO-Corrido (M.C. Valdez) ★ Ideal 634

SI TU ME QUIERES-Canción (Emilio Cáceres) ★ Ideal 637

NO TIENES VERGÜENZA-Canción (M.C. Valdez) ★ Ideal 637

NUESTRO OLVIDO-Canción ★ Ideal 656

UN MAR DE LAGRIMAS-Canción ★ Ideal 656

JUANITA Y MARIA MENDOZA con el Conjunto de Valerio Longoria. Valerio Longoria-accordion; con bajo sexto y contrabajo. September 1951.

QUE CHIQUITITAS-Corrido (Rubén Méndez del Castillo) ★ Ideal 642

TE ABORREZCO MAS Y MAS-Canción (M.C. Valdez) ★ Ideal 642

TU DESTINO-Canción (José V. Franco) ★ Ideal 650

EL GÜERO CANDELARIO-Corrido (M.C. Valdez) ★ Ideal 650

DESTROZAS MI QUERER-Canción (Valerio Longoria) ★ Ideal 685

AMOR Y DESPRECIO-Canción (M.C. Valdez) ★ Ideal 685

LYDIA MENDOZA con el Conjunto Los Rebeldes. Saxophone, clarinet, guitar & bass. October, 1951.

INFAME TRAICION-Canción (M.M. Carreón) ★ Ideal 659

TRISTE ES LA VIDA-Canción (José V. Franco) ★ Ideal 659

JUANITA MENDOZA con el Conjunto de Al Méndez. Two reeds, guitar, bass and piano (on some). This conjunto sounds exactly like Los Rebeldes. October, 1951.

LOCA SI, TONTA NO-Canción (M.C. Valdez) ★ Ideal 662-A

TE VAS O TE QUEDAS-Canción (José Alfredo Jiménez) ★ Ideal 662-B

LYDIA MENDOZA con el Conjunto de Al Méndez. October, 1951.

PRISIONERA-Canción (José Alfredo Jiménez) ★ Ideal 670

CONTESTACION A DESOLACION-Canción Fox (Valdez-Morante) ★ Ideal 670

YA NO TENGO CORAZON-Canción Fox (Lauro Monreal Carrión) ★ Ideal 681

ALBURES-Canción ★ Ideal 681

QUE VOY HACER-Vals Canción (José V. Franco) ★ Ideal 694

SECRETO DE AMOR-Canción (M.C. Valdez) ★ Ideal 694

JUANITA Y MARIA MENDOZA con el Conjunto Ideal
Trumpet, saxophone, guitar, bass and piano. November, 1951.

EL MUCHACHO DECIDIDO-Canción (M. Valdez) ★ Ideal 676

AUNQUE SEAS BORRACHO-Canción (Arturo G. Gonzales) ★ Ideal 676

JUANITA MENDOZA con el Conjunto Ideal. November, 1951.

QUE PASO-Ranchera (Iris García) ★ Ideal 745

ES MENTIRA-Canción (M.C. Valdez) ★ Ideal 745

JUANITA Y MARIA MENDOZA con el conjunto de Narciso Martínez. December, 1951.

TRES PUÑALADAS-Canción (Víctor Cordero) ★ Ideal 690

TAN SOLO UN MOMENTO-Canción (Jesús FaBella) ★ Ideal 690

PEDACITO DE MI SER-Canción (NC) ★ Ideal 739

SE LLEGO TU DIA-Bolero (Juan García) ★ Ideal 739

JUANITA Y MARIA MENDOZA con el Conjunto Ideal.
Includes trumpets, clarinet, piano, congo, guitar and bass. February, 1952.

CONTESTACION DE EUFEMIA PA' LUTERIO-Ranchera (Rubén Fuentes) ★ Ideal 712

MI CABALLO ALAZAN-Porro (C. Saucedo) ★ Ideal 712

PALOMA QUERIDA-Ranchera (J.A. Jiménez) ★ Ideal 718

GOLONDRINA AVENTURERA-Ranchera (Víctor Cordero) ★ Ideal 718

DESDE QUE TE FUISTE-Bolero (José Franco) ★ Ideal 727

JULIA, JULIA-Canción (Juan M. Verduzco) ★ Ideal 727

LA ISLA CAPRI-Canción Fox ★ Ideal 855

FASCINACION-Canción Schottis (Manuel Valdez) ★ Ideal 855

LYDIA MENDOZA y su guitarra (requinto by Enrique Rodríguez). March, 1952.

CONTESTACION A AMOR QUE MALO ERES-Bolero (Marquette-Morante) ★ Ideal 732, ILP 120(33), Fony 114(M)(33)

ACABAME DE MATAR-Bolero (F. Cuéllar) ★ Ideal 732, ILP 120(33), Fony 114(M)(33)

CARIÑO CIEGO-Tango (José Morante) ★ Ideal 743, ILP 120(33), Fony 114(M)(33)

TU SABES BIEN-Ranchera (Jesús Ramos) ★ Ideal 743, ILP 120(33)

TINIEBLAS-Bolero (Pablo D. Codesal) ★ Ideal 752, ILP 120(33), Fony 114(M)(33)

AMOR EN DUDA-Ranchera (José Morante) ★ Ideal 752, ILP 120(33), Fony 114(M)(33)

JUANITA Y MARIA MENDOZA con sus guitarras (with string bass). July, 1952.

UN MAR DE VINO-Ranchera (Rafael Cardona) ★ Ideal 776

AMARGO RECUERDO-Ranchera (Mariano Peña) ★ Ideal 776

DICEN QUE SOY-Ranchera (Rafael Cardona) ★ Ideal 783

POR JUGAR UN ALBUR-Ranchera (Mariano Peña) ★ Ideal 783

UN HOMBRE CASADO-Ranchera (José Morante) ★ Ideal 787
TU TIENES LA CULPA-Ranchera (Mariano Peña) ★ Ideal 787
TU LLANTO BEBERAS-Ranchera (NC) ★ Ideal 795
LA ROGONA-Ranchera (NC) ★ Ideal 795

LYDIA MENDOZA con su guitarra. July, 1952.
QUE HICISTE CON MIS BESOS-Ranchera (Mariano Peña) ★ Ideal 784
NO ME BUSQUES MAS-Ranchera (Mariano Peña) ★ Ideal 784

LYDIA MENDOZA con el conjunto de Narciso Martínez. July, 1952.
POR CAUSA DE UN AMOR-Bolero (Lorenzo Caballero) ★ Ideal 797
CUANDO SE PIERDE LA MADRE-Canción (Esteban Ortiz) ★ Ideal 797
HOY QUE VUELVO-Ranchera (Lorenzo Caballero) ★ Ideal 805
AMAR ES VIVIR-Bolero (Víctor Cordero) ★ Ideal 805

JUANITA Y MARIA MENDOZA con Narciso Martínez. July, 1951.
POR QUERERTE TANTO-Canción ★ Ideal 848
NOCHES ETERNAS-Canción ★ Ideal 848

JUANITA Y MARIA MENDOZA con Los Conquistadores.
Includes piano accordion. (Note: Los Conquistadores is the name of José Morante's conjunto.) September, 1952.
CONTESTACION A LA INTERESADA-Ranchera (S. Flores & Morante) ★ Ideal 804
PARRANDA LARGA-Ranchera (Judith Reyes) ★ Ideal 804
AMOR DE MI PASION-Bolero (M.C. Valdez) ★ Ideal 812
PALOMA HERIDA-Ranchera (Pablo Valdovinos) ★ Ideal 812
SENDOS OPUESTOS-Ranchera (José Morante) ★ Ideal 819
POS YA ESTARA-(Martínez) ★ Ideal 819
MIS DOS AMORES-Ranchera (J. Morante) ★ Ideal 828
DE MIS BRAZOS TE FUISTE-Ranchera (J. Morante) ★ Ideal 828
BESOS CANSADOS-Canción (Pepe Morante) ★ Ideal 871
TRANQUILIZATE MI AMOR-Canción (Morante) ★ Ideal 871
EL PERDIDO-Canción (Morante & Martínez) ★ Ideal 883
CUENTO DE AMOR-Canción (M.C. Valdez) ★ Ideal 883
NO QUIERO CASADOS-Canción (Daniel Garcés) ★ Ideal 908
TU VIDA Y TU SUERTE-Canción (Gilberto Parra) ★ Ideal 908
LA ARREPENTIDA-Canción (Tomás Ortiz) ★ Ideal 919
A TI TE TOCA-Canción (José Morante) ★ Ideal 919
EL CONQUISTADOR (José Morante) ★ Ideal 934
SOMBRAS Y ANGUSTIAS (José Morante) ★ Ideal 934
MALDITO VICIO ★ Ideal unissued(?)
POR SI ME OLVIDAS (José Alfredo Jiménez) ★ Ideal unissued(?)

JUANITA Y MARIA MENDOZA con el Conjunto de Tony De La Rosa.
Includes trumpet, saxophone and rhythm section. With very little accordion, except "Tú creías" and "No me quiera mi ranchera," which feature very nice accordion by Tony De La Rosa. October, 1953.

SERENATA HUASTECA-Huapango (José Alfredo Jiménez) ★ Ideal 986

MI NOVIO-Porro (Daniel Garcés) ★ Ideal 986

TU CREIAS-Ranchera (Daniel Garcés) ★ Ideal 992

NO ME QUIERA MI RANCHERA-(NC) ★ Ideal 992

SU AMOR-Ranchera (Daniel Garcés) ★ Ideal 997

AMOR DE MIS AMORES-Ranchera (Daniel Garcés) ★ Ideal 997

JUANITA Y MARIA MENDOZA con el conjunto de Chuy Compeán. Chuy Compeán-saxophone with Tony De La Rosa on accordion. 1954.

LAS QUE SE QUIEREN-(Daniel Garcés) ★ Ideal 1007

QUIEREME-Bolero (J. Mendoza) ★ Ideal 1007

SERAS PERDONADA-Ranchera (Genaro Solís) ★ Ideal 1020

ACUERDATE DE MI-Ranchera (Daniel Garcés) ★ Ideal 1020

PRENDA PRESTADA-Ranchera (Daniel Garcés) ★ Ideal 1024

POR ELLA-Ranchera (Daniel Garcés) ★ Ideal 1024

LYDIA MENDOZA con el conjunto de Narciso Martínez. April, 1954.

SI FUE POR ESO-Bolero (Zúñiga y Sandoval) ★ Ideal 1059, FL 9055(33)

SIN QUERER-Bolero (Conde Drácula) ★ Ideal 1059

MEDALLA DE DIOS-Ranchera (Aurelio García B.) ★ Ideal 1066, FL 9055(33)(C), ARH CD 361

VI PASAR-Ranchera (Aurelio García B.) ★ Ideal 1066

JUANITA Y MARIA MENDOZA con el Conjunto de Chuy Compeán. Includes saxophone, accordion, guitar and bass. April, 1954.

VAMONOS-Ranchera (José A. Jiménez) ★ Ideal 1072

HAY UN MOMENTO-(José A. Jiménez) ★ Ideal 1072

LA TRAGEDIA DE BIGOTES-Corrido (M.C. Valdez) ★ Ideal 1080

OLVIDAME-Ranchera (Garcés y Maber) ★ Ideal 1080

LAS QUEJAS DE ZENAIDA-Ranchera (M.C. Valdez) (Original title on tape shows ZENOBIO Y ZENAIDA) ★ Ideal 1084

NECESITAS DE LAS COPAS-Ranchera (Garcés-Mober) [as by Juanita Mendoza] ★ Ideal 1084

JUANITA Y MARIA MENDOZA con el conjunto de Tony De La Rosa. Includes accordion, bajo sexto and bass. 1954.

PORQUE TE VAS-Fox Canción (Víctor Cordero) ★ Ideal 1076

QUIEREME-(M.S. Acuña) ★ Ideal 1076

CAMINA Y CAMINA-Ranchera (José Morante) ★ Ideal 1088

EN OTROS TIEMPOS-Ranchera ★ Ideal 1088

LYDIA MENDOZA con el conjunto de Tony De La Rosa. 1954.

PORQUE PENSAR EN TI-Bolero (Manuel Imperial) ★ Ideal 1092

ES INUTIL-Bolero (Víctor Cordero) ★ Ideal 1092

AMOR MALDITO-Bolero (Carlos Crespo) ★ Ideal 1103

AUNQUE ME ODIES-Bolero (José Morante) ★ Ideal 1103, ARH CD/C 343

JUANITA Y MARIA MENDOZA con el conjunto de Tony De La Rosa. 1954.

AUTOBUSES DE REYNOSA-Ranchera (Paco De La Garza) ★ Ideal 1150

ANDO CERQUITA-Ranchera (Paco De La Garza) ★ Ideal 1150

PUENTES QUEMADOS-Ranchera (José Morante) ★ Ideal 1161, ARH CD/C 343

LAGRIMAS LLORO-Ranchera (NC) ★ Ideal 1161

LYDIA MENDOZA (vocal and guitar) con el Conjunto de Gilberto López. Accordion, with bajo sexto, bass and drums. San Benito, TX, April 21, 1964.

CARIÑO SIN CONDICION-Canción (Antonio Antojo) ★ Ideal 2158, ILP 143(33)

YA SIN FE-Bolero (Meléndez y Villareal) ★ Ideal 2158, ILP 143(33)

EL SILENCIO DE LA NOCHE-Ranchera (José Alfredo Jiménez) ★ Ideal 2165(45), ILP 143(33)

EN REDASTE MI VIDA-Ranchera ★ Ideal 2165(45), ILP 143(33)

CUANDO TE VUELVA A VER-Ranchera (Luly Ramos) ★ Ideal 2179, 2393(45), ILP 143(33)

AMOR BONITO-Ranchera (Lydia Mendoza) ★ Ideal 2179, 2393(45), ILP 143(33), ARH CD/C 343

UNA AVENTURA-Bolero (DAR) ★ Ideal 2201(45), ILP 143(33)

PERDONAME-Bolero (DAR) ★ Ideal 2201(45), ILP 143(33)

TU DESTINO-Ranchera (Desconocido) ★ Ideal 2218(45), ILP 143(33), ARH CD/C 341

MI DELITO-Canción (Rafael Hernández) ★ Ideal 2218(45), ILP 143(33)

PA' QUE ME DICES COSAS-Ranchera (DAR) ★ Ideal 2265(45), ILP 143(33)

LA RAFAELITA-Corrido (Miguel Martínez-F. Avitia) ★ Ideal 2265(45), ILP 143(33)

MENDOZA FAMILY DISCOGRAPHY: SECTION 5

FALCON RECORDS

LYDIA MENDOZA con su guitarra y conjunto. Gallardo-bass. McAllen, TX, August 17, 1950.

F-1182 ★ BESANDO LA CRUZ-Ranchera (Chucho Monge) ★ Falcón 097, 1011(45), EP 48(45), LP 136(33), LP 1010(M)(33)

F-1183 ★ ANGEL DE MIS ANHELOS-Canción (Jesus Fabella) ★ Falcón 097, 1011(45), EP 48(45), LP 136(33), LP 1010(M)(33)

F-1188 ★ INVIERNO EN ABRIL-Bolero (Rafael Ramírez) ★ Falcón 106, LP 2029(33)

F-1189 ★ QUE ME IMPORTA-Canción (Lydia Mendoza) ★ Falcón 106

LAS HERMANAS MENDOZA: Juanita y María con guitarras.

F-1184 ★ CUATRO CAMINOS-Ranchera (José Alfredo Jiménez) ★ Falcón 091

F-1185 ★ YO FUI EL PRIMERO-Canción (Leonor Mendoza) ★ Falcón 091

F-1186 ★ ME EQUIVOQUE-Canción (Chucho Navarro) ★ Falcón 101

F-1187 ★ INGRATA Y MALVADA-Canción (Lydia Mendoza) ★ Falcón 101

LAS HERMANAS MENDOZA: Juanita y María con el conjunto Los Donneños. Ramiro Cavazos-bajo sexto, Rafael Gaspar-bass, Lupe Torres-guitar, Mario Montes-accordion. September 8, 1950.

F-1205 ★ GOLONDRINA DE OJOS NEGROS-Canción (Víctor Cordero) ★ Falcón 110

F-1206 ★ POR UNA INGRATA MUJER-Canción (NC) ★ Falcón 110

F-1207 ★ TE ARREPENTIRAS, MUJER-Canción (Lydia Mendoza) ★ Falcón 118

F-1208 ★ CIELO AZUL-Canción (NC) ★ Falcón 175

F-1209 ★ AMBICION-Canción Fox ★ Falcón 118

F-1210 ★ ME PERTENECES-Canción (NC) ★ Falcón 164

F-1211 ★ DESENGAÑO-Canción (NC) ★ Falcón 164

F-1212 ★ MIS SUEÑOS-Canción (NC) ★ Falcón 175

LYDIA MENDOZA con su guitarra y conjunto.
Eugenio Gutiérrez-bass; accordion, saxophone, bajo sexto. January 11, 1951.

F-1262 ★ UN DIA NUBLADO-Ranchera (José Alfredo Jiménez) ★ Falcón 129, LP 2029(33)

F-1263 ★ LA QUE SE FUE-Ranchera (José Alfredo Jiménez) ★ Falcón 129, LP 2029(33)

F-1264 ★ IMPOSIBLE OLVIDARTE-Ranchera ★ Falcón 138

F-1265 ★ YO FUI EL CULPABLE-Ranchera (José Torres) ★ Falcón 138

JUANITA Y MARIA MENDOZA y guitarras.
Rafael Gaspar-bass. January 10, 1951.

F-1266 ★ EL COBARDE-Ranchera (José A. Jiménez) ★ Falcón 117

F-1267 ★ CUANDO SALGO A LOS CAMPOS-Ranchera ★ Falcón 117

F-1268 ★ AMARGADO DE LA VIDA ★ Falcón unissued

F-1269 ★ VIDA MARCADA ★ Falcón unissued

LYDIA MENDOZA con su guitarra y el Conjunto Ranchero de Oscar Guerra.
Oscar Guerra-trumpet, Carmona-clarinet, Tavio-sax, Carlos-guitar, Gallardo-bass.
May 30, 1951.

F-1300 ★ COMO UN CRIMINAL-Ranchera (José A. Jiménez) ★ Falcón 165

F-1301 ★ NO SE HA PERDIDO NADA-Bolero ★ Falcón 168, 1113(45), LP 149(33)

F-1302 ★ VIEJOS AMIGOS-Ranchera (José A. Jiménez) ★ Falcón 157, LP 2029(33)(33)

F-1303 ★ LEJOS DE TI-Canción ★ Falcón 157, LP 2029(33)(33)

F-1304 ★ TANTO COMO TE AME-Canción (NC) ★ Falcón 168, 1113(45), LP 1010(M)(33), LP 136(33)

F-1305 ★ MI RECOMPENSA-Canción (NC) ★ Falcón 165

LYDIA MENDOZA con su guitarra y el Conjunto de Oscar Guerra.
Oscar Guerra-trumpet, G. Jesse-bongos, G. Williams-bass, Beto Contreras, David
Gamboa. September 12, 1951.

F-1342 ★ CUANDO EL DESTINO-Ranchera (José A. Jiménez) ★ Falcón 182, F 1513(45), LP 136(33), LP 1010(M)(33)

F-1343 ★ TRES PUÑALADAS-Ranchera (Víctor Cordero) ★ Falcón 182, F 1513(45), EP 48(45), LP 136(33), LP 1010(M)(33)

F-1344 ★ DOS CAMINOS (José A. Jiménez) ★ Falcón 187

F-1345 ★ VUELVE A MI-Bolero (Esteban Ortiz) ★ Falcón 196

F-1346 ★ TU RECOMPENSA-Bolero (Rubén Ortiz) ★ Falcón 196

F-1347 ★ SIN FE-Bolero (María Alice Sandoval) ★ Falcón 187

LYDIA MENDOZA con su guitarra y conjunto. September 24, 1952.

F-1537 ★ EN MIS PENSAMIENTOS (Benny Villaseñor) ★ LP 2029(33), LP 2056(33)

F-1538 ★ GUITARRAS DE MEDIA NOCHE (J. A. Jiménez) ★ LP 2056(33)

F-1539 ★ CORAZON PARTIDO-Bolero (Fuentes-Cervantes) ★ Falcón 270, LP 2056(33)

F-1540 ★ POR QUE VOLVISTE-Ranchera (José A. Jiménez) ★ Falcón 270, LP 2056(33)

F-1541 ★ MIEL AMARGA-Ranchera (Cuco Sánchez) ★ Falcón 274, LP 2056(33)

F-1542 ★ POR UNA GITANA (Oscar García) ★ Falcón 274, LP 2056(33)

F-1543 ★ UN SECRETO-Bolero (Daniel Garcés) ★ Falcón 286, Falcón 286(45)

F-1544 ★ LA ULTIMA COPA-Ranchera (José Morante) ★ Falcón 286, Falcón 286(45), EP 66(45), LP 136(33), LP 1010(M)(33)

LYDIA MENDOZA con su guitarra y el conjunto Los Halcones.
With Pete Arando, George Jesse, Cruz Ortiz, R. Zenteno, Oscar Guerra and Gonzalo de León-violin. January 31, 1953.

F-1604 ★ CUANTO AMOR-Ranchera (Manuel Pomián) ★ Falcón 304, LP 2029(33)(33)

F-1605 ★ EL DESCONSOLADO-Ranchera (Rodolfo de la Garza) ★ Falcón 304, LP 2029(33)(33)

F-1606 ★ INSTANTE-Bolero (Rodolfo de la Garza) ★ Falcón 316

F-1607 ★ YO SE MUY BIEN-Canción (Rodolfo de la Garza) ★ Falcón 316

LYDIA MENDOZA con su guitarra y el conjunto Los Tejanos.
Oscar Guerra, Cruz Ortiz, Pete O., Pedro Ayala-accordian and David Gamboa. May 18 & 19, 1953.

F-1651 ★ MI ULTIMA CARTA-Ranchera (Víctor Cordero) ★ Falcón 331, 1579(45), LP 2056(33)(33)

F-1652 ★ LA NOCHE DE MI MAL-Ranchera (José Alfredo Jiménez) ★ Falcón 331, 1579(45), LP 2056(33)(33)

F-1653 ★ TE AMARE VIDA MIA-Ranchera (Cuco Sánchez) ★ Falcón 334, LP 2029(33)(33)

F-1654 ★ LE PIDO A LA SUERTE-Ranchera (J.A. Jiménez) ★ Falcón 334, LP 2029(33)(33)

F-1655 ★ SIN TENER POR QUE-Ranchera (Homero McDonald) ★ Falcón 343, LP 2029(33)(33)

F-1656 ★ POBRECITO CORAZON-Bolero (Daniel Garcés) ★ Falcón 343

F-1657 ★ SOY (LO QUE SOY)-Bolero (NC) ★ Falcón 353, LP 2056(33)(33)

F-1658 ★ CUANDO TU LO QUIERAS-Canción (Rafael Ramírez) ★ Falcón 353, LP 2056(33)(33)

(Note: F-1651 on Falcon 1579(45) is retitled "LA ULTIMA CARTA."
LP 2056(33), entitled "LA ALONDRA DE LA FRONTERA," was issued in both Mexico and the United States with two titles missing from the Mexican version.)

LOS TRES REYES.
Juanita Mendoza-vocal, Daniel Garcés-vocal, Valdez, Raúl, Mike Garza, Toby Torres, Hugo González-bajo sexto and Fred Flores. Falcón Recording Session #470. March 1, 1958.

F-2557 ★ COMO HAS CAMBIADO (Garcés & Angelina) ★ F 759(45)

LOS TRES REYES.
Juanita Mendoza-vocal, Daniel Garcés-vocal, Bocho R., Raúl Moreno, Félix González Robledo. Falcón Session #487. May 19, 1958.

F-2605 ★ MONEDA EN EL AIRE-Ranchera (Judith Reyes) ★ F 813(45)

F-2606 ★ LA MENSA-(Fidel A. Vista) ★ F 785(45)

F-2607 ★ BUENOS CONSEJOS-(Manuel González) ★ F 785(45)

F-2608 ★ TU INGRATO DESDEN-Ranchera (Daniel Garcés) ★ F 925(45)

(Note: Reverse sides of F 759, F 813 and F 925 are by Los Tres Reyes, without Juanita Mendoza.)

HERMANAS MENDOZA: Juanita y María.
With Enrique Rodríguez and Henry Ojeda. Falcón Recording Session #686. June 7, 1960.

F-3312 ★ UNA NOCHE ME EMBRIAGUE-Ranchera (M.C. Valdez) ★ F 1012(45), Bronco 006(33)

F-3313 ★ LA JACALERA-Ranchera (NC) ★ F 1034(45), Bronco 006(33)

F-3314 ★ CARTA DE AMOR-Ranchera (M.C. Valdez) ★ F 1034(45), Bronco 006(33)

F-3315 ★ EL AMOR QUE SOÑE-Ranchera (Daniel Garcés) ★ F 1012(45), Bronco 006(33)

LYDIA MENDOZA y su guitarra.
With Los Hermanos Prado, Mario Saenz-bass and M. García. July 7, 1960.

F-3360 ★ MAL HOMBRE-Canción (NC) ★ F 1066(45), LP 136(33), LP 1010(M)(33)

F-3361 ★ CELOSA-Canción Schottis (Pablo Rodríguez) ★ F 1041(45), LP 136(33), LP 1010(M)(33)

F-3362 ★ BARAJA MARCADA-Ranchera (Pepe Albarrán) ★ F 1019(45), LP 136(33), LP 1010(M)(33)

F-3363 ★ AMOR DE MADRE-Canción (NC) ★ F 1066(45), EP 66(45), LP 136(33), LP 1010(M)(33), LP 1029(M)(33)

F-3364 ★ COMO GOLONDRINA-Ranchera (Juan Flores) ★ F 1041, LP 136(33)

F-3365 ★ SENDA GRIS-Ranchera (Juan Flores) ★ F 1051, LP 136(33)

F-3366 ★ FALTA TU AMOR-Bolero (José L. Alvarez) ★ F 1019(45), LP 149(33), LP 1013(M)(33)

F-3367 ★ QUIERO PEDIRTE (Title on LP 1013(M)(33): QUIERO PEDIRTE UN FAVOR)-Bolero (Bety y Pablo Reynoso) ★ F 1051(45), LP 149(33), LP 1013(M)(33)

F-3368 ★ LYDIA HUAPANGO-(Agustín Mendoza) ★ F LP 136

LYDIA MENDOZA.
With Los Hermanos Prado (sax and trumpet) and Mario Saenz-bass, Falcón Session #742. April 19, 1961.

F-3529 ★ COMO SAN PEDRO A CRISTO-Ranchera (Antonio Cantoral) ★ F 1075(45), LP 149(33), LP 1013(M)(33)

F-3530 ★ PARA MORIR IGUALES-Ranchera (José Alfredo Jiménez) ★ F 1075(45), LP 149(33), LP 1013(M)(33)

F-3531 ★ LA GUIA-Ranchera (DAR) ★ F 1091(45), LP 149(33), LP 1013(M)(33)

F-3532 ★ ¿POR QUE TE VAS?-Ranchera ★ F 1091(45), LP 149(33), LP 1013(M)(33)

F-3533 ★ ALGUN DIA-Bolero (Hermanos González) ★ F 1136(45), LP 149(33), LP 1013(M)(33)

F-3534 ★ PLEGARIA-Canción (DAR) ★ F 1136(45), LP 149(33), LP 1013(M)(33)

F-3535 ★ TODO ES FALSO-Ranchera (DAR) ★ F 1100(45), LP 149(33), LP 1013(M)(33)

F-3536 ★ PAJARITO HERIDO-Canción (DAR) ★ F 1100(45), EP 48(45), LP 149(33), LP 1013(M)(33)

(Note: Falcón LP 149 is the same as LP 1013(M).)

HERMANAS MENDOZA: Juanita y María con guitarras.
Lydia Mendoza-guitar, Fabián M. Garza. Falcón Recording Session #753. July 10, 1961.

F-3565 ★ VUELA PALOMA-Ranchera (Juan Gaytán) ★ F 1095(45), Bronco 006(33)

F-3566 ★ UN DIA CON OTRO-Ranchera ★ F 1095(45), Bronco 006(33)

F-3567 ★ CUATRO VICIOS ★ F 1120(45), Bronco 006(33)

F-3568 ★ ¿QUE TENDRE YO? (Juan Gaytán) ★ F 1120(45), Bronco 006(33)

LYDIA MENDOZA y su guitarra.
With Gamabil Villareal. Falcón Recording Session #787. January 29, 1962.

F-3665 ★ CUANTO TE QUIERO-Canción Vals (DAR) ★ F 1222(45), LP 2056(33)

F-3666 ★ DESTINO CRUEL-Ranchera (Leonor Mendoza) ★ F 1222(45), LP 2056(33)

F-3667 ★ MARIA ANGELINA-Canción (Jesús Fabella) Ranchero (M.S. Acuña)." ★ F 1171(45), LP 2056(33)

F-3668 ★ PERO AY QUE TRISTE-Canción (Leonor Mendoza) ★ F 1171(45), EP 66(45), LP 2056(33)

HERMANAS MENDOZA: Juanita y María.
Lydia Mendoza-guitar, Fabián M. Garza. Falcón Recording Session #799. McAllen, TX., March 14, 1962.

F-3715 ★ TE QUIERO PORQUE TE QUIERO-Ranchera (Luis Moreno) ★ F 1180(45), Bronco LP 006(33)

F-3716 ★ TE LO JURO POR DIOS-Ranchera (NC) ★ F 1180(45)

F-3717 ★ OJITOS SOÑADORES-Ranchera (NC) ★ F 1159(45), Bronco LP 006(33)

F-3718 ★ POR ULTIMA VEZ-Ranchera (Juan M. Gaytán) ★ F 1159(45), Bronco LP 006(33)

LYDIA MENDOZA con el Conjunto de Marco Antonio Ramírez.
Marco Antonio Ramírez-drums, Israel Segura-bass, Mario Saenz-bajo sexto, Wally González-accordion, Rafael Cantú-sax, Antonio Prado-sax. Falcón Session #1410, August 6, 1968.
The following F matrix numbers recorded at this session appear on the Master Tape Box for LP 4012 as R prefix numbers. About 1970 Falcón sold the company to Royalco, but a few years later re-aquired the material. At the time of the deal with Royalco, the company began to prefix all masters with an R.

F-6168 ★ ESTA NOCHE (Rodolfo de la Garza) ★ LP 4012(33), LP 149(33), LP 3045(M)(33)

F-6169 ★ NUMERO 13 (de la Garza) ★ LP 4012(33), LP 3045(M)(33)

F-6170 ★ EN TUS BRAZOS (Pedro Becerra) ★ LP 4012(33), LP 3045(M)(33)

F-6171 ★ YA SIN TI (Pedro Becerra) ★ LP 4012(33), LP 3045(M)(33)

F-6172 ★ VOLVI LA ESPALDA-Bolero (Fuentes-Gil) ★ F 1797(45), LP 4012(33), LP 3045(M)(33)

F-6173 ★ MI FRANQUEZA-Bolero (Lydia Mendoza) ★ LP 4012(33), LP 3045(M)(33)

F-6174 ★ LLORA CORAZON-Bolero (Pedro E. Becerra) ★ F 1797(45), LP 4012(33), LP 3045(M)(33)

F-6175 ★ NO VUELVO A ROGAR-Bolero (Eloy Saldívar) ★ F 1827(45), LP 4012(33)

F-6176 ★ LA ULTIMA MIRADA-Bolero Ranchero (Eloy Saldívar Brambila) ★ LP 4012(33), LP 3045(M)(33)

F-6177 ★ AMOR Y CELO-Ranchera (Pedro E. Becerra) ★ F 1827(45), LP 4012(33), LP 3045(M)(33)

F-6178 ★ DIA TRAS DIA (NC) ★ LP 4012(33), LP 3045(M)(33)

F-6179 ★ LA MUJER DEL PUERTO (Manuel Esperón) ★ LP 4012(33), LP 3045(M)(33)

(Note: There are often at least two cuts missing on the Mexican versions of Falcón LPs, therefore some of the titles listed for LP 4012 may not appear on LP 3045(M)(33). LP 4012 also was issued as an 8-track tape F8T 4012. The title of LP 4012 is LLORAR CORAZÓN.)

LYDIA MENDOZA.

R-1112 ★ A MANERA DE ORACION-Vals (Ernesto R. Díaz) ★ F 1897(45), LP 4004(33), LP 3031(M)(33)

R-1113 ★ PERDON YO PIDO-Bolero (Lydia Mendoza) ★ F 1897(45), LP 4004(33), LP 3031(M)(33)

R-1114 ★ MADRE LINDA (Alberto Brambila) ★ LP 4004(33), LP 3031(M)(33)

R-1115 ★ MADRECITA MEXICANA (Carmelita Molina) ★ LP 4004(33), LP 3031(M)(33)

R-1116 ★ DI MI CARIÑO A MI MADRE-Ranchera (Bonifacio Mosquida) ★ F 1899(45), LP 4004(33), LP 3031(M)(33)

R-1117 ★ MADRECITA (Daniel Peña) ★ LP 4004(33)

R-1118 ★ FLORES DE MAYO (Trinidad Santana) ★ LP 4004(33), LP 3031(M)(33)

R-1119 ★ DUERME DUERME DUERME (Rafael Ramírez) ★ LP 4004(33), LP 3031(M)(33)

R-1120 ★ AMOR DE LOS AMORES ★ LP 4004(33), LP 3031(M)(33)

R-1121 ★ MADRE (Roberto Cantoral) ★ LP 4004(33), LP 3031(M)(33)

R-1122 ★ CANTO A MI MADRE-(Jesús Torres Padilla) ★ LP 4004(33), LP 3031(M)(33)

R-1123 ★ CANTA PAJARILLO CANTA-Bolero (P. Delis-A. Legal) ★ F 1899(45), LP 4004(33)

(The title of LP 4004(33) is FLORES DE MAYO.)

LYDIA MENDOZA.

R-1275 ★ FELIZ NAVIDAD-Cumbia (José Feliciano) ★ LP 4017(33)

R-1276 ★ ARBOLITO ARBOLITO-Vals (NC) ★ LP 4017(33)

R-1277 ★ YA VIENE LA NAVIDAD-Cumbia (Tony Acosta) ★ LP 4017(33)

R-1278 ★ NOCHE DE PAZ-Vals (Frank Gruber) ★ LP 4017(33)

R-1279 ★ LLORANDO EN NAVIDAD-Bolero (Lydia Mendoza) ★ F 1922(45), LP 4017(33)

R-1280 ★ RECUERDOS DE NAVIDAD-Bolero (Marco A. Laines) ★ LP 4017(33)

R-1281 ★ MI CANCION DE NAVIDAD-Vals (Pepe Albarrán) ★ LP 4017(33)

R-1282 ★ CAMPANAS DE NAVIDAD-Bolero (Tony Acosta) ★ LP 4017(33)

R-1283 ★ AMARGA NAVIDAD-Ranchera (J.A. Jiménez) ★ LP 4017(33)

R-1284 ★ ES NAVIDAD-Bolero (Roberto Chiofalo) ★ LP 4017(33)

R-1285 ★ FELIZ AÑO NUEVO-Ranchera (Lalo Guerrero) ★ F 1922(45), LP 4017(33)

R-1286 ★ ESTA NAVIDAD-Bolero (Bobby Capó) ★ LP 4017(33)

(The title of LP 4017(33) is MI CANCION DE NAVIDAD.)

LYDIA MENDOZA con los Alegres de Terán.

R-1698 ★ VIRGEN DEL TEPEYAC (Sebastián Curiel) ★ F 1973(45), LP 4037(33)

R-1699 ★ OH MARIA MADRE MIA ★ LP 4037(33)

R-1700 ★ VIVA MARIA ★ LP 4037(33)

R-1701 ★ HIMNO GUADALUPANO ★ LP 4037(33)

R-1702 ★ MEXICO LINDO (Salomé Tenorio) ★ F 1973(45), LP 4037(33)

R-1703 ★ JUAN DIEGO [Ermita en el Tepeyac] (Pepé Albarrán) ★ LP 4037(33)

R-1704 ★ PERDON, PERDON ★ LP 4037(33)

R-1705 ★ PLEGARIA GUADALUPANA ★ LP 4037(33)

R-1706 ★ Unknown Title ★ Falcón Unissued

R-1707 ★ Unknown Title ★ Falcón Unissued

R-1708 ★ Unknown Title ★ Falcón Unissued

R-1709 ★ Unknown Title ★ Falcón Unissued

R-1710 ★ OH VIRGEN SANTA ★ LP 4037(33)

R-1711 ★ ADIOS REINA DEL CIELO ★ LP 4037(33)

R-1712 ★ MAÑANITAS A LA VIRGEN ★ LP 4037(33)

R-1713 ★ JUAN DIEGO (Valladares Trejo) ★ LP 4037(33)

(The title of LP 4037(33) is UN CANTO A LA VIRGEN.)

LYDIA MENDOZA con mariachi.

R-1766 ★ ASOMATE A LA VENTANA (Alejandro Flores) ★ LP 4033(33)

R-1767 ★ PUEBLITO VIEJO (José A. Morales) ★ F 1983(45), LP 4033(33)

R-1768 ★ LA TARDE ERA TRISTE-Canción Popular (NC) ★ LP 4033(33)

R-1769 ★ TE AMO (Jorge Anez) ★ LP 4033(33)

R-1770 ★ SOBERBIA (José A. Morales) ★ LP 4033(33)

R-1771 ★ CANORA AVECILLA (Pablo J. Valderrama) ★ LP 4033(33)

R-1772 ★ ME LLEVARAS EN TI (Jorge Villamil) ★ LP 4033(33)

R-1773 ★ OJOS MIRADME (José Macías) ★ LP 4033(33)

R-1774 ★ SERENITA DE MAYO (Gabriel E. Casas) ★ LP 4033(33)

R-1775 ★ MIS FLORES NEGRAS (Julio Flores) ★ LP 4033(33)

R-1776 ★ TODITO EL AÑO (C. Estava-A. Dalmar) ★ F 1983(45), LP 4033(33)

R-1777 ★ LOS MIRLOS-Popular Criolla (NC) ★ LP 4033(33)

(The title of LP 4033(33) is UN CANTO A COLOMBIA: LA ALONDRA DE LA FRONTERA.)

(Note: Matrix numbers R-1778-89 were apparently unused.)

LYDIA MENDOZA con el Conjunto Los Ayala.

R-1882 ★ ABREME EL CIELO (B. Saldarriaga) ★ LP 4049(33)

R-1883 ★ SERENATA A MI MADRE (Oscar Castro) ★ LP 4049(33)

R-1884 ★ MAMITA MIA (B. Saldarriaga) ★ F 1993(45), LP 4049(33)

R-1885 ★ DESVELO (Bolívar-Vinueza) ★ LP 4049(33)

R-1886 ★ ADIOS MADRE MIA (César Castro) ★ F 1993(45), LP 4049(33)

R-1887 ★ DESCONSUELO (B. Saldarriaga) ★ LP 4049(33)

R-1888 ★ DOBLEN CAMPANAS (B. Saldarriaga) ★ LP 4049(33)R-1889 ★ MADRE MIA (R. Caseda) ★ LP 4049(33)

R-1990 ★ AUSENTE MADRE MIA (J. C. Villafuerte) ★ LP 4049(33)

R-1991 ★ DOS CLAVELES (J. Barros) ★ F 1991(45), LP 4049(33)

R-1992 ★ MI ORFANDAD (A. Muriel) ★ LP 4049(33)

R-1993 ★ CARIÑO DE MADRE (César Castro) ★ F 1991(45), LP 4049(33)

(The title of LP 4049(33) is MAMITA MIA.)

MENDOZA FAMILY DISCOGRAPHY: SECTION 6
Sombrero/Norteño/Lira/Tesoro/Buena Vida, Pegaso,
Del Valle, Universal, El Toro, Popular/Lyga, Magda, Del Sur,
El Zarape, Reloj, Atlas, Del Pajarito, Arhoolie, DLB

SOMBRERO/NORTEÑO/LIRA/TESORO/BUENA VIDA RECORDS
(Produced by José Morante)

HERMANAS MENDOZA: Juanita y María con el Conjunto Monte Carlo. San Antonio, TX, August, 1956.

So 101+ ★ MUJER PAPELERA-Ranchera (Manuel Valdez) ★ Sombrero 101+

So 101- ★ CONTESTACION A GRITENME PIEDRAS DEL CAMPO-Ranchera (José Morante) ★ Sombrero 101-

JUANITA Y MARIA MENDOZA con el Conjunto de el Azote Norteño "Manuel Guerrero."
Manuel Guerrero-accordion. San Antonio, TX, late 1956.

SO 103+ ★ UNAS COPAS DE LICOR-Ranchera (M.C. Valdez) ★ Sombrero 103, 126(45), LP 2012(33)

SO 103- ★ DESTINO MARCADO-Ranchera (José Morante) ★ Sombrero 103, 126(45), LP 2012(33)

HERMANAS MENDOZA: Juanita y María con Chencho López y Los Alteños.

EL SOLDADO MARIHUANO-Corrido (Tradicional) (Issued as UN SOLDADO BIEN TRONADO on Buena Vida) ★ Sombrero 2300(45), Buena Vida LP 317(33)

MI PENSAMIENTO-Ranchera (NC) (Issued as MIS PENSAMIENTOS on Buena Vida) ★ Sombrero 2300(45), Buena Vida LP 317(33)

CONTESTACION A VOY VAGANDO-Ranchera (DAR-arr: Morante) ★ Sombrero 2354(45)

MARIA MENDOZA con los Alteños.

EL PALOMO FLOJO (CONTESTACION A PALOMA LOCA)-Ranchera (arr: Morante) ★ Sombrero 2354(45)

JUANITA MENDOZA con Flaco Jiménez y sus Caminantes. ca. 1965.
MI NOVIO ES HIPPI-Cómica (NC) ★ Lira 1957(45)B, Buena Vida LP 317(33)

JUANITA MENDOZA con los Gavilanes del Norte.
CONTESTACION A QUE TAL SI TE COMPRO-Ranchera (C. Reyna) ★ Lira 1957(45)A

LYDIA MENDOZA con los Conquistadores.
Los Conquistadores: Chepe Soliz, Guevara, Valdez and José Morante. ca. 1966.
EL LLANTO DE MI MADRE (Salomé Gutiérrez) ★ Norteño 270(45)
PARA ADORARTE A TI (arr: Lydia Mendoza) ★ Norteño 270(45)
PARA MI PADRE Canción (José Morante) ★ Norteño 272(45)

LYDIA MENDOZA con Los Alteños de José Eulogio Flores.
SEGUIRE ESPERANDO-Bolero (Salomé Gutiérrez) ★ Norteño 276(45)

LYDIA MENDOZA con el Conjunto Aguila (Medina y Saldaña).
HAY UNOS OJOS-Ranchera (Salomé Gutiérrez) ★ Norteño 272(45), LP 809(33)
HAZ LO QUE QUIERAS-Bolero (Salomé Gutiérrez) ★ Norteño 282(45), Buena Vida LP 310(33), Cass 8-310, Buena Vida LP 317(33)
MARIA MARIQUITA ES MIA-Rédova (arr: Lydia Mendoza) (Issued as MARIA MARIQUITA on Buena Vida) ★ Norteño 282(45), Buena Vida LP 317(33)
EL RENCOR-Ranchera (DAR) ★ Norteño 285(45)
SENTIMIENTO-Ranchera (DAR) ★ Norteño 285(45)

LYDIA MENDOZA y Los Huracanes de Texas.
PLEGARIA A MI MADRE-Ranchera (Lydia Mendoza) ★ Norteño 303(45)
NUNCA CREAS QUE TU AMOR ME DOMINE-Ranchera (NC) ★ Norteño 303(45)

LYDIA MENDOZA y su guitarra.
CARMEN CARMELA-Ranchera (Tradicional) ★ Norteño 300(45), LP 812(33)
NAVE PERDIDA-DOS PUERTAS-Ranchera (DAR) ★ Norteño 300(45), LP 812(33)
QUERIDA ABUELITA-Canción (Lydia Mendoza) ★ Norteño 309(45), 8TR 817
CORAZON DE PIEDRA-Ranchera (Lydia Mendoza) ★ Norteño 309(45), Canon LP DCN-17(M)(33), 8TR 817
LOS ROSALES DE MI MADRE ★ Norteño 318(45), 8TR 817
CONTESTACION A LA DEL MORAL ★ Norteño 318(45), 8TR 817
MAL HOMBRE-Tango (DAR) ★ Norteño 381(45), LP 812(33), 8TR 817
ADIOS VIEJA ESCALERA-Ranchera (DAR) ★ Norteño 381(45)
JOAQUIN MURRIETA-Corrido (arr: Lydia Mendoza) ★ Norteño 387(45), 8TR 822, Cass 822
JESUS CADENA-Tragedia (DP) ★ Norteño 387(45), 8TR 822, Cass 822

LOS MENDOZAS: Lydia y Manuel con Los Trovadores del Bajío.
Fiddle, guitar, bass.
COPITAS DE VINO ★ Norteño 395(45)
PERO PALOMA ★ Norteño 395(45)

LYDIA MENDOZA y su guitarra con Los Conquistadores. 1978.
BONITO MONTERREY-Corrido Brambila (arr: Lydia Mendoza) ★ Norteño 411(45), Tesoro 506(M)(45)

LYDIA MENDOZA con su guitarra y ritmos. 1978.

LA JAIBERA-Rumba (DAR) ★ Norteño 411(45), Tesoro 506(M)(45)

HERMANITAS MENDOZA: Juanita, María y Lydia con el Conjunto Aguila. August, 1967.

GREGORIO CORTEZ-Corrido (NC) ★ Sombrero 2291(45), LP 2012(33), Buena Vida LP 319(33)

LOS CASADOS-Corrido (NC) ★ Sombrero 2291(45), LP 2012(33)

LA JACALERA-Ranchera Cómica (NC) ★ Sombrero 2308(45), LP 2012(33)

LA HIJA DESOBEDIENTE-Corrido (NC) ★ Sombrero 2308(45), LP 2012(33)

HERMANAS MENDOZA: Juanita y Lydia con Los Alteños.

TRES BUENOS CONSEJOS-Ranchera (arr: L. Mendoza) ★ Sombrero 2312(45), LP 2012(33)

PAREJITOS MUY PAREJITOS-Ranchera (NC) ★ Sombrero 2312(45), LP 2012(33)

HERMANAS MENDOZA: Juanita y Lydia con el Conjunto Aguila.

SAN ANTOÑITO-Ranchera (NC) ★ Sombrero 2316(45), LP 2012(33)

RAMON RAMON-Ranchera (NC) ★ Sombrero 2316(45), LP 2012(33)

DELGADINA-Corrido (NC) ★ Sombrero LP 2012(33), Buena Vida LP 319(33)

TOMA ELISA EL PUÑAL-Ranchera (NC) ★ Sombrero LP 2012(33)

HERMANAS MENDOZA: Lydia y María con sus guitarras. San Antonio, TX, 1982.

TENIA MI PRIETO-Ranchera (Lydia Mendoza) ★ Norteño 422(45)

POBRE DE MI CORAZON-Bolero (DAR) ★ Norteño 422(45)

LYDIA MENDOZA con su guitarra y el Conjunto Aguila y los Alteños de J.E. Flores. San Antonio, TX, c. 1960s.

ESO TAMBIEN SE AGRADECE-Ranchera (José A. Morante) ★ Norteño LP 809(33), 8TR 809

FELIZ CUMPLEAÑOS-Vals (DAR) ★ Norteño LP 809(33), 8TR 809

CELIA-Canción (arr: Lydia Mendoza) ★ Norteño LP 809(33), 8TR 809

TANGO NEGRO-Tango (DAR) ★ Norteño LP 809(33), 8TR 809

NO ME VENGAS A LLORAR-Canción (arr: Lydia Mendoza) ★ Norteño LP 809(33), 8TR 809

LYDIA MENDOZA (vocal and guitar).

LA BODA NEGRA-Canción (DAR) ★ Norteño LP 809(33), 8TR 809

LYDIA MENDOZA accompanied by Los Conquistadores (guitars).

DELICIOSA Y TRANQUILA-Ranchera (arr: Lydia Mendoza) ★ Norteño LP 809(33), 8TR 809

EL PUÑAL DE TU DESDEN-Colombiana (NC) ★ Norteño LP 809(33), 8TR 809

AMAR SIN ESPERANZA-Canción (NC) ★ Norteño LP 809(33), 8TR 809

LA SOMBRA DE MI PENA-Ranchera (Salomé Gutiérrez) ★ Norteño LP 809(33), 8TR 809

NO HAS DE SER MIA-Ranchera (Salomé Gutiérrez) ★ Norteño LP 809(33), 8TR 809, Norteño 276(45)

(Note: Title of LP 809(33) is Lydia Mendoza, LA ALONDRA DE LA FRONTERA.)

LYDIA MENDOZA y su guitarra (and bass).

LADRILLO-Tango ★ Norteño LP 812, 8TR 812

TU ME ENSEÑASTE A TODO-Fox Trote (M.C. Valdez) ★ Norteño LP 812, 8TR 812

COSAS QUE SUCEDEN-Bolero ★ Norteño LP 812, 8TR 812

LA NORTEÑA-Canción ★ Norteño LP 812, 8TR 812

LA MANCHA-Ranchera ★ Norteño LP 812, 8TR 812

CAMA VACIA-Tango ★ Norteño LP 812, 8TR 812

LYDIA MENDOZA y su guitarra.
Accompanied by conjunto: accordion, saxophone/clarinet, bass and drums.

UN CORAZON DE MADERA-Ranchera (Salomé Gutiérrez) ★ Norteño LP 812, 8TR 812

QUE LINDO BESAS-Fox Trote ★ Norteño LP 812, 8TR 812

TU SENDERO-Canción (José Morante) ★ Norteño LP 812, 8TR 812

(Note: Title of Norteño LP 812, 8TR 812: LYDIA MENDOZA Y SU GUITARRA DE ORO.)

LYDIA MENDOZA.
Vocal accompanied by amplified 12-string guitar plus a second guitar.

DESOLACION-Bolero Ranchera (M.C. Valdez) ★ Norteño Internacional LP 204(33), 8TR NRC 204

AMELIA AMELIA-Ranchera (DAR) ★ Norteño Internacional LP 204(33), 8TR NRC 204

LA CUMBANCHA-Bolero (A. Lara) ★ Norteño Internacional LP 204(33), 8TR NRC 204

HOMBRE HOMBRE-Ranchera (arr: Lydia Mendoza) ★ Norteño Internacional LP 204(33), 8TR NRC 204

A MANO CON LA VIDA-Ranchera (José A. Morante) ★ Norteño Internacional LP 204(33), 8TR NRC 204

PREGUNTA-Bolero (DAR) ★ Norteño Internacional LP 204(33), 8TR NRC 204

MORIR POR TU AMOR-Vals (DAR) ★ Norteño Internacional LP 204(33), 8TR NRC 204

OLVIDA QUE ME AMASTE-Ranchera (DAR) ★ Norteño Internacional LP 204(33), 8TR NRC 204

DOS LAGRIMITAS-Vals (DAR) ★ Norteño Internacional LP 204(33), 8TR NRC 204

GITANA-Bolero (DAR) ★ Norteño Internacional LP 204(33), 8TR NRC 204

(Note: Title of Norteño Internacional LP 204(33), 8TR NRC 204: 20 EXITOS DE SIEMPRE. All selections are very short (under 2 minutes). Side B by Rita Vidaurrie.)

LYDIA MENDOZA. 1960s.

UNA SOLA CAIDA ★ Cañón (M) LP DCN-17(33), Norteño 8TR 817

NO JUEGUES CON MI AMOR ★ Cañón (M) LP DCN-17(33), Norteño 8TR 817

LOS BARANDALES DEL PUENTE ★ Cañón (M) LP DCN-17(33), Norteño 8TR 817

MAÑANITAS A MI PADRE ★ Cañón (M) LP DCN-17(33), Norteño 8TR 817

POR UN AMOR ★ Cañón (M) LP DCN-17(33), Norteño 8TR 817

ANGEL DE MIS SUEÑOS ★ Cañón (M) LP DCN-17(33), Norteño 8TR 817

MIL VIDAS ★ Cañón (M) LP DCN-17(33), Norteño 8TR 817

NOCHES DE ANGUSTIA ★ Cañón (M) LP DCN-17(33), Norteño 8TR 817

(Note: Title of Cañón (M) LP DCN-17(33), Norteño 8TR 817: LYDIA MENDOZA.)

LYDIA MENDOZA. 1970s.

LEY DEL CONTRABANDO ★ Lira/Norteño 8TR 822, Cass 822

CARGA BLANCA ★ Lira/Norteño 8TR 822, Cass 822

POTRO LOBO GATEADO ★ Lira/Norteño 8TR 822, Cass 822

VALENTIN DE LA SIERRA ★ Lira/Norteño 8TR 822, Cass 822

LUZ ARCOS ★ Lira/Norteño 8TR 822, Cass 822

LA PRISION DE COLORADO ★ Lira/Norteño 8TR 822, Cass 822

A MI VIEJO SAN ANTONIO ★ Lira/Norteño 8TR 822, Cass 822

EL REPATRIADO ★ Lira/Norteño 8TR 822, Cass 822

(Note: Title of Lira/Norteño 8TR 822, Cass 822: CON CORRIDOS Y CORRIDOS.)

LAS HERMANITAS MENDOZA: Juanita, María and Lydia accompanied by conjunto.

LAS ISABELES-Ranchera ★ Buena Vida LP 317(33)

ADELAIDA-Ranchera ★ Buena Vida LP 317(33)

GABINO SANTOS MEDINA-Tragedia (arr: Lydia Mendoza) ★ Buena Vida LP 319(33)

CORRIDO DE RIVERA-Corrido (PD) ★ Buena Vida LP 319(33)

CORRIDO DE VALENTINA-Corrido (arr: Hermanas Mendoza) ★ Buena Vida LP 319(33)

CORRIDO DE LA NUEVA RAZA-Corrido (NC) ★ Buena Vida LP 319(33)

HIJA DE LA MALA VIDA-Corrido (DAR) ★ Buena Vida LP 319(33)

CONSEJOS TE HE DE DAR-Corrido (arr: Lydia Mendoza) ★ Buena Vida LP 319(33)

MIS PENSAMIENTOS-Ranchera (DAR) ★ Buena Vida LP 319(33)

LAS MUCHACHAS MODERNAS-Corrido (NC) ★ Buena Vida LP 319(33)

(Note: Title of Buena Vida LP 317(33): LAS TRES GRANDES VOLUME 2: CHELO (Silva), LYDIA MENDOZA Y HERMANAS MENDOZA.)

(Note: Title Buena Vida LP 319(33): LAS ALONDRAS DE LA FRONTERA: LAS HERMANAS MENDOZA: JUANITA, MARIA Y LYDIA.)

LYDIA MENDOZA con conjunto.

POR QUE ME ENGAÑASTE ★ Buena Vida LP 310(33), Cass 8-310

ES MI DESTINO ★ Buena Vida LP 310(33), Cass 8-310

HERMANAS MENDOZA: Juanita y María.

VERSOS DE MI CASAMIENTO ★ Buena Vida LP 310(33), Cass 8-310

(Note: Title of Buena Vida LP 310(33): LAS GRANDES DE TEXAS: CHELO SILVA, LYDIA MENDOZA, HERMANAS MENDOZA. (All of Side A is by Chelo Silva).)

LYDIA MENDOZA San Antonio, TX, ca. 1981.

CONSEJO A LA MUJER ★ Tesoro Cass 704(M)

TRISTEZA INFINITA ★ Tesoro Cass 704

CASTIGA TIRANO ★ Tesoro Cass 704

MAL HOMBRE-Tango [with electric guitar] ★ Tesoro Cass 704

AL ENCONTRARTE ★ Tesoro Cass 704

LEJOS ★ Tesoro Cass 704

NO ME ABANDONES ★ Tesoro Cass 704

AQUEL AMIGO ★ Tesoro Cass 704

EL LIRIO ★ Tesoro Cass 704

NO ES CULPA MIA ★ Tesoro Cass 704

EL NOVILLERO ★ Tesoro Cass 704

TE VAS ★ Tesoro Cass 704

AUNQUE ME DUELA EL ALMA ★ Tesoro Cass 704

CORAZON YA NO LE LLORES ★ Tesoro Cass 704

UNA MANCHA MAS ★ Tesoro Cass 704

(Note: Title of Tesoro Cass 704: 15 EXITOS DE LYDIA MENDOZA.)

Most of these titles originally were recorded for release in Colombia, but Lydia lost the address of the man who had requested them there, and they were released by Morante on his Tesoro label in Mexico.

GAVIOTA RECORDS

LYDIA MENDOZA con su guitarra y el Conjunto Gaviota.
Orchestra arrangements with saxophone, bass, guitar, percussion, and accordion.
Corpus Christi, TX, ca. 1955.

GA 1012-A-1 ★ SI SUPIERAS COMO TE ODIO-Bolero (Johnny Herrera) ★ Gaviota 1012(78)

GA 1012-2 ★ PARA TI VIVIRE-Vals Canción (Johnny Herrera) ★ Gaviota 1012(78)

GA 1013-1 ★ QUE DIFERENTE-Bolero Tejano (Johnny Herrera) ★ Gaviota 1013(78)

GA 1013-2 ★ VEN, CORAZON-Canción Vals (Johnny Herrera) ★ Gaviota 1013(78)

(Note: 500 copies of each of the above were pressed.)

LYDIA MENDOZA con su guitarra. Gregory, TX, June, 1975.

DE RODILLAS VENDRAS ★ Gaviota LP 1001(33)

ESTA NOCHE ME VOY ★ Gaviota LP 1001(33)

TENEMOS QUE SUFRIR ★ Gaviota LP 1001(33)

LO DE NOSOTROS ★ Gaviota LP 1001(33)

AMOR Y CORAZON ★ Gaviota LP 1001(33)

QUE ★ Gaviota LP 1001(33)

EN ESTA NOCHE BUENA ★ Gaviota LP 1001(33)

CON ESTA COPA ★ Gaviota LP 1001(33)

QUE BONITA MADRUGADA ★ Gaviota LP 1001(33)

QUIERO PAGAR ★ Gaviota LP 1001(33)

POR NINGUN MOTIVO ★ Gaviota LP 1001(33)

DAME LA MANO ★ Gaviota LP 1001(33)

(Note: Title of Gaviota LP 1001(33): LYDIA MENDOZA INTERPRETA A JOHNNY HERRERA)

(All songs composed by Johnny Herrera.)

PEGASO RECORDS

LYDIA MENDOZA con el Conjunto Los Alteños de José Eulogio Flores.
San Antonio, TX, ca. late 1950s.

EL QUE PIERDE UNA MUJER-Bolero (Luis Arcaraz) ★ Pegaso 519(45), Tambora (M) 226(45)

SI TU SUPIERAS-Ranchera (Baldomero Saucedo) ★ Pegaso 519(45)

DEL VALLE RECORDS

MARIA MENDOZA con el conjunto de El Tejano Díaz. McAllen, TX, 1959.

V-0209 ★ OLVIDE TU PASADO-Bolero Ranchero (Ray Monsiváis) ★ Del Valle 203(45)

V-0210 ★ A LA PURA VUELTA Y VUELTA-Canción Polka (Ray Monsiváis) ★ Del Valle 203(45)

EL TACUACHITO ★ Del Valle Unissued

LINDA ROSA DE CASTILLA ★ Del Valle Unissued

UNIVERSAL RECORDS

LYDIA MENDOZA con Luis Sepulveda y su conjunto. Los Angeles, CA, early 1960s.

TK 4 ★ NO MALDIGAS EL DESTINO-Bolero (Carlos Estrada Lira) ★ Universal 223(45)-A

TK 6 ★ CIEGO DE AMOR-Tango (Carlos Estrada Lira) ★ Universal 223(45)-B

EL TORO RECORDS

LYDIA MENDOZA y conjunto.
Accordion, guitar, bass and drums. Probably San Antonio, early 1960s.

DI 402 ★ AUNQUE ME DUELE EL ALMA-Ranchera (DAR) ★ El Toro 5002(45)

DI 403 ★ UN MOMENTO MAS-Bolero (Flores) ★ El Toro 5002(45), Tambora (M) 226(45)

POPULAR/LYGA RECORDS
(Label operated by Gastón Ponce in Houston, Texas)

LYDIA MENDOZA con el conjunto de Pablo Garza.
With accordion, bajo sexto, bass, and drums. early 1960s

pop 073A ★ QUE DIFERENTES SON MIS NOCHES-Bolero (Johnny Herrera) ★ Popular 073(45)-A, Lyga 4(45)-A,
Firmamento Cass 1021

pop 073B ★ ANDO TOMANDO MIS COPAS-Ranchera (Juan Gaytán) ★ Popular 073(45)-B, Lyga 4(45)-B,
Firmamento Cass 1021

LYDIA MENDOZA con su guitarra. Houston, TX, 1964.

LH 2083 ★ POR TU VIDA Y LA MIA-Ranchera (NC) ★ Popular 079(45), Firmamento Cass 1021

LH 2084 ★ SALUD DINERO Y AMOR-Ranchera (NC) ★ Popular 079(45), Firmamento Cass 1021

LYDIA MENDOZA. Houston, TX, early 1970s.

CARGA BLANCA-Corrido (NC) ★ Lyga 1(45), *Coyote LP 001, Firmamento Cass 1021

EN LAS ESQUINAS DE ENFRENTE-Ranchera (NC) ★ Lyga 1(45), Firmamento Cass 1021

LH 2466 ★ sev EL PUENTE ROTO-Ranchera (NC) ★ Lyga 2(45), Firmamento Cass 1021

LH 2467 ★ TORMENTO INGRATO-Ranchera (NC) ★ Lyga 2(45), Firmamento Cass 1021

LYDIA MENDOZA con Lorenzo Caballero.

LH 2506 ★ MARGARITA MARGARITA-Ranchera ★ Lyga 3(45)A, Firmamento Cass 1021

LH 2507 ★ DOS CORAZONES ★ Lyga 3(45)B, Firmamento Cass 1021

(Note: Coyote LP 001 is titled: CORRIDOS DE AQUÍ Y DE ALLÁ.)

MAGDA RECORDS

LYDIA MENDOZA.
Vocal and amplified guitar with orchestra including alto saxophone, bass, percussion, and organ. San Antonio, TX, ca. 1960s.

BORRATE-Bolero (DAR) ★ Magda 171(45), Magda LP 514(33), Super Mex 8TR 12

DIOS DE BARRO-Bolero (DAR) ★ Magda LP 514(33), Super Mex 8TR 12

VALENTE QUINTERO-Corrido (DAR) ★ Magda LP 514(33), Super Mex 8TR 12

EL HIJO DESOBEDIENTE-Corrido (DAR) ★ Magda LP 514(33), Super Mex 8TR 12

SOY COMO SOY-Bolero (DAR) ★ Magda LP 514(33), Super Mex 8TR 12

FORJADOR DE ILUSIONES-Bolero (DAR) ★ Magda LP 514(33), Super Mex 8TR 12

ROSITA ALVIREZ-Corrido (DAR) ★ Magda LP 514(33), Super Mex 8TR 12

VUELVE-Bolero (DAR) ★ Magda LP 514(33), Super Mex 8TR 12

AUNQUE ME HAGAS LLORAR-Ranchera (DAR) ★ Magda 171(45), Magda LP 514(33), Super Mex 8TR 12

SANTA AMALIA-Corrido (DAR) ★ Magda LP 514(33), Super Mex 8TR 12

LA MANO NEGRA-Corrido (DAR) ★ Magda LP 514(33)

VALENTIN DE LA SIERRA-Corrido (DAR) ★ Magda LP 514(33)

(Note: Title of Magda LP 514(33): LA ALONDRA DE LA FRONTERA-CANTA CORRIDOS-ROSITA AL-VIREZ.)

DEL SUR RECORDS

LYDIA MENDOZA.
Vocals and amplified guitar accompanied possibly by bass guitar. Pepe Maldonado sings vocal duets. South Texas, ca. 1971-72.

TU CAMINO Y EL MIO-Ranchera (DAR) [duet] ★ Del Sur 126(45), Del Sur LP 1005(33), Discolando LP 8434(33)

DICES BIEN MIO-Ranchera (DAR) ★ Del Sur 126(45), Del Sur LP 1005(33), Discolando LP 8434(33)

ACUERDATE DE MI-Ranchera (DAR) ★ Del Sur LP 1005(33), Discolando LP 8434(33)

AMOR CELOSO-Ranchera (DAR) ★ Del Sur LP 1005(33), Discolando LP 8434(33)

ANGEL DE MIS ANHELOS-Ranchera (DAR) ★ Del Sur LP 1005(33), Discolando LP 8434(33)

MARIPOSA FUGAS-Ranchera (DAR) ★ Del Sur LP 1005(33), Discolando LP 8434(33)

TODOS LOS DIAS QUE AMANECE-Ranchera (DAR) ★ Del Sur LP 1005(33), Discolando LP 8434(33)

TE QUIERO CON LA VIDA-Ranchera (DAR) ★ Del Sur LP 1005(33), Discolando LP 8434(33)

CUANDO ESCUCHES ESTE VALS-Canción Vals (DAR) ★ Del Sur LP 1005(33), Discolando LP 8434(33)

POR UNA MUJER CASADA-Ranchera (DAR) ★ Del Sur LP 1005(33), Discolando LP 8434(33)

CUATRO LEGUAS-Ranchera (DAR) ★ Del Sur LP 1005(33), Discolando LP 8434(33)

ESPERO TU REGRESO-Bolero (DAR) ★ Del Sur LP 1005(33), Discolando LP 8434(33)

(Note: LP/Cass 1005 title: TU CAMINO Y EL MIO. LP 8434 title: DEL CORAZON DE LA MUSICA NORTEÑA.)

LYDIA MENDOZA.
Vocal and guitar with bass, drums and accordion.

AMOR SANTO-Bolero (DAR) ★ Del Sur 170(45)

ABORRECEME-Ranchera (DAR) ★ Del Sur 170(45)

NO QUIERO NADA A LA FUERZA-Ranchera (DAR) ★ Del Sur 178(45)

CUARTO TRISTE-Bolero Ranchera (DAR) ★ Del Sur 178(45)

LA CRUZ DE MIS BRAZOS ★ Del Sur 301(45), R y N Cass 1170

CELOS MENTIROSOS ★ Del Sur 301(45), R y N Cass 1170

LYDIA MENDOZA. Mission, TX, 1983.

DESTINO CRUEL ★ Del Sur Cass 1049, 8TR 1049, R y N Cass 1158

SOLO LO DEJO AL RECUERDO ★ Del Sur Cass 1049, 8TR 1049, R y N Cass 1170

CUATRO MILPAS ★ Del Sur Cass 1049, 8TR 1049, R y N Cass 1158

COMO LE HAGO ★ Del Sur Cass 1049, 8TR 1049, as COMO LE HAGO PA' OLVIDARTE on R y N Cass 1170

DIME QUE QUIERES DE MI ★ Del Sur Cass 1049, 8TR 1049, R y N Cass 1170

AMOR DE MADRE ★ Del Sur Cass 1049, 8TR 1049, R y N Cass 1158

YA ME CANSE DE ESTE AMOR ★ Del Sur Cass 1049, 8TR 1049, R y N Cass 1158

BIENVENIDA ★ Del Sur Cass 1049, 8TR 1049, R y N Cass 1158

FELIZ AÑO NUEVO ★ Del Sur Cass 1049, 8TR 1049

SOLO RUINAS Y CENIZAS ★ Del Sur Cass 1049, 8TR 1049, R y N Cass 1170

(Note: Title of Del Sur Cass 1049, 8TR 1049: DESTINO CRUEL.)

LYDIA MENDOZA.

UNA NOCHE MAS ★ R y N Cass 1158 ★ NO ME ABANDONES ★ R y N Cass 1158

AMOR BONITO ★ R y N Cass 1158

SIGUE VENDIENDO TU AMOR ★ R y N Cass 1158

MAL HOMBRE ★ R y N Cass 1158

TE AME UNA SOLA VEZ ★ R y N Cass 1158

AUNQUE TE DE CORAJE ★ R y N Cass 1158

CONSEJO A LAS MUJERES ★ R y N Cass 1158

TE VAS ★ R y N Cass 1158

ENTRE COPA Y COPA ★ R y N Cass 1158

(Note: Title of R y N Cass 1158: 15 EXITOS DE LIDIA MENDOZA: LA ALONDRA DE LA FRONTERA.)

LYDIA MENDOZA.

RECORDANDO ★ R y N Cass 1170

AQUEL AMIGO ★ R y N Cass 1170

NO ES CULPA MIA ★ R y N Cass 1170

CORAZON YA NO LE LLORES ★ R y N Cass 1170

AL ENCONTRARTE A TI ★ R y N Cass 1170

CASTIGO TIRANO ★ R y N Cass 1170

AUNQUE ME DUELA EL ALMA ★ R y N Cass 1170

EN UNA SEPULTURA ★ R y N Cass 1170

POR ELLA NOMAS POR ELLA ★ R y N Cass 1170

(Note: Title of R y N Cass 1170, vol. 2: LA ALONDRA DE LA FRONTERA—15 EXITOS)

EL ZARAPE RECORDS

LYDIA MENDOZA. Dallas, TX, ca. 1970.

POR EL AMOR A MI MADRE ★ El Zarape LP 1028(33)

HUMILLADA ★ El Zarape LP 1028(33)

NO SUPISTE COMPRENDERME ★ El Zarape LP 1028(33)

MI UNICO CAMINO ★ El Zarape LP 1028(33)

LUIS PULIDO ★ El Zarape LP 1028(33)

EL MARINERO ★ El Zarape LP 1028(33)

MANAÑITAS A MI MADRE ★ El Zarape LP 1028(33)

CABARETERO ★ El Zarape LP 1028(33)

CALLEJON SIN SALIDA ★ El Zarape LP 1028(33)

UNA CANCION A MI MADRE ★ El Zarape LP 1028(33)

(Note: Title of El Zarape LP 1028(33): POR EL AMOR A MI MADRE.)

LYDIA MENDOZA con el Mariachi Monumental Sahuayo, Pedro García director. Dallas, TX, 1970s.

CARITA DE VIRGEN-Ranchera (DAR) ★ El Zarape LP 1055(33)

CONFIANZA-Ranchera (Oscar Treviño) ★ El Zarape LP 1055(33)

EL CHISME-Ranchera (Oscar Treviño) ★ El Zarape LP 1055(33)

EL RINCON-Ranchera (DAR) ★ El Zarape LP 1055(33)

LA CRUZ QUE LABRASTE (DAR) ★ El Zarape LP 1055(33)

TE QUIERO-Ranchera (Oscar Treviño) ★ El Zarape LP 1055(33)

NI LA DISTANCIA-Ranchera (Oscar Treviño) ★ El Zarape LP 1055(33)

LINDA MORENA-Ranchera (Oscar Treviño) ★ El Zarape LP 1055(33)

BESANDO LA CRUZ-Ranchera (Chucho Monje) ★ El Zarape LP 1055(33)

LLORANDO EN SILENCIO-Ranchera (Linda Almanza) ★ El Zarape LP 1055(33)

AMOR SOÑADO-Bolero (Lydia Mendoza) ★ El Zarape LP 1055(33)

SI YA NO ME QUIERES-Ranchera (Lydia Mendoza) ★ El Zarape LP 1055(33)

(Note: Title of El Zarape LP 1055(33): LYDIA MENDOZA CON EL MARIACHI MONUMENTAL SAHUAYO.)

RELOJ RECORDS

LYDIA MENDOZA. Delray Beach, FL, ca. 1970.

MADRECITA DE MI SER ★ Reloj LP 1008(33)

TODO POR TI ★ Reloj LP 1008(33)

PERDON MADRECITA ★ Reloj LP 1008(33)

AMOR DE MADRE ★ Reloj LP 1008(33)

OH MADRE QUERIDA ★ Reloj LP 1008(33)

CARIÑO SIN CONDICION ★ Reloj LP 1008(33)

CANTO A MI MADRE ★ Reloj LP 1008(33)

MADRECITA MIA ★ Reloj LP 1008(33)

MADRECITA CONSENTIDA ★ Reloj LP 1008(33)

MI MADRECITA QUERIDA ★ Reloj LP 1008(33)

MUCHOS DIAS DE ESTOS DIOS ME NEGO ★ Reloj LP 1008(33)

HASTA EN MI TUMBA ACUERDATE DE MI ★ Reloj LP 1008(33)

(Note: Title of Reloj LP 1008(33): REGALO A MI MADRE-TODO POR TI.)

ATLAS RECORDS

LYDIA MENDOZA.

Vocal and guitar with accordion and bass. TX, early 1980s.

LH-17954 ★ MALA JUGADA (Lydia Mendoza) ★ Atlas 102(45)

LH-17955 ★ PILAR VILLAGOMEZ (Lydia Mendoza) ★ Atlas 102(45)

DEL PAJARITO

LYDIA MENDOZA con su guitarra. Phoenix, AZ, 1970s.

DEJENME LLORAR-Bolero (Homero Aguilar) ★ JRS-16 (22924A)(45)

BESOS Y COPAS-Ranchera (Víctor Cordero) ★ JRS-16 (22924B)(45)

ARHOOLIE RECORDS

LYDIA MENDOZA. (vocal and guitar). Galveston, TX, December, 1975.

MAL HOMBRE-Tango (NC) ★ Arhoolie LP 3005(33)

PERO HAY QUE TRISTE ★ Arhoolie LP 3005(33)

(Note: Arhoolie LP 3005 is the sound track recording of the film: CHULAS FRONTERAS)

LYDIA MENDOZA. (Vocal and guitar.) San Antonio, TX, May 13, 1979.

MUJER PASEADA ★ Arhoolie LP 3012(33), Cass 3012

AMOR BONITO (Lydia Mendoza) ★ Arhoolie LP 3012(33), Cass 3012

SIN FE ★ Arhoolie Cass 3012

OLVIDARTE JAMAS ★ Arhoolie LP 3012(33), Cass 3012

NO ES CULPA MIA ★ Arhoolie LP 3012(33), Cass 3012

MI PROBLEMA ★ Arhoolie LP 3012(33), Cass 3012

NO PUEDO DEJAR DE QUERERTE ★ Arhoolie Unissued.

ROSARIO NOCTURNO ★ Arhoolie Unissued.

AUNQUE VENGA MUY BORRACHO ★ Arhoolie LP 3012(33), Cass 3012

COLLAR DE PERLAS ★ Arhoolie LP 3012(33), Cass 3012

LUIS PAULIDO ★ Arhoolie LP 3012(33), Cass 3012

MARGARITA ★ Arhoolie Unissued.

ZENAIDA ★ Arhoolie Unissued.

TANGO NEGRO ★ Arhoolie LP 3012(33), Cass 3012

SILVERIO PEREZ ★ Arhoolie LP 3012(33), Cass 3012

MALAGUEÑA SALEROSA ★ Arhoolie LP 3012(33), Cass 3012

OJITOS VERDES ★ Arhoolie LP 3012(33), Cass 3012

BESANDO LA CRUZ ★ Arhoolie LP 3012(33), Cass 3012

HACE UN AÑO ★ Arhoolie LP 3012(33), Cass 3012

(Note: Arhoolie 3012 title: LA GLORIA DE TEXAS)

DLB RECORDS

LYDIA MENDOZA y su guitarra. San Antonio, TX, February 15, 1983.

ENTREVISTA CON SALOME GUTIERREZ (Interview with Salomé Gutiérrez) ★ DLB LP 1094(33), Cass 1094

MAL HOMBRE (Lydia Mendoza) ★ DLB LP 1094(33), Cass 1094, Cass 6006, Cass 8006

CELOSA-Ranchera (Lydia Mendoza) ★ DLB 803(45), DLB LP 1094(33), Cass 1094, Cass 6006, Cass 8006

CUANDO ESCUCHES ESTE VALS (S. Garrido) ★ DLB LP 1094(33), Cass 1094, Cass 6006, Cass 8006

DIME, MAL HOMBRE ★ DLB LP 1094(33), Cass 1094

FELIZ CUMPLEAÑOS ★ DLB LP 1094(33), Cass 1094

PAJARITO HERIDO (Lydia Mendoza) ★ DLB LP 1094(33), Cass 1094, Cass 6006, Cass 8006

EL LIRIO (Lydia Mendoza) ★ DLB LP 1094(33), Cass 1094, Cass 6006, Cass 8006

(Note: DLB LP 1094 title: LYDIA MENDOZA: LA ALONDRA DE LA FRONTERA: COLECCION DE ORO DE CINCUENTA AÑOS.)

LYDIA MENDOZA. San Antonio, TX, August 20, 1983.

ACERCAME A TU VIDA ★ DLB Cass 1113

BESANDO LA CRUZ ★ DLB Cass 1113

CUANDO ESTEMOS VIEJOS ★ DLB Cass 1113

EL TERMOMETRO ★ DLB Cass 1113

FLOR DE FLORES ★ DLB Cass 1113

FIRMAMENTO ★ DLB Cass 1113

CAPRICHOS DEL DESTINO ★ DLB Cass 1113

LA DEL MOÑO COLORADO ★ DLB Cass 1113

RUINAS Y CENIZAS ★ DLB Cass 1113

TRIGUEÑITA ★ DLB Cass 1113

(Note: The title of DLB Cass 1113 is TODA UNA EPOCA. All items on DLB Cass 1113 have Jorge Infante-electric piano, overdubbed.)

LYDIA MENDOZA. San Antonio, TX, May 15, 1984.

PERO AY QUE TRISTE (Lydia Mendoza) ★ DLB Cass 1139, Cass 6006, Cass 8006

MUNDO ENGAÑOSO (S. Macías) ★ DLB Cass 1139, Cass 6006

YA ME CANSE DE ESTE AMOR (Lydia Mendoza) ★ DLB Cass 1139, Cass 6006

HAZME PARA UN LADO (Salomé Gutiérrez) ★ DLB Cass 1139, Cass 6006

TUS DESPRECIOS (Lydia Mendoza) ★ DLB Cass 1139, Cass 6006

TANGO NEGRO (DAR) ★ DLB Cass 1139, Cass 6006

LAS ISABELES (Leonor/Lydia Mendoza) ★ DLB Cass 1139, Cass 6006

AMOR DE MADRE (Lydia Mendoza) ★ DLB Cass 1139, Cass 6006

UN NUEVO AMANECER (Lydia Mendoza) ★ DLB Cass 1139, Cass 6006

REMORDIMIENTO (Salomé Gutiérrez) ★ DLB Cass 1139, Cass 6006

(Note: Title of DLB Cass 1139: LYDIA MENDOZA: LA ALONDRA DE LA FRONTERA. Title of DLB Cass 8006: LYDIA MENDOZA: 15 EXITOS.)

LYDIA MENDOZA. San Antonio, TX, May 6, 1985.

CUANTO TIENES CUANTO VALES ★ DLB Unissued

LA CHUPARROSA ★ DLB Unissued

CUANDO SE TIENE (Lydia Mendoza) ★ DLB Unissued

NO PUEDO DEJAR DE QUERERTE (Leonor Mendoza) ★ DLB Unissued

CINCO POR UNA SON CINCO ★ DLB Unissued

LA FERIA DE LAS FLORES ★ DLB Unissued

EL JARDIN DE LOS CEREZOS (Salomé Gutiérrez) ★ DLB Unissued

LYDIA MENDOZA. San Antonio, TX, September 9, 1985.

EL GENERAL FRANCISCO VILLA-Corrido ★ DLB Unissued

LA YEGUA PAJARERA-Corrido ★ DLB Unissued

LOS TEQUILEROS-Corrido ★ DLB Unissued

ARTURO GARZA TREVIÑO-Corrido (Salomé Gutiérrez R.) ★ DLB Unissued

VALENTE QUINTERO-Corrido ★ DLB Unissued

NETO PEREZ-Corrido (Salomé Gutiérrez) ★ DLB Unissued

EL DIA DE SAN JUAN-Corrido ★ DLB Unissued

EL GATO NEGRO-Corrido (Salomé Gutiérrez) ★ DLB Unissued

JACINTO TREVIÑO-Corrido ★ DLB Unissued

LYDIA MENDOZA. San Antonio, TX, August 24, 1986.

LLORANDO EN NAVIDAD (Lydia Mendoza) ★ DLB Unissued

PERDON YO PIDO ★ DLB Unissued

DELICIOSA (Leonor Mendoza) ★ DLB Unissued

AQUELLAS CARICIAS (Leonor Mendoza) ★ DLB Unissued

DELGADINA (Leonor Mendoza) ★ Arhoolie Cass 3012

YO NO ESPERO (Leonor Mendoza) ★ DLB Unissued

TODOS DICEN QUE NUNCA (Leonor Mendoza) ★ DLB Unissued

LYDIA MENDOZA vocal and guitar with accordion and bass. San Antonio, TX, 1987.

CORRIDO DE LA PLAZA DEL ZACATE (Manuel y Lydia Mendoza) ★ DLB 874(45)

MAS VALE SOLO QUE MAL ACOMPAÑADO (Lydia Mendoza) ★ DLB 874(45)

Bibliography

Cancionero mexicano: canciones mexicanas y canciones que han tenido gran popularidad en México. 2 vols. México: Libro-Mex Editores, 1980.

Esparza Sánchez, Cuauhtémoc. *El Corrido zacatecano.* Colección Científica: Historia 46. México: Instituto Nacional de Antropología e Historia, 1976.

Geijerstam, Claes af. *Popular Music in Mexico.* Albuquerque: University of New Mexico Press, 1976.

Gil, Carlos B. "Lydia Mendoza: Houstonian and First Lady of Mexican American Song." *Houston Review* 3 (1981): 250–60.

Griffith, James F. "Lydia Mendoza: An Enduring Mexican-American Singer." *Ethnic Recordings in America: A Neglected Heritage.* Studies in American Folklife 1. Washington: American Folklife Center, Library of Congress, 1982. 102–31.

McDowell, John Holmes. "The *Corrido* of Greater Mexico as Discourse, Music, and Event." *"And Other Neighborly Names": Social Process and Cultural Image in Texas Folklore.* Ed. Richard Bauman and Roger D. Abrahams. Austin: University of Texas Press, 1981. 44–75.

Miller, Dale. "Lydia Mendoza: The Lark of the Border." *Guitar Player* 22.8.224 (August 1988): 38–41.

Morales, Alfonso, et al. *El país de las tandas: teatro de revista 1900–1940.* México: Museo Nacional de Culturas Populares, 1984.

Paredes, Américo. *A Texas-Mexican Cancionero: Folksongs of the Lower Border.* Urbana, IL: University of Illinois Press, 1976.

Peña, Manuel. *The Texas-Mexican Conjunto: History of a Working-Class Music.* Austin: University of Texas Press, 1985.

Reina Schement, Jorge, and Ricardo Flores. "The Origins of Spanish-Language Radio: The Case of San Antonio, Texas." *Journalism History* 4.2 (1977): 56–61.

Romero Flores, Jesús. *Corridos de la revolución mexicana.* México: B. Costa-Amic, 1977.